LEFT-OF-CENTRE PARTIES AND TRADE UNIONS IN THE TWENTY-FIRST CENTURY

Left-of-Centre Parties and Trade Unions in the Twenty-First Century

Edited by

ELIN HAUGSGJERD ALLERN

and

TIM BALE

OXFORD
UNIVERSITY PRESS

OXFORD
UNIVERSITY PRESS

Great Clarendon Street, Oxford, OX2 6DP,
United Kingdom

Oxford University Press is a department of the University of Oxford.
It furthers the University's objective of excellence in research, scholarship,
and education by publishing worldwide. Oxford is a registered trade mark of
Oxford University Press in the UK and in certain other countries

Published in the United States of America by Oxford University Press
198 Madison Avenue, New York, NY 10016, United States of America

British Library Cataloguing in Publication Data

Data available

Library of Congress Control Number: 2016948584

ISBN 978–0–19–879047–1

Printed in Great Britain by
Clays Ltd, St Ives plc

Acknowledgements

We have shared a fascination with the relationships between political parties and interest groups in democracies for a decade. The first fruit of our collaboration was a workshop at the ECPR Joint Sessions in Lisbon in 2009, which led to a special issue of the journal, *Party Politics*. The specific idea for the project on which this book is based first occurred to us in the spring of 2011, during a series of conversations at the University of Sussex where one of us was then teaching and the other had come as a visiting fellow in order to develop a joint research proposal on parties and interest groups. We decided that looking at left-of-centre parties and trade unions—long one of the best-known, politically most important, and most talked-about relationships—would be a great first stage in such a project, the second stage of which is ongoing as we write. That decision led to us rounding up a posse of country experts drawn from scholars specializing either in parties or in trade unions/interest groups, or in some cases both.

Since then, and through the course of what has been a complex and challenging project to pull together, we feel we have got to know all of them. Clearly this volume could never have materialized without their expertise, their commitment, and their being prepared to put up with our demands! We would like to thank them all—and, no doubt, the colleagues, friends, and families who stand behind them, as well as the people in parties and trade unions all around the world who agreed to fill in their questionnaires and meet them for interviews. Social science relies on the cooperation of those it studies in order to come up with accurate and, we hope, interesting findings, so we appreciate that help immensely.

We also appreciate all the hard work of the editorial and production teams at Oxford University Press, especially Dominic Byatt, who helped us enormously by securing some very useful academic feedback on the initial proposal and book manuscript draft. We hope that what has eventually emerged is all the better for us taking it on board. We would also like to thank colleagues for the comments on various manuscript drafts received on conferences, workshops, and research seminars during the writing process.

Predictably, but importantly, we would like to thank friends and colleagues at Queen Mary University of London and at the University of Oslo, which deserves a special mention for providing the financial wherewithal needed to make all this happen. In April 2014, we were able to invite all of the country experts to Oslo to discuss the results of the party–union surveys before completing the datasets and drafting the book chapters. Thanks are also due to the European Consortium of Political Research, which funded a very helpful ECPR Research Session at the European University Institute in Florence during the early stages.

An even more special mention should go to the excellent research assistants in Oslo who helped us, oftentimes above and beyond the call of duty: Lars Petter Berg, Eirik Hildal, Maiken Røed, and Torill Stavenes. They have all provided invaluable assistance, at various stages of the process. Simon Otjes deserves special thanks for not only co-writing an excellent country chapter but also for being an invaluable co-author on the methodological and the cross-national chapters. The scaling analysis of existing party–union links was his idea and turned out to be a very fruitful way forward.

As usual, however, our biggest debt is due to our respective families for their love, support, and forbearance: we can only imagine how difficult the pair of us are to live with sometimes!

EHA, University of Oslo, and TB,
Queen Mary University of London,
September 2016

Contents

List of Figures   ix
List of Tables   xiii
List of Contributors   xvii

1. The Relationship between Left-of-Centre Parties and Trade Unions   1
    Elin Haugsgjerd Allern and Tim Bale

2. Mapping Party–Trade Union Relationships in Contemporary
    Democracies   26
    Elin Haugsgjerd Allern, Tim Bale, and Simon Otjes

3. The Australian Labor Party and the Trade Unions:
    'Til Death Do Us Part'?   54
    Phil Larkin and Charles Lees

4. A Dying Embrace? Interlocked Party–Union Directorates
    in Austria's Cartel Democracy   70
    Kurt Richard Luther

5. Finland: Strong Party–Union Links under Challenge   93
    Tapio Raunio and Niko Laine

6. Left-wing Parties and Trade Unions in France   112
    Nick Parsons

7. Growing Apart? Trade Unions and Centre-left Parties
    in Germany   130
    Tim Spier

8. Parties and Labour Federations in Israel   149
    Ronen Mandelkern and Gideon Rahat

9. Left-of-Centre Parties and Trade Unions in Italy: From Party
    Dominance to a Dialogue of the Deaf   170
    Liborio Mattina and Mimmo Carrieri

10. The Legacy of Pillarization: Trade Union Confederations
    and Political Parties in the Netherlands   186
    Simon Otjes and Anne Rasmussen

11. Two Branches of the Same Tree? Party–Union Links in Sweden
    in the Twenty-First Century   206
    Jenny Jansson

12. Strong Ties between Independent Organizations: Unions and
    Political Parties in Switzerland   226
    Roland Erne and Sebastian Schief

13. No Place Else To Go: The Labour Party and the Trade Unions
    in the UK   246
    Paul Webb and Tim Bale

14. Still So Happy Together? The Relationship between Labour
    Unions and the Democratic Party   264
    Christopher Witko

15. The Relationship between Left-of-Centre Parties and Trade
    Unions in Contemporary Democracies   280
    Elin Haugsgjerd Allern, Tim Bale, and Simon Otjes

16. Variations in Party–Union Relationships: Explanations
    and Implications   310
    Elin Haugsgjerd Allern, Tim Bale, and Simon Otjes

Bibliography   343
Index   369

List of Figures

3.1. Total link scores of central party organization–trade union relationships (0–20) — 64

3.2. Rating of overall degree of closeness/distance (average score) between the party and union confederation, last five years (*c*.2008–13) — 65

4.1. Total link scores of central party organization–trade union relationships and legislative party–trade union relationships (0–20/0–12) — 85

4.2. Rating of overall degree of closeness/distance (average score) between the party and union confederation, last five years (*c*.2008–13) — 86

5.1. Share of SDP and VAS MPs in 2013/14 that hold or have held positions as officials or staff in the confederations of unions at the national level — 103

5.2. Total link scores of central party organization–trade union relationships and legislative party–trade union relationships (0–20/0–12) — 104

5.3. Rating of overall degree of closeness/distance (average score) between the party and union confederation, last five years (*c*.2008–13) — 105

6.1. Total link scores of central party organization–trade union relationships and legislative party–trade union relationships (0–20/0–12) — 124

6.2. Rating of overall degree of closeness/distance (average score) between the party and union confederation, last five years (*c*.2008–13) — 125

7.1. Share of SPD and Die Linke MPs in 2014 with union membership or current/former positions as officials or staff in the unions at the national or local level — 141

7.2. Total link scores of central party organization–trade union relationships and legislative party–trade union relationships (0–20/0–12) — 143

7.3. Rating of overall degree of closeness/distance (average score) between the party and union confederation, last five years (*c*.2008–13) — 144

8.1. Share of Labour, Likud, and Meretz MKs that hold or have held positions as officials or staff in the confederations of unions at the national level — 162

8.2. Total link scores of central party organization–trade union relationships and legislative party–trade union relationships (0–20/0–12) — 163

8.3. Rating of overall degree of closeness/distance (average score) between the party and union confederation, last five years (*c*.2008–13) — 164

9.1. Total link scores of central party organization–trade union relationships and legislative party–trade union relationships (0–20/0–12) — 178

9.2. Rating of overall degree of closeness/distance (average score) between the party and union confederation, last five years (*c*.2008–13) — 178

10.1. Share of PvdA, SP, and CDA MPs in 2013/14 that hold or have held
      positions as officials or staff in the confederations of unions at the
      national level   198

10.2. Total link scores of central party organization–trade union relationships
      and legislative party–trade union relationships (0–20/0–12)   198

10.3. Rating of overall degree of closeness/distance (average score) between
      the party and union confederation, last five years (*c.*2008–13)   200

11.1. Share of SAP and VP MPs that hold or have held positions as officials
      or staff in the confederations of unions at the national or local level   217

11.2. Total link scores of central party organization–trade union relationships
      and legislative party–trade union relationships (0–20/0–12)   219

11.3 Rating of overall degree of closeness/distance (average score)
      between the party and union confederation, last five years (*c.*2008–13)   220

11.4. LO, TCO, and Saco members voting for SAP (%)   222

11.5. Support for union–party cooperation among LO members, 1988–2011   223

12.1. Share of SP and CVP MPs in 2013/14 that hold or have held positions
      as officials or staff in unions at the federal or regional level   237

12.2. Total link scores of central party organization–trade union relationships
      and legislative party–trade union relationships (0–20/0–12)   239

12.3. Rating of overall degree of closeness/distance (average score) between
      the party and union confederation, last five years (*c.*2008–13)   240

13.1. Total link scores of central party organization–trade union relationships
      and legislative party–trade union relationships (0–20/0–12)   257

13.2. Rating of overall degree of closeness/distance (average score) between
      the party and union confederation, last five years (*c.*2008–13)   258

14.1. Total link scores of central party organization–trade union relationships
      and legislative party–trade union relationships (0–20/0–12)   273

15.1. Frequency of total organizational link scores of central party
      organization–trade union relationships (0–20)   289

15.2. Frequency of total organizational link scores of legislative party
      group-trade union relationships (0–12)   289

15.3. Frequency of total organizational link scores of party–trade union
      relationships (0–20)   289

15.4. Total link scores of central party organization–trade union
      relationships and legislative party–trade union relationships: the main
      centre-left party and its traditional union ally/allies and other union
      confederations/unions (0–20/0–12), mean values, N = 42/38   291

15.5. Total link scores of central party organization–trade union relationships:
      the major left-of-centre party and the traditional union ally/allies,
      by country (0–20), N = 20   293

15.6. Total link scores of legislative party group–trade union relationships: the major left-of-centre party and the traditional union ally/allies, by country (0–12), mean values, N = 16   293

15.7. Total link scores of central party organization–trade union relationships: the major left-of-centre party and other union confederations/unions, by country (0–20), N = 22   294

15.8. Total link scores of legislative party group-trade union relationships: the major left-of-centre party and other union confederations/unions, by country (0–12), mean values, N = 22   294

15.9. Total link scores of party–trade union relationships: the major left-of-centre party and its traditional union ally/allies compared to the major left-of-centre party and other unions, by country (0–20), N = 40   296

15.10. Distribution of total link scores of CPO–trade union relationships by country (0–20)   296

15.11. Distribution of total link scores of LPG–trade union relationships by country (0–12)   297

15.12. Distribution of total organizational link scores of party–trade union relationships by country (0–20)   298

15.13. Share of parties/unions reporting the different overall degrees of closeness/distance of party–trade union relationships the last five years (*c.*2008–13), N = 65   303

15.14. Rating of overall degree of closeness/distance (average score) between the major old left-of-centre party and its traditional union ally/allies, last five years (*c.*2008–13)   304

16.1. Strength of party–union links (additive score) and share of unions members voting for the left-of-centre party (US excluded)   324

16.2. Strength of party–union links (additive score) and resources offered by unions to the left-of-centre party (additive score)   325

16.3. Strength of party–union links (additive score) and union density   327

16.4. Strength of party–union links (additive score) and level of trade union fragmentation   328

16.5. Strength of party–union links (additive score) and level of corporatism (degree of routine involvement)   330

16.6. Strength of party–union links (additive score) and extent of state subsidies to parties' national organizations   331

16.7. Strength of party–union links (additive score) and strength of party finance regulations   332

List of Tables

1.1. Alternative conceptualizations of party–interest group (trade union) relationships   10

2.1a. Country selection and various contextual variables   31

2.1b. Country selection and various contextual variables   32

2.2. Sub-groups of links providing contact between parties (CPO/LPG) and unions at the national level, with items listed in hierarchical order of strength   41

2.3. Left-of-centre party–trade union relationships: item and scale scalability values   43

A2.1. List of countries, political parties, confederations and unions, and party-union pairs   48

A2.2. Scale scalability (H) values for confederations and individual unions   52

A2.3. Scale scalability (H) values per country   52

3.1. Overlapping organizational structures between party central organization and union confederation as of 2013–14   58

3.2. Reciprocal, durable inter-organizational links between party central organization/legislative group and union confederation, last five years (c.2008–13)   60

3.3. One-way, occasional links at the organizational level between party central organization/legislative group and union confederation, last five years (c.2008–13)   62

4.1. Overlapping organizational structures between party central organization and union confederation, as of 2013–14   76

4.2. Reciprocal, durable inter-organizational links between party central organization/legislative group and union confederation, last five years (c.2008–13)   78

4.3. One-way, occasional links at the organizational level between party central organization/legislative group and union confederation, last five years (c.2008–13)   81

5.1. Reciprocal, durable inter-organizational links between party central organization/legislative group and union confederation, last five years (c.2008–13)   99

5.2. One-way, occasional links at the organizational level between party central organization/legislative group and union confederation, last five years (c.2008–13)   101

5.3. The party choice of trade union members in Eduskunta elections, 1991–2015   108

6.1a. Reciprocal, durable inter-organizational links between party central organization/legislative group and union confederation, last five years (*c*.2008–13)   116

6.1b. Reciprocal, durable inter-organizational links between party central organization/legislative group and union confederation, last five years (*c*.2008–13)   117

6.2a. One-way, occasional links at the organizational level between party central organization/legislative group and union confederation, last five years (*c*.2008–13)   119

6.2b. One-way, occasional links at the organizational level between party central organization/legislative group and union confederation, last five years (*c*.2008–13)   120

7.1. Reciprocal, durable inter-organizational links between party central organization/legislative group and union confederation, last five years (*c*.2008–13)   135

7.2. One-way, occasional links at the organizational level between party central organization/legislative group and union confederation, last five years (*c*.2008–13)   139

8.1. Overlapping organizational structures between party central organization and union confederation, as of 2013–14   154

8.2. Results of Elections to the Histadrut conference, 1956–2012   156

8.3. Elections to the Histadrut Chair   157

8.4. One-way, occasional links at the organizational level between party central organization/legislative group and union confederation, last five years (*c*.2008–13)   159

9.1. One-way, occasional links at the organizational level between party central organization/legislative group and union confederation, last five years (*c*.2008–13)   174

10.1. Reciprocal, durable inter-organizational links between party central organization/legislative group and union confederation, last five years (*c*.2008–13)   191

10.2. One-way, occasional links at the organizational level between party central organization/legislative group and union confederation, last five years (*c*.2008–13)   195

11.1. Reciprocal, durable inter-organizational links between party central organization/legislative group and union confederation, last five years (*c*.2008–13)   212

11.2a. One-way, occasional links at the organizational level between party central organization and union confederation, last five years (*c*.2008–13)   215

11.2b. One-way, occasional links at the organizational level between legislative group and union confederation, last five years (*c*.2008–13)   216

12.1. Overlapping organizational structures between party central organization and union confederation, as of 2013–14 233

12.2. Reciprocal, durable inter-organizational links between party central organization/legislative group and union confederation, last five years (*c*.2008–13) 234

12.3. One-way, occasional links at the organizational level between party central organization/legislative group and union confederation, last five years (*c*.2008–13) 235

13.1. Overlapping organizational structures between party central organization and union confederation, as of 2013–14 250

13.2. Reciprocal, durable inter-organizational links between party central organization/legislative group and union confederation, last five years (*c*.2008–13) 253

13.3. One-way, occasional links at the organizational level between party central organization/legislative group and union confederation, last five years (*c*.2008–13) 255

14.1. One-way, occasional links at the organizational level between party central organization/legislative group and union confederation, last five years (*c*.2008–13) 270

15.1. Left-of-centre party–trade union relationships: shares of party-union dyads relying on different link types 286

15.2. Descriptive statistics: total organizational link scores (0–12/20) 288

15.3. Share of MPs in 2013/14 that hold or have held positions as officials or staff in the confederations of unions at the national level 299

15.4. Changes in personnel overlaps and transfers at the national level over time: major left-of-centre party–traditional union ally and other left-of-centre party–traditional union ally 301

15.5. Existence of links between trade union confederation/union and (any) other parties during the last five years (*c*.2008–13), according to trade union 306

16.1. Descriptive statistics: dependent and independent variables 321

16.2. Correlations between independent variables and strength of party–union links (additive score) 322

A16.1. Missing cases from cross-sectional analysis 339

A16.2. List of independent variables (operationalization and sources) 339

List of Contributors

Elin H. Allern is Professor of Political Science at the University of Oslo. She specializes in comparative party and interest group politics.

Tim Bale is Professor of Politics at Queen Mary University of London, where he specializes in British and European party politics.

Mimmo Carrieri is Professor of Economic Sociology at Sapienza University of Rome, where he specializes in unions and industrial relations.

Roland Erne is the Jean Monnet Chair of European Integration and Employment Relations at University College Dublin.

Jenny Jansson is a researcher at the Department of Government, Uppsala University, where she specializes in Swedish politics and labour history.

Niko Laine is a PhD candidate in political science at the University of Tampere.

Phil Larkin is Adjunct Associate Professor of Public Policy in the Institute for Governance and Policy Analysis at the University of Canberra. He specializes in legislatures, parties, and public policy.

Charles Lees is Professor of Politics at the University of Bath where he specializes in comparative politics and policy.

Kurt Richard Luther is Professor of Comparative Politics at Keele University and Guest Professor at Tongji University in Shanghai. He specializes in European party politics.

Ronen Mandelkern is Lecturer in Political Science in Tel Aviv University where he specializes in comparative and Israeli political economy.

Liborio Mattina is former Professor of Political Science and Comparative Politics at the University of Trieste. His main fields of research are interest groups and democratic theory.

Simon Otjes is a researcher at the Documentation Centre Dutch Political Parties at University of Groningen where he studies Dutch and European party politics.

Nick Parsons is Reader in French at Cardiff University where he specializes in French and European industrial relations and social policy.

Gideon Rahat is Professor of Political Science at the Hebrew University of Jerusalem where he specializes in democratic political institutions and Israeli politics.

Anne Rasmussen is Professor at the Department of Political Science, University of Copenhagen, and affiliated to the department of Public Administration at Leiden University. She specializes in interest representation, party politics, and political responsiveness.

Tapio Raunio is Professor of Political Science at the University of Tampere where he specializes in comparative European politics.

Sebastian Schief is Senior Lecturer at the University of Fribourg, Switzerland, in the Department of Social Sciences, where he specializes in industrial relations, social policy, precariousness, and working time and work organization.

Tim Spier is Assistant Professor of Political Science at the University of Siegen, Germany, mainly working in the fields of political sociology, especially political parties, interest groups, electoral behaviour, and coalitions.

Paul Webb is Professor of Politics at the University of Sussex, where he specializes in British and comparative party and electoral politics. He is co-editor of the journal *Party Politics*.

Christopher Witko is Associate Professor of Political Science at the University of South Carolina where he studies American politics and public policy.

1

The Relationship between Left-of-Centre Parties and Trade Unions

Elin Haugsgjerd Allern and Tim Bale

INTRODUCTION

Comparative party and interest group politics represent long-established fields of political science. It is widely agreed that both parties and interest groups matter for how democracy works, but also that the relationship between them is one of the keys to understanding representative government itself (Schattschneider 1942; 1960; Neumann 1956, 412–13; Duverger 1954/1972; Almond and Powell 1966; Katz and Mair 1995; Thomas 2001b, 2001c, 1; Beyers et al. 2008). Historically, examples of close party–interest group relationships abound, but perhaps the best known—because it was supposedly the most intimate—is the relationship between left-of-centre parties and trade unions (see, for instance, Duverger 1954/1972, 17ff.; Padgett and Paterson 1991, 177–85; Ebbinghaus 1995; Poguntke 2015). Whether rooted in a shared history, culture, and ideology (see Minkin 1991) or more a 'marriage of convenience' (see Warner 2000), the common wisdom is that their relationship helped socialist, social democratic, and labour parties win power and ensured the working class achieved huge gains in terms of full employment, the welfare state, and labour market regulation.

The classic party–union relationships were found in Northern Europe, in the United Kingdom and Scandinavia, but also in Commonwealth countries in Oceania (Duverger 1954/1972; Rawson 1969, 314). In Europe, the links between the parties and unions varied in organizational strength (Duverger 1954/1972; Padgett and Paterson 1991). In predominantly Catholic nations like France and Italy, trade unions have always been less strongly linked to political parties, and the principal ones were originally most closely aligned to communist rather than socialist or social democratic parties (Padgett and Paterson 1991, 184; Daley and Vale 1992/93). Moreover, unions in some countries were split along religious lines, as in the Netherlands and Belgium, where Catholic parties were not only dependent on the Church and religious organizations, but appeared as federations of Catholic workers' unions and cooperatives, peasants' associations, associations of industrialists, and others (Duverger 1954/1972, 6; Rawson 1969, 313; von Beyme 1985, 192). Links between left-of-centre parties and unions have also traditionally existed in mature democracies in Asia, like Japan (Hrebenar 2001, 171). In the US, of course, there was no connection to a socialist working-class party although there were less institutionalized connections to centrist, middle-class parties—usually the Democrats (Epstein 1967, 152; Thomas 2001d; Witko 2009).

Duverger (1954/1972) maintained that the original degree of closeness— i.e. whether an interest group was formally affiliated to the party or not— appeared to be correlated to the national cleavage and organizational structure, the core voters' need for more political resources, and, in the case of collective membership, whether the party or the interest group was established first. Rawson (1969, 315ff.) also argued that a key variable was whether the party's origin was external: if an organization had been involved in the formal founding of the party, it was more likely to accept or demand formal affiliation. The fact that Norwegian and Swedish unions were affiliated only at the local level reflects the fact that the Labour Party was established before the Confederation of Trade Unions. The Danish case—where the trade union movement developed earlier and collective membership has never existed (Bille and Christiansen 2001)—is an exception that Rawson related to influence from Germany and the tradition of guilds, among other things (Rawson 1969, 326).[1] Later, von Beyme (1985) emphasized the significance of party ideology. For example, he argues that the syndicalist and anarchist elements in Latin socialist parties called for a territorial base, while the British model was in line with the country's tradition of more national, 'guild socialism'. According to Ebbinghaus (1995), divisions between secular and religious identities nurtured a cleavage between reformist and revolutionary unions. In Southern Europe, such fragmentation of the labour movement resulted in organizational weakness and bias towards protest rather than bargaining (Gumbrell-McCormick and Hyman 2013, 136).

In recent decades, however, both wings of the historical labour movements have, it seems, seen their interests diverge, meaning that party–union links become less mutually useful, not least due to structural changes in the economy and labour market. According to Howell et al. (1992, 5) the political exchange between the two sides has consisted of two bargains—an economic bargain that 'concerns issues of employment and wage restraints', and a political bargain that 'links voting behaviour and protective legislation'. In their view, the post-war period has altered the calculus for both actors:

While the interests and constituencies of party and union overlapped during the first three decades of the postwar period, the crisis of the Fordist political economy, beginning in the late 1960s, and the barely visible contours of a post-Fordist political economy today, have encouraged a collapse in the material bases of the close relationship between unions and left parties. The interests of left parties and trade unions today are, not surprisingly, different from their interests during the long postwar boom.

The decline of Keynesianism, a wave of 'neoliberalism', the growing power of the European Union, increased income inequalities in Western countries (Atkinson 1999; Piketty 2014), and the recent economic crisis in many advanced industrial societies, have apparently made adherence to traditional left-wing policies even more difficult (see e.g. Häusermann 2010). Social democracy, under electoral and fiscal pressure, has either lost its radical edge or its original meaning and many of the parties which once professed it have moved into the centre, unable or unwilling to offer the kinds of policies that used to be taken for granted—not least by trade unions (De Waele et al. 2013; Bailey et al. 2014). As a result, these left-of-centre parties might now be regarded as embarrassing encumbrances rather than natural allies (see e.g. Taylor 1993; Piazza 2001; Upchurch et al. 2009; Hyman and Gumbrell-McCormick 2010; Gumbrell-McCormick and Hyman 2013).

By the same token, some of those unions have become less attractive for parties as their membership has declined. Traditional blue-collar unions organize less of the workforce than they used to. The traditional working class has shrunk and a more pluralist middle class, which might dislike the traditional party–union alliance, has expanded (Koelbe 1992; Gumbrell-McCormick and Hyman 2013, 138–9). Since 1970, union density has fallen on average in advanced industrial societies (Wallerstein and Western 2000, 357–8; Visser 2006; Gumbrell-McCormick and Hyman 2013, 5; Kelly 2015), a development which Piazza (2001) more specifically connects to the process of globalization, i.e. the increasing importance of international trade and investment to national GDP. He presents evidence that union density is negatively affected by globalization and has not been significantly related to the recent success of centre-left parties: 'organized labour is not the electoral (or workplace) force as it used to be' (Piazza 2001, 426).[2]

In brief, the left-of-centre parties no longer have the vote-mobilizing potential in traditional voter groups that they once had (Nieuwbeerta 1996, 356; Achterberg 2006). Close relationships with trade unions do not seem very attractive even if some argue that social democrats still need to rely on core voters to succeed (Karreth et al. 2012, 815), and that strong unions might remain an electoral asset for such parties (Kunkel and Pontusson 1998; Allern 2010, 288ff.; Francia 2012). In economies based on a large public sector, the dilemma for social democrats is perhaps especially pronounced. Voters employed in public administration and services are highly unionized, but often in employees' organizations outside the traditional trade union movement. Besides, unions left with core members in declining sectors like heavy industry may easily develop militant preferences, in turn making them even less attractive to social democratic parties (Howell 2001, 16–18). Unions, for their part, are predicted to instead seek enduring alliances with other non-party organizations in order to pool resources (Gumbrell-McCormick and Hyman 2013, 145). In short, more heterogeneous constituencies have made it less attractive to preserve traditional alliances between left-of-centre parties and trade unions.

All this accords with, and almost certainly has its roots in, Otto Kirchheimer's *catch-all party* thesis, according to which political parties, from the late 1950s onwards, were beginning to accentuate the interests and values that brought together, rather than separated, different parts of society, thereby weakening their original roots in structural and cultural cleavages (Kirchheimer 1966, 186). In a more pluralist society, both parties and interest groups preferred more autonomy from each other lest they repel voters or other parties (Kirchheimer 1966, 193). Binding ties with traditional allies would give way to access to numerous and different interest groups to secure both electoral support and workable government policy (Kirchheimer 1966, 190–1, 194). Likewise, interest groups would prefer weaker connections with multiple parties. Yet Kirchheimer's work, based first and foremost on a consideration of social democratic parties, was more a series of striking speculations than research rooted in any systematic collection of data, and the studies that have followed have qualified rather than simply echoed his message (see e.g. Thomas 2001e, 270–2). As will become clear, we still lack sufficient systematic empirical evidence across countries to draw clear conclusions about the accuracy (or otherwise) of the conventional wisdom that the old ties within the labour movement have eroded and been replaced by more pluralist, weak links.

In this book, therefore, we aim to examine systematically the nature of the relationships between the left-of-centre parties and trade unions and the factors that shape them in contemporary democratic politics. Thus, by 'left-of-centre parties' we mean the social democratic/labour/socialist/communist parties associated with the old historical labour movement and their effective splinter groups (see Chapter 2 for details). Generally, we hope to build bridges between the study of interest groups and parties. More specifically, we aim to interrogate the common wisdom that today's left-of-centre parties and unions are virtually separated, to explain variation in the current state of play between them, and to throw light on differences between previous and contemporary relationships. Covering twelve mature democracies in Europe, North America, and Oceania—countries that were democratized for the first time before or in the 1940s and have been continuously democratic since then—we aim to see whether or not we find a similar pattern of relationships across the world. Our country selection (which we go on to unpack in more detail in Chapter 2) allows us to capture different types of settings, country sizes, and continents/ regions, and to discuss examples of both previously intimate and more distant party–union relationships.

In this introductory chapter we provide the general conceptual and theoretical background to our study. The main goal of the book is to assess and analyse today's relationships between left-of-centre parties and trade unions based on a framework inspired by a general cost–benefit model of resource exchange and transaction costs theory. This book moves beyond the conventional discussion of general tendencies and trends to explore the variation that exists, mainly across space. However, we do this against a backdrop of a scholarly debate focusing, mainly inductively, on long-term developments. Accordingly, we first present this debate on stability and change within the literature on parties, interest groups, and industrial relations, arguing that no clear conclusions regarding the strength of connections can be drawn due to the wide range of understandings and indicators adopted. Thereafter we summarize and review alternative ways of conceptualizing 'party–union'-relationships and present the one that we use in this comparative study: namely how parties and trade unions are connected and interact as organizations. After discussing how we may understand their approach to one another, we specify our hypotheses on the variation that our research on party–union links reveals.

THE DEBATE ON LONG-TERM DECLINE

After a decline of interest in organized political actors in the 1970s and 1980s, both the comparative study of political parties and organized interests has experienced a revival in recent decades. But the scholars working on parties and interest groups have traditionally not been the same people (see Allern and Bale 2012a) and, partly as a result of this, the relationship between parties and interest groups has been largely overlooked by political scientists (but see Thomas 2001a; Poguntke 2006; Rasmussen 2012; Rasmussen and Lindeboom 2013). Nonetheless, there seems to be little doubt among them that the formerly integrated relationship between the old left-of-centre parties and trade unions has declined: after all, such changes would seem to be fairly well-documented across countries (cf. Padgett and Paterson 1991, 216ff.; Thomas 2001e).

Perhaps the best-known example of decline (though by no means termination) is the British Labour Party—an organization that famously 'grew out of the bowels' of the trade union movement (see Minkin 1991). Over time the number of affiliated unions has decreased (Webb 1994, 114–15), and throughout the 1990s the trade unions' formal voting power in the party's decision-making and selection bodies was reduced (Jordan and Maloney 2001; Quinn

2002, 223)—a process which, after it seemed to have stalled for more than a decade, suddenly began again in 2013.[3] Other recent examples of significantly weakened party–trade union links are apparently found in Scandinavia (Sundberg 2003), and in Australia and New Zealand (Katz 2001, 73–4) but in some countries they arguably go further back: the formal affiliation of trade unions to the Belgian socialist party, for example, was changed 'to a straight individual direct membership in 1945' (Epstein 1967, 148).

Yet continuity, and indeed variation, also seems to exist. Streeck and Hassel (2003, 343) argue that party–union relations in Western Europe have been remarkably stable in a _long-term_ perspective, whereas Padgett and Paterson (1991, 220) emphasized in the early 1990s that the pace of change in labour parties' relationships with trade unions seemed to differ from country to country. Sundberg's (2001; 2003) comparative study of the Scandinavian labour and farmers' parties from the late 1990s concludes that both party types had less close relations with the respective unions than before, but that agrarian party links with farmers' unions had weakened the most. Moreover, it seems as if the Danish Social Democratic Party and trade unions have grown further apart than their Swedish and Norwegian counterparts (Allern et al. 2007; 2010; Christiansen 2012). In the German case, scholars have also pointed to stability despite tensions (e.g. Jacoby and Behrens 2014, 2).

A broader comparative survey of thirteen European and Latin American countries at the turn of the millennium also suggests that the degree of change varies (Thomas 2001a). Thomas (2001e, 270–2) found a clear decline in the historical links between social democratic parties and trade unions in democracies that have had strong left-of-centre governing parties (as in Britain, Sweden, Israel, and even in a relatively recent democracy like Spain), but could find no general trend towards weaker links with traditionally closely connected interest groups. Indeed, he concludes that there exists no single pattern of party–interest group relationships within or across countries today, even if the links between political parties and interest groups in general seem rather weak (see also Wilson 1990, 159ff.).

Of course, the heterogeneity uncovered by Thomas may be related to the fact that he employed a broad definition of relationship and did not study the various aspects of it in any detail. In contrast, Poguntke (1998; 2000; 2002) concentrated on three relatively specific types of 'organizational linkage'— organized ways of linking citizens' preferences to elite decisions—in his comparative study of parties in eleven European countries between 1960 and 1989: party membership organization, external and internal collateral organizations, and new social movements (Poguntke 2002, 47f.; Poguntke 2006). Interestingly, he revealed a good deal of stability in ties to collateral organizations over time, although, in his most detailed analysis, Poguntke points to the important difference between party-created and external groups, finding, as he hypothesized he would, that 'on average, external collateral organizations have become less relevant over time whereas internal collateral organizations have increased at roughly the same rate' (1998, 176–8).

Thus, while Poguntke's study generally supports Kirchheimer's argument that parties' links with their traditionally associated interest groups are in decline, he actually finds few cases where close relationships between parties and unions have been completely severed (Poguntke 2002, 59). According to those who subscribe to the *cartel party thesis* (the next step, if you like, after Kirchheimer) proposed by Richard Katz and Peter Mair (1995; 2009; see also Blyth and Katz 2005), this may only be a matter of time. Parties, it is assumed, will become part and parcel of the state and, it is argued, parties which originated in interest groups, including trade unions, have distanced themselves from them because their policy offers are externally constrained by, for example, fiscal crisis, and because they rely increasingly on the state rather than civil society (and firms and individuals) for their funding. For their part, interest groups, because parties are apparently now putting the onus on them to make demands on the state directly (Katz and Mair 1995, 23), supposedly prefer more room for manoeuvre and may not want to run the risk of being tainted by association with this or that party. Although some links between trade unions and social democratic parties may remain, the argument runs, not only do the unions deal directly with the 'bourgeois', centre-right parties when the latter are in power, they also deal with social democratic parties that are in office (and often defending policies antithetical to trade unions) in much the same way.

Recent work putting such claims to the empirical test confirms that party–union links have indeed continued to decline in many cases (e.g. Bellucci and Heath 2012; Lizzi 2014), but also suggests that there is enough evidence of variation to prompt us to question the existence (or at least the strength) of a general trend towards distance to civil society (Quinn 2010; Allern and Bale 2012b; Parsons 2015; Poguntke 2015; Celis et al. 2015). However, since the existing studies apply different measurements and are often very small N-studies (Allern and Bale 2012b; van Biezen and Poguntke 2014; but see Poguntke 2015), further research is needed to help us describe and analyse more systematically and more precisely the degree of distance/closeness in those relationships across countries.

THE CONCEPT AND DIMENSIONS OF RELATIONSHIPS

One of the major reasons why it is difficult to draw clear conclusions across cases is the fact that existing studies adopt such a broad range of understandings and indicators of the links between parties and trade unions. In the literature, individual parties and interest organizations involved in relationships are often described as being 'aligned', 'interlinked', 'tied', and 'connected' as organizations. However, what this means in practice is unclear and contested, although we can try to bring some sense of order to the confusion.

In the sociological literature which dominated political science in the 1950s and 1960s, for example, both political parties and interest groups—and the relationship between them—were seen as manifestations of underlying social cleavages (e.g. Lipset and Rokkan 1967), but the studies were relatively unconcerned with the organizational structure of party–group relationships (Rokkan 1966, 105ff.). Not surprisingly, the latter were of more interest to those taking a structural yet also institutional approach to political parties (cf. Ware 1996, 7–10). In Duverger's seminal work on European political parties, for example, links with interest groups are a focal point. The socialist mass party emerged outside the national assemblies on the basis of trade union movements, cooperatives, and friendly societies (Duverger 1954/1972).

According to Duverger, the strongest links were manifested by parties with an indirect structure: these could be parties whose members were collectively, not individually, affiliated through the trade unions (as in, for example, the British Labour Party). Exactly how parties might be linked to the aligned interest groups when there is no such membership was not elaborated upon (Duverger 1954/1972; Rawson 1969, 316; von Beyme 1985), although Duverger (1968, 455–8) later distinguished between no links, formal or informal subordination of interest group to party, formal or informal subordination of party to interest group, or egalitarian (permanent or ad hoc) cooperation between interest group and party.

The literature on socialist parties in particular has, more specifically, shown that individual parties and trade unions could be closely connected through, for example, liaison committees, leadership and membership overlap and interchange, and a wide arena of common collective activities (see e.g. Harrison 1960; Kassalow 1963; Elvander 1980; Koelbe 1987, 256; Padgett and Paterson 1991, 177–85).

Later, a wider range of indicators were used, including the transfer of finances and other material resources (see e.g. Kvavik 1976; Wilson 1990; Sundberg 2003). Sometimes 'relationship' is applied in a highly abstract sense, for example by pointing to a degree of ideological affinity (Poguntke 2006). Von Beyme (1985, 191) suggests that a major distinction is made between loose cooperation, with contact mainly limited to party finance and election campaigns, and organizational integration through collective membership of party members. Yishai (2001) argues that party links with 'civil associations' have historically had three manifestations: ideological overlap, party use of social organizations to provide social services, and economic support from civil associations.

Other party scholars are not primarily concerned with how parties and unions/interest groups are linked as organizations. Heaney (2010) defines, for example, party–group relationships based on how parties and interest groups act or compete as 'brokers' vis-à-vis each other. In the case of social democratic parties, Kitschelt (1994, 225) emphasizes trade union control of leadership appointments and thereby puts emphasis on power relations, as does Mavrogordatos (2009) by making a distinction between independence, group dependence, party dependence, and interdependence (cf. Duverger 1968, 455–8; Hayward 1980, 5–6). Some identify party strategies vis-à-vis interest groups, for instance in terms of affiliation, alliances, and co-optation (Schwartz 2005). Likewise, interest group scholars have mainly focused on groups' strategies towards parties and, in particular, on the relative importance of contact with parties or parliamentary groups compared to interaction with other political actors or institutions (e.g. Binderkrantz 2005). Thomas (2001c, 19–21; 2001e, 281–4), on the other hand, analyses party–interest group relationships along multiple dimensions: in terms of differing degrees of ideological affinity or adversity, of organizational links or lack thereof, as well as in terms of strategies and power relations between parties and interest groups by differentiating between the integration model, the dominant party model, the cooperation/proximate ideology model, the separation/pragmatic involvement model, the non-involvement model, the competition/rivalry model, and the conflict/confrontation model.

The relationship between political parties and trade unions, then, appears to be a multidimensional phenomenon, and how to study it is open to debate. Table 1.1 (adapted from Allern and Bale 2012a) sums up the various alternative understandings of party–group relationships in general, mentioned here with examples of links/relations and some, mostly European, empirical studies within each category. In this book, we will concentrate on party–trade union relationships in the limited organizational sense. In everyday language, 'relationship' denotes 'the way in which two or more people, groups, countries, etc., talk to, behave toward, and deal with each other'. 'The relation' is what connects or binds 'participants in a relationship' (*Merriam-Webster Dictionary*).

Likewise, we assume the notion of 'party–union relationship' refers to the extent to which, and the manner in which, parties and trade unions are connected as organizations, as well as to how they deal with each other. A relationship, then, primarily consists of links that connect trade unions to the party's members, decision-makers, and/or decision-making bodies, i.e. links that open up for contact and potentially provide communication about information, know-how, opinions, and policy views between parties and trade unions. In other words, party–union links are *those means by which a party and a trade union may interact repeatedly*—such as corporate membership, joint committees, or regular elite contact (cf. Allern 2010). Neither financial donations nor what the two organizations involved may or may not share in terms of ideology are considered as part and parcel of that relationship; instead both these things are treated as *independent variables*—factors (and not of course the only factors) which shape and even drive relationships.

Table 1.1. Alternative conceptualizations of party–interest group (trade union) relationships[1]

Examples	Interaction/ contact	Material	Ideological	Strategic	Power balance
Links/ relations	Collective membership, liaison committee, ad hoc meetings, leadership overlap	Financial donations, transfer of labour, shared resource pools	Degrees of ideological affinity	Competition, co-optation, cooperation, etc.	Independence, group dependence, party dependence
Studies	Duverger (1954/1972); Kirchheimer (1966); von Beyme (1985); Thomas (2001a); Poguntke (2002); Sundberg (2003); Allern et al. (2007); Witko (2009); Allern (2010); Rasmussen (2012); Rasmussen and Lindeboom (2013); Poguntke (2015)	Kvavik (1976); Wilson (1990); Yishai (2001); Sundberg (2003); Koger et al. (2010)	Thomas (2001a); Yishai (2001); Poguntke (2006)	Thomas (2001a); Schwartz (2005); Verge (2012); Otjes and Rasmussen (2015)	Duverger (1968); Kitschelt (1994); Morlino (1998); Mavrogordatos (2009); Lizzi (2014)

[1] This is a modified and updated version of the equivalent table presented in Allern and Bale (2012a). Some studies, like Sundberg (2003) and Thomas (2001a), combine the different understandings.

We aim to study the links that can provide mutual decision-making, planning, and/or coordination of activities—or simply involve regular communication about political issues. By mapping such links we are able to compare the *organizational closeness of relationships*, i.e. the strength/weakness of organizational links between, on the one hand, the party in question and, on the other, the (confederations of) trade unions on the other. As will become clear, we assume the dimension of 'closeness/distance' primarily to reflect *the extent to which relationships—dyads—are institutionalized*: i.e. the degree to which the contact *is being incorporated into a formalized and/or structured system or set of arenas in which interaction takes place.*

This is about both the kind and the number of connections—the extent of durable and/or organized links in this sense. Yet we should also keep in mind that regular contact might also be established through completely informal connections (at the individual level). In Chapter 2, we further discuss how to measure the degrees and dimensionality of closeness and range of party–union relationships as defined here. We concentrate on connections potentially providing contact between left-of-centre parties and trade unions on the formal organizational level—such as, for example, collective membership, joint committees and seminars promoting dialogue. This mapping is partly based on written sources, including party and union statutes, and partly based on a survey/structured interviews conducted among key informants in the parties and trade unions examined. In addition, we cover the individual level by looking, where we can, at the number of the different parties' legislators who hold or have previously held positions in trade unions.

Based on such links/ties, *pairs* of parties and groups make up *dyads*: two organizations maintaining a politically significant relationship. However, as we go on to note, they can of course be linked, too, with more than one actor on the party/group side. We are also interested in the *overall range of old left-of-centre party–trade union relationships*, mainly seen from the party side, the question being 'is a left-of-centre party only or primarily linked to its traditional union ally, or has it established more or less equal links with a wide range of employee organizations?' But we will also (albeit briefly) touch upon the relationships trade unions have with other parties, be they green, new left, centre-right, or populist (radical) right. In countries where Catholic unions have traditionally been close to Catholic/Christian democratic parties, we map these relationships separately in the country analyses (see Chapter 2). For reasons of tractability, we concentrate on the national/leadership level of politics, openly acknowledging that, in doing so, we risk losing potentially important interactions in federal states and at the local level in all of the polities we look at. The unitary/federal and centralization/decentralization dimension(s) will instead be treated as an independent variable.

THE FOUNDATIONS OF RELATIONSHIPS: THEORY AND HYPOTHESES

In contrast to much of inductive party literature (Kirchheimer 1966; Katz and Mair 1995), we emphasize that differences in the national context might make different rates of change and specific patterns of contemporary party–union relationships more or less likely. For instance, structural changes, such as new employment patterns, have not occurred at the same rate everywhere (Thomas 2001a; Allern 2010). Even if close relationships between parties and unions have become generally less use*ful* due to such changes, they have not necessarily become use*less* in all cases, and party–union links might still be perceived as quite valuable by some of those involved. Second, parties and unions are capable of acting upon and influencing the contexts in which they operate. For example, unions might be capable of accommodating new interests and recruiting new employee groups when the traditional ones are in decline. Even if one believes that structural and institutional factors matter, there is no determinism implied here. Our first hypothesis (H1), then, is that *the links between old left-of-centre parties and trade unions are generally not very strong, but that significant variation exists in the strength of links, and in the range of each side's relationships with others, both within and across countries.* Anticipating that our data confirms this, the next question is 'what conditions make strong links more or less likely?' We focus initially on the issue of organizational closeness in what follows, but will briefly get back to the issue of range later on.

We generally assume that what happens—and perhaps also what has happened historically—at the actor level is crucial for how left-of-centre party–trade union relationships materialize. The question is how can we depict parties' and unions' basic approach towards each other? Parties are by definition political actors, operating mainly within the political arena. Trade unions primarily concern themselves with the labour market. Indeed, in the US, political engagement has historically been seen as a sign of 'immaturity', while union members in Europe today often criticize the political attachments of their organizations (Gumbrell-McCormick and Hyman 2013). On the other hand, many scholars would argue that unions need to get involved in politics to pursue their basic goals: 'at a very minimum, unions have to influence the ways the state shapes the rules of the game in the labour market, including their own right to exist, to bargain collectively and to mobilize collective action' (Gumbrell-McCormick and Hyman 2013, 133; see also Svensson and Öberg 2002). In most advanced industrial democracies, political action is used as a complement to economic bargaining (Cella and Treu 2001).[4] That said: what would motivate unions to keep or establish institutionalized relationships with political parties, and what would stimulate parties to form organizational alliances with labour market actors and interest groups like trade unions?

A Cost–Benefit Exchange Model

It is widely agreed that common political interests based on a shared ideology laid the ground for historically close party–union relationships, but that the basis soon become a more pragmatic alliance (Taylor 1993, 134; Howell et al. 1992, 4). To pursue a market analogy, we can generally presuppose that, politically speaking, party–trade union relationships are based on the instrumental exchange of various 'goods' or 'resources'. In brief, political parties need votes, monetary support, and organizational assistance, while unions in turn want members but above all rely on parties for favourable legislation and congenial policy (Howell et al. 1992, 5; Warner 2000, 29, 99; McLean 1987, 70; Schwartz 2005, 44; Allern et al. 2007).[5] For parties, establishing relationships with trade unions can serve as a way of increasing or maintaining electoral support as organizational elites may try to persuade their members to vote for specific parties and support parties with financial donations and labour, especially during the campaign period (Allern et al. 2007). For unions, links with parties may serve as a way to recruit new members and to provide influence over parties' policymaking decisions and public policy outputs.

Interest groups like trade unions have been described as policy maximizers, at least compared to parties (Berry 1997; Schlesinger 1984; Quinn 2002), who balance the seeking of votes, office, and policy (Strøm 1990). Moreover, they have a relatively narrow scope of interests and may be rather inflexible in their policy demands. In contrast, party leaders, we assume, assess the costs and benefits of having more or less close relationships with interest groups for the pursuit of access to office and maximization of policy by means of votes (cf. Allern et al. 2007). Major parties seeking office tend to cast their net wider than unions and need to be flexible and open to logrolling as regards policy. For parties, the potential costs of a close relationship with the unions—besides time invested and generally reduced freedom of action—include possible drawbacks like repelling other voter groups and limiting the party's coalition options. Moreover, strong links with particular interest groups like unions involve the risk of making policy promises that collide with other (and possibly more important) policy preferences. For trade unions, alienating members and the effective removal of their right to 'seek out the highest bidder' among all parties are potential disadvantages, in addition to the costs of any resources they invest in the relationship (cf. Kirchheimer 1966, 193; McLean 1987, 70; Warner 2000, 165–6). Close organizational relationships might also increase the risk of conformity, making both sides less adaptable (Schwartz 2005, 54).

As a consequence, parties and unions that do not have much to offer each other in terms of 'goods'—i.e. cases where the costs of being (closely) linked are likely to exceed the benefits for each actor—presumably enjoy significantly weaker links, if any. The size of benefits and costs involved may, of course, fluctuate and change over time. When the exchange of resources occurs efficiently, we may expect close party–group relationships—in terms of over-lapping structures or strong inter-organizational links—to remain. But when 'one side in the exchange can no longer deliver the goods that the other side seeks, or if those goods become less valuable to the recipient, the institutional links will presumably become weaker, as the costs of being closely linked . . . . are likely to exceed the benefits for each actor' (Allern et al. 2010, 4; see also Bates et al. 1998, 8; Hall and Taylor 1996, 942–46; Christiansen 2012).

This market analogy can be taken further. Warner (2000), for example, argues that interest groups like trade unions are similar to firms.[6] They may choose to incorporate the supplier (the political party) or create an equivalent (a new party) in order to obtain the product, instead of frequently 'buying' it in the market. Lobbying politicians and their parties ad hoc involves transaction costs. To the extent that most benefits exchanged by an interest group and a political party are 'specific to their particular relationship, one might expect to find the group creating its own party or taking over an existing one' (Warner 2000, 29–30). The same logic applies to parties if they are interested in attracting or maintaining the support of a particular section of society, and they might also be interested in institutionalizing a relationship with a particular interest organization instead of asking for meetings ad hoc. Warner emphasizes that whereas the establishment of new parties is quite rare, a similar mechanism can lead both interest groups and political parties to establish *enduring alliances*—'contracts of exchange'—in order to decrease transaction costs, another of which is the need to ensure party leaders keep their policy promises (Warner 2000, 28–30, 100–5). As in the political exchange between party leaders and members (cf. Strøm and Müller 1999, 16–8), key problems are imperfect information and non-simultaneity.

However, unlike scholars using similar theory on party organizations, Warner (2000, 163–4, 97) does not explicitly depict links as an *organizational* phenomenon to overcome problems of enforcement. In contrast, Quinn (2002) assumes that parties—again analogous to business firms—incorporate interest groups in their organizational structure in order to guarantee stability in the provision of monetary support and labour. For their part, interest groups join such 'institutionalized frameworks' to make the parties' supply of policy more reliable. If interest groups anticipate that parties will break promises, they may effectively undersupply resources like labour and financial support. Hence, it might also be useful for parties to establish 'credible compensation mechanisms' with interest groups. Specifically, Quinn (2002; 2010) suggests that, in the case of the Labour Party and trade unions in the UK, the formal affiliation, representation, and voting rights of the trade unions have provided greater stability and reliability in the party's and the unions' exchange of finances, labour, and policy. Inter-organizational links like permanent liaison committees and formal or tacit cooperation agreements may fill a similar institutional function. Such mechanisms can also be used to secure stable exchange of information between the two sides. In other words, particularly strong links between parties and interest groups can be seen as 'aggregations of rules with members...agreeing to follow those rules in exchange for such benefits as they are able to derive from their membership within the structure' (Peters 1999, 47).

Actor-level Hypotheses

In what follows, we deduce some hypotheses on what might explain whether left-of-centre parties and trade unions are involved in close or more distant relationships today, primarily based on the cost–benefit exchange model already described. Thus we concentrate here on the strength of links and we use pairs of parties and unions as our unit of analysis. As noted earlier, we assume the dimension of closeness/distance primarily reflects *the extent to which relationships—dyads—are institutionalized*: that is, the degree to which contact is incorporated into a structured and highly formalized system (arena) for interaction.

For the sake of analytical parsimony, we do not examine variation in parties' primary goals. The main question is whether the strength of contemporary party–union links is correlated to the size of benefits 'exchanged', in line with the general assumptions already described. Faced with a set of trade unions, we assume that a party assesses the membership size, the voting record of organization members, and the amount of monetary and organizational resources on offer. In this context, it seems likely that those original blue-collar unions—the traditional union allies of left-of-centre parties—that have been able to recruit new employee (white-collar) groups, are generally more attractive than those who have not. But we assume such differences will be reflected in today's union membership numbers. Likewise, faced with a set of parties, we assume that a trade union assesses the given party's supply of potential recruits (through, say, its willingness to formally recommend union membership to its own members), the party's policies, and record, plus the its chances of staying in or getting access to government and/or playing a pivotal role in parliament (Otjes and Rasmussen 2015, 4). Hence, both parties' record in office and share of seats in the legislative might play a part.

Mapping the achievement of specific policy-related goals is beyond the scope of this study, but we presume that a centrist ideological profile on the part of a party will make such rewards less likely and thus weaken its appeal to its traditional (blue-collar) trade union ally.[7] Obviously, the individual competitive situation of old left-of-centre parties and trade unions vis-à-vis different constituencies might affect the calculus as well: however, for the sake of simplicity, we focus here on the actual resource exchange. Accordingly, *we assume differences in the closeness of party–union relationships will vary systematically according to the different benefits that can be exchanged for the pursuit of goals on each side* (H2):

- In cases where the old left-of-centre party recommends union membership in its statutes, party–union links are likely to be stronger than in cases where the party does not recommend union membership (H2a).

- The closer to the centre the party is located along the socio-economic left–right axis, the weaker the links between that party and the trade union (H2b).
- The more time (years/days) a left-of-centre party has spent in office in recent years, the stronger the links with between this party and trade unions tend to be (H2c).
- The higher the number of seats a left-of-centre party has won in recent years, the stronger the links between this party and trade unions tend to be (H2d).
- The larger the share of organized employees affiliated to a union, the stronger the links between that union and the left-of-centre party/left-of-centre parties tend to be (H2e).
- The more union members who have voted for the left-of-centre party/parties at the most recent elections, the stronger the links between that union and the party/parties in question tend to be (H2f).
- The more donations and organizational support a trade union has made and provided to the left-of-centre party/parties in recent years, the stronger the links between the two sides tend to be (H2g).

Based on the exchange model, one would furthermore assume that party–union-pairs that *mutually* provide each other with significant resources are more likely to be characterized by strongly institutionalized interaction than those with a less reciprocal and weaker resource exchange overall. It could thus be argued that the model implies that the more resources a left-of-centre party is able to provide a trade union overall, and the more resources this union can offer the party overall, the stronger the links between them. However, for the sake of simplicity, we limit ourselves to, suggesting rather more modestly that *resources offered by parties and unions are equally important for the strength of links between left-of-centre parties and trade unions* (H3).

That said, it is by no means certain that all *types* of party/union resources are equally important. According to transaction costs theory, the degree of 'asset specificity' will matter. Exclusivity in value increases the probability for very strong links (integrated or fairly close relationships, if you like). A group may easily prevent a party from using its organizational facilities and the same goes for human capital: after all, unions are able to instruct or at least encourage their activists to stop working for the party in question. In contrast, financial donations (unless they are not donations but loans) cannot be redeployed once given and consumed by the party. Votes have the same value for all parties, but the value depends on how hard the competition is for those votes—are they valued by other parties? Moreover, if union members are used to voting for a specific party, they can be hard to 'deprogram' (Warner 2000, 29–30). Seen from the party's point of view, the provision of stable access to government can easily be denied and transferred to other groups, whereas an established rule encouraging party members to affiliate to a specific union and specific policy rewards can be regarded as similar to financial donations: they are hard to redeploy, at least in the short term. Hence, one might theorize that the close organizational relationships are more likely to exist alongside a degree of asset specificity. Focusing, for the sake of simplicity, on votes, members and money, we suggest that:

- *The correlations are stronger between the strength of party–union links and the unions' financial party contributions, the share of union members voting for the party in recent years, and recommendation of union membership in party statutes than the correlations between the strength of party–union links and other resource variables* (H4).

Also, according to an exchange model, parties will evaluate these benefits in light of what they have to 'pay' for support (Warner 2000, 184)—above all, in terms of *the risk of repelling significant member/voter groups and/or coalition partners*. In addition to this comes the size of *policy sacrifices* both sides have to make while negotiating, although sadly we lack data to explore those here.[8] We assume that such specific and variable costs involved in a relationship must be lower than the benefits for parties to choose strong links instead of opting for greater distance. Put differently, high costs will reduce the value of the benefits. Whether this is the case, would, however, be hard to tell for certain, but focusing on the views of voters, we may more modestly hypothesize that:

- *Party–union links tend to be weaker in cases where a relatively large propor-tion of voters hold a negative view of (i.e. low confidence in) trade unions than in cases where a smaller proportion of voters hold such a view* (H5).

Finally, at the party/union-level, existing studies suggest we should also take historical factors into account when trying to explain contemporary relation-ships, since these might constrain parties' and unions' inclination to calculate costs and benefits. Certainly, institutions may not always be the product of rational design, and may not always deliver optimal payoffs to the actors that they involve (Pierson 2000, 477–86). The strength of historical links might have slowed the pace of change towards looser, wider-ranging relationships and thus weakened any correlation between cost–benefit balance and the degree of contemporary closeness. Thus, we finally put forward:

- *In cases where a union's origins were based on partisan considerations party/union-links are likely to be stronger today than in cases with non-partisan roots, and in cases that were originally characterized by strong links —links regulated by party/union statutes—the links are, in particular, likely to be stronger links today* (H6).

Finally, as regards the *range* of each side's relationships, we see this as related to the exchange described earlier: the more equally distributed union resources are in the eyes of the parties, the more likely it is that left-of-centre parties have established (equal) links to a wide range of unions (and vice versa). However, in the explanatory analysis in Chapter 16, we will focus on the strength of links between pairs of individual parties and union confederations/unions.

Country-level Hypotheses

Left-of-centre parties and trade unions are nested in different societies and political systems, and there is bound to be variation at the country level. The general incentives for party–union links may vary, and country-level factors can also affect the value of specific party–union resources. For instance, the value and thus the effect of union donations to parties is probably weaker in countries with generous public party funding than in countries with limited or no state subventions to parties. In empirical work such multi-level relations could be modelled via an interaction effect between resources offered and the specific country-level variable. However, notwithstanding the fact that we expect the country-level variables to constrain the relationship between resources and party–group ties, we do not formulate hypotheses outlining the specific interaction effects, since the limited number of cases we are dealing with (in Chapter 16) is insufficient to allow us to test such hypotheses empirically.

In terms of social/economic conditions, it can be argued that the general strength of unions probably plays a part: if unions are generally strong, in terms of total membership and limited fragmentation, this is likely to increase parties' general interest in trade unions as organized actors. More specifically, the actual value of what individual unions might 'exchange' with parties is probably influenced by these factors as well. Even if an individual union is strong compared to other unions, this does not help much if unions are weak overall. Moreover, high union fragmentation makes it less likely that one trade union (confederation) is able to offer a large share of votes to the left-of-centre party/parties. Thus, we hypothesize:

- *Left-of-centre parties and unions in countries with relatively high union density tend to have stronger links than parties and unions in countries with weaker union density* (H7a).
- *Left-of-centre parties and unions in countries with low trade union fragmentation tend to have stronger links than parties and unions in countries with higher trade union fragmentation* (H7b).

In addition, the national competitive situation of parties will probably affect how much parties can offer the union side. Multiple competitors make it less likely that one party is able to offer stable/regular access to government. Such fragmentation also makes it generally less easy to predict future benefits/costs of specific party–union links.

- *Left-of-centre parties and unions in countries with a relatively high number of effective left-of-centre parties tend to have weaker links than parties and unions in countries with fewer or one such party* (H8).

Another general reason that party–union relationships might differ at the country level is that enduring institutional constraints might make different ways of interacting more or less useful. Different systems imply different incentive—or disincentive—structures for party and interest group organization and behaviour. Both the institutional setting of representative and policymaking institutions and direct and indirect state regulations limit the range of strategic options (see e.g. Müller 2002, 252). There are three institutional aspects which we think deserve particular attention.

First, the existence of *corporatist arrangements* could present a regulatory limit to party and interest group organization and behaviour, affecting the value of the resources the two sides can exchange. 'Corporatism' has been defined in multiple ways, but often refers to a political economic system in which economic and other policy decisions are achieved through negotiation between centralized corporate bodies representing interest groups. In particular, under corporatism wages are determined through collective negotiations between the representatives of employers and workers (see e.g. Siaroff 1999). When more power is located in corporate arrangements (Yishai 1991, 10), parties become less attractive target groups for interest organizations, and party–union links appear less likely in general (Rasmussen and Lindeboom 2013). Similarly, Rommetvedt et al. (2012), find that the decline of corporatism has led to a revival of lobbying directed towards elected representatives in Denmark and Norway. If this is generally the case, it would perhaps also make parties more attractive targets for unions. In contrast, however, Anthonsen et al. (2011) argue that the causal direction might (as) well be the opposite. Since unions might be 'tempted to seek direct political influence instead of bargaining with employer organizations', strong party–union links probably undermine corporatism, especially in polarized political environments—as corporatist modes of policymaking presumably depends on the pattern of party competition (Anthonsen and Lindvall 2009).

Others, however, have maintained that the relationship is not conflictual and is positive: strong corporatism enables parties to win and maintain office more efficiently. Even when out of government, parties may influence public policy through their associated interest group(s) (Müller 2002, 269; see also Thomas 2001e, 276), and strong corporatist arrangements have previously been associated with close party–union relationships empirically (e.g. Padgett and Paterson 1991, 178, 192). If this is right, then the decline of corporatism witnessed in recent decades as the growth of the public sector has complicated the process of centralized wage bargaining (Hernes 1991, 247–55; Wallerstein and Western 2000; Gumbrell-McCormick and Hyman 2013, 5) may have weakened the incentives towards strong party–union links. Yet the degree of corporatism/ pluralism still varies across countries, and we therefore suggest that:

- *The overall strength of links between left-of-centre parties and trade unions varies across countries according to the degree of corporatism/pluralism* (H9).

Second, *state funding of parties* might limit the value of interest group donations to parties. It is an important trend in contemporary political finance (Casas-Zamora 2005) and, despite a degree of convergence, there is still variation in financial regimes (Müller 2002, 263; Koß 2010) which is highly relevant for the issue of links with interest groups. As Katz and Mair (1995) implicitly suggest, the *size* of public subventions may create various incentive structures for party relations to civil society. Parties that receive generous state support may be less enthusiastic about the benefits of close relationships with trade unions—both traditional ones and others—than parties in systems where public subventions are more modest (cf. Thomas 2001e, 276). Therefore:

- *Left-of-centre parties and trade unions in countries with relatively generous public funding tend to have weaker links than parties and unions in countries with only moderate, limited or no state subventions to parties (at the national level)* (H10).

Finally, the *legal and constitutional regulation of interest groups* is likely to play a part (Thomas 2001e, 276–7). The extent of regulations varies between countries, with American parties and groups being particularly heavily regulated (Thomas 2001e, 84). Such rules make financial contributions donated by trade unions to parties more sensitive or less likely (Müller 2002, 269). Given that donations motivate parties to nurture links with unions, we suggest that:

- *Left-of-centre parties and trade unions in countries with no legal rules limiting private financial contributions (including trade union donations) to (national) parties tend to have stronger links than parties and unions in systems with such rules* (H11).

If such rules exist, they may affect the amount resources groups can offer parties in a negative way.

We conclude this chapter by briefly mentioning some of the general institutional factors that have been argued to affect party–interest group relationships and that ideally serve as control variables. *State structure* is probably the most relevant part of the general institutional setting. A federal structure—in contrast to a unitary state—constrains the development of strong national party organizations for numerous reasons. Due to the transfer of power to local levels in federal systems, parties in those systems generally tend to allocate resources at the sub-national level, at the expense of national activities (Müller 2002, 253). Parties need freedom to take account of local variations, and they do not have the necessary organizational capacity at the national level.[9] The same argument applies to trade unions, and a 'federalized' party structure might itself strengthen this tendency. The party example *par excellence* is seen in the loosely organized, non-programmatic parties of the US, where the structure of government allows fifty diverse states to regulate the political parties (Foster and Muste 1992, 12–13). Accordingly, it may be that well-organized links between, in particular, national extra-parliamentary parties and trade unions are less likely in federal states than in unitary states. However, the correlation is not necessarily strong. Germany is an example of a federal state that has well-organized parties and historically fairly close relationships between parties and trade unions (see e.g. Padgett and Paterson 1991, 180–2). A less radical hypothesis is that federal systems promote a greater *variety* of relationships than do unitary systems, especially if party organizations are loosely structured (Thomas 2001e, 274–5).

Parliamentary government—as opposed to separation of powers—is another major institutional constraint that might promote some patterns of relationships more than others. According to Thomas (2001e, 274–5), parliamentary government has tended to encourage strong links between specific parties and interest groups, like left-of-centre parties and trade unions, whereas separation of powers has been associated with supra-partisan interest groups. When numerous power centres exist, it might be risky for trade unions to be strongly linked with one specific party (see e.g. Wilson 1990, 162; Witko 2009, 227). Interest groups like trade unions must always cultivate access to all sides, so they will hesitate to favour one party's candidates before elections (Rozell et al. 2006, 14–15). However, frequent alternation in government and minority government may weaken the differences between the two institutional settings in this regard. In such a parliamentary environment, trade unions cannot base their influence on friendly relationships with one party only. Parties that are out of power may have very little impact on the executive (cf. Selle 1997, 159; Thomas 2001e, 274–5).

Moreover, it has been argued that the party system matters for party–interest group relationships. Conventional wisdom suggests that strong links between particular parties and interest groups are more likely to occur in countries with numerous parties than in two-party systems, due to more complicated patterns of party competition. Parties would have greater incentives to try to form loose connections across groups when there is only one major competitor (Allern 2010: 99–100). However, in systems with many different parties, allying with just one or two of them would theoretically represent something of an opportunity cost for unions. Moreover, party system fragmentation makes it generally less easy to envisage future benefits/costs of specific party–union links. Hence, one might expect a negative correlation between the number of (effective) parties and the strength of (exclusive) links between left-of-centre parties and trade unions.

SUMMARY OF MAIN RESEARCH QUESTIONS

Our first task, before investigating these hypotheses, however, is to provide a detailed description of contemporary relationships between left-of-centre parties and trade unions in mature democracies across the world. This should help us address the hypotheses detailed in this chapter and our main research questions, namely:

- To what extent are left-of-centre parties and trade unions involved in structured organizational relationships: what characterizes the strength of links between them?

- If these parties are linked with trade unions, what sort of unions are they linked with? Are they linked to other employee organizations in addition to or even instead of their traditional ally?

- Are contemporary trade unions closely linked with just one left-of-centre party or do they prefer weaker connections with multiple parties, perhaps including parties which are not on the left of the political spectrum? Or do they keep their distance from political parties in general?

Second, we can only hope to get at change over time—and therefore at the issue of how much those relationships have flourished or floundered—by taking a snapshot of what is going on today and comparing that to what we already know about historical relationships from, say, party–union statutes, informants' personal recollections, and of course secondary literature. We need to ask the following questions:

- To what extent have such relationships changed over time? Are we seeing the attenuation or even the wholesale disintegration of previously intimate relationships?

- Is it the same story everywhere? Or do some close relationships remain intact while others have withered? Is there variation in party-trade union links both within and between countries?

Third, anticipating that our data indicate that variation actually exists across dyads and countries, we want to ask and answer the following questions:

- To what extent do factors at the party and union level play a part? Do party–union relationships vary in line with the expectations of a cost–benefit exchange model?

- To what extent do country-level variables affect variation in left-of-centre party–trade union relationships? Do relationships differ systematically across different contexts?

Finally, if briefly, we also aim to throw light on the political significance of party–union links. The relationships we measure are not truly important unless they have political consequences. Do they make a difference to the policy-related decisions made by political parties and/or trade unions? And, finally: in what way do party–group relationships seem to shape democratic governance? If parties and trade unions still enjoy relationships with each other, can we presume that they do in fact take account of each other's opinions on policy? We therefore asked our country teams to look briefly at the following questions when concluding their chapters: do party–union links seem to influence the policy decisions made by any of those involved, and to what extent do unions influence government decisions through such more or less institutionalized frameworks?

Left-of-centre parties involved in close organizational relationships with trade unions are often accused by opponents of being little more than the trade union movement's loyal and obedient 'political wing'. In contrast, the assumption that strong party–union links can make for a lower level of strikes and a greater level of progress is widespread on the left of the political spectrum, and presumes that unions modify their policy views through their interaction with parties. It has been argued, for instance, that social democratic parties have historically swapped policies favourable to unions in the short term for industrial peace and assistance in policy implementation (Howell 2001, 13). The country case analyses presented in this book should throw some light on these issues, too.

PLAN OF THE BOOK

The descriptive research questions, theoretical propositions, and hypotheses presented in this introduction constitute the guiding analytical framework of this volume. In Chapter 2, we elaborate the analytical dimensions to be mapped, discuss how to measure the closeness and range of party–union relationships empirically, and present our cases, data, and methods in detail. We argue that the key aspect of closeness might be one-dimensional or multidimensional, based on two or three main categories of links: namely overlapping organizational structures (statutory links like collective affiliation of unions and representation rights), formal inter-organizational links (like joint committees), and informal inter-organizational links (like leadership and personnel overlaps). Moreover, we set out to check the assumed hierarchy and dimensionality empirically using (Mokken) scaling analysis, and are able to assign an overall scale of closeness to the vast majority of dyads we examine.

The chapters that come after Chapter 2 contain case studies of twelve contemporary mature democracies in Europe, North America, and Oceania. Each of the country chapter starts by giving a brief summary of what the relationship between left-of-centre parties and trade unions looked like in the late nineteenth and the first half of the twentieth century. In the countries where union confederations and unions have historically been close to a centre-right party, this relationship is discussed as well. Each chapter then supplies the reader with a short contextual description informed by the country-level factors presented in this chapter, mainly based on comparative data on structural changes and the institutional setting presented in Chapter 2. How have historical relationships been challenged by social developments? What are the general—social and institutional—constraints on party–trade union relationships today? The main part of each country chapter is a detailed empirical assessment of the relationship between contemporary left-of-centre parties and all the major confederations of trade unions in the polity under examination.

By using the same conceptualization for describing both historical and contemporary links, we get closer than ever to describing stability and change in the traditional alliance in each of the twelve countries. Authors also discuss what factors appear to be the drivers behind the developments revealed, as well as how we can understand the contemporary level of closeness/distance as seen from both sides. The essence of the framework elaborated in this chapter—not least on resource exchange—informs and frames these discussions. In conclusion, each author briefly comments on the apparent political significance of the remaining links. Do stronger links in the organizational sense seem to mean more political influence, or can equally 'influential' relationships materialize informally?

In the final two chapters of the book we analyse contemporary party–union relationships across all cases. In Chapter 15 our aim is to offer a systematic overview of the strength of party–union links in the twelve selected countries. We first summarize the main conclusions of the empirical assessments presented in the preceding country chapters. Thereafter, we systematically and in detail compare party–union links across all dyads and countries, visualizing our findings wherever possible. Next, we add data on informal links (such as MPs' union backgrounds) and discuss the relationship between the links at the two levels. We also compare our objective measures of those links with the perceptions of those involved. In the last section of the chapter we summarize our findings and lessons learned for the debate on how centre-left parties and trade unions relate to each other in the twenty-first century.

In Chapter 16, we move on to explain what we find, focusing in particular on the relationship between left-of-centre parties and their traditional trade union allies. The aim is to explore the hypotheses presented in this chapter regarding what one might conceive of as the core dyad(s). First we summarize the points made in the country chapters. Then we move on to investigate systematically the relationships across cases, beginning with a look at factors at the party/union level and moving on to an examination of country-level (structural and institutional) variables. Finally, we discuss what country analyses tell us about the 'so what' question (political significance of changes and variation in links). We conclude by discussing the theoretical, public policy, and partisan strategic implications of the book's findings.

NOTES

1. The choice of local collective membership in Norway is also related to the fact that some unions were still dominated by liberals at the time of the establishment of a confederation (Allern 2010).
2. Piazza (2001) argues that he thereby explains delinking of the relationship between labour parties and unions, but it should be noted that he does not operationalize it in terms of organizational links. The dependent variables measured are 'left party power' and 'the policy orientation of the primary centre-left, social-democratic party(ies) with regard to social democratic values' (2001, 420).
3. Note that the three-way electoral college, which gave trade unions a considerable say in the choice of Labour's leader, was, under Ed Miliband's leadership, abandoned in favour of a one member-one vote system—a system that led to the election a radical left-winger, Jeremy Corbyn, in September 2015. This marked swing to the left subsequently encouraged a couple of small, particularly militant trade unions to (re)affiliate to the Labour Party.
4. For an informative account of the complex and sometimes contradictory historical relationship between the two roles, see Gumbrell-McCormick and Hyman (2011, 133–6) and Ebbinghaus (1995).
5. Unlike Warner (2000), we do not include the more abstract party goods of 'the reputation for being its party', and 'campaign training of staff', as they are hard to measure. 'Voter education' is not treated separately, but endorsements and encouraging members to support is seen as a means used to provide votes.
6. See Allern (2010: 83ff.) for more detail on this perspective inspired by the 'theories of transaction costs of economic exchange'.
7. In other words, we will not systematically investigate whether parties that have in recent years advocated a legal framework favourable or neutral to union organization and collective bargaining tend to have stronger links to unions than parties that have accepted a more hostile framework (compared to others and over time). That said, country analyses might be more specific in this regard.
8. Even if parties prioritize office-maximization over policy in cases of trade-offs, and are not policy-maximizers as interest groups allegedly are, both sides in a potentially intimate relationship probably calculate this option in light of their *basic* ideological orientation (cf. Warner 2000: 184). Close relationships—with overlapping organizational structures or particularly strong inter-organizational links—are more likely when basic positions overlap (cf. Howell et al. 1992, 4) as such links are particularly binding and thus costly in terms of loss of freedom of manoeuvre. However, this is also a difficult proposition to explore empirically due to lack of comparative data on the ideological (policy) positions of trade unions.
9. Wilson (1990, 166–7) argues that the weak degree of formalization of American parties as membership organizations makes them easy to influence for interest groups. American political parties possess few resources themselves and are strongly dependent on external support.

2

Mapping Party–Trade Union Relationships in Contemporary Democracies

Elin Haugsgjerd Allern, Tim Bale, and Simon Otjes

INTRODUCTION

In Chapter 1 we presented the descriptive research questions and theoretical propositions that guide this empirical study of the relationship between left-of-centre parties and trade unions. The overall aim is to interrogate the common wisdom which claims that traditional left-of-centre party–trade union relationships are no longer close and exclusive. But we also want to look at variation and try to explain the current state of play as well as the trends.

Studies of party–union links have long suffered from a lack of agreement on how to conceptualize 'relationships' and measure their 'closeness', and this has prevented clear conclusions from being drawn. We therefore try to be very specific, asking to what extent and how parties and trade unions are connected as organizations, and how they behave towards and deal with each other. Party–union links are those means by which a party and an interest group may interact repeatedly—such as corporate membership, joint committees, or regular elite contact. This specificity allows us to maintain a clear focus across cases.

In what follows, we first define what we mean when we talk about the closeness or distance between parties and trade unions and the range of relationships each of them may or may not enjoy with other organizations. We then show how we operationalize all this. Second, we present our case selection—the countries, parties, and trade unions to be studied. We discuss the selection's limitations as well as its plus points, and conclude that, taken as a whole, it enables us to generate several interesting insights into the relationship between left-of-centre parties and trade unions in mature democracies. We also show how our country cases score on most of the contextual variables presented in Chapter 1, based on existing comparative datasets. Finally, we briefly summarize how the original data on relationships have been collected and systematized for this book and the datasets on which it draws, focusing both on the mapping of party–union statutes and the construction of a questionnaire to key informants on both sides. We also discuss how to measure the strength of (formal) links quantitatively with one or more aggregate scores. In sum, this chapter provides an essential backdrop for reading and interpreting the empirical evidence collected and presented by our country teams in the chapters that follow.

THE CONCEPT OF CLOSENESS: BASIC CATEGORIZATION OF LINKS

The study of party–interest group relationships in terms of organizational closeness is not an entirely novel enterprise. However, we will argue that existing approaches have been unable to cover all the possible permutations—ranging from full integration to complete detachment. A new conceptualization is needed—one specified in terms of concrete links. This can provide us with a basis for trying to create aggregate measures of the strength of at least formal links.

Poguntke (2006, 397–8) argues that European parties may have more or less close relationships with *collateral organizations*. These can be corporately linked to the party (through collective membership), through being formally affiliated (through guaranteed representation in decision-making bodies) or informally linked (through exclusive negotiations) based on a broad commonality of interests. As long as ancillary organizations are excluded, this classification is certainly useful when trying to measure fairly close or very close party–interest group relationships.

There is obviously a fundamental difference between organizations that are, according to the party statutes, partly incorporated in the party structure, on the one hand, and formally independent groups, on the other. Likewise, parties can have *ex officio* seats in other organizations, or else they have no such connections. However, parties can have a fairly close relationship with an interest group without links like collective membership and formal affiliation. Historically there are, for instance, many examples of trade unions that have been strongly linked with a social democratic party without being incorporated in the party's structures (Padgett and Paterson 1991, 179–85).[1] We need a conceptual tool which specifies non-statutory links that promote contact between parties and interest groups in the pure organizational sense, namely without the notion of belonging to the same political camp. Put differently, the distinction between formal versus informal links is not sufficient because it cannot capture the importance of some non-statutory links, especially if they cut across ideological affinity.

True, relations not regulated by party statutes are less formal than those which are: as Poguntke (2006) points out, integration of interest groups into the party structure establishes a special relationship. But we also want to capture 'official' contacts with groups which are not written into the party rules. The relationship between formally autonomous parties and trade unions is not necessarily unofficial and poorly organized, and non-statutory links may constitute significant structures promoting interaction and contact between parties and interest groups (cf. Minkin 1991, xv). Therefore, we think, a useful basic distinction can be made between *overlapping organizational structures* (such as corporate membership or formal affiliation) on the one hand and *inter-organizational links* for contact (such as liaison committees) on the other.

We also recognize that significant links can materialize outside well-organized settings (Kitschelt 1989, 231–3), as emphasized by American scholars (Herrnson 2009; Witko 2009).[2] However, such links are more contingent upon political circumstances and leadership personalities (Poguntke 1998, 156–7), and therefore probably create a less binding, more flexible relationship (cf. Schwartz 2005, 44). They may, but do not necessarily, revolve around tacit norms for representation or contact. Personnel overlaps—namely the extent to which party elites hold positions in unions and vice versa—appear, in particular, to be different from other measures, which are about frameworks and activities. In theory, care might be taken to ensure that the two hats worn by the same person are not mixed up in formal meetings (see e.g. Yishai 1991, 131). But those overlaps should still be included as a separate category since they open up multiple opportunities for contact between decision makers.

Finally, it should be noted that overlapping organizational structures and unorganized links promoting contact are by definition reciprocal, although it could be argued that in cases where only one of the sides enjoys *ex officio* seats on the other's decision-making bodies the formal representation is one-sided. Collective membership does not represent an arrangement for contact between the party and the union itself (cf. Poguntke 2002, 50), but collective membership often guarantees one-sided/mutual representation in national decision-making bodies, and has been seen as indicative of parties 'made up by unions' (Duverger's notion of 'indirect parties').

To conclude, we believe we should distinguish between the following major classes of links:

- *Overlapping organizational structures*: Links regulated by party and/or union statutes (e.g. *ex officio* representation in executive bodies).
- *Inter-organizational links*:
  - Reciprocal, durable links: joint party–union arrangements (e.g. joint committees).
  - One-way, occasional links: party/union-arranged meetings (and invitations to party/union events).

- Reciprocal, occasional links: Regular formal (i.e. official) meetings at the individual level.
- *Individual-level links* (e.g. personnel overlaps and regular informal meetings).

We assume such links may exist between trade unions and both parties' central organization and legislative group, even if they are probably stronger outside the latter since unions cannot be formally affiliated to a legislative party group. The categorization refers to the *dyads*, that is, pairs of parties (or 'party faces') and interest groups. Therefore, corporatist bodies, where party and union elites meet with each other but also with the government, do not count and are treated as exogenous to party–union relationships. So, *pace* Valen and Katz (1964, 313–15) and Kvavik (1976, 97), is the joint management of agencies such as educational organizations and newspapers.

The party and union in question do not need to enjoy links of all three kinds to qualify as having a relationship. That said, statutory links generally suggest a higher degree of closeness, since such links probably involve a higher degree of commitment between the two sides. Arguably, overlapping structures are required before the two sides can be said to enjoy a completely integrated relationship organizationally. By the same token, at least some durable inter-organizational links are needed before a relationship can be said to be fairly close in the organizational sense. A relationship that would consist of only occasional organizational links could be described as less close, yet not distant due to the regularity of activities involved. A relationship without even a few occasional links should be considered distant or inactive/non-existent at the organizational level.

Although we should emphasize the fact that we believe there is a hierarchy between the three main categories or levels, this does not imply that we assume *a priori* that formal links are more significant politically than those generated at the individual level. This is, at the end of the day, an empirical question. Patterns that are kept 'informal' for some reason may be self-reproducing and perfectly 'organized'. The hierarchy we suggest simply means that we think some links are stronger than others in a technical organizational sense—likely but not guaranteed to involve a different degree of commitment. By mapping the number of types and links we are able to cover all the possible permutations—ranging from full integration to complete detachment. However, we pay most attention to links measured at the organizational level (the links shaded grey in Table 2.2). As noted in Chapter 1, for reasons of tractability, we concentrate on the national/leadership level of politics, fully acknowledging that in doing this we are forced to discount potentially important interactions in federal states and at the local level in all of the polities we look at.

Before aggregating an overall score, we investigate whether or not the different kinds/types of links can be captured in one dimension (see the section on 'Measuring the Overall Strength of Organizational Links' for the links each category denotes in practice).

CASE SELECTION: A MULTI-LEVEL DESIGN

The 'cases' of this book are parties and trade unions, or their relationships. However, they operate—and are nested—in different countries. As mentioned in Chapter 1, our focus is on mature democracies, i.e. countries that were democratized for the first time before or in the 1940s, and have been continuously democratic since then, on three continents: Australia, Austria, Finland, France, Germany, Israel, Italy, the Netherlands, Sweden, Switzerland, the United Kingdom, and the US.

Countries Selected

The selection of countries ensures that we study parties and unions that operate in national-level settings across several continents that differ in some potentially significant respects. They are all economically developed, industrialized, and urbanized, and as Lijphart (1999) points out, all of them belong to the Western, originally Judeo-Christian world. But they also vary along several relevant system-level variables. The key differences, reflecting the hypotheses on country-level variables discussed in Chapter 1, are presented in Tables 2.1a and 2.1b.

The differences are relatively small as far as employment patterns/class structure goes, but we see that Finland and Sweden are characterized by relatively high union density, whereas France and the US are at the other end of the scale, marked by low union density. Austria has a low, indeed the lowest, level of union fragmentation, whereas France is at the other extreme where the probability that any two union members are in the same confederation is particularly low. Here it is worth noting, however, that some of the countries with low fragmentation, like the United Kingdom, may have only one peak association but that this is not necessarily strong. The average number of left-of-centre parties has increased but varies across the selected countries: whereas there is only one significant left-of-centre party in the US and UK (Democrats and Labour), there are multiple competitors in other countries.

As far as corporatism goes, we see that despite a trend of decline, there is still significant variation across countries (see Table 2.1b). According to Martin and Swank's composite measure of corporatism, the most corporatist state today is Austria, whereas the least corporatist (most pluralist) are the United

Table 2.1a. Country selection and various contextual variables[1]

Year/country	Size of working class (sector)[2a]		Size of working class (occupation)[2b]		Size of lower service segment[2c]			Degree of class voting[3]		Size of public sector[4]		Union density[5]		Union fragmentation[6]		Left party fragmentation[7]	
	1960	2008	1969	2008	1969	1995	2008	1961–70	1981–90	2000	2013	1960–5	2011	1960–5	2011	1960–4	2013
Australia	48.7	20.1 (12)	41.9	25.9	16.5	13.6 (97)	15.0	29.3	19.4	15.1	14.3 (12)	49.1	18.0	2.9	1.9 (08)	1.0	1.0
Austria	49.6 (69)	28.0 (11)	36.2 (84)	30.4	19.7 (84)	13.1	13.9	27.4	18.3	–	–	67.0	28.1 (10)	1.0	1.0 (10)	1.1	1.9
Finland	44.8	26.2	31.6 (77)	28.3	19.6 (77)	14.8 (00)	15.6	50.2	35.7	22.2	24.4 (11)	35.2	69.2 (09)	3.9	2.8	2.4	3.4
France	48.8 (62)	22.8 (06)	–	30.2	–	12.2 (03)	12.5	18.3	11.7	25.0	17.9	19.7	7.6 (08)	4.3	7.9	1.9	1.9
Germany	56.8	30.7 (09)	39.0 (70)	30.5	19.9 (70)	10.8	12.2	24.8	13.4	16.4	14.3 (11)	33.7	18.5 (10)	1.5	1.6	1.0	2.3
Israel	42.9 (69)	19.7 (11)	37.4 (70)	15.6	20.1 (70)	16.8	16.3	–	–	17.3	16.5 (08)	74.0 (69)	34.0 (06)	–	–	2.1	3.1
Italy	48.8 (62)	30.5 (10)	–	34.3	–	15.7	11.4	14.5	13.1	15.3	16.0	25.5	35.1 (10)	2.8	3.4	1.8	1.5
Netherlands	38.0 (75)	18.5	32.7 (77)	23.6	20.7 (77)	12.6	14.1	14.7	15.5	20.4	21.3 (11)	38.7	18.2	4.2	2.2	1.2	1.9
Sweden	41.0 (70)	21.8	37.7 (70)	25.6	21.5 (70)	18.1 (97)	19.0	40.7	32.7	29.0 (01)	25.8	69.4	54.6	1.7	2.9 (10)	1.2	1.4
Switzerland	35.3 (86)	23.0 (09)	–	24.1	–	12.3	13.2	–	12.8	14.7 (01)	17.3	34.2	17.8 (09)	2.7	3.4 (10)	1.0	1.0
United Kingdom	50.2	18.1 (12)	–	17.9	–	17.7	15.8	38.3	23.4	18.0	21.5	38.7	25.8	1.8	1.4	1.0	1.0
United States	38.2	21.6 (02)	35.3 (70)	21.8	18.5	27.6 (03)	28.0	7.7	8.1	14.8	14.6 (08)	29.1	11.3 (09)	1.7	2.7 (09)	1.0	1.0

Table 2.1b. Country selection and various contextual variables[1]

Year/country	Corporatism[8a] 1960	Corporatism[8a] 2000	Routine involvement of unions and employers' organizations in government[8b] 1960	Routine [...] 2013	State funding to parties (2013)[9] Permanent	State funding Electoral	Party finance restrictions (2013)[10] Individuals	Corporations	Trade unions	Foreign	Federalism[11] 1960–5	Federalism 2008–14	Parliamentary government[12] 1960–5	Parliamentary 2008–14	Electoral system[13] 1972	Electoral 2005	Effective number of parties[14] 1960	Effective 2011
Australia	−0.2	−0.3	0	1	No	Yes	No	No	No	No	1	1	0	0	4	4	3.0	3.3
Austria	0.6	0.5	2	2	Yes	No	No	No	No	Yes	1	1	1	1	3	3	2.5	4.8
Finland	0.5	0.4	0	1	Yes	No	Yes	Yes	Yes	Yes	0	0	1	1	3	3	5.2	6.5
France	−0.2	−0.4	0	0	Yes	Yes	Yes	Forbidden	Forbidden	Forbidden	0	0	0	1	2	2	6.1	4.1
Germany	−0.04	−0.1	1	1	Yes	No	No	No	No	Yes	2	2	0	0	4	4	3.6	5.6
Israel	–	–	2	0	Yes	Yes	Yes	Forbidden	Forbidden	Forbidden	0	0	0	0	3	3	5.2	7.3
Italy	0.3	0.3	0	1	No	Yes	Yes	Yes	Yes	Yes	0	0	0	0	4	4	3.9	3.8
Netherlands	1.0	0.01	2	2	Yes	No	No	No	No	No	0	0	0	0	3	3	4.5	7.0
Sweden	1.0	0.4	2	1	Yes	No	No	No	No	No	0	0	0	0	3	3	3.3	4.8
Switzerland	−0.1	−0.2	2	2	No	No	No	No	No	No	2	2	2	2	3	4	5.0	6.4
United Kingdom	−0.5	−1.1	0	0	No	No	No	No	No	Forbidden	0	0	0	0	1	1	2.3	3.7
United States	−1.5	−1.6	0	0	No	Yes	Yes	Forbidden	Forbidden	Forbidden	2	2	2	2	1	2	2.0	2.2

Notes

[1] Details regarding measurements and sources are, with a few exceptions, not provided in the tables' notes but in the Appendix to Chapter 16 (Table A16.2). The year of estimate is provided in parenthesis when it differs from that stated in the second row. A hyphen indicates that data are missing from the source(s) used. For Germany, pre-1990 figures are for the Federal Republic of Germany.

2a Share of employees working in the industrial sector (except Israel and Switzerland, see end of note). Figures from 1960 are based on ISIC rev. 2 (categories 2–5: mining and quarrying, manufacturing, electricity, gas and water, and construction). The Finnish 1960 figure is based on category 3 and 5 only; the Italian figure is based on category 3 only. Figures from 2008 are based on ISIC rev. 3 (categories C–F: mining and quarrying, manufacturing, electricity, gas and water, and construction). For Israel, the figures concern the share of civilians employed in the industrial sector. For Switzerland, the figures concern employment in the industrial sector. Sources: Bank of Israel Report 2013 (2014); OECD (2014).

2b Share of employees working in industrial occupations. Figures from 1969 are based on ISCO-68 (categories 7–9: production and related workers, transport equipment operators, and labourers). Figures from 2008 are based on ISCO-88 (categories 7–9: craft and related trade workers, plant and machine operators, and assemblers and elementary occupations). The Israeli 2008 figure does not include category 7; the British and American figures do not include category 9. Source: ILO Labour Statistics (2014).

2c Share of employees working in sales and services. Figures from 1969 and 1995 are based on ISCO-68 (category 5: service workers and shop and market sales workers). Figures from 2008 are based on ISCO-88 (categories 4–5: sales workers and service workers). Note that the 2008 figures are not directly comparable to the ones from 1969 and 1995 since they are based on a less inclusive classification scheme. Source: ILO Labour Statistics (2014).

3 Level of class voting measured by the Alford Index. Source: Nieuwbeerta (1996: 356).

4 Public sector employment as a share of the labour force. Public sector employment covers all employment of the general government sector as defined in the System of National Accounts plus employment of public corporations. Source: OECD (2011; 2013b; 2015).

5 Share of employees who are members of a trade union. The 1960–5 figures are a calculated mean. The Israeli 1969 figure concerns party membership in the general Histadrut among wage and salary workers. In addition, about 5 per cent of wage and salary workers were organized in trade unions that were not part of Histadrut. Sources: Cohen et al. (2003, 695); Mundlak et al. (2013); OECD (2013a).

6 Effective number of unions. The 1960–5 figures are a calculated mean. Source: Visser (2015).

7 Effective number of left parties on the votes level. Sources: Swank (2013); Döring and Manow (2016).

8a Standard-score index of employer organization, union organization (index of union density, union peak association power, as for employers, and policy-process integration of labour), and the level of collective bargaining. Source: Martin and Swank (2012a; 2012b).

8b Coded: (0) no concertation, involvement is rare or absent, (1) partial concertation, irregular and infrequent involvement, and (2) full concertation, regular and frequent involvement. Source: Visser (2015).

9 Existence of permanent and electoral state subsidies. Source: Casas-Zamora (2005, 19–20), updated by means of International IDEA (2016) and other sources (coded by us).

10 Existence of restrictions on donations to parties from individuals, corporations, trade unions, and foreign actors. Note that in Germany, the restrictions for foreign actors do not apply to EU nationals. In Italy, the restrictions for individuals do not apply if the donations are to the parties' routine expenses; for corporations, specific types of donations are forbidden. Source: Casas-Zamora (2005, 19–20), updated by means of International IDEA (2016) and other sources (coded by the authors).

11 Coded: (0) non-federal, (1) weakly federal, and (2) strongly federal. Source: Armingeon et al. (2014).

12 Coded: (0) parliamentary, (1) mixed (semi-presidential), and (2) presidential democracy. Note that France went from parliamentary to mixed (semi-presidential) in 1965. Source: Cheibub et al. (2010).

13 Type of electoral system for legislative elections. Coded: (1) plurality (first past the post), (2) majority, (3) proportional representation (PR), and (4) mixed systems (combination of PR and either plurality or majority). This option includes situations in which a single chamber contains seats selected by different methods, or situations in which all of the seats in a chamber are chosen by the same method, but each chamber is selected through different methods. Source: Regan et al. (2009). For Israel: Gideon Rahat.

14 Effective number of parties on the votes level. Source: Armingeon et al. (2014).

States and the United Kingdom. If we concentrate on routine involvement of trade unions and employers' organizations in government decisions on social and economic policy, we see that Austria, the Netherlands, and Switzerland are characterized by 'full concertation, regular and frequent involvement', whereas France, Israel, the United Kingdom, and the United States are at the other end of the spectrum, marked by 'no concertation, involvement is rare or absent'. The question is whether and how this affects party–union relationships, as discussed in Chapter 1.

When it comes to state subventions, Switzerland and the United Kingdom stand out with virtually no public support to parties, whereas four countries in our selection both provide general support and election support: Austria, France, Italy, Australia, and Israel. In France, Israel, and the US, donations from trade unions to parties are forbidden, and in Italy there are limitations, whereas in all other countries such transfers are completely legal. However, it should be noted that, although the American system limits private financial contributions, it has been unable to place limits on campaign expenditures. As a result, parties and interest groups have tried to find ways around the regulations. One such are the independent political action committees (PACs) attached to interest groups whose purpose is fundraising for candidates. That said, parties in two countries both depend more strongly on unions' financial support than others and are also allowed to receive such donations, namely in Switzerland and the United Kingdom, although legislation recently mooted by the UK's Conservative government looks as if it may reduce such funding to the Labour Party in the long term. The selected countries also differ as regards state structure and the relationship between the legislature and the executive.

In other words, the countries we have included certainly vary along the variables highlighted in Chapter 1. Our priority in this book is to give a broad overview of party–union links in mature democracies in different parts of the world and to explore variation at the level of parties and unions. How and indeed whether this variation turns out to matter will be one of the key questions addressed in Chapter 16. Although one challenge we have to surmount is the mismatch between a large number of country-level variables and a limited number of country cases, we think there is enough variation and there are enough cases to generate new insights on how party–union relationships vary across different settings. The contextual information is also used by country experts when they describe the system-level conditions, and changes herein, for links between left-of-centre parties and trade unions in a comparative perspective.

Political Parties Examined

As noted in Chapter 1, the party focus of this study are the social democratic/labour/socialist/communist parties associated with the historic labour movement. This means that 'old' left-of-centre parties are included, while new left parties—for instance, those that first got going in the 1970s—are excluded. But if splinter groups from old left parties have established new significant left parties (after the Second World War), these have been included as well as they can be argued to have roots in the old labour movement.

Since we will look at today's relationships in the light of historical facts, we limit ourselves to parties with enduring representation in parliament by excluding left-of-centre parties that made what turned out to be only a passing appearance on the political scene in the post-war period. Moreover, to be included, parties have to have held seats in one of the last three legislative terms. As a result, between one and three left-of-centre parties are studied in every country.

In addition, in cases where trade unions were split historically and where some unions have had strong links to non-socialist parties (such as Christian democratic parties) that still exist, these parties are included in the country analyses in order to give a more complete country description seen from the unions' point of view. But because we focus on the labour movement, the comparative element of our work only addresses the old social democratic/ labour/socialist/communist parties. Information on links to other parties, however, will be described in order to cast light on the cross-national comparison of old left-of-centre party–trade union relationships. After all, historical closeness to other parties might be one explanation for relative distance to left-of-centre parties today.

We look both at *extra-legislative central party organizations* (CPOs) and at *legislative party groups* (LPGs), since parties in some countries (for instance, the UK) only have relatively weak and politically insignificant organizations outside the national legislature and, as a result, by no means all significant contact will take place on a party headquarters to union headquarters basis. In this way, we can also compare across two 'faces' of parties, and touch more directly upon public decision-making rather than just on party programmes and manifestos.

Trade Unions Surveyed

A trade union is an association of labourers/employees in a particular trade, industry, company, institution, or organization created for the purpose of securing improvements in pay, benefits, working conditions, and/or social and political status through collective bargaining. Changes and variety in the trade union world have, in many countries, been more pronounced than they have been in the party system. As a result, we include both old unions and unions that have been founded (sometimes as the result of mergers of older unions) relatively recently. In this way, we might be able to see whether left-of-centre parties have widened the range of their relationships from blue-collar unions to include different types of employees (on an equal footing).

At the same time, we have chosen to narrow the universe we aim to cover to peak associations, at least where they exist. Hence, *in each country all today's union confederations are included*, no matter when they were founded. In this way, we can generalize about the peak associations, and will cover unions with different interest profiles: both white collar (administration and service) and blue collar (industry and business), as well as both public and private sector unions—and unions with partisan and non-partisan origins.

A few identification/selection issues should be noted. In the countries where peak associations are few and far between and/or relatively unimportant—in the US, the UK, and Australia—we have included 4–5 major individual unions (including 'super-unions' that recent processes of consolidation have produced) as equivalents, making sure we covered both white-collar and blue-collar, public and private sector, unions. In Austria, where the peak association is strong but there is only one, the three largest unions, in terms of membership, are also included in order to capture variation in union profiles. In Germany, where one out of three peak associations completely dominates (DGB), and the two others (DBB and CGB) are not full-blown alternatives, we have instead included four individual unions for the same reason. In France, the number of confederations is particularly high, and including every single one might have significantly reduced the chance that the parties would complete our survey. Here we have therefore excluded one fragmented peak association (G10) and one managerial one (CGC-CFE).[3]

The Party-Union Dyads

The primary unit of analysis is *pairs of parties and confederations/unions* (i.e. party-union dyads). Or more precisely, we have identified one set of pairs consisting of relationships between the party CPOs and individual confederations/unions, and one set consisting of relationships between party LPGs and confederations/unions. In other words, every party CPO and every party LPG is 'paired' with all the confederations/unions studied in the given country. To illustrate: if there is one party and three confederations, as in the Italian case, there will be 3 + 3 party-union dyads: the three relationships between the Democratic Party's CPO and the confederations—CGIL (Italian General Confederation of Labour), CISL (Italian Confederation of Workers' Trade Unions), UIL (Italian Union of the Labour)—and three relationships between the Democratic party's LPG and CGIL, CISL, and UiL respectively. A complete list of parties, confederations/unions and party-union pairs/dyads is included in the Appendix at the end of this chapter. There are 81 (CPO) + 81 (LPG) left-of-centre party-union pairs to be mapped altogether in the cross-country analyses, although not all will be included in the scaling analysis due to missing values (i.e. 'unclear values', see section on 'Measuring the Overall Strength of Organizational Links'). A complete list of parties, confederations/unions, and party-union pairs/dyads is included in the Appendix at the end of this chapter.

DATA COLLECTION: COMBINING MULTIPLE SOURCES

The datasets underpinning this book are based on multiple sources. First, the statutes of the organizational units involved have been collected and country experts have also searched for other relevant organizational documents (like annual reports) and reliable secondary sources. Second, we have elicited both information and evaluations through questionnaires—mainly about organizational facts—sent to key informants in both parties and the union confederations/unions. Each country team started by identifying a contact person/key informant in each organization and invited them to participate in advance, selected according to formal position: The secretary-general (elected or employed) in the party's/parties' central organization or his/her equivalent, head of staff in the party's/parties' legislative group, and the leader (elected) or secretary-general in the given peak association/unions. In most cases the informants were party/union officials of very high rank. However, in some cases country experts found it necessary, and just as informative, to talk to people a little lower down the pecking order. The main point was to get access to a particularly well-informed person who could respond *on behalf of* its party/organization. In a couple of countries it was very difficult to get responses back, and country experts conducted a structured interview instead.

As already explained, we mapped links between unions and both the party in central office and the party in public office (and in particular the legislature), and decided to seek information directly from the latter rather than assuming one key informant could cover both. Therefore we constructed three generic versions of the questionnaire: one for the union confederations/unions, one for the parties' legislative group, and one for the extra-legislative party organization. Among other things, we have asked both the parties and the confederations/unions about the existence of every link type and created a data set of dichotomous link variables. So the questions were mainly identical, and in this way we increased the validity by having two sources. Moreover, we are able to see whether the parties and unions evaluate their relationship differently when it comes to their own *perceptions of closeness*, and in this way also include both formal and informal meetings. It is not a given, for example, that they have a shared view on how 'close' they are even though the formal status of the relationship is clear. Diverging views on relationships is a key issue in dyadic data analysis (e.g. in psychology). In addition, in the union questionnaire we included a couple of questions regarding links to *other* parties in general (even if these are not included in the study as separate units).[4]

The survey was conducted in the autumn of 2013, but in a few cases the questionnaires were sent out at the end of 2013/beginning of 2014. However, we do not consider this time gap to be a major problem, as most questions deal with situations over the last five years. The questionnaires were translated from British English into US English, Dutch, Finnish, French, German, Hebrew, Italian, and Swedish by both language professionals and country experts.

The total response rate was about 70 per cent, among both parties and unions. When returned, the data were input into three country data files by the project's research assistants: one for confederations/unions, one for the legislative parties, and one for the extra-legislative parties. After checking by country experts, three comparative datasets were then created based on these files. Thereafter, these three comparative datasets provided the basis for creating one dyadic dataset across countries (see section on 'The Problem of Missing and Diverging Party/Union Answers'). Responses to open-ended questions and the specification of 'other alternatives' etc., were translated by the country teams and then inserted in a joint text (Word) file with responses attached to unique unit numbers.[5]

Third, biographical data have—if available—been collected from encyclopaedias and the websites of parliament/MPs (see country chapters for details) during winter/spring 2013/14 to see what proportion of them hold or have held positions (as officials or staff) in different trade unions. The aim was to map only the permanent representatives and deputy representatives who attended for the entire term (e.g. for a minister), and to include positions at both the national and local level, but to distinguish between them as we focus on the national level of politics.

As for the independent variables, these data are based on our party/union surveys and imported from, or calculated based on, reliable, publicly available comparative datasets (see details in Chapter 16, including the Appendix).

THE PROBLEM OF MISSING AND DIVERGING
PARTY/UNION ANSWERS

A few methodological problems, and one joint solution, should be noted. The total response rate was an impressive 70 per cent, among both parties and unions, but the willingness/ability to respond varied between countries: ranging from a 100 per cent response rate in Finland and Switzerland to less than

20 per cent returned questionnaires in the case of US and Australia. In a study where we are surveying a complete but limited universe (not a random large N-sample), that is of course a challenge. The preparation of the data files has also, naturally, revealed some missing answers and, in addition, divergent party/union answers to identical questions in some countries. The possibility of differing views is one of the reasons why we thought it was important to ask both sides, and this aspect of the research design is partly what makes our study innovative. However, we do not think that party–union relationships are merely social constructions, and our main aim is to map organizational facts: links that either exist or do not exist. Despite room for interpretation and perception regarding the less institutionalized links, we sought, wherever possibly, to discover the actual truth.

Whatever the reasons for unreturned questionnaires, missing answers and divergent party/union responses, we decided to consider the three datasets created from the survey as the official version of the relationship that the two sides decided to report. Party/union responses to similar questions may be identical or they may not. Those who did not respond were also included with missing only. Next, in the dyadic dataset we constructed variables that capture convergence/divergence. Then, in addition we included variables with 'defini-tive' expert codings regarding the organizational facts, accepting that, where responses contradict each other or have proven impossible to obtain, the country specialists should answer according either to information available from public sources (the ideal) or else an expert judgement call on their part. What seems likely to be the truth in cases where answers differ/are missing? This is to be considered a 'coded judgment' by the country expert, based on *both* the surveys *and* other sources. If the party and union in a given case both responded and agreed, this value was as a general rule used for the expert coding. We have in this dyadic file also created a variable to measure the degree of confidence, ranging from 0 to 100. The country experts were asked to choose 'unclear/don't know' if they weren't confident about their codings (less than 40 degrees). The average degree of confidence is across all countries is 93. The range goes from a minimum value of 46 to the maximum 100, but no country has a mean degree-of-confidence score lower than 75.

The closeness of the relationships involving the party CPOs and the party LPGs are assessed separately in each step of the analysis, as these are different party units and not all links relevant for the CPOs apply to the LPGs—an obvious example being the collective affiliation of unions. When comparing dyads we distinguish between their basic features in terms of type of party/union 'members':

Party side (SideP_IDx):

- Major old left-of-centre party (socialist, social democrat or equivalent).
- Communist or other left-of-centre party with origins in the old left.

- Other left-of-centre party with origins in the old left.

Union side (SideU_IDx):

- Traditional left-of-centre union ally.
- Traditional right-of-centre union ally.
- Other.

By 'traditional ally' we mean a confederation/union that has been known for having a fairly close/close relationship with one or more left-of-centre parties *or* a centre-right party (such as the Catholic parties/Christian Democrats). These variables were coded by country experts, in line with our general conceptualization. The dyads/pairs in which we are most interested are the relationships between the CPOs/LPGs of the major old left-of-centre parties (socialist, social democrat, or equivalent) and the confederations and/or major unions closely associated with the historical labour movement.

DEGREE OF CLOSENESS AND RANGE: INDICATORS OF LINKS

Our aim is to measure the extent to which links create a structured and highly formalized system that enables contact between the organizations involved based on the conceptualization presented in the previous section. Table 2.2 presents the dichotomous link variables that guided the mapping of party-union statutes and construction of questionnaires. The table's columns cover extra-legislative and legislative party together, but note that the links labelled 'collective membership' and 'invitation to the party's annual congress' are only relevant in the case of the extra-legislative party organization. Based on what we know, we have also assumed that *ex officio* representation of unions is irrelevant in the case of parties' legislative groups. The list is not exhaustive; but it is extensive and based on a review of existing literature (see e.g. Duverger 1954/1972; Valen and Katz 1964; Kriesi and van Praag 1987; Kitschelt 1989; Padgett and Paterson 1991; Quinn 2002; Poguntke 2002; 2006; Sundberg 2003). In addition we asked whether 'official social media connections (such as mutual followers on twitter)' exist, but this turned out to be a problematic item (generating mostly missing values) and is thus excluded from the analysis. We believe social media connections are best studied by data generated directly from social media.

Our primary focus is organizational, but we also include less formal links insofar as they are politically relevant. Hopefully, this means we avoid giving a really fine-grained analysis for old, strongly institutionalized links, while links which are probably crucial these days due to developments in ICT are simply

Table 2.2. Sub-groups of links providing contact between parties (CPO/LPG) and unions at the national level, with items listed in hierarchical order of strength (measures at the organizational level in shaded area)

Overlapping organizational structures	Inter-organizational links	Individual-level links
National/local collective affiliation (membership) of a union* (assuming parties are not affiliated to unions) The party enjoys representation rights in the union's national decision-making bodies (one or more): ▪ National congress ▪ National executive ▪ Board of representatives The union enjoys representation rights in the party's national decision-making bodies (one or more): ▪ National congress ▪ National executive ▪ National council	*Reciprocal, durable—joint arrangements/agreements:* Tacit (*de facto* official) agreements about mutual representation in national decision-making bodies Permanent joint committee(s) Temporary joint committee(s) Formal (written) agreements about regular meetings between party and union Tacit (*de facto* official) agreements about regular meetings between party and union Joint conferences Joint campaigns *One-way, occasional—party/group-arranged meetings:* Invitation to party to participate in the organization's national congress Invitation to organization to participate in the party's national congress/conference Invitations to organization to participate in the party's ordinary meetings, seminars, and conferences Invitations to party to participate in ordinary organization meetings, seminars, and conferences Invitations to organization to special consultative arrangements initiated by the party Invitations to party to special consultative arrangements initiated by the organization *Reciprocal, occasional—formal (i.e. official) meetings at the individual level:* ▪ Formal face-to-face meetings or telephone/video calls ▪ Speakers at each other's seminars/conferences ▪ Formal written letters (including electronic)	*Meetings:* Various forms of informal (i.e. unofficial) contact of political relevance between individual representatives and spokesmen: ▪ Informal written communication like personal letters, memos ▪ Informal written communication via SMS, e-mail and social media (Facebook, Twitter etc.) ▪ Informal face-to-face meetings ▪ Informal oral contact via telephone/Skype etc. *Personnel:* Personal overlaps in—or transfers to—the party's/union's decision-making bodies:** ▪ Party/union top elite members who hold or have held office in union/party (share of overlap between bodies in sum) ▪ Party/union top elite members who are or have been staff members at the national or local levels in party/union

* Local collective membership is included although it is not per se a national feature. The reason is that collective membership at the local level indirectly implies a potentially strong formal 'bottom-up' link to the national party organization *and* it is regulated by national party statutes.

** Overlapping regular memberships are not included, as the focus is on links opening up for contact between parties and interest groups, i.e. the organizational level or decision-making elite level.

bundled into a residual category, labelled 'informal'. Personnel overlaps—namely the extent to which party elites hold positions in unions and vice versa—may be different from other measures, which are about frameworks and activities. But, since one can argue that 'being' is as important as 'doing' in any relationship, they should ideally be included, not least because they open up multiple opportunities for contact between decision makers.

However, we will only be able to get a crude measure of personnel overlaps/ transfer and we will not be able to map formal and informal meetings at the individual level—just the key informants' views on what kind of contact they find most common.[6] Therefore our total quantitative scores will summarize those links measured at the organizational level, based on party statutes and information provided by our key informants, and the data we have on other (informal) kinds of links at the individual level will be presented separately. That said, we try to look at the relationship between links at the organizational level and those materializing at the individual level: are statutory and inter-organizational links supplemented and reinforced by informal personnel links, or do such ties seem to be something which compensates for weak links at the organizational level?

Finally, we are interested in the overall range of individual parties' and unions' relationships: are left-of-centre parties only or primarily linked to their traditional union ally or have they established (equal) links with a wide range of employee organizations and unions with and without a partisan history? We will also briefly touch upon the relationship of trade unions with other (green, new left, new/radical right, or centre-right) parties in general.

MEASURING THE OVERALL STRENGTH OF ORGANIZATIONAL LINKS

Next, we need to consider how we can aggregate and measure the strength of organizational-level—statutory and formal inter-organizational—links. We would like to know whether an additive index is justified given the structure of the responses. In Table 2.2 the possible links are hierarchically ordered internally from stronger to weaker in terms of the degree of 'institutionalization' involved (see shaded area). It could be argued that our basic distinction implies the following: in order to have a completely integrated relationship overlapping structures are required; to have a (fairly) close relationship at least some formal and durable inter-organizational links are needed; a purely ad hoc relationship, however, consists of only occasional organizational links. But the relationships between and within these categories of links are by no means given, so we will start by testing this empirically.[7] Does the relationship between the various links appear to be hierarchical, as we assume, and do they tap a one-dimensional scale of 'closeness' or multiple scales? In order to integrate the items—the kinds of organizational-level links included in the questionnaire (see Table 2.3)—to a scale, one would need to know whether all the items empirically measure the same underlying concept. Do the most institutionalized (strongest) links preclude—even render superfluous—links at a lower level or do they instead nurture more links?

It might be that parties and trade unions tend either to have overlapping structures or inter-organizational links, thereby making addition across the main categories we have identified less meaningful (see e.g. Rasmussen and

Table 2.3. Left-of-centre party–trade union relationships: item and scale scalability values[1]

Variable (link items)	Party CPO-unions		Party LPG-unions		Party-unions	
	H_i	(%)	H_i	(%)	H_i	(%)
Collective union affiliation to party (local/national)	1.00	1	–	–	1.00	2
Union delegates at party conference	0.89	3	–	–	0.89	3
Party delegates at union conference	1.00	1	–	–	1.00	2
Party *ex officio seats* in union executive	n/a	0	–	–	–	–
Union *ex officio seats* in party executive	n/a	0	–	–	–	–
Party *ex officio seats* in union council	n/a	0	–	–	–	–
Union *ex officio seats* in party council	n/a	0	–	–	–	–
Tacit agreement about mutual representation	0.86	19	0.62	6	0.88	21
Permanent joint committee(s)	0.78	16	0.52	11	0.83	15
Temporary joint committee(s)	0.83	12	0.55	6	0.94	11
Formal agreement about regular meetings	0.74	4	0.81	3	0.95	3
Tacit agreement about regular meetings	0.85	35	0.66	20	0.86	38
Joint party-union conferences	0.78	18	0.41	8	0.82	20
Joint party-union campaigns	0.69	16	0.55	15	0.66	20
Party invited to union's conference	0.82	46	0.70	42	0.81	52
Union invited to party's conference	0.71	60	–	–	0.62	59
Union invited to party's ordinary meetings, seminars, etc.	0.75	51	0.79	48	0.81	53
Party invited to union's ordinary meetings, seminars, etc.	0.72	47	0.76	45	0.79	50
Union invited to party's special consultative arrangements	0.74	69	0.68	76	0.82	79
Party invited to union's special consultative arrangements	0.76	51	0.50	50	0.43	59
H	0.78		0.64		0.80	
Standard error	0.06		0.06		0.05	
N	68		66		66	

[1] This table concerns the relationships between communist, social-democratic, and other old left-of-centre parties and all confederations of trade unions/selected unions in every country (pairs of individual parties and confederations/unions). The empty cells (-) represent links we assume are mostly not applicable in the case of LPGs and that we have not surveyed.

Lindeboom 2013). A similar question concerns the association between different types of inter-organizational links: do units with the strongest links also tend to have the weaker kind too? The different types of link are not necessarily mutually exclusive. If that is the case, then having fewer 'institutional' links *in addition* to stronger ones might increase the degree of closeness. We therefore use a scaling analysis to explore the dimensionality empirically. We assume the link items *mirror* one or more fundamental ways of being connected so that we can expect items mirroring the same underlying dimension/concept to go together. Do some clusters of items cohere, but not all items?

The choice of scaling method has strong implications for the results that one gets: ultimately, data reduction is a process of creation (Coombs 1964). Researchers choose specific scaling methods and construct certain spaces. It is important to choose a method that fits the structure of the data that one examines. The data we have here are dichotomous: specific kinds of links either do or do not occur. This means that correlation-based methods such as factor analysis cannot be used here: they are mainly appropriate for data with a normal distribution. Instead, we employ Mokken scaling (Mokken 1971; van Schuur 2003), a method that was specifically developed for dichotomous data—such as, for correct and incorrect answers in exams. Mokken wanted to assesses the extent to which items with correct and incorrect answers could be integrated into a single scale, running from easy items (that most people answer correctly) to difficult items (that most people answer incorrectly). In other words, his scale incorporated a hierarchical element, while its quality can be judged on the number of errors: namely the number of times people who answer the difficult questions correctly get the easy questions wrong—expressed in the H-value.

In our context, Mokken scaling would mean that a single scale runs from the more common weaker (occasional) links to the strongest (most institutional) uncommon ones. Hence, we will test whether pairs of parties and trade unions that have unusually strong links also enjoy the links that occur in many party–union relationships. If all items line up, then we can construct a single scale. The strength of the scale is expressed in the H-value. An H-value below 0.3 is unacceptable. An H-value below 0.4 is poor. An H-value below 0.5 is mediocre and an H-value above 0.5 is good. We can also zoom into the relationship between one item and the other items in the scale. This is expressed in the H_i-value. It is important to note that in Mokken scaling analysis, as most kinds of regression analysis, cases with one or more missing values (i.e. 'unclear'/'don't know' in our case) are removed from the analysis. This means that 68/66 of the dyads (84/82 per cent) are included in the scaling analysis of the dyads involving unions and the party's central organizations and legislative party groups respectively.

Since we cover the entire population of surviving left-of-centre parties and peak associations (major unions) in the countries concerned, there are no sampling errors involved. However, we should keep in mind that those dyads including individual unions are slightly underrepresented compared to those including confederations. Moreover, the excluded relationships are not evenly distributed between countries. Only four out of eight of the Austrian party-union pairs are included in the scaling analysis, and only three out of six Italian dyads. In the case of the United Kingdom, the scaling analysis only covers the relationship of Labour's CPO with the only British 'confederation' (TUC) and one individual union (GMB), and in parliament only the relationships between Labour and two individual unions (GMB and Unite). In the case of Sweden, two of sixteen dyads are excluded (including the previous communist party, *Vänsterpartiet*). In the Swiss case, one dyad involving the main Social Democratic Party, LPG, and the confederation SGB, the traditional union ally, is excluded. Finally, in the Australian case the scaling analysis only includes the relationships between the Labour Party's central organization and the only Australian confederation of trade unions (ACTU) and one individual union (ANMF). A complete of list of included units can be seen in Table A2 in this chapter's Appendix.

Table 2.3 provides an overview of the scaling results for the remaining cases. First we look at the dyads involving the parties' central party organizations (CPO). The H-value for the scale for these dyads is very high (H value of 0.78). Every individual item relates sufficiently strongly to the other items, as the H_i-values show. The results are somewhat weaker for the dyads involving legislative party groups (LPGs), with a lower number of possible links, but the scale is still 'good' (H value of 0.64). Every individual item has sufficiently strong relations with the other items in the scale. We also see that some (the strongest) links are unusual, others (the weaker ones) are more common, and some could even be said to be prevalent. We will get back to the frequency of links in detail in the descriptive cross-national analysis in Chapter 15.

In the column to the right, we provide a scaling analysis based on values of the CPO-union dyads and LPG-union dyads combined. We assigned the values as follows: a value of 1 if a union link exists either with the LPG or the CPO and value of 0 if there is no link with either of them. For other cases, namely where there is a 0 ('no link') and at least one entry of 'unclear/don't know' as a coded judgement, a missing value is entered. The result was 66 valid cases. We see the links items scale very well (H = 0.80).

Next we zoom into the difference between confederations and individual trade unions. In our data we have sixteen dyads involving an individual trade union and about fifty including confederations, within and outside the legislative arena. As for analysis of the CPO and LPG dyads combined, we have forty-six dyads including confederations and twenty including individual unions. This gives us six types of party-union groups (see Table A2.2 in the Appendix). For all four groups the H-value is sufficient.

To conclude, the scaling results are strong at the transnational level. Therefore, we have created an additive overall score of 'organizational closeness', by counting the number of 'yes values' for all the links used in the scaling analysis for all those dyads without any 'unclear values'. On the basis of the scaling analysis, a low score points to the existence of only weak (if common) ties, whereas the highest scores point to the existence of both weaker (common) and strong (less common) ties. We are, in line with the scaling analysis, able to assign an overall scale of closeness to 84/82 per cent of the cases. Links exist in the excluded cases as well, but it is not possible to assign an overall score due to one or more 'unclear values'. Since we assume the strongest links (those creating overlapping structures) are not applicable in the case of LPGs and hence have not been surveyed, we calculate separate total scores for the party-union pairs involving CPOs and LPGs, with 20 and 12 as maximum scores respectively. In Chapter 15 we will show that the two additive indexes are strongly correlated, and we calculate a combined score across 'party faces', running from 0 to 20, in order to get one score for the relationships between union confederations/ unions and the party/parties at large (for 82 per cent of the cases). The combined score will be what we focus on in the statistical analysis at the end of the book (Chapter 16).

We have also checked the results for individual countries, and they are more varied (see Table A2.3 in the Appendix). At least two dyads (with no missing values) are required to be assigned a scalability value. Moreover, there must be sufficient variance on the items: if there is zero variance on any item, no scale is produced. As a consequence, we cannot report individual scalability for Austria, Australia, Italy, the United Kingdom, Israel, and the union-LPG dyads of Switzerland. Of the remaining countries with sufficient valid cases, we find very strong scales in Finland, the Netherlands, Sweden. and France. The United States' dyads involving the central party organization of the Democrats still have sufficient scaling scores but they are much lower. The scales for dyads involving the US union-LPG and the German union-LPG dyads are insufficient. This means that in these countries the items relate somewhat differently than they do in the rest of the cases. Hence, one should be careful when disaggregating the data and examining the scales at the national level. We will focus our attention at the actual underlying data. That said, we see that we have scalability values for all countries for the analysis based on values of the CPO-union dyads and LPG-union dyads combined, and that these H-values are high in all countries (between 0.64 and 1.00).

THE ISSUE OF POLITICAL SIGNIFICANCE

An exploration of the extent to which party–union links have consequences for political decision-making, and whether degrees of organizational closeness matter for party–union patterns of influence, is beyond the scope of this book. Nevertheless, we will briefly address this issue towards the end of each country analysis (see Chapter 1). In this way, we also highlight that the strength of links may over time affect party-union resources. An initial indication can perhaps be provided by looking more closely at the content of the contact that goes on, based on secondary sources or information from additional interviews. Some meetings and correspondence might be fairly trivial and non-political in character, while contact in other cases may be marked by real attempts to influence decision makers (Svensson and Öberg 2002, 305).

A big question, of course, is whether the unions with which the parties interact actually influence political decisions. Do they, for instance, lead the party to formulate a policy proposition differently than would have been the case in the absence of any contact? And how much influence do parties have on the stances of trade unions? To reveal such changes of position is, not surprisingly, a very difficult task methodologically: a change in a party's policy preferences corresponding to the stance of a union (and vice versa) does not necessarily mean that the other side has caused this change. The party, for example, may have reached a similar conclusion independently, or other actors may have had an impact, for instance through the mass media. Clearly, a full exploration of this subject would require the examination of a host of possible intervening factors and would call for analyses of a wide range of specific policy fields.[8] Our rather more modest goal, however, is simply for the country teams to discuss whether the links generally seem to have a real impact based on their national expertise, including new knowledge obtained through their data collection.

CONCLUSION

Our goal is to understand how parties and trade unions are connected as organizations, by concentrating on specific links (be they overlapping organizational structures or other opportunities for interaction) that should allow us, ultimately, to look cross-nationally at organizational closeness/distance (the strength of links) between parties and trade unions and the range of each side's relationships (the variety of associates). In this chapter we have focused on how we define and operationalize both these dimensions. We have also presented our case selection and discussed its limitations as well as its advantages. And we have explained how the original data on relationships have been collected and systematized via the mapping of party-union statutes and a questionnaire to key informants on both sides. Lastly, after showing how we measure the overall strength of links quantitatively, we have discussed the question of their political significance. Chapters 15 and 16 will put all this together so we can paint a composite picture of the contemporary relationships between left-of-centre parties and trade unions. Before we can do that, however, we need to drill down further into the cases themselves.

APPENDIX

Table A2.1. List of countries, political parties, confederations and unions, and party-union pairs[1]

Country	Party name	Confederation name	Union name	Pair/dyad
Australia	ALP (Australian Labor Party)	ACTU (Australian Council of Trade Unions)	SDA (Shop Distributive and Allied Employees Association) ANMF (Australian Nursing Federation) AEU (Australian Education Union) CPSU (Community and Public Sector Union) AWU (Australian Workers' Union)	ALP (CPO)/ACTU *ALP (CPO)/SDA* ALP (CPO)/ANMF *ALP (CPO)/AEU* *ALP (CPO)/CPSU* *ALP (CPO)/AWU* *ALP (LPG)/ACTU* *ALP (LPG)/SDA* *ALP (LPG)/ANMF* *ALP (LPG)/AEU* *ALP (LPG)/CPSU* *ALP (LPG)/AWU*
Austria	SPÖ (Social Democratic Party of Austria)	ÖGB (Austrian Trade Union Federation)	GÖD (Public Services Union) PRO-GE (Union of Production Workers) GPA-djp (Union of Salaried Private Sector Employees and of Printers, Journalists and Paper Workers)	*SPÖ (CPO)/ÖGB* *SPÖ (CPO)/GÖD* SPÖ (CPO)/PRO-GE SPÖ (CPO)/GPA-djp *SPÖ (LPG)/ÖGB* *SPÖ (LPG)/GÖD* SPÖ (LPG)/PRO-GE SPÖ (LPG)/GPA-djp
Finland	SDP (Social Democratic Party of Finland) VAS (Left Alliance)	SAK (Central Organization of Finnish Trade Unions) STTK (Finnish Confederation of Professionals) AKAVA (Confederation of Unions for Professional and Managerial Staff in Finland)	SDP (CPO)/SAK SDP (CPO)/STTK SDP (CPO)/AKAVA SDP (LPG)/SAK SDP (LPG)/STTK SDP (LPG)/AKAVA VAS (CPO)/SAK VAS (CPO)/STTK VAS (CPO)/AKAVA VAS (LPG)/SAK VAS (LPG)/STTK VAS (LPG)/AKAVA
France	PS (Socialist Party) PCF (French Communist Party)	CGT (General Confederation of Labour) FO (General Confederation of Labour— Workers' Force) CFDT (French Democratic Confederation of Labour)	PS (CPO)/CGT PS (CPO)/FO PS (CPO)/CFDT PS (CPO)/CFTC PS (CPO)/UNSA

			CFTC (French Confederation of Christian Workers)	PS (CPO)/FSU
				PS (CPO)/USS
			UNSA (National Union of Autonomous Unions)	PS (LPG)/CGT
				PS (LPG)/FO
			FSU (United Trade Union Federation)	PS (LPG)/CFDT
			USS (Solidarity Trade Union)	PS (LPG)/CFTC
				PS (LPG)/UNSA
				PS (LPG)/FSU
				PS (LPG)/USS
				PCF (CPO)/CGT
				PCF (CPO)/FO
				PCF (CPO)/CFDT
				PCF (CPO)/CFTC
				PCF (CPO)/UNSA
				PCF (CPO)/FSU
				PCF (CPO)/USS
				PCF (LPG)/CGT
				PCF (LPG)/FO
				PCF (LPG)/CFDT
				PCF (LPG)/CFTC
				PCF (LPG)/UNSA
				PCF (LPG)/FSU
				PCF (LPG)/USS
Germany	SPD (Social Democratic party of Germany) Die Linke (The Left)	DGB (German Trade Union Confederation)	IG Metall (Industrial Metal Workers' Trade Union) Ver.di (United Services Trade Union) IG BCE (Trade Union for Mining, Chemicals and Energy Industries) GEW (German Education Union)	SPD (CPO)/DGB
				SPD (CPO)/IG Metall
				SPD (CPO)/Ver.di
				SPD (CPO)/IG BCE
				SPD (CPO)/GEW
				SPD (LPG)/DGB
				SPD (LPG)/IG Metall
				SPD (LPG)/Ver.di
				SPD (LPG)/IG BCE
				SPD (LPG)/GEW
				Die Linke (CPO)/DGB
				Die Linke (CPO)/IG Metall
				Die Linke (CPO)/Ver.di
				Die Linke (CPO)/ IG BCE
				Die Linke (CPO)/GEW
				Die Linke (LPG)/DGB
				Die Linke (LPG)/IG Metall
				Die Linke (LPG)/Ver.di
				Die Linke (LPG)/ IG BCE
				Die Linke (LPG)/GEW
Israel	Labour Meretz	Histadrut (The New Labour Federation) HL (The National Labour Federation) KL (Power to the Workers)		Labour (CPO)/Histadrut
				Labour (CPO)/HL
				Labour (CPO)/KL
				Labour (LPG)/Histadrut
				Labour (LPG)/HL
				Labour (LPG)/KL
				Meretz (CPO)/Histadrut
				Meretz (CPO)/HL

(continued)

Table A2.1. Continued

Country	Party name	Confederation name	Union name	Pair/dyad
				Meretz (CPO)/KL
				Meretz (LPG)/Histadrut
				Meretz (LPG)/HL
				Meretz (LPG)/KL
Italy	PD (Democratic Party)	CGIL (Italian General Confederation of Labour) CISL (Italian Confederation of Union Workers) UIL (Union of Italian Workers)		PD (CPO)/CGIL PD (CPO)/CISL *PD (CPO)/UIL* *PD (LPG)/CGIL* PD (LPG)/CISL *PD (LPG)/UIL*
Netherlands	PvdA (Labour Party) SP (Socialist Party) GreenLeft	FNV (Dutch Trade Union Movement) CNV (Christian National Trade Union Confederation) MHP (Confederation for Middle and Higher Personnel)		PvdA (CPO)/FNV PvdA (CPO)/CNV PvdA (CPO)/MHP PvdA (LPG)/FNV PvdA (LPG)/CNV PvdA (LPG)/MHP SP (CPO)/FNV SP (CPO)/CNV SP (CPO)/MHP SP (LPG)/FNV SP (LPG)/CNV SP (LPG)/MHP GreenLeft (CPO)/FNV GreenLeft (CPO)/CNV GreenLeft (CPO)/MHP GreenLeft (LPG)/FNV GreenLeft (LPG)/CNV GreenLeft (LPG)/MHP
Sweden	SAP (The Social Democrats) VP (The Left Party)	LO (Trade Union Confederation) TCO (Swedish Confederation of Professional Employees) Saco (Swedish Confederation of Professional Associations) SAC (Central Organization of Swedish Workers)		SAP (CPO)/LO SAP (CPO)/TCO SAP (CPO)/Saco SAP (CPO)/SAC SAP (LPG)/LO SAP (LPG)/TCO SAP (LPG)/Saco SAP (LPG)/SAC VP (CPO)/LO *VP (CPO)/TCO* *VP (CPO)/Saco* VP (CPO)/SAC VP (LPG)/LO VP (LPG)/TCO VP (LPG)/Saco VP (LPG)/SAC
Switzerland	SP (Social Democratic Party of Switzerland)	SGB (Swiss Federation of Trade Unions) Travail.Suisse (Umbrella Group for Workers' Unions) KV (Swiss Association of Commercial Employees)		SP (CPO)/SGB SP (CPO)/ Travail.Suisse SP (CPO)/KV *SP (LPG)/SGB* SP (LPG)/ Travail.Suisse SP (LPG)/KV

United Kingdom	Labour Party	TUC (Trades Union Congress)	Unite UNISON GMB (Britain's General Union) NUT (National Union of Teachers) USDAW (Union of Shop, Distributive and Allied Workers)	Labour Party (CPO)/TUC *Labour Party (CPO)/Unite* *Labour Party (CPO)/UNISON* Labour Party (CPO)/GMB *Labour Party (CPO)/NUT* *Labour Party (CPO)/USDAW* *Labour Party (LPG)/TUC* Labour Party (LPG)/Unite *Labour Party (LPG)/UNISON* Labour Party (LPG)/GMB *Labour Party (LPG)/NUT* *Labour Party (LPG)/USDAW*
United States	Democratic Party	AFL-CIO (American Federation of Labour and Congress of Industrial Organizations) CTW (Change to Win)	SEIU (Service Employees International Union) AFT (American Federation of Teachers) UBC (United Brotherhood of Carpenters) UAW (United Auto Workers)	Democratic Party (CPO)/AFL-CIO Democratic Party (CPO)/CTW Democratic Party (CPO)/SEIU Democratic Party (CPO)/AFT Democratic Party (CPO)/UBC Democratic Party (CPO)/UAW Democratic Party (LPG)/AFL-CIO Democratic Party (LPG)/CTW Democratic Party (LPG)/SEIU Democratic Party (LPG)/AFT Democratic Party (LPG)/UBC Democratic Party (LPG)/UAW

[1] Units excluded from the scaling analysis of CPO-union and LPG-union dyads are in italics.

Table A2.2. Scale scalability (H) values for confederations and individual unions

	Party CPO-union dyads	N	Party LPG-union dyads	N	Party -unions	N
Confederation	0.76	52	0.68	50	0.84	46
Individual union	0.92	16	0.57	16	0.61	20

Table A2.3. Scale scalability (H) values per country

	Party CPO-union dyads		Party LPG-union dyads		Party-union dyads	
	H	N	H	N	H	N
Austria	NA	2	NA	2	1.00	4
Finland	1.00	6	0.56	6	0.91	4
France	0.87	14	1.00	14	0.98	12
Germany	0.65	10	-0.19	10	0.80	9
Italy	NA	2	NA	1	1.00	3
Netherlands	0.90	9	0.74	9	1.00	5
Sweden	1.00	6	1.00	8	0.96	8
Switzerland	0.77	3	NA	2	1.00	3
United Kingdom	NA	2	NA	2	0.64	4
United States	0.31	6	-0.13	6	1.00	3
Australia	NA	2	NA	0	1.00	5
Israel	NA	6	NA	6	0.69	6

NOTES

1. Poguntke's notion of 'independent' or 'informal' collateral organization acknowledges this, but emphasizes exclusiveness and permanent exchange (van Biezen et al. 2012) and includes an ideological element in terms of a 'broad commonality of interests' (Poguntke 2006).

2. More precisely, Kitschelt (1989, 231) distinguishes between arms-length relations, selective communication, organized ties, and clientelism. The first type denotes a minimum of contact, the others increasing density of communication and coordination. The problem is, however, that the categorization is not one-dimensional, although it is presented as such. The issue of arms-length relations implicitly refers to frequency of contact, while clientelism denotes a situation where the movement organization tries to shift the burden of protest mobilization to the party (Kitschelt 1989, 232–3). Kitschelt also adds that 'cultural interpenetration'—a continuous flow of symbols and ideas—may compensate for weak organized ties (1989, 246). However, ideological overlap is not treated as an indicator of links in this context, since the major phenomenon to be explained is parties' links for contact with interest organizations.

3. The choice of including both individual unions and confederations in the same analysis means that one will, in a sense, count an individual union twice. We have chosen to do so, however, since unions and peak associations are involved in distinct relationships with parties despite not being independent of each other.

We can check whether the results differ between the relationships involving individual unions and confederations.

4. In some cases, it was very difficult to get responses back, and country experts conducted a structured interview instead.

5. All these datasets, and questionnaires and code books, will be made publicly available via Elin H. Allern's university website <http://www.sv.uio.no/isv/english/people/aca/elinal/>.

6. The intensity of links—frequency of meetings and overlaps, etc.—at both the organizational and individual level, of both formal and informal contact, is obviously important but can be difficult to get at. It is beyond the scope of this study to assess the strength of each individual kind of link in this sense.

7. It is worth noting that only five central party organizations, three legislative party organizations, and seven unions mentioned that they also had 'other kinds of links'. Moreover, not all of the 'alternatives' were clearly different from those we listed, and these borderline cases might have been covered by expert judgments, on which our scaling is based.

8. For a review of the literature on measuring power and influence, see Baumgartner and Leech (1998, 58ff.).

3

The Australian Labor Party and the Trade Unions

'Til Death Do Us Part'?

Phil Larkin and Charles Lees

The Australian Labor Party (ALP) is an explicitly 'labourist' party that was created by the union movement which emerged in the pre-federation Australian colonies. Much to the dismay of the landed political classes, the party imported a culture of unity and solidarity from the unions that ran counter to the established parliamentary culture of the day. The party also developed a strong extra-parliamentary machine, endowed with a variety of mechanisms to ensure that its elected representatives, who were explicitly regarded as delegates of the wider labour movement, acted in accordance with positions officially agreed through the party's bureaucratic processes. As a result, ALP MPs found themselves in a kind of 'double-lock': bound both by decisions taken in the parliamentary caucus and also by the decisions taken in the party organization outside parliament. The unions played a central role in this extra-parliamentary machine. What characterizes the relationship between the Australian Labor Party and trade unions today?

BACKGROUND AND CONTEXT

When describing contemporary politics in Australia, Jaensch (1983) refers to the 'ubiquity, pervasiveness, and centrality of party in Australia' that dates back to the early years of party system consolidation following Federation in 1901. Political parties came relatively late to Australia. A recognizable party system only developed in the years between 1890 and 1910, several decades after the pre-federation colonies had established functioning bicameral legislatures with elected lower houses and a relatively encompassing franchise. The pre-eminence of these democratically elected lower houses, the geographical dispersion of the population, along with the economic prosperity of the nineteenth century meant that the stimulus to party formation was lacking (see, *inter alia*, Loveday et al. 1977 and Aitken 1982). It took the end of this prosperity in the late 1880s, and resultant divisions around free trade and protectionism, to create the conditions for the eventual emergence of the first party-like organizations. And it was this economic turmoil and associated industrial unrest that prompted the union movement to pursue direct representation via the establishment of labour parties after 1891.[1] Prior to this, unions' political activity had, like other organized interests, been primarily focused on lobbying government or individual MPs. But by federation and the establishment of an Australia-wide labour party (it became the Australian *Labor* Party in 1912), labour parties were established in all the colonies except Tasmania. By 1909, the basic dynamic of the Australian party system was established and persists to this day: a *de facto* two-party system with the ALP the dominant force on the centre-left facing a strong non-Labor competitor on the centre-right. The union movement provided extra-parliamentary organization but, initially at least, this did not extend to exerting close control over their elected representatives: the predominant cadre party culture continued.

One key aspect of the party's operation which lies outside of its formal constitutional structures, but which plays a crucial role in its operations and decision making, is the system of party factions. All parties have divisions within them, but the ALP's factions are so peculiarly institutionalized and well organized that it is claimed they represent 'parties in miniature, incorporating a fee-paying membership, their own regular conferences, their own newsletters, elected office holders, and the imposition of factional discipline on their members once policies have been debated and decided upon' (McAllister 1991, 211). The roots of the factions were loosely ideological and they have maintained their 'Left', 'Centre', and 'Right' labels. But more recent commentary has downplayed the role of ideology, as personality and patronage have become more important in their operation.

The factions structure internal party competition to a remarkable extent. Leigh argues that the current system emerged in the 1980s out of the need to regulate and make predictable competition for front-bench portfolios (Leigh 2000). For while it is an ALP prime minister's responsibility to allocate individual ministers to specific portfolios, prime ministers are nominally constrained in whom they can choose from by the party caucus vote. From the mid-1980s onwards the factions eschewed open ballots within caucus and started agreeing the number of front-bench positions their respective groups were entitled to on the basis of their nominal caucus strength. But the process was given additional momentum by the organizational structure and, particularly, the executive decision-making role of the State or Territory and National

Conferences: since the decisions that are taken there are binding, there was a clear incentive to try to control their outcome. The resulting factional carve-up has now extended to cover not only the Commonwealth front bench but also the selection of candidates to stand for election to the Commonwealth and State or Territory parliaments and even to positions in the secretariats at the various levels of party organization. But factional competition is not always as orderly as this process would suggest, and has frequently boiled over into outright and very public hostility, both within States but also between factions at national level.

The operational basis of factional power lies with the affiliated unions. For example, the Australian Workers Union (AWU) and the Shop, Distributive and Allied Employees Association (SDA) are mainstays of the Labor Right faction, while the Australian Manufacturing Workers Union is allied to the Left faction. Unions thus affiliate to the factions as well as to the party. With the membership numbers of the affiliated unions deployed by the union leaders, they have become key factional powerbrokers whose support can be decisive in deciding a pre-selection contest for a parliamentary seat or an elected parliamentarian's subsequent promotion to the front bench.

While the factional system may have been intended to structure internal party competition, it has often been the source of intra-party instability, with internal competition played out through the pre-selection (and inevitable deselection) of parliamentary candidates. There is a perception that unions' role in this process is oligarchic in nature. After a period of considerable leadership instability, in 2013 the reinstated ALP leader Kevin Rudd introduced reforms to reduce the role of the factions, and by extension the unions, in selecting the party leader. As well as requiring a super-majority in caucus to force a leadership challenge (75 per cent in government, 60 per cent in opposition), rather than being decided entirely in caucus, Rudd's reforms meant that rank-and-file members now comprise 50 per cent of the votes in any leadership election. On taking office, the centre-right Abbott government launched the Royal Commission on Trade Union Governance and Corruption, which had a remit to investigate all unions but made special reference to several of the large, ALP-affiliated ones including the AWU, the Construction, Forestry, Mining and Energy Union (CFMEU), the Electrical Trade Union (ETU), the Transport Workers Union (TWU), and the Health Services Union (HSU). ALP MP Craig Thomson had been the centre of a drawn-out corruption case relating to his time as HSU National Secretary prior to the ALP's election defeat in 2013.

The difficulty with the perception of union dominance of Labor is that union membership, and specifically membership of the affiliated unions, has both shrunk and become less representative of the wider electorate. The decline in union membership in the late twentieth century in Australia has been dramatic. Between 1966 and 1986, the proportion of the workforce who reported being members of a union fluctuated between 45 per cent and 52 per cent (Leigh 2006, 539). But over the last thirty years the figure has fallen precipitously, from 43 per cent of males and 35 per cent for females in 1992 to just 18 per cent for both in 2011 (Australian Bureau of Statistics 2011).

The number of union members affiliated to the ALP has also declined. Union affiliation to the party remains dominated by the traditional 'blue collar' unions. The problem for the ALP is that this situation is unlikely to change, with little prospect of currently unaffiliated unions joining up in the foreseeable future (Bracks et al. 2010, para. 4.6).

RELATIONSHIPS TODAY: MAPPING OF LINKS

There was a poor response rate to the survey, which was sent twice to the ALP, the Australian Council of Trade Unions (ACTU), and the five largest unions. Of those bodies approached, ACTU, the Australian Education Union (AEU), and the Australian Nursing and Midwifery Federation (ANMF) do not affiliate to the ALP (though many of the members of ACTU do affiliate). There is no mechanism by which unions can affiliate to the legislative party; unions may sponsor individual members of the ALP caucus but not affiliate as such.

Only the ACTU and ANMF responded to our approaches. From this we deduce that the union–ALP link, always the subject of controversy, was even more sensitive than usual. However, such is the prominence of the union link, it has been possible to find alternative sources of information to complete much of the survey.

Overlapping Organizational Structures: Statutory Links

The statutory links between the union movement and the party's central organization are well documented (see Table 3.1). As already explained, the ALP has traditionally vested considerable authority in its extra-parliamentary party apparatus, and parliamentary representatives were regarded as delegates of the wider labour movement. ALP party caucus discipline remains strong, and floor-crossing by ALP MPs is extremely rare.

Individual ALP members affiliate to local branches, which are embedded within State/Territory party organizations. Local branches can send delegates to their respective State or Territory Conferences, which are usually held annually. Nationally, the supreme authority within the party remains the National Conference, held every three years and to which delegates from the State and Territory organizations are sent. The National Executive is in charge of the day-to-day running of the party, with the National Conference

Table 3.1. Overlapping organizational structures between party central organization and union confederation, as of 2013–14[1]

Party-confederation dyad—CPO	ALP-ACTU		ALP-AEU		ALP-ANMF		ALP-AWU*		ALP-CPSU*		ALP-SDA*	
	P/U	CJ	P/U	CJ	P/U	CJ	P/U	CJ	P/U	CJ	P/U	CJ
National/local collective affiliation (membership) of a union	No	No	n.d.	No	No	No	n.d.	Yes	n.d.	Yes	n.d.	Yes
The party enjoys representation rights in at least one of the union's national decision-making bodies[2]	No	No	n.d.	No	No	No	n.d.	No	n.d.	No	n.d.	No
The union enjoys representation rights in at least one of the party's national decision-making bodies[2]	n.d.	No	n.d.	No	n.d.	No	n.d.	No	n.d.	No	n.d.	No

[1] There are no LPG cells in this table as we assumed the questions (link types) do not apply to the legislative party group and they were thus not asked. 'P/U' indicates responses from party/trade union questionnaires and 'CJ' signifies the authors' 'coded judgment' based on alternative sources in cases of diverging or missing P/U answers. 'c.d.' means contradictory data (diverging P/U answers), 'n.d.' means no data (informant didn't know/ missing), and 'n.a.' means not applicable in this case. * indicates affiliated unions.

[2] See Chapter 2 for a description of the specific rights/bodies that have been mapped.

restricted to major constitutional change and to ratifying the party's platform. The Conference does, however, appoint the National Executive. Unions that choose to do so affiliate at the level of State and Territory branches and can then send delegates to the conferences. Representation of individual unions is in rough proportion to the size of their membership. However, while the extent of unions' influence is based on the size of the membership, the actual input of rank and file union members into the governance of the party is negligible. In practice, union votes are deployed by union leaders at their discretion (Parkin 1983, 22).

The decisions of the State and Territory and National Conferences bind their parliamentary parties and, on taking office, parliamentarians are required to pledge to uphold those decisions. But the local branches provide only 50 per cent of the delegates to the State or Territory Conferences: affiliated unions are also entitled to 50 per cent. In turn, votes at National Conference are evenly split between the State and Territory delegates and those from affiliated unions. In fact, however, the 50 : 50 split between union and party membership delegates represents a significant decline in union dominance. Prior to the 1970s, up to 85 per cent of State and Territory Conference delegates could come from trade unions.

This dominance of the State and Territory Conference in turn yielded effective control of the National Conference and the subsequent selection of the National Executive. The policy platform, which the parliamentary party was pledged to uphold, was drawn up by a committee nominated by the State and Territory Conferences and from which the parliamentary caucus members were excluded—the infamous '36 faceless men' whom Liberal leader Robert Menzies once said dictated policy to the parliamentary ALP. In 1980, this was reduced to a formal 75:25 per cent split between union and party delegates, and subsequently to a 60:40 split and then to the current 50:50. Nonetheless, even at its reduced level, the effect of this is to entrench a major role for the affiliated trade unions in general (and, in individual States and Territories, of some unions in particular) in party decision-making. Consequently, while the local branch party might remain the *de jure* building block of the party, the *de facto* role of the individual membership in determining the direction of the party is negligible. The delegates of the local branches can submit motions to change party policy for consideration and debate at their State or Territory or National Conference. But in practice, the decisions taken at the conferences will have been the result of prior negotiations between the party leadership, the large affiliated unions, and the party secretariats.

So unions have a central role in decision making in the ALP and are ensured a significant presence at the National Conference and on the National Executive (though, unlike at State and Territory level, at neither is a distinction made between union delegates and others). The National Executive currently includes several union delegates. Union delegates are also well represented on the party's various administrative and policy committees.

Inter-organizational Links: Reciprocal and Durable

Table 3.2 presents the occurrence of durable inter-organizational links. The poor response rate to the party–union survey has made completing some of our mapping exercise difficult, as has the relative opaqueness surrounding the detail of the mechanics of party–union links. It is ironic that, while the relationship between the ALP and the affiliating unions is probably closer and more institutionalized than any other in our comparative study, it is also one of the most tricky to study.

In spite of the absence of statutory links between them, it is unsurprising to find a relatively close working relationship between Australia's trade union confederation, the ACTU, and the ALP, with a range of reciprocal, durable organizational links at both central and legislative party levels, including joint committees and regular meetings. Notably though, they did not always share joint campaigns. This was particularly noticeable in the fight against Work-Choices, the controversial industrial relations reforms that John Howard's

Table 3.2. Reciprocal, durable inter-organizational links between party central organization/legislative group and union confederation, last five years (c.2008–13)[1]

Party-confederation dyad—CPO	ALP-ACTU		ALP-AEU		ALP-ANMF		ALP-AWU*		ALP-CPSU*		ALP-SDA*	
	P/U	CJ	P/U	CJ	P/U	CJ	P/U	CJ	P/U	CJ	P/U	CJ
Tacit agreements about one-sided/mutual representation in national decision-making bodies	No	No	n.d.	No	No	No	n.d.	No	n.d.	No	n.d.	No
Permanent joint committee(s)	Yes	Yes	n.d.	No.	No	No	n.d.	n.d.	n.d.	n.d.	n.d.	n.d.
Temporary joint committee(s)	Yes	Yes	n.d.	n.d.	No	No	n.d.	n.d.	n.d.	n.d.	n.d.	n.d.
Formal agreements about regular meetings between party and organization	Yes	Yes	n.d.	n.d.	No	No	n.d.	n.d.	n.d.	n.d.	n.d.	n.d.
Tacit agreements about regular meetings between party and organization	Yes	Yes	n.d.	Yes	No	No	n.d.	Yes	n.d.	Yes	n.d.	Yes
Joint conferences	Yes	Yes	n.d.	n.d.	No	No	n.d.	n.d.	n.d.	n.d.	n.d.	n.d.
Joint campaigns	No	No	n.d.	n.d.	No	No	n.d.	n.d.	n.d.	n.d.	n.d.	n.d.

Party-confederation dyad—LPG	ALP-ACTU		ALP-AEU		ALP-ANMF		ALP-AWU*		ALP-CPSU*		ALP-SDA*	
	P/U	CJ	P/U	CJ	P/U	CJ	P/U	CJ	P/U	CJ	P/U	CJ
Tacit agreements about one-sided/mutual representation in national decision-making bodies	No	No	n.d.	No	No	No	n.d.	No	n.d.	No	n.d.	No
Permanent joint committee(s)	Yes	Yes	n.d.	No	No	No	n.d.	n.d.	n.d.	n.d.	n.d.	n.d.
Temporary joint committee(s)	No	No	n.d.	n.d.	No	No	n.d.	n.d.	n.d.	n.d.	n.d.	n.d.
Formal agreements about regular meetings between party and organization	n.d.	n.d.	n.d.	n.d.	No	No	n.d.	n.d.	n.d.	n.d.	n.d.	n.d.
Tacit agreements about regular meetings between party and organization	Yes	Yes	n.d.	Yes	No	No	n.d.	Yes	n.d.	Yes	n.d.	Yes
Joint conferences	No	No	n.d.	n.d.	No	No	n.d.	n.d.	n.d.	n.d.	n.d.	n.d.
Joint campaigns	No	No	n.d.	n.d.	No	No	n.d.	n.d.	n.d.	n.d.	n.d.	n.d.

[1] 'P/U' indicates responses from party/trade union questionnaires, 'CJ' signifies the authors' 'coded judgment' based on alternative sources in cases of diverging or missing P/U answers. 'c.d.' means contradictory data (diverging P/U answers), 'n.d.' means no data (informant didn't know/missing), and 'n.a.' means not applicable in this case. * indicates affiliated unions.

Coalition government introduced in 2006. The reforms prompted a high-profile campaign from ACTU and featured prominently in the 2007 general election that saw the Coalition ousted. While the ALP was the main beneficiary of ACTU's campaign, the party was kept at a distance from it. The unaffiliated ANMF appears to maintain a cordial but somewhat distant working relationship with the ALP.

The affiliated unions were non-respondents but, nevertheless, we know they wield significant power within the ALP machine. As such, it seems inconceivable that there are not tacit agreements about regular meetings and consultations, for instance. The unions will also have delegates at the National Conference, though they will not formally sit as delegates of their union. They will also be well represented at State and Territory conferences and wield further power through the factional system. Indeed, the links are almost certainly stronger at State/Territory than at national level.

Inter-organizational Links: One-way and Occasional

Where we can be relatively certain about the statutory links even without the responses from the affiliated unions, capturing the occasional, inter-organizational links is inevitably less certain and more speculative. Some aspects of these links are clearly visible, though, as shown in Table 3.3. The National Conferences of the large unions are regularly addressed by senior party figures, for instance. We can be less certain of other aspects of the links. But, as with the reciprocal and durable links, the statutory position that large affiliated unions hold within in the party, as well as their position in the factional system, means that they will be frequently consulted by the party at national and State/Territory level. In short, we can be certain of inter-organizational links even if we can be less sure of the exact form that these links take.

Individual-level Links: Personnel Overlaps and Transfers

One of the most visible and controversial aspects of the ALP–union link is the way in which it impacts on the selection of candidates for seats in the national legislature via the system of factions. The precise mechanisms vary between the States and Territories and between upper and lower house seats, but for the most part selection is shared between a plebiscitary element and either the State/Territory conference or a central committee, a subset of the State conference, and it is through these central components that the union weight which underpins factional power becomes significant.[2] The central selection bodies essentially reflect the relative strength of the factions in the State at that

Table 3.3. One-way, occasional links at the organizational level between party central organization/legislative group and union confederation, last five years (c.2008–13)[1]

Party-confederation dyad—CPO	ALP-ACTU		ALP-AEU		ALP-ANMF		ALP-AWU*		ALP-CPSU*		ALP-SDA*	
	P/U	CJ	P/U	CJ	P/U	CJ	P/U	CJ	P/U	CJ	P/U	CJ
Invitation to party to participate in the organization's national congress	No	No	n.d.	Yes	Yes	Yes	n.d.	Yes	n.d.	Yes	n.d.	Yes
Invitation to organization to participate in the party's national congress/conference	Yes	Yes	n.d.	n.d	No	No	n.d.	No	n.d.	No	n.d.	No
Invitations to organization to participate in the party's ordinary meetings, seminars, and conferences	No	No	n.d.	n.d	Yes	Yes	n.d.	Yes	n.d.	Yes	n.d.	Yes
Invitations to party to participate in ordinary organization meetings, seminars, and conferences	Yes	Yes	n.d.	n.d	Yes	Yes	n.d.	Yes	n.d.	Yes	n.d.	Yes
Invitations to organization to special consultative arrangements initiated by the party	No	No	n.d.	n.d	Yes	Yes	n.d.	Yes	n.d.	Yes	n.d.	Yes
Invitations to party to special consultative arrangements initiated by the organization	No	No	n.d.	n.d	No	Yes	n.d.	Yes	n.d.	Yes	n.d.	Yes

Party-confederation dyad—LPG	ALP-ACTU		ALP-AEU		ALP-ANMF		ALP-AWU*		ALP-CPSU*		ALP-SDA*	
	P/U	CJ	P/U	CJ	P/U	CJ	P/U	CJ	P/U	CJ	P/U	CJ
Invitation to party to participate in the organization's national congress	Yes	n.a.	n.d.	Yes	Yes	n.a.	n.d.	Yes	n.d.	Yes	n.d.	Yes
Invitation to organization to participate in the party's national congress/conference	n.a.	n.a.	n.a.	n.a.	n.a.	n.a.	n.a.	n.a.	n.a.	n.a.	n.a.	n.a.
Invitations to organization to participate in the party's ordinary meetings, seminars, and conferences	No	No	n.d.	n.d	No	No	n.d.	Yes	n.d.	Yes	n.d.	Yes
Invitations to party to participate in ordinary organization meetings, seminars, and conferences	Yes	Yes	n.d.	n.d	Yes	Yes	n.d.	Yes	n.d.	Yes	n.d.	Yes
Invitations to organization to special consultative arrangements initiated by the party	No	No	n.d.	n.d	Yes	Yes	n.d.	Yes	n.d.	Yes	n.d.	Yes
Invitations to party to special consultative arrangements initiated by the organization	No	No	n.d.	n.d	No	No	n.d.	Yes	n.d.	Yes	n.d.	Yes

[1] 'P/U' indicates responses from party/trade union questionnaires, 'CJ' signifies the authors' 'coded judgment' based on alternative sources in cases of diverging or missing P/U answers. 'c.d.' means contradictory data (diverging P/U answers), 'n.d.' means no data (informant didn't know/missing), and 'n.a.' means not applicable in this case. *indicates affiliated unions.

time, usually ensuring the successful candidate is effectively selected centrally rather than locally. Preselection of candidates for seats and the power of patronage it hands the factional leaders is a key means by which the factional system in the ALP is maintained.

As a party founded to express union interests, the party's elected members have traditionally been closely linked with and affiliated to the union movement. This has provided a great deal of political ammunition to the ALP's opponents over the years. In the campaign for the 2007 federal election, for instance, the number of ALP frontbench members with union connections was explicitly highlighted by the Coalition. In fact, the last ALP cabinet in 2013 included former ACTU national secretary Greg Combet, former ACTU presidents Simon Crean (a former ALP leader) and Martin Ferguson, and former AWU secretary Bill Shorten, as well as many more with strong union connections. After the fall of the Labor government and the subsequent resignation of Kevin Rudd, Shorten assumed the party leadership. Former union staffers are well represented in the current parliamentary party, with all the affiliated unions surveyed having former staff in the Commonwealth Parliament. Indeed, of the 80 ALP members of the Commonwealth Parliament, 43 have previously worked for a union and/or ACTU in some capacity. Almost half of the ALP's MPs in the current parliament and almost all of its senators—twenty-one out of a total of twenty-five—have previously worked for a union.[3]

Recruitment of unionists into the ranks of the ALP has been dominated by the affiliated unions and private sector blue collar unions that have traditionally been at the heart of the ALP–union relationship, although the actual roles played by Labor politicians in their respective unions vary significantly: there are a number of local organizers, for example, but also former national secretaries. Still, regardless of seniority, it would seem that a post of some sort in the secretariat is probably the single most popular route to a seat in the Commonwealth Parliament. It is a pattern repeated at State/Territory level too.

Overall Degree of Closeness and Range

The affiliated unions retain a prominent formal role, for instance through guaranteed representation at State and Territory and National Conferences, but also a more informal but no less significant role through the factional system. The lack of responses from them has made it difficult to see the fine detail of the relationship, and we are unable to calculate a total organizational link score for the affiliated unions (see Figure 3.1). However, it is clear that, in some areas, the leaders of the large affiliated unions are a significant voice in the decision-making process and that the links are intimate and durable.

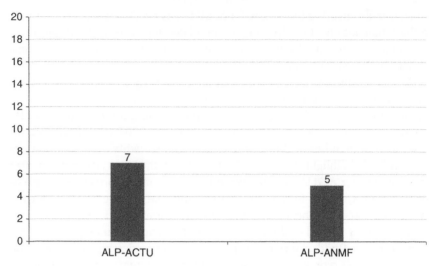

Figure 3.1. Total link scores of central party organization–trade union relationships (0–20).

The most visible aspect of the link is through the factional deals over the pre-selection of candidates for elections. As we have seen, employment in a union remains a common route to a parliamentary seat. Affiliated unions are also well represented on the party's National Executive: of the twenty elected members of the current Executive, twelve are union officials.[4] The three affiliated unions included here all have representatives on the executive. The affiliated unions remain an integral part of the internal life of the ALP. Quite how integral, however, is contingent and debatable. The national secretary of the affiliated HSU reportedly went as far as to claim that affiliated union control of candidate selection was such that it gave them at least the equivalent influence within the party as a junior minister in a state government (Dorling and McKenzie 2010). Many union officials are significant players within the party. Yet, this has not prevented rule changes that have reduced the unions' formal role within the party. Nor has it prevented the general trajectory of policy away from the many unions' preferred positions.

The relationship between the party and the ACTU is close. However, there are no statutory links, nor any tacit agreements about representation. The total organizational link score is 7. Even during Accord—the high-point of Australian corporatism under the premiership of former ACTU President Bob Hawke—the relationship was a contractual one between separate parties rather than a process internalized within the party. However, while the affiliated unions remain a significant voice within the ACTU, it is perhaps reflective of the changing pattern of Australian trade unionism that the last three presidents of the Council have been from unaffiliated unions. Figure 3.2

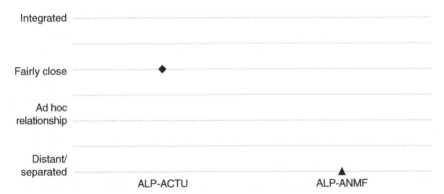

Figure 3.2. Rating of overall degree of closeness/distance (average score) between the party and union confederation, last five years (*c*.2008–13).[1]

[1] The ratings reflect the union's rating only since ALP did not answer the survey.

shows that the ACTU itself regards its relationship with the ALP as 'fairly close'. There is clearly a high degree of regular contact through meetings and joint committees, for instance. Furthermore, the future career paths of its senior officials would suggest a strong link. Of its ten past presidents, four have become MPs (including former party leaders, Bob Hawke and Simon Crean), one represented the ALP in the Victorian Assembly, one stood for election (albeit unsuccessfully), and another was president of a State branch of the party. The ACTU may lack formal links but there are clearly strong and enduring informal links.

The ANMF, the unaffiliated union which completed the survey, obtained a link score of 5, but seemed at pains to emphasize its relative distance from the party and to contrast its position from those of the affiliated unions (see Figure 3.2). Its response stressed professional terms upon which it engaged with the ALP, much as it engages with any other party.

We may conclude, then, that links still exist between the ALP and trade unions, not least with the ACTU and with the party's traditional allies among the individual unions. What might explain this relative stability in party–union relationships?

EXPLAINING THE RELATIVE STABILITY

Both the nature of the modern ALP and the role played by the unions within it are contested at a number of levels. In broad ideological terms, it can be argued that the focus on the interests of a relatively small, traditionally white and male, section of the population ignores other sources of inequality. In strategic terms, unions in general, and those affiliating to the ALP in particular, are seemingly in decline, so to afford them a continued, privileged place is to constrain the party's capacity to appeal to the median voter (Jaensch 1989). It might also constrain the accommodation to neoliberalism that some would suggest has been made inevitable by the impact of global capitalism (Lavelle 2005). And in pragmatic terms, the particular organizational culture to which union affiliation has contributed—the factionalism and consequent emphasis on patronage over talent and internecine battles for position—has proved a distraction to the party's core business of both fighting and winning elections and also providing Australia with effective government thereafter. Former ALP Prime Minister Bob Hawke, who was himself a president of the ACTU before becoming leader of the ALP, earned a stiff rebuke from the then ALP leader Julia Gillard when he claimed in 2012 that union influence over the party had become 'stifling' (Wright 2012), while former leader Mark Latham (2005, 254) echoed Menzies' jibe that the party leadership was at the mercy of 'faceless men', claiming that he was 'not opposed to unionism per se, just the idea of six union secretaries sitting around a Chinese restaurant table planning the future for everyone else'.

The counterargument put forward by those who regard the union link as synonymous with the party's ideological compass, is that the distancing has gone too far already. These voices would argue that the party leaders who have been most keen to minimize the union link do so because it constrains their capacity to adopt neoliberal, pro-business policies in place of union-based democratic socialism. Since the end of the post-war boom in the 1970s, the party has sought to accommodate business interests, advocating wage restraint for the unions, decentralizing wage bargaining, and dismantling industrial protection. This has culminated in a situation where the distance politically between the two has widened to the point where the unions are expected to lobby 'their government' just like any other interest group. Party leaders do not conceive of themselves as part of the wider labour movement—representing the interests of labour is not on their agenda (see, for example, Lavelle 2010).

Nevertheless, the official party line remains that the party–union link is a defining feature that must be maintained. An internal review of the ALP, conducted by three of its grandees in 2010, concluded that 'Australia's union movement remains at the bedrock of the Australian Labor Party. The affiliation of trade unions is a key characteristic that makes Labor different from other progressive parties around the world' (Bracks et al. 2010, para. 10.1).

From the party's perspective, while some ALP leaders may regard the union link as a constraint, there would be significant financial implications in endangering this relationship. The unions continue to make a decisive financial contribution to the party through both direct donation and also through the affiliation of individual members, although this reliance has reduced over time, particularly after the introduction of public funding for political parties in the 1980s. There is of course a counterfactual argument to be made here, namely the possibility that the closeness of the union–party relationship has constrained the party's capacity to attract a greater volume of private donations from a wider range of donors.

Policy differences have also often put the relationship under strain. In particular, the apparent tension between concerns for the protection of ordinary union members and the apparent imperatives of a globalizing economy has hampered coherent policy formulation. For example, Gough Whitlam's attack on protectionism in the early 1970s flew in the face of continued union support for continued, high import tariffs (Leigh 2002). Indeed, the wider process of economic liberalization has created tensions between the unions and the ALP, both in and out of government: for instance, during the period of intense debate over the macroeconomic reforms introduced under Hawke and Keating and, in opposition, in the run-up to the signing of the Free Trade Agreement with the USA in 2004, which was supported by the ALP leadership but opposed by the unions.[5] More recently, the social conservatism of some unions has contrasted with the more progressive official party line. For example, the SDA was a particularly vehement opponent of the ALP's recent championing of the gay marriage. Attempts by the party to adopt more environmentally friendly policies have also encountered union resistance. As the reduced reliance on union funding since the 1980s, and an absence of alternatives, has reduced their capacity directly to dictate the terms of policy to the ALP in the manner that might previously have been the case, so the ALP has been more willing to pick fights with the unions in order to accumulate wider political capital.

CONCLUSION

The relationship between the ALP and its affiliated unions seems to present something of a paradox. The ALP is the creation of the union movement and institutional links between the affiliated trade unions and the ALP remain strong. The unions nominate 50 per cent of the delegates to main conferences, maintain places on various committees including those involved in policy development, and, in most States and Territories, those involved in the selection of candidates to stand for parliament at both State/Territory and Commonwealth level. While it may have been reduced, it is undeniable that the unions retain a major position within the formal party structure. And through the factional system, the unions (or at least some of them) are able to exert further influence over the party, particularly through the selection of candidates for parliament. Their position within the party is sufficient for former leaders to bemoan their influence, suggesting that they can at least constrain the scope for the party to develop policy that appeals to a wider constituency.

Labor's affiliated unions, then, have maintained their ability to exert a degree of *ex ante* control over the party's activities, and the fact that the relationship between the two in Australia continues in the face of supposedly universal pressures towards 'delinking' (Piazza 2001) would support this assertion. Yet, at the Commonwealth level at least, the union link has seemingly done little to impede the gradual adoption of a more economically liberal, catch-all strategy aimed at the median voter. Indeed, it has been argued that the Blairite Third Way emphasis on economic liberalization in the UK was pre-empted by the macro-economic reforms of the ALP governments of Hawke and Keating (see, for example, Pierson and Castles 2002).

The relative distance of the Commonwealth ALP from the unions may go some way to explaining this apparent paradox. With union affiliation at State or Territory level, direct union control of the Commonwealth party is harder: the union movement may have created labour parties in the pre-federation colonies, but the Commonwealth party was the creation of those parties rather than the unions that founded them. With economic policy a federal competency, this allows Commonwealth ALP governments a degree of latitude in the pursuit of economic liberalization that their State and Territory counterparts might not enjoy. But, through the factional control of pre-selection, the unions still have the means to influence the Commonwealth party through their *ex ante* control of candidates (and, indeed, their *ex post* power to replace sitting members).

Nevertheless, the impact of the structural changes that have supposedly encouraged social democratic parties and unions to delink elsewhere have worked to weaken the capacity of the affiliated unions to control the ALP. While the tools to exert control over the party remain, the unions have ultimately been reliant on the ALP to win office and have consequently found themselves relatively powerless to oppose its adoption of median voter strategies in order to do so. The union campaign against the Coalition's Work-Choices industrial relations reforms illustrates this. The campaign was run independently of the ALP and included both ALP-affiliated and unaffiliated unions. The campaign was seen as very successful and contributed to the defeat of John Howard's long-lived Coalition government. Yet, the unions ultimately had to settle for the ALP's alternative—labelled 'WorkChoices-lite' by critics—that modified rather than abandoned the Coalition's policy. The Greens' opposition to WorkChoices was far stronger and, unlike the ALP, they committed to abandon WorkChoices in its entirety and return to the *status quo ante* in the (somewhat far-fetched) event that they won office. It is no surprise therefore that some unions have flirted with other parties. Some have speculated that union support for the ALP might become rather more conditional were the distancing we have already seen to go much further (Cook nd: 109–10).

Clearly, while there may be electoral pressure on the leadership to balance union interests with others, including business, the relationship between the Australian trade unions and the ALP is clearly not 'like any other interest group' (Lavelle 2010, 55). For any student of the ALP, the union relationship remains fundamental to both explaining how the party sees itself and also the way in which it operates.

NOTES

1. The strikes of 1890 clearly played a role in giving the new Labor parties momentum, though the decision to form them preceded the strikes. In Queensland, the Trades and Labor Council had fielded candidates in elections in the 1880s and, in 1899, following the collapse of the coalition government, saw the world's first, though very short-lived, labour government.

2. Only the ACT and in NSW lower-house candidate preselections are entirely decided by a plebiscite of local members. Section N.40 of the NSW Party rulebook allows the State Administrative Committee to impose a candidate when *it* determines the party is on a 'campaign footing...or in other urgent situations'. The clause has been interpreted liberally on a number of occasions <http://www.crikey.com.au/2009/09/30/special-report-how-to-become-a-federal-mp-part-1-alp/>.

3. Based on biographical information given on the Commonwealth Parliament website. It should be noted that we do not distinguish between the levels of office held: the ALP caucus includes former union national secretaries but also those who held relatively junior roles early in their careers.

4. <http://www.alp.org.au/national_executive>. In addition to the elected members, the party leader, president and vice-presidents, secretary, and the president of Young Labor all serve in an *ex officio* capacity.

5. Although they were to use the unions in the pursuit of liberalization through the corporatist Accord.

4

A Dying Embrace?

Interlocked Party–Union Directorates in Austria's Cartel Democracy

Kurt Richard Luther

INTRODUCTION

From the late nineteenth century, present-day Austria developed distinct so-cialist, Christian democratic, and German-national subcultures, each containing one or more parties and various auxiliary associations, including a multitude of highly partisan trade unions (Wandruszka 1954).[1] In February 1934, the grow-ing political conflict of the First Republic peaked in armed clashes between socialist and conservative-fascist forces, whereupon the Christian-Social gov-ernment proscribed the Social Democratic Workers' Party of Austria and its allied Free Trade Unions and created a one-party state and single state-oriented trade union federation. After the 1938 *Anschluss*, all trade unionists were transferred to the National Socialist German Labour Front. In 1945, at the birth of the Second Republic, the elites of the still mutually hostile socialist and Christian-democratic subcultures opted to build a metaphorical arch over the gulf separating these 'pillars', making Austria a near-archetypal 'consoci-ational democracy' (Lijphart 1968b; 1969). Together with the then influential Austrian Communists, they simultaneously founded the reformist Austrian Trade Union Federation (*Österreichischer Gewerkschaftsbund*, or ÖGB).

In such 'classic consociationalism' (Luther 1999a, 6–15), pillar parties pro-mote vertical encapsulation ('pillarization') and political mobilization via organizational penetration and the exercise of hierarchical control over the provision of incentives. They are also the pivotal actors in the ubiquitous system of inter-subcultural accommodation, the structural features of which include grand coalition, proportionality, and segmental autonomy. Trade unions cooperate with pillar parties in intra-subcultural exchange relationships that help consolidate their respective pillars and in the system of overarching accommodation and proportional division of spoils, often via 'interlocking directorates' (Lijphart 1968b). In Austria, trade unions have permeated their members' working lives and been especially prominent in the neo-corporatist arena, where the ÖGB remains one of the five privileged peak interest group associations, or 'social partners' (Luther 1999a, 66–8), that long exercised an effective veto in key areas of social and economic policy (Tálos 2008). Another is the Chamber of Labour (*Arbeiterkammer* or AK), which all workers are required by statute to join and which functions as a sort of think tank. It is closely linked to the social-democratic subculture's party and its trade union.

Despite its nominal non-partisanship, the ÖGB is a multi-partisan organization, within which regular elections are contested by 'fractions' closely linked to the two mass-membership pillar parties. The same applies to its legally subordinate sectoral unions. In line with the principles of proportionality and segmental autonomy respectively, those elections determine the distribution of internal resources and allocate political control to the strongest fraction.[2] The social democratic *Fraktion Sozialdemokratischer GewerkschafterInnen im ÖGB* (FSG) predominates at the level of the ÖGB and in six of the currently seven individual unions. Christian-democratic trade unionists are mobilized mainly by the *Fraktion Christlicher Gewerkschafterinnen und Gewerkschafter im ÖGB* (FCG), which dominates one union, but is also represented in the other six and at the level of the ÖGB (Karlhofer 2006). The FSG and FCG provide benefits for their members and have close relations with the *Sozialdemokratische Partei Österreichs* (SPÖ) and the Christian-democratic *Österreichische Volkspartei* (ÖVP) respectively.

BACKGROUND AND CONTEXT

Since 'classic consociationalism', there have been profound changes to Austria's consociational architecture, to the socio-economic and party-political context of party–trade union relations, as well as within and between those organizations. From 1966 to 1983, grand coalition—the most obvious symbol of consociational democracy—was replaced by single-party government and then by the SPÖ's short-lived coalition with the Freedom Party of Austria (FPÖ). Yet the consensual style and proportional division of spoils characteristic of consociational democracy continued, especially in the not-so-visible neo-corporatist arena. Until the early 1980s, Austria's largely social-democratic economic consensus delivered the highest levels of economic growth in OECD (Organisation for Economic Co-operation and Development) Europe, an extensive welfare state, low inflation, and comparatively very low levels of unemployment and of industrial conflict (Lauber 1992).

Having come to associate social partnership with economic success, political stability, and social harmony, most Austrians were content to accept their opaque system of government by an elite cartel of pillar parties and allied peak interest groups. Indeed, pillarization continued, and in the 1970s total pillar party membership reached the remarkable equivalent of about a quarter of the electorate (Luther 1999b, 46). This helped ensure that well into the 1980s, the SPÖ and ÖVP together regularly won 90–95 per cent of national election votes and seats.

Yet by the 1980s, the limits of 'Austrokeynesianism' had become apparent: the budget deficit and unemployment were rising rapidly, the financial viability of Austria's generous welfare state was questioned, and many of the exceptionally large, highly unionized, and arguably overstaffed nationalized industries faced collapse. The attendant threats to the clientelistic outputs associated with consensualism (and in particular to those the SPÖ provided for 'its' trade unionists) help explain the populist reorientation of the FPÖ, which under Jörg Haider immediately doubled its vote (1986: 9.7 per cent). The pillar parties' response to the economic and populist challenge was to revert from 1987 to 1999 to the increasingly awkward embrace of grand coalition government, now under SPÖ leadership. They first pursued budget consolidation, deregulation, and privatization—a market-oriented strategy that met with resistance from SPÖ trade unionists, as did initially the government's decision to apply for European Community membership. Austria's 1995 accession to the post-Maastricht Treaty European Union marked another shift in the economic context of Austrian politics by *inter alia* further reducing the policy autonomy of the elite cartel of pillar parties and interest groups, as well as its capacity to provide material benefits to subcultural (trade union) clients. In turn, the total number of votes the unions could mobilize for 'their' parties fell.

Though grand coalition government had been restored and a weaker system of social partnership persisted, the encapsulated pillar identities of classic Austrian consociationalism had, since the 1970s, gradually been diluted by factors such as a changed occupational structure, secularization, urbanization, rising levels of education, and alterations in the structure of political communication. During the 1990s, the FPÖ's strategy of populist vote maximization ever-more successfully exploited the protest potential of Austria's increasingly dealigned, anti-establishment electorate. At the 1999 general election, the combined pillar party share of the vote and of seats comprised merely 60 per cent and 64 per cent respectively. The FPÖ became the second largest electoral force by 415 votes (level pegging with the ÖVP on 26.9 per cent), and eclipsed the SPÖ as the most popular party among blue-collar voters (by 48 to 35 per cent). Though the FPÖ's advance was less pronounced among unionized workers, the apparent electoral realignment of Austria's working class posed a profound challenge for the historically close relationship between the

SPÖ and Austria's blue-collar unions. That challenge was exacerbated by the formation in February 2000 of an ÖVP–FPÖ coalition led by Wolfgang Schüssel, who had a strong neoliberal agenda and little sympathy for Austria's extra-constitutional social partnership (Luther 2012). The SPÖ found itself excluded from government for only the second time since 1945. Moreover, unlike then, neither it nor its FSG-dominated ÖGB and AK allies could rely on exercising significant policy influence (let alone a policy veto) through the neo-corporatist channel. The ÖVP–FPÖ government's confrontational style and corporatism-sceptic orientation was exemplified in 2003, when it pushed through pension reform with little regard for the views of social partners and entered into an all-out confrontation with the unions that resulted in Austria's highest ever annual number of days lost to strikes. The sight of the Chairman of the FCG-dominated Public Services Union casting his parliamentary vote in support of the reforms, briefly threatened to split to ÖGB on partisan lines. The party system appeared to be shifting to a bipolar logic, with the prospect of consensus replaced by confrontation between neoliberal and corporatism-sceptic right-of-centre governments on the one hand and two left-of-centre parties (the Greens and the SPÖ), with a much-reduced role for neo-corporatism and the traditionally influential peak interest groups, including the ÖGB.

Majority opinion in the leaderships of the SPÖ, ÖGB, and FSG-dominated sectoral unions remained implacably opposed to the coalition and committed to maintaining the proximity of most unions to the SPÖ, as well as to re-establishing the role of social partnership.[3] Yet some started to consider alternative scenarios, including SPÖ Chairman Alfred Gusenbauer, who was keen to enhance the relative importance of the political over the corporate channel and 'liberate' his party from what he regarded as the politically stifling embrace of its increasingly outdated subcultural auxiliary associations and of its unions in particular. Neither the pillar parties nor the unions were the organizations they had been during classic consociationalism. When Gusenbauer became Chairman in 2000, total pillar party membership was 40 per cent down on its 1970s peak. In international comparison, Austria's party membership density remains exceptionally high, but by Gusenbauer's 2008 resignation, it had reduced to 'merely' 17 per cent (van Biezen et al. 2012, 29). ÖGB membership had also shrunk, from a 1981 peak of 1.7 million to 1.4 million in 2000. In March 2006, it was revealed that in 2000, corruption, embezzlement, and illicit speculation in Caribbean tax havens had brought a major ÖGB-owned bank (the BAWAG) close to insolvency, and in response the ÖGB President (simultaneously an SPÖ MP) had secretly mortgaged the union's strike fund. He now immediately retired from all trade union and political positions and was summarily dismissed by the ÖGB, which suffered an existential crisis and massive loss of political capital. By 2014, its membership had fallen to 1.2 million, the lowest since the late 1940s. Concerned at reputational damage to the SPÖ and instrumentalizing the crisis to undermine his intra-party union critics, Gusenbauer outlawed the practice of ÖGB and sectoral union presidents standing on its electoral lists. This generated major resentment among the unions and helps explain their much-reduced efforts at voter mobilization during the October 2006 general election campaign. The SPÖ performed less well than expected, but was narrowly able to re-enter government as senior partner in a SPÖ/ÖVP coalition, which signalled the beginning of the end of Schüssel's neoliberal and anti-corporatist experiment. Yet the pillar parties' renewed embrace was predicated on a further reduced share of votes and seats (55 per cent and 59 per cent respectively). Gusenbauer's strained relations with the SPÖ's union wing contributed to his 2008 premature loss of the party Chairmanship and Chancellorship. These were assumed by Werner Faymann, who presented himself as a defender of the party's traditional blue-collar clientele and reversed Gusenbauer's injunction on union presidents standing on SPÖ election lists. Yet he could not halt the continued erosion of the pillar parties, which at the 2013 election could muster merely 50.1 per cent of votes and 51 per cent of seats, while a strengthened FPÖ re-established its plurality among blue-collar voters.

RELATIONSHIPS TODAY: MAPPING OF LINKS

We focus on the two parties' links to the ÖGB and to three sectoral unions, selected because they have the largest memberships,[4] organize different types of workers, and vary in their dominant fraction. Austria's biggest blue-collar union (the ÖGB's third-largest) is the FSG-dominated Union of Production Workers (PRO-GE), created in 2009 via a merger of the Metal, Energy, Textile and Food Workers' Union and the Chemical Workers Union. The Public Services Union (GÖD) is the only union with an FCG-majority directorate. It organizes central government employees and a few others in the public sector. The largest sectoral union is the Union of Salaried Private Sector Employees and of Printers, Journalists and Paper Workers (GPA-djp), whose members work mainly in the non-manual private sector. The FSG dominates the GPA-djp's directorate and has twice as many shop stewards as the FCG, yet a plurality of shop stewards is elected on independent lists.

The evidence underpinning this chapter supplements the questionnaire findings with internal party and union documents, plus structured interviews undertaken in summer 2014 with (in part) senior party and union inform-ants.[5] Those interviews and the large number of contradictory or incomplete questionnaire responses underscore the challenge of capturing the peculiar Austrian case within the project's framework. To have relied solely on a project questionnaire predicated on the assumptions that parties are largely single actors (which the ÖVP is not) and that unions and parties are separate organizations, between which relations must be direct, would have led to the conclusion that Austria has few party–union links, if any. Yet in reality, there are very widespread, long-standing, and in part intense party–union links, especially with the SPÖ. The dominant fractions of each union are the unions' political face and it is through them (rather than the unions as corporate entities) that unions have traditionally interlocked with the SPÖ's and ÖVP's (central) organizations and legislative groups (*Klubs*). Virtually all relations between the ÖGB and these parties run along separate tracks forged by 'their' fraction. Strong links also exist between each sectoral union directorate and 'its' party, but those between parties and sectoral unions with politically incongruent directorates (i.e. SPÖ-GÖD, ÖVP-PRO-GE, and ÖVP-GPA-djp) are insubstantial and will thus not be discussed further. To capture Austrian reality, we will treat parties' relationships to union fractions as functional equivalents of party–union links. That decision is strongly supported by the interview information and provides insight into many inconsistencies in questionnaire responses.

Party/union survey responses reported in Table 4.1 suggest that there are no overlapping structures between Austria's unions and parties' central organization. However, for the reasons explained earlier, we should qualify this description (see table column with 'coded judgments' (C/J)). As will become clear, it can be argued that statutory links exist between SPÖ and ÖGB, between ÖVP and ÖGB, and also between ÖVP and GÖD.

SPÖ statutes (§9) had long recommended SPÖ members join the FSG, detailed extensive SPÖ-FSG co-operation (e.g. §§43 and 61) and allocated the FSG 50 delegates to the SPÖ's conference (§35(4)) and seats in the SPÖ's Extended Presidium, Party Council and Women's Section (§§53, 56, and 59). FSG statutes *inter alia* required FSG functionaries to be SPÖ members and granted seats in the national FSG Executive (§§5 and 8) to two members of the SPÖ Executive and to the Leader of the SPÖ *Klub*. The FSG was thus effectively interlocked with the SPÖ, as were by extension the FSG-controlled union directorates. In 2012, FSG statute revisions removed all mentions of the SPÖ and its rights of representation. Simultaneously, the SPÖ's statutes erased references to the FSG, which they supplanted with a new legal entity: 'Trade Unionists in the SPÖ' (GewSPÖ), which comprises the self-same individuals (including all FSG office-holders) and exercises identical rights. The purpose of this bilateral statute change was to keep the FSG organizationally embedded in the SPÖ, while circumventing new party funding legislation that would have prevented it keeping confidential its use of ÖGB resources to support the party.

This new construct has some parallels with those mediating ÖVP–union relations. The ÖVP's highly complex indirect structure (Müller 2006) includes a relatively lightweight central party organization that seeks to coordinate nine provincial branches and three functional 'Leagues': of Business (ÖWB),

Table 4.1. Overlapping organizational structures between party central organization and union confederation, as of 2013–14[1]

Party-confederation dyad—CPO	SPÖ-ÖGB		SPÖ-PRO-GE		SPÖ-GPA-djp		SPÖ-GÖD		ÖVP-ÖGB		ÖVP-PRO-GE		ÖVP-GPA-djp		ÖVP-GÖD	
	P/U	CJ	P/U	CJ	P/U	CJ	P/U	CJ	P/U	CJ	P/U	CJ	P/U	CJ	P/U	CJ
National/local collective affiliation (membership) of a union	No	No	c.d.	No	No	No	No	No	No	No	c.d.	No	No	No	No	No
The party enjoys representation rights in at least one of the union's national decision-making bodies[2]	n.d.	No	No	No	No	No	n.d.	No	n.d.	No	No	No	No	No	No	No
The union enjoys representation rights in at least one of the party's national decision-making bodies[2]	No	Yes	No	No	No	No	No	No	No	Yes	No	No	No	No	No	Yes

[1] There are no LPG cells in this table as we assumed the questions (link types) do not apply to the legislative party group and they were thus not asked. 'P/U' indicates responses from party/trade union questionnaires and 'CJ' signifies the authors' 'coded judgment' based on alternative sources in cases of diverging or missing P/U answers. 'c.d.' means contradictory data (diverging P/U answers), 'n.d.' means no data (informant didn't know/missing/unclear), and 'n.a.' means not applicable in this case.

[2] See Chapter 2 for a description of the specific rights/bodies that have been mapped.

Agriculture (ÖBB), and of Employees (ÖAAB). The Leagues provide the bulk of ÖVP membership, and have independent legal status and extensive rights that ensure they significantly shape the internal life of the ÖVP's organization and *Klub* (e.g. §§11, 23, 27, and 33 of ÖVP Statutes). Formal rules and long-standing conventions guarantee an intricate system of proportional representation and resource allocation, including individual League legislative caucuses ('Working Groups') that convene prior to meetings of the overall ÖVP *Klub*.[6] These enable the Leagues to operate within the ÖVP as quasi-interest group lobbies. The Leagues maintain strong links to their specific interest group allies, including in the neo-corporatist system. Relations with organized labour are mediated through the ÖAAB, which is linked to the ÖGB and GÖD through the FCG, with which it operates shared lists at AK elections, but also in a small number of union elections. In 1951, the FCG was hived off from the ÖAAB to enable the former to operate within the unions as a less overtly partisan body. Yet current ÖAAB statutes (§61) still call on members actively to support the FCG's trade union work, while the FCG encourages its members to join the ÖAAB.[7]

Inter-organizational Links: Reciprocal and Durable

The questionnaire responses reported in Table 4.2 fail to capture the complex pattern of durable inter-organizational links, which are significantly underpinned by overlapping leadership. Although the 2012 FSG statute revisions removed the reciprocity of SPÖ-ÖGB representation in national decision-making bodies, this relationship remains very strong. By convention, the SPÖ conference elects to the SPÖ Executive four or five social democratic ÖGB Executive Committee members, including the ÖGB president, the FSG-ÖGB chairman and the chairman of the largest blue-collar union, who are then all elected to the SPÖ's Executive Committee. In 2014, two further ÖGB Executive Committee members sat on the SPÖ Executive. There are also durable ÖGB links to the *Klub*. Until Gusenbauer's short-lived 2006 ban, all ÖGB presidents were also SPÖ MPs. Indeed, from 1971–86, the ÖGB president held the position of president of parliament, formally the second-highest office of state. From 2008, the ÖGB president opted not to stand for parliament, but the ÖGB is again represented in the *Klub* by the FSG-ÖGB chairman and the chairman of the largest blue-collar union. In 2014, the social democratic ÖGB vice-president was also an SPÖ MP. Such dense overlapping leadership means that the additional types of specifically union–party organizational links listed in Table 4.2 are largely superfluous. An interviewee made an analogous argument regarding the SPÖ's organizational links to the sectoral unions. As PRO-GE is the largest blue-collar union, its chairman is by convention a member of the SPÖ and ÖGB Executives Committees, as well as

Table 4.2. Reciprocal, durable inter-organizational links between party central organization/legislative group and union confederation, last five years (c.2008–13)[1]

Party-confederation dyad—CPO	SPÖ-ÖGB		SPÖ-PRO-GE		SPÖ-GPA-djp		SPÖ-GÖD		ÖVP-ÖGB		ÖVP-PRO-GE		ÖVP-GPA-djp		ÖVP-GÖD	
	P/U	CJ	P/U	CJ	P/U	CJ	P/U	CJ	P/U	CJ	P/U	CJ	P/U	CJ	P/U	CJ
Tacit agreements about one-sided/mutual representation in national decision-making bodies	No	Yes	No	Yes	c.d.	Yes	No	n.d.	No	Yes	No	No	No	No	c.d.	Yes
Permanent joint committee(s)	No	n.d.	No	No	No	No	No	No	No	n.d.	No	No	No	No	c.d.	n.d.
Temporary joint committee(s)	No	Yes	No	No	c.d.	Yes	c.d.	n.d.	No	n.d.	No	No	No	No	c.d.	n.d.
Formal agreements about regular meetings between party and organization	No	n.d.	No	No	No	No	No	No	No	n.d.	No	No	No	No	c.d.	n.d.
Tacit agreements about regular meetings between party and organization	No	Yes	No	Yes	c.d.	Yes	c.d.	n.d.	No	n.d.	No	No	c.d.	n.d.	c.d.	n.d.
Joint conferences	No	n.d.	No	No	c.d.	No	c.d.	n.d.	No	n.d.	No	No	c.d.	n.d.	c.d.	n.d.
Joint campaigns	No	n.d.	No	No	c.d.	No	c.d.	n.d.	No	n.d.	No	No	No	No	c.d.	n.d.

Party-confederation dyad—LPG	SPÖ-ÖGB		SPÖ-PRO-GE		SPÖ-GPA-djp		SPÖ-GÖD		ÖVP-ÖGB		ÖVP-PRO-GE		ÖVP-GPA-djp		ÖVP-GÖD	
	P/U	CJ	P/U	CJ	P/U	CJ	P/U	CJ	P/U	CJ	P/U	CJ	P/U	CJ	P/U	CJ
Tacit agreements about one-sided/mutual representation in national decision-making bodies	No	Yes	No	Yes	No	No	No	n.d.	n.d.	n.d.	No	n.d.	No	n.d.	No	n.d.
Permanent joint committee(s)	No	n.d.	No	No	No	No	No	n.d.	n.d.	n.d.	No	n.d.	No	n.d.	No	n.d.
Temporary joint committee(s)	No	n.d.	No	No	No	No	No	n.d.	n.d.	n.d.	No	n.d.	No	n.d.	No	n.d.
Formal agreements about regular meetings between party and organization	No	n.d.	No	No	No	No	No	n.d.	n.d.	n.d.	No	n.d.	No	n.d.	No	n.d.
Tacit agreements about regular meetings between party and organization	No	n.d.	No	No	c.d.	Yes	No	n.d.	n.d.	n.d.	No	n.d.	No	n.d.	No	n.d.
Joint conferences	No	n.d.	No	No	c.d.	No	No	n.d.	n.d.	n.d.	No	n.d.	Yes	n.d.	No	n.d.
Joint campaigns	No	n.d.	No	No	No	No	No	n.d.	n.d.	n.d.	No	n.d.	No	n.d.	No	n.d.

[1] 'P/U' indicates responses from party/trade union questionnaires, 'CJ' signifies the authors' 'coded judgment' based on alternative sources in cases of diverging or missing P/U answers. 'c.d.' means contradictory data (diverging P/U answers), 'n.d.' means no data (informant didn't know/missing/unclear), and 'n.a.' means not applicable in this case.

an SPÖ MP. For its part, the SPÖ-GPA-djp relationship is cemented by its chairman's membership of the same thee key bodies and currently holding the chairmanship of the FSG-ÖGB, by virtue of which he additionally acts as a key interlocutor between the SPÖ and all six FSG-dominated unions. Moreover, GPA-djp's managing director is one of the ÖGB Executive Committee members elected to the SPÖ Executive.

Though its union relationships are less extensive and intensive, the ÖVP (ÖAAB) also has durable union links figuring overlapping leadership. They flow mainly though the ÖAAB organization, but also into its *Klub*. Those between the ÖVP(ÖAAB) and FCG-ÖGB are enshrined in the ÖAAB statutes (§24j), which grant an *ex officio* seat on the ÖAAB Executive (its highest decision-making body) to the FCG-ÖGB chairman, who in the latter capacity is automatically an ÖGB Executive Committee member. By convention, at least one further FCG member of the ÖGB Executive Committee sits on the ÖAAB Executive. Since GÖD always holds the FCG-ÖGB chairmanship and is the strongest FCG component by far, both seats go to its members. The ÖAAB Statutes (§24i) also provide an explicit GÖD-ÖVP(ÖAAB) link in the form of an *ex officio* Executive seat for its chairman. The durable links and pivotal role of overlapping leadership in a country permeated by multi-functionaries was long personified in Fritz Neugebauer. The GÖD's powerful chairman since 1997, he was an MP from 2002 until late 2013 and for the last five years also the parliament's second president. From 2003 until 2009, he was simultaneously chairman of the ÖAAB and thus both leader of that League's legislative caucus and deputy leader of the overall ÖVP *Klub*. Both the chairman of GÖD and the chair of the FCG-ÖGB are linked into the central organization of the national-level ÖVP by virtue of their co-optation on to its Executive.

We enquired into the extent to which unions regarded themselves as political actors and whether individuals simultaneously in party and union national decision-making bodies had a predominantly party or union identity. In their questionnaire responses, the SPÖ and ÖVP(ÖAAB) central organizations agreed 'fully' that their party represents the interests of specific social groups, but the SPÖ *Klub* was only 'partially' convinced, which interviews suggest reflects its sense of responsibility to incorporate a broader range of interests into legislative outcomes. The FSG-dominated unions' questionnaires indicated they see themselves as 'full-blown' political actors, an assessment replicated in their party interlocutors, but interviewees stressed those unions' social democratic affinity did not translate into uncritical support for the SPÖ. Meanwhile, GÖD rejected characterization as a political actor and interviews found FCG officials with seats on both party and union decision-making bodies strongly identified as union representatives. On the social democratic side, where overlapping leadership is more extensive, subjective identity is less clear-cut. In general, the interviews found the highest-level union members of the interlocking party–union directorates (e.g. the ÖGB president and FSG chairman) identify strongly as union representatives, while union officials owing their party position (e.g. in the *Klub*) mainly to a party selectorate are less inclined to do so.

Inter-organizational Links: One-way and Occasional

Table 4.3 reports a significant number of contradictory responses to questions about the existence of occasional links between party and union organizations. They largely result from the challenges of capturing in a questionnaire designed for this project's wide range of countries the peculiarities of the Austrian case, including above all the key role of the unions' fractions.[8] Moreover, it seems likely that respondents' reluctance to contradict the official narrative of union non-partisanship resulted in underreporting of links.

It was impossible to resolve all ensuing issues, but interviews and internal party and union documents enable us confidently to offer judgements (recorded under 'C/J') in nine cases of reported contradictions concerning SPÖ–union links and alternative responses for six others. This multi-method approach generates a clear and consistent picture of the occasional inter-organizational links between the SPÖ central party office and the ÖGB, GPA-djp and PRO-GE, as well between those unions and the SPÖ *Klub*. They each span the range of types identified in Table 4.3 and, as interviewees from those organizations stressed, are not confined to symbolic interaction, but often entail detailed substantive discussions of policy and strategy. Some are bilateral, but many include participation from multiple unions, or simultaneously from the SPÖ's central organization and *Klub*. A stark contrast exists between the wide-ranging types of occasional links the SPÖ central party organization has to the three FSG-dominated unions and the complete absence of such links to the GÖD. This highlights the important role partisan (in)congruence plays in determining party–union links. That the SPÖ *Klub* questionnaire nonetheless reports occasional intra-organizational links to GÖD might seem a contradiction, but is related to the importance of GÖD's membership for much legislative business (see section on 'Explaining Strong and Continued Links').

It unfortunately proved impossible to obtain questionnaires from the FCG-ÖGB and from the ÖVP(ÖAAB) *Klub*, or to conduct an interview within the latter. However, our other sources (including internal documents and interviews with the FCG Chairman and Deputy GÖD Chairman) do permit us to resolve nine contradictory questionnaire responses and offer six alternative judgements (see 'C/J' columns in Table 4.3). In turn, that allows us to confirm some significant patterns in the unions' occasional inter-organizational links to the ÖVP(ÖAAB). Above all, it is clear that the ÖVP(ÖAAB) party

Table 4.3. One-way, occasional links at the organizational level between party central organization/legislative group and union confederation, last five years (c.2008–13)[1]

	SPÖ-ÖGB		SPÖ-PRO-GE		SPÖ-GPA-djp		SPÖ-GÖD		ÖVP-ÖGB		ÖVP-PRO-GE		ÖVP-GPA-djp		ÖVP-GÖD	
	P/U	CJ	P/U	CJ	P/U	CJ	P/U	CJ	P/U	CJ	P/U	CJ	P/U	CJ	P/U	CJ
Party-confederation dyad—CPO																
Invitation to party to participate in the organization's national congress	Yes	Yes	Yes	Yes	Yes	Yes	c.d.	No	No	Yes	c.d.	No	c.d.	n.d.	c.d.	Yes
Invitation to organization to participate in the party's national congress/conference	No	Yes	c.d.	Yes	c.d.	Yes	No	No	No	Yes	c.d.	No	Yes	Yes	Yes	Yes
Invitations to organization to participate in the party's ordinary meetings, seminars, and conferences	No	Yes	c.d.	Yes	Yes	Yes	No	No	No	Yes	Yes	No	Yes	Yes	Yes	Yes
Invitations to party to participate in ordinary organization meetings, seminars, and conferences	Yes	Yes	Yes	Yes	Yes	Yes	c.d.	No	No	Yes	c.d.	No	No	No	c.d.	Yes
Invitations to organization to special consultative arrangements initiated by the party	No	Yes	c.d.	Yes	c.d.	Yes	No	No	No	Yes	c.d.	No	No	No	Yes	Yes
Invitations to party to special consultative arrangements initiated by the organization	No	Yes	c.d.	Yes	c.d.	Yes	No	No	No	Yes	c.d.	No	c.d.	n.d.	c.d.	Yes
Party-confederation dyad—LPG																
Invitation to party to participate in the organization's national congress	Yes	Yes	Yes	Yes	Yes	Yes	Yes	n.d.	n.d.	n.d.	Yes	n.d.	Yes	n.d.	Yes	Yes
Invitation to organization to participate in the party's national congress/conference	n.a.	n.a.	n.a.	n.a.	n.a.	n.a.	n.a.	n.a.	n.a.	n.a.	n.a.	n.a.	n.a.	n.a.	n.a.	n.a.

(continued)

Table 4.3. Continued

Party-confederation dyad—CPO	SPÖ-ÖGB		SPÖ-PRO-GE		SPÖ-GPA-djp		SPÖ-GÖD		ÖVP-ÖGB		ÖVP-PRO-GE		ÖVP-GPA-djp		ÖVP-GÖD	
	P/U	CJ	P/U	CJ	P/U	CJ	P/U	CJ	P/U	CJ	P/U	CJ	P/U	CJ	P/U	CJ
Invitations to organization to participate in the party's ordinary meetings, seminars, and conferences	Yes	Yes	Yes	Yes	Yes	Yes	Yes	n.d.	n.d.	Yes	Yes	n.d.	Yes	n.d.	Yes	Yes
Invitations to party to participate in ordinary organization meetings, seminars, and conferences	Yes	Yes	Yes	Yes	Yes	Yes	Yes	n.d.	n.d.	n.d.	Yes	n.d.	Yes	n.d.	Yes	Yes
Invitations to organization to special consultative arrangements initiated by the party	Yes	Yes	Yes	Yes	Yes	Yes	Yes	n.d.	n.d.	Yes	Yes	n.d.	Yes	n.d.	Yes	Yes
Invitations to party to special consultative arrangements initiated by the organization	Yes	Yes	Yes	Yes	Yes	Yes	n.d.	n.d.	n.d.	n.d.	Yes	n.d.	Yes	n.d.	Yes	Yes

[1] 'P/U' indicates responses from party/trade union questionnaires, 'CJ' signifies the authors' 'coded judgment' based on alternative sources in cases of diverging or missing P/U answers. 'c.d.' means contradictory data (diverging P/U answers), 'n.d.' means no data (informant didn't know/missing/unclear), and 'n.a.' means not applicable in this case.

organization maintains a large range of occasional union links to GÖD. Like the social democrats (and in part for analogous reasons), the ÖVP(ÖAAB) *Klub* also has links to GÖD. Notwithstanding the questionnaire responses from the ÖVP(ÖAAB) *Klub*, it is our judgement (reinforced by interviews with the FCG-ÖGB chairman) that the FCG-ÖGB has occasional organizational links both to the ÖVP(ÖAAB)'s central party organization and to its legislative group. Again drawing on the interviews with Christian Democratic interlocutors, it seems that with the exception of those involving GÖD, the quality of the ÖVP(ÖAAB)'s occasional inter-organizational links to the unions is generally less substantial than those which exist between the SPÖ and the unions.

Individual-level Links: Individual Contacts and Personnel Overlaps and Transfers

Individual-level contact was investigated by both questionnaires and interviews. Too few responses were received regarding ÖVP(ÖAAB)–union contacts to do more than confirm they are mainly with GÖD, and that party organization and union-agreed informal contacts (e.g. meetings and telephone calls) are the most frequent, yet seminars and informal letters apparently also figure prominently in GÖD's communication both with the party's organization and its *Klub*. The questionnaires offered clear and consistent answers regarding the types of (in)formal contact in unions' contacts to the SPÖ's party organization and *Klub*. All union respondents and the SPÖ party organization reported formal meetings and teleconferences to be the most common form of party–union contact, followed by formal (electronic) letters. The unions and SPÖ *Klub* agreed their most frequent type of contact was informal (meetings, phone calls, etc.), and were virtually unanimous that the second most frequent was participation in joint seminars or conferences. Interviews suggested this pattern of *Klub*–union contact reflects the centrality in Austria's consensual legislative system of a combination of informal bilateral communication to test out potential compromise and more discursive, transparent dialogue between individuals representing key stakeholders. Interviewees from both SPÖ party units and all three FSG-dominated unions typically reported that formal contacts were important, but the informal were the most influential and took place at least weekly and often daily. The greater importance of informal contacts was echoed in the GÖD interview, which also reported more-than-weekly contacts to the ÖVP(ÖAAB) *Klub*. Social democratic and Christian-democratic interviewees were keen to stress that their contacts with the other organization were always to key interlocutors, rather than to the organization as such. Especially on the social-democratic side, the most senior party and union interviewees emphasized both the ease with which key individuals (including those holding governmental office, or positions in ministerial cabinets) could be contacted, and that in some meetings party participants (also) attended in their capacity as the party's representatives in public executive office.

Personnel overlaps and transfers clearly help explain this. Having discussed overlapping leadership, we will now mainly address other types of individual-level personnel overlap, concentrating on the social-democratic side, where our information is most extensive. There have always been strong personnel links between the SPÖ *Klub* and trade unions. In spring 2014, some 27 per cent of SPÖ MPs held or had recently held positions as union officials or staff. Whether by serendipity or (more likely) by design, their numbers roughly reflected the relative size of the FSG-dominated sectoral unions. Five were linked to the GPA-djp (its chairman, another Executive member, and three MPs with regional roles) and four to the PRO-GE (its chairman, another Executive member, and two shop stewards). Two MPs (had) held positions in the similarly-sized Union of Municipal Employees (*Gewerkschaft der Gemeindebedienstete*), and two others had done so in the Transport and Services Union (*Vida*). The former pair included the ÖGB's vice-president (simultaneously chair of its Women's Section), while the latter comprised an Executive member and a regional chairman. The chairman of the smaller Construction and Woodworkers Union (*Bau-Holz*) was also an MP. There was no MP with a union background in the tiny (51,000-member) Union of Postal and Telecommunication Workers.

This legislative group overlap is of course replicated throughout the broader mid-level SPÖ and union elite by virtue of the effective interlocking of the FSG (to which union staff and officials belong) and the recently created GewSPÖ. There are also overlaps at the highest level, between SPÖ holders of national executive office and (former) union officials. The latter have regularly held key SPÖ ministerial portfolios, including the ministries of social affairs (which unions covet most) and of infrastructure. In 2014, the previous ÖGB president was the SPÖ's serving social affairs minister, and that September the ÖGB's earlier mentioned vice-president left parliament to become health minister.

Overall Degree of Closeness and Range

We are able to assign an overall organizational score to four of the party–union dyads studied here. Figure 4.1a and 4.1b show that the relationship between SPÖ's central organization and PRO-GE obtains a total link score of 8 (out of 20), whereas the SPÖ-CPO and GPA-djp seem to be connected by nine link types. The scores are slightly lower in the legislative arena, but then the maximum score is only 12. Hence, these figures show that numerous links exist, and that there is no significant difference between the SPÖs links with

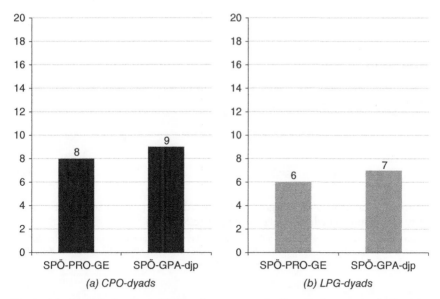

Figure 4.1. Total link scores of central party organization–trade union relationships and legislative party–trade union relationships $(0–20/0–12)$.[1]

[1] The theoretical maximum link score is 20 for the CPO-dyads and 12 for LPG-dyads since some link items are unlikely to apply to the legislative party group and were thus not included in this part of the survey. However, when comparing dyads involving CPOs with those involving LPGs, one should still keep in mind that the latter's maximum involves fewer links than the former's top scores.

the major blue-collar union PRO-GE and its organizational connections with the non-manual private sector union GPA-djp.

The perception data on actors' own ratings of distance/closeness by and large confirms this, and suggests that the relationship between the SPÖ and the peak association ÖGB is as close, or closer, than the relationship between the SPÖ and individual unions, whereas ÖVP and related trade unions are described as involved in more distant relationships (see Figure 4.2). The ÖVP (ÖAAB) party organization's questionnaire characterized its relationship to GÖD as 'ad-hoc' and those it has to all other unions as 'distanced', while all three sectoral unions described their relationship to the ÖVP(ÖAAB) as merely 'ad-hoc'. That largely corresponds with the interviewees' accounts.

When questionnaire responses are complemented with interview findings, it is apparent that the ÖVP(ÖAAB)'s union links are far less close than those of the SPÖ. Given that the directorates of the ÖGB, GPA-djp, and PRO-GE are FSG-dominated, it is unsurprising the ÖVP(ÖAAB)'s relationship to them is not close. Perhaps more unexpected is that the ÖVP(ÖAAB)'s relationship to the FCG-dominated GÖD should be deemed by both organizations' questionnaires to be merely 'ad hoc' and is characterized in the SPÖ *Klub*'s

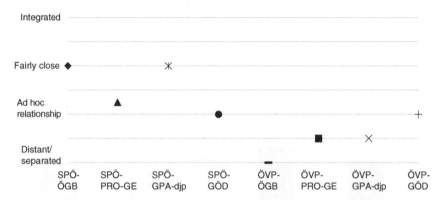

Figure 4.2. Rating of overall degree of closeness/distance (average score) between the party and union confederation, last five years (*c.*2008–13).[1]

[1] Ratings in-between two categories reflect that the party and union responses to the survey question differed. None of the ratings differed with more than one category. The SPÖ-ÖGB, SPÖ-GÖD, and ÖVP-ÖGB ratings reflect the party's rating only because of missing union answers.

questionnaire as 'distanced', yet in that of the SPÖ central party office as 'fairly close'. These seemingly paradoxical responses are largely explainable by the particular role of GÖD and the ÖVP's multifaceted nature. Numerous interviewees emphasized that because GÖD organizes central government civil servants, whose employment rights are often legally entrenched, any government wishing to make even modest changes within Austria's federal ministries or wider public administration must negotiate with it from an early stage. Within both the SPÖ and ÖVP, as well as in the Austrian media, GÖD's acknowledged skill at defending its members' interests is often portrayed as a prime obstacle to long-overdue structural reforms.

In short, GÖD is regarded by both of these government-oriented parties as a frequently necessary, but not much-loved interlocutor. Second, the ÖVP's unique organization results in the ÖAAB (and thus the FCG-GÖD representatives there) being structurally embedded in the overall party and in the ÖAAB's legislative caucus, yet the ÖAAB is itself but one of the three intra-party Leagues constantly lobbying to promote the competing interests of their respective client groups. The ÖAAB, and especially GÖD, encounter opposition—and at times downright hostility—from the market-oriented Business League, which has little sympathy for unions and even less for civil servants. Indeed, the GÖD interviewee judged his union's relationship to the ÖVP to have become more distant in recent years. As the current ÖVP leader was from the ÖAAB, this attests to the latter's relative intra-party weakness and the abiding dominance of the ÖVP by its Business League.

The greater closeness and stability of relations between the SPÖ and the ÖGB, GPA-djp, and PRO-GE is attributable in part to overlapping structures and durable links. Yet, as both union and SPÖ interviewees stressed, a more profound explanation lies in Austrian pillarization. The social-democratic pillar of which both are key components has for over one hundred years been strongly identified with, and normatively committed to, workers' representation. Pillarization generated a dense network of local, district, and provincial party and trade union (youth) organizations and a multiplicity of auxiliary associations focusing on a range of sports and leisure activities, most with extensive with overlapping memberships. Notwithstanding depillarization, the overwhelming majority of individuals who have comprised the national-level party and union leaderships were socialized and remained active within such pillar organizations, where they originally formed personal contacts and networks that most of them nurtured throughout their party and/or union careers.

A further explanation for the closeness derives from the SPÖ's status as a near-perpetual governing party. SPÖ interviewees characterized the SPÖ's relationship to the blue-collar PRO-GE as especially close. They attributed this not only to symbolism, but also to many of the PRO-GE's highly unionised production workers being employed in nationalized industries. The government portfolio with responsibility for this sector is traditionally held by the SPÖ, which means it regularly needs to consult the unions and when in government can still exercise some clientelism. SPÖ interviewees considered the party's relationship to PRO-GE to be at least as close as that to the GPA-djp (which the SPÖ values *inter alia* because of the GPA-djp's size), and concluded that these two were the SPÖ's closest relationships to any of the seven sectoral unions.

The range of ÖVP(ÖAAB)–union relationships is much narrower. Although the FCG holds a 'watching brief' for the Christian Democrats at the level of the ÖGB, within which convention dictates that FCG support is required for numerous key decisions, including the overall allocation of resources, the Christian Democrats' major union relationship is with GÖD. Conversely, the social democrats maintain, through the FSG, very significant links to the ÖGB, GPA-djp, and PRO-GE, as well as a politically insubstantial presence in GÖD. The contrast between the two parties' range of union links is even greater if one includes those to the four sectoral unions excluded from this study. Each of these is FSG-dominated, and between them they organize over 400,000 blue-collar and white-collar workers employed in the public and private sectors, as well as in local government. Though we cannot go into detail, the interviews confirmed the SPÖ has strong links to all four. In sum, the proportion and variety of unions linked to the SPÖ is very wide-ranging, while the ÖVP(ÖAAB)'s links are very narrow in respect of both criteria. Looking at the links from the perspective of the individual unions, the overall picture (including in respect of the unions not considered in detail here) is that each union has only one significant party link, the conduit for which is the union's dominant fraction. The contact between non-dominant union fractions and 'their' party should be regarded not as a relationship between the union and that party, but merely as a politically largely insignificant way in which the latter monitors the internal affairs of that union and helps ensure a proportional division of spoils.

EXPLAINING STRONG AND CONTINUED LINKS

Four interconnected contextual factors largely account for the nature and durability of Austria's party–union links. The first comprises Austria's social democratic and Christian-democratic subcultures, where overlapping party and union organizational networks fostered partisan alignment and socialized future elites. The second is a predominantly accommodative decision-making culture traceable to the Second Republic's consociational origins. Also very important has been Austria's neo-corporatist arena, where the pillar parties and their interest group allies exercised hegemonic control and the organizational leaderships replicated the pattern of interlocking party–union directorates. The fourth factor has been a duopolistic party system, enabling the virtually permanent governmental incumbency of the unions' main pillar party ally, usually in coalition with the ÖVP. Together, these factors provided favourable conditions for lasting and mutually advantageous party–union exchange relationships, especially on the social democratic side.

For the unions, the prime benefit of party–union links derives from guaranteed incorporation into government decision-making across the political and neo-corporatist arenas. All three sectoral union questionnaires identified taxation; equal opportunities; as well as healthcare and social affairs as their 'very important' policy areas. PRO-GE and GPA-djp both additionally cited economic affairs; employment and labour market; finance and competition; and childcare, education, and youth. GÖD's distinctive membership meant it alone prioritized justice, police, and home affairs; public administration; and the military, while the GPA-djp's clientele was mirrored in it also identifying as 'very important' energy and 'information society and media'. Yet social democratic interviewees judged 'their' unions to be largely preoccupied with moderating the fallout from the financial and economic and crises, and they were, at best, only moderately reassured by the SPÖ chairman's repeated assertions the SPÖ-led coalition was weathering the storm better than most European countries. They all agreed that close party–union links guaranteed the long-term, systematic inclusion of union interests in Austrian political decision-making, which they felt had enabled unions not only significantly to resist neoliberal pressures, but also to make lasting and positive contributions to enshrining *inter alia* labour-friendly macroeconomic and employment-related policies.

Such policy outcomes are also regarded as benefits of party–union links by the SPÖ and ÖVP (ÖAAB) organizations and *Klubs*, but not by the overall ÖVP. Accordingly, the FCG's relationship to the ÖVP (ÖAAB) generates fewer benefits in policy areas that unions traditionally value than the social democratic party–union link. A second benefit to parties of their union links has been their ability to draw on the latter's substantial resources. Political sensitivities made it impossible to acquire details of financial contributions and meant no party questionnaires answered the party funding questions. Yet the GPA-djp reported providing the SPÖ with indirect funding and staff support during elections, while PRO-GE conceded giving both pillar parties material resources at elections. Meanwhile, GÖD recorded indirectly funding the ÖVP (ÖAAB) and individual politicians, as well as providing staff, material, and premises during elections. Interviewees explained that the fractions' use of union resources to assist 'their' party is subject to political constraints, reflecting the consensual and proportionality principle: there has to be prior inter-fractional agreement to on the size of the pot at fractions' disposal and discretion in its use. Resource transfer typically includes support in kind and fractions using 'educational' funds as indirect party subsidies, mainly to disseminate policy positions favouring 'their' party. Social democratic interviewees stressed that the ÖGB and SPÖ can no longer sit down prior to election campaigns to decide a budget and each organization's contribution, but argued there remain ways unions can financially support SPÖ campaigns; however, union attempts to negotiate more MPs in return threatened the party leadership's limited scope to influence the *Klub*'s composition.

A further traditional benefit of union links, as far as parties are concerned, is votes. Social democratic interviewees differed in their estimation of the unions' value in direct vote mobilization, but union membership has long been a key determinant of voting behaviour and benefited the SPÖ. Typically, its electorate had nearly twice as many unionized than non-unionized voters, while the ÖVP's contained only about 20 per cent (Kritzinger et al. 2013, 80–4). However, the SPÖ's net vote benefit is now much lower than it used to be. The share of union members in the labour force is much reduced and the populist FPÖ has made significant inroads into the blue-collar vote, achieving a plurality in 1999 and again in 2013. As yet, its advances among unionized voters have been less dramatic. Such enormous voter shifts would have been inconceivable thirty years ago and are attributable to fundamental change in two factors underpinning Austria's stable party–union links. As Austria's subcultural pillars have continued to collapse, the parties' partisan foundations have dramatically weakened. Massively increased electoral competition, above all from populist parties, has put an end to Austria's two-party system, generated high levels of public scepticism of government by elite cartel, and threatens to deprive the pillar parties of even a combined plurality.

Such contextual changes have altered parties' and unions' internal politics and calculations of the costs and benefits of their links. The unions' fractional dominance may appear robust, but is often more vulnerable than it looks. Within the GPA-djp, officials elected on non-fractional/independent lists have for some time constituted a plurality, and though still less numerous elsewhere are a growing phenomenon, the causes of which include long-term occupational structure change, partisan dealignment, and depoliticization. Independents do not yet have fractional status, and some union directorates manipulate procedural regulations to prevent such threats to their dominance. However, interviewees report that union leaders are aware that perceptions of unions being overly 'political' undermine their internal legitimacy. They are thus increasingly willing to challenge demonstratively 'their' party in the name of defending union members' interests, but also to respond to FPÖ encroachment by adopting anti-immigrant and anti-EU positions. One FSG interviewee added that the party link can be disadvantageous when SPÖ performance is 'weak' (e.g. regarding union demands for a 'wealth tax'), and the SPÖ will in future not always be in government, so prudence dictates unions keep their distance. Another ascribed the current ÖGB president's decision to not stand for the SPÖ *Klub* to his desire to strengthen ÖGB's claims to be non-partisan and (perhaps more credibly) to avoiding being required to vote for legislation that contradicts ÖGB positions. Some in the SPÖ welcomed unions pressuring the party to adopt more radical, worker-friendly policies, maintaining this would benefit both wings of Austria's labour movement. For others, the costs of their party's close union links increasingly outweigh the benefits. For them, the party's electoral weakness has been exacerbated by those links, narrowing its core electoral support to the shrinking number of unionized workers. They claimed Faymann's reversal of Gusenbauer's exclusion of union chairmen from the SPÖ *Klub* limited the party's policy flexibility, aggravated tensions within the coalition and increased the grand coalition's reputation for immobilism. They further argued that the intra-party weight of the structurally entrenched, well-organized and resourced unions reduces social democracy's policy breadth and limits its capacity to broaden its electoral base, thus threatening to electorally marginalize the party further. In sum, one of the paradoxical consequences of strong party–union links is that the more the party's membership and the electorate shrink, the stronger the unions are.

The relative merits of competing positions on the benefits of close party–union relations are less important than that the capacity to provide reciprocal benefits will probably soon be severely undermined. The pillar parties' widely expected loss of their electoral and parliamentary plurality means the other factors underpinning those relations will no longer apply. The non-pillar parties, at least one of which they would be obliged to coalesce with, have never been included in the neo-corporatist system, and some strongly oppose it. Moreover, at least one of them has demonstrated little commitment to consensus politics. Accordingly, even if neo-corporatism survives, the pillar parties will probably lose their hegemony there, and the accommodative style of Austrian decision-making exemplified in party–union relations and the broader social partnership system will also be threatened.

CONCLUSION

To capture the reality of contemporary Austrian party–union relationships, this chapter has recognized the peculiarities of the Austrian case by treating parties' links to union fractions as functional equivalents of party–union links and targeting the analysis on the politically most relevant: those between parties and dominant union fractions. Given Austria's tradition of social democratic and Christian-democratic unionism, we examined the party–union links of both pillar parties: SPÖ and ÖVP. On the union side, we included the trade union confederation (ÖGB) and three sectoral unions, selected because of differences in the partisanship of their dominant fraction, their membership size, and the ÖGB's varied occupational profile.

There are enduring, extensive, and intensive party–union links that make Austria different from other countries studied in this volume. Though the relationship between the unions and the SPÖ has been far more profound, there are also longstanding links to the Christian-democratic ÖVP(ÖAAB). A key feature of both sets of links has been a dense pattern of overlapping directorates, which constitute a cornerstone of the Second Republic's opaque system of government by an elite cartel of pillar parties and allied peak interest groups. The party–union relationships include overlapping structures, inter-organizational links that are reciprocal and durable, as well as many others that are occasional. At the individual level, contacts are often frequent and informal, partly because of Austria's small size and the concentration of key party and union actors in one relatively small city. The motivations behind party–union links rest primarily on shared policy goals in policy fields that unions traditionally value (e.g. employment and labour market, social affairs, and taxation). Yet the links have also provided parties with other benefits, including resources and votes.

We identified four interconnected contextual factors that had largely accounted for the nature and durability of Austria's party–union links. These are subcultural pillarization; a culture of accommodative decision-making; SPÖ-ÖVP hegemony in Austria's neo-corporatist arena; and a two-party system that permitted near-permanent (joint) pillar party incumbency. The recent acceleration of depillarization and declining partisanship highlight Austria's transition from a consociational to a cartel democracy (Lijphart 1968b), where the elite cartel no longer bridges encapsulated, mutually hostile, and deferential subcultures. Moreover, rapid party system fragmentation suggests the cartel parties will soon lose their parliamentary and governmental majority, and thus the capacity credibly to promise their union allies durable access to power and the provision of policy benefits. Yet the system of interlocking party–union directorates keeps those organizations locked in a tight embrace that was for many years mutually advantageous, but which critics argue now leaves the SPÖ captured by 'its' unions and incapable of the policy flexibility required to counter its political decline. For their part, the unions face their own internal pressure and cling on to cartel politics for fear of something worse. It remains possible that the SPÖ will find ways of loosening the embrace sufficiently to be able to appeal beyond its shrinking heartland. Yet in its present form, the life of Austria's long-lasting elite cartel appears to be moving to an end. If so, the parties and unions may well find that theirs is a dying embrace.

NOTES

1. I would like to thank Gemma Loomes for her help in generating the data files from the questionnaire results.
2. Analogous processes apply within three other social partners: the AK, Federal Chamber of Business, and Chambers of Agriculture. Unlike the ÖGB and the Association of Austrian Industrialists, they can rely on compulsory membership.
3. Meanwhile, the single FCG-dominated union's relations to the neoliberal oriented ÖVP were challenging.
4. PRO-GE: 229,776 (19 per cent); GÖD 236,892 (20 per cent), and GPA-djp 277,792 (23 per cent) of the ÖGB's membership on 31 December 2014.
5. The key informants include:
   (1) SPÖ former Chairman;
   (2) SPÖ Legislative Group Leader;
   (3) ÖGB-FSG official responsible for organization;
   (4) ÖGB-FSG official responsible for communication;
   (5) PRO-GE chairman;
   (6) GÖD deputy chairman;
   (7) GPA-djp managing director;
   (8) FCG chairman (and deputy ÖGB president);
   (9) Official of the ÖVP's Austrian Employees' League (*Österreichischer Arbeitneh-merinnen- und Arbeitnehmerbund*, or ÖAAB).
6. In 2014, the ÖAAB caucus comprised eighteen of the ÖVP's total forty-seven seats.
7. Precise data on FCG-ÖAAB membership overlap are unavailable, but interviewees claimed that about half the ÖAAB's total membership of approximately 250,000 comprise GÖD members, while *c.*90 per cent of FCG members are simultaneously ÖAAB members.
8. For example, the questionnaire asks parties to describe links with different 'unions', whereas the unions (whose questionnaires were completed by fraction members) are asked to describe links between 'your organization' and the party.

5

Finland

Strong Party–Union Links under Challenge

Tapio Raunio and Niko Laine

INTRODUCTION

Links between trade unions and political parties in Finland before the Second World War were very strong, but at the same time the trade union movement was internally fiercely politicized, with social democrats and communists fighting for influence. In fact, this high level of politicization and conflict characterized the young country as a whole. Having gained independence in 1917, Finland experienced a short but very bitter civil war between Whites and Reds in 1918, a strong right-wing extremist *Lapua* movement in the 1930s, and wars against the Soviet Union and Germany between 1939 and 1945 which actually brought the divided nation together in the face of a common enemy.

The blue-collar trade union movement grew in tandem with the leftist parties. The Social Democratic Party (SDP) was created in 1899 while the Finnish Federation of Trade Unions was established in 1907. In the 1920s the trade union movement and leftist parties basically operated together in workers' associations. However, the trade union movement was internally divided, with often bitter fighting between communists and more moderate wings of the movement. Finding themselves in the minority and dissatisfied with the hard-line approach of the communists, the Social Democrats left the Finnish Federation of Trade Unions in 1929, establishing in October 1930 the Confederation of Finnish Trade Unions (SAK). The SDP's departure actually saved parts of the trade union movement from government repression as that same year the Eduskunta (the unicameral national parliament), under pressure from the *Lapua* movement, banned the communist-dominated Finnish Federation of Trade Unions as well as numerous other socialist organizations. The ban on socialist organizations effectively paralyzed the Communist Party, while the Social Democrats in the heated circumstances of the 1930s rejected cooperation with the communists and entered the first red–green coalition with the Agrarian Union, the predecessor of the Centre Party, in 1937. This set an important precedent for post-Second World War coalitions crossing the left–right divide that became the standard type of government in Finland. Towards the end of the 1930s, SAK had also managed to overcome, at least temporarily, many of its internal problems and it was able to push through some important labour market reforms. Moreover, in the midst of the Winter War against the Soviet Union in 1940, SAK and the Confederation of Finnish Employers (STK) announced their 'January engagement' (*tammikuun kihlaus*), signalling that previous barriers to cooperation had ceased to exist and recognizing the right of workers to organize themselves.

After the Second World War, however, both industrial relations as a whole and the trade union movement itself continued to be characterized by conflicts. Inside SAK, acrimony continued between communists and social democrats, but perhaps more difficult were the splits in the social democratic group of the confederation, with some unions forming a breakaway confederation the Finnish Trades Organization (SAJ) in 1960. This mirrored, and was indeed closely linked to, the division inside the SDP where in 1959 a minority formed the Social Democratic Opposition (*Työväen ja Pienviljelijäin Sosialidemokraattinen Liitto*, TPSL) that existed until 1973 when it rejoined the SDP. In 1969, however, unification was achieved when the statutes of SAK were changed, allowing member unions more independence in decisions concerning collective bargaining and industrial action. SAK also adopted its current name, the Central Organization of Finnish Trade Unions. A year before that, in 1968, the first comprehensive incomes policy agreement was signed, paving the way for more consensual industrial relations and wide-ranging corporatist arrangements (Bergholm 2005; 2007; Mickelsson 2007).[1]

This chapter examines links between trade unions and left-of-centre parties in Finland. From the union side the analysis also covers the Finnish Confederation of Professionals (STTK) and the Confederation of Unions for Professional and Managerial Staff in Finland (AKAVA), but the main focus is on links between SAK and the two leftist parties, the SDP and the Left Alliance (VAS). The main argument is that while the electoral strength of the leftist parties has declined quite dramatically, the organizational links between SAK and the parties of the left have remained largely intact. At the same time, SAK has been forced to cast its net wider, redirecting its resources into other channels of influence. The same applies increasingly to the Social Democrats, as the party is clearly losing its grip on the working class vote while struggling to formulate goals or an identity that would appeal to broader sections of the electorate.

BACKGROUND AND CONTEXT

The links between parties and trade unions received heightened media attention in spring 2014 when Social Democrats elected a new leader, with the challenger Antti Rinne narrowly beating the incumbent party chair Jutta Urpilainen by 257 to 243 votes. Rinne, a trade union leader with no previous parliamentary experience, was very much perceived as the 'trade union candidate', and the unions of both metal-workers and paper-workers supported him. His victory was interpreted by many as reflecting a yearning on the part of the rank-and-file for a return to more leftist politics after two decades of politics during which the party had, both voluntarily and under strong external and budgetary constraints, embraced more market-friendly policies. Whatever the reason, the tight leadership contest brought to the fore three questions that are relevant for contextualizing the links between unions and left-of-centre parties: the decline of the left, structural transformation, and corporatism.

In the 2015 Eduskunta elections, the SDP captured only 16.5 per cent of the vote, its lowest ever share. The Social Democrats have not been as strong in Finland as in the other Nordic countries, but they were the largest party in all Eduskunta elections held from 1907 to 1954, and from 1966 onwards they finished first in every election apart from those held in 1991, 2003, 2007, 2011, and 2015. The peak was achieved in the 1995 elections with 28.3 per cent of the vote, the highest vote share for a single Finnish party in the post-war period. Yet the collective vote share of the leftist parties has declined quite dramatically in recent decades. Whereas the SDP and the predecessor of Left Alliance, the Finnish People's Democratic Union (FPDU), won between them over 45 per cent of the vote at all except one election between 1945 and 1966 (when they won together 48.3 per cent of the vote), by 2015 the electoral strength of the left had decreased to 23.6 per cent. The FPDU's decline began in the late 1960s and support for the Left Alliance has declined gradually since the 1995 elections, with the party winning 7.1 per cent of the vote in the 2015 elections.

The dilemma facing the SDP is, of course, shared by centre-of-left parties across Europe. At its core are two interlinked questions: whether to defend traditional leftist economic goals or endorse more market-friendly policies, and who the party represents. This debate about the party's ideology and identity flared up after the 1991 elections, which ushered in a centre-right coalition, and coincided with a serious recession in the early 1990s that followed the collapse of the Soviet Union. With unemployment reaching at worst nearly 20 per cent of the workforce, and with Social Democratic voters particularly afflicted by the bad times, the SDP and the trade unions closely attached to it began to emphasize the virtues of budgetary discipline and monetary stability alongside traditional social democratic goals such as universal social policies and job creation. Since trade with the Soviet regime had accounted for around 15–20 per cent of overall national trade, the demise of the communist bloc increased trade dependence on EU countries. As a result, internal party debates about ideology, the possibility of joining the EU, and the need to restore economic well-being became closely entangled. In those circumstances, the gradual move towards the right was made as much out of necessity as out of deliberate choice.

However, when in government—as the leading cabinet party from 1995 to 2003 and as the second largest coalition party in 2003–7 and 2011–15—the SDP implemented economic reforms that frustrated its left-leaning supporters (Mickelsson 2007; Raunio 2010). The Left Alliance, founded in 1990, is in a largely similar situation. VAS brings together a variety of leftists and former communists, and the party is also internally divided on the left–right axis, with the leadership advocating 'green-left' ideological moderation, while the working class voters more closely linked to trade unions oppose such centrist moves (Zilliacus 2001; Dunphy 2007). As its waning electoral support indicates, the party has found it difficult to cater for the needs of both traditional working class voters and the more urban, new 'green-left' supporters.

Importantly, both the SDP and VAS are operating in the context of a fragmented party system where pragmatic cooperation and compromises are the norm. Cabinet formation has something of an 'anything goes' feel to it, and governments are typically surplus majority coalitions that bring together parties from the left and the right (Arter 2009a). After 1966–70, the centre-right parties have held the majority of Eduskunta seats, often by a comfortable margin. This presents a challenge for the trade unions, particularly for SAK, as leftist parties are not as influential in Finnish politics as they once were.

Finland has also experienced major structural transformation that is evident not only in party politics but also in the trade union movement (Karvonen 2014). Until the Second World War, Finland was predominantly a rural society, with the primary sector (agriculture and forestry) playing a major role economically. Thereafter markets for pulp and the paper industry boomed, and war reparations to the Soviet Union made it necessary to expand the share of the metal industry in industrial output. However, the industrial sector of the economy never became as important as in Great Britain, Germany, or many other central European states. From the 1970s on, Finland rapidly became a post-industrial society where the tertiary sector (private and public services) engaged more than half of the labour force. In 2011, about 74 per cent of the labour force was employed in the tertiary sector. These major changes in occupational structures are obviously reflected in trade unions (Böckerman and Uusitalo 2006; Bergholm 2012; Bergholm and Bieler 2013). Essentially, the blue-collar SAK, while still numerically the largest confederation, is facing more competition from the STTK and AKAVA, which are politically quite different organizations.

The SAK has twenty-one individual member unions, with approximately 1 million members in private and public sectors. Nearly half of them—about 455,000—work in manufacturing and construction industries, while 335,000 members are employed in private services and 240,000 in the public sector. The SDP is the dominant party, with most of the unions controlled by Social Democrats. Left Alliance is the other major political force in SAK, but its influence has declined in recent decades. According to recent surveys, the populist Finns Party (formerly True Finns) enjoys considerable support among trade union members. But, in spite of a major electoral triumph in 2011 (when it took 19.1 per cent of the vote), and a similarly strong showing in 2015 (when it took 17.7 per cent), it has, so far at least, failed to achieve any real organizational breakthrough inside SAK.

The STTK has over 600,000 members in eighteen unions, with some of the largest unions consisting of nurses, health and social care professionals, and clerical employees. Its roots lie in the Intellectual Employment Union, founded in 1922, while STTK was established in 1946. While there is considerable variation between the unions, STTK is overall much less penetrated by party politics than SAK, and in the 2015 elections it did not fund any parties or individual candidates. According to both STTK's (2013) own barometer and the surveys conducted in connection with Eduskunta elections, the loyalty of members towards Social Democrats is decreasing, and nowadays the distribution of party support among STTK members reflects quite well the distribution of party support among the population as a whole. However, the chair of STTK has always been a Social Democrat.

AKAVA, originally established in 1950, has thirty-five member unions representing workers with university, professional, or other high-level education. It has about 585,000 members, roughly half of whom work in the private sector. In AKAVA the strongest party is the National Coalition, but like the STTK, it is internally much less prone to party-political battles than SAK.

Despite the societal changes mentioned earlier, Finland has been a strongly corporatist country since 1968 and remains so today. While the core issue of these centralized agreements was wages, the negotiations were often extended to labour market and social policy questions (Kyntäjä 1993), and were generally thought to work in favour of the more moderate, social democratic camp in the trade unions. That said, there was a temporary weakening of corporatism in the early 1990s, caused mainly by the economic recession that followed the dissolution of the Soviet Union. From the mid-1990s, however, the SDP-led cabinets of Paavo Lipponen (1995–2003) emphasized the importance of collective wage bargaining and corporatism, not least because the cooperation of the trade unions was seen as essential, not just for joining the EU in the first place, but in order to meet the criteria for Economic and Monetary Union (EMU) and to maintain economic discipline once in the Eurozone (Raunio 2010). The main employers' organization is the

Confederation of Finnish Industries (EK) that adopted its current name in 2004. Inside the EK the most influential party is the National Coalition. The EK decided unilaterally to abandon tripartite collective wage talks in 2007 when Finland was governed by a centre-right coalition (Bergholm and Bieler 2013). However, since 2011 centralized wage agreements have been reintroduced, no doubt thanks to the SDP re-entering government between 2011 and 2015.

While the system of collective wage talks is not as comprehensive as before, with such bargaining often delegated to the level of individual unions, many labour market agreements and laws are effectively decided in tripartite negotiations between the employers' federations, the trade unions, and the government. Collective agreements are universally binding, that is, they also cover those not belonging to unions. Trade union density has also risen over the decades, reaching its peak during the severe recession of the early 1990s, and over 70 per cent of the workforce now belongs to unions (Böckerman and Uusitalo 2006; see Chapter 2). Through comprehensive wage agreements and the overall change in direction of political consensus, a high level of industrial disputes has given way to a more conciliatory style of conflict resolution—a change that can be measured in the number of work days lost annually to industrial action dropping to just 152 during the first nine years of the 2000s (Karvonen 2014, 39).

RELATIONSHIPS TODAY: MAPPING OF LINKS

In Finland relationships are not regulated in the rules of procedure of either leftist parties (SDP, VAS) or trade unions. This was not always the case: in the first decades of independence individual unions were members of the parties, with the last union leaving the SDP in the 1950s. Now links are based on multifaceted cooperation that has become firmly institutionalized over the decades. There are no written rules or integrated relationships, yet there are daily contacts, joint working groups, and strong personnel overlaps. The Social Democrats and SAK in particular are formally independent of one another, yet in reality their relationship is very close.[2]

Inter-organizational Links: Reciprocal and Durable

Both the survey and additional interviews with party and union officials confirm the existence of tacit agreements between Social Democrats and SAK (see Table 5.1). This applies to mutual representation in decision-making bodies, permanent and temporary joint committees, joint campaigns and

Table 5.1. Reciprocal, durable inter-organizational links between party central organization/legislative group and union confederation, last five years (c.2008–13)[1]

Party-confederation dyad—CPO	SDP-SAK		SDP-STTK		SDP-AKAVA		VAS-SAK		VAS-STTK		VAS-AKAVA	
	P/U	CJ	P/U	CJ	P/U	CJ	P/U	CJ	P/U	CJ	P/U	CJ
Tacit agreements about one-sided/mutual representation in national decision-making bodies	c.d.	Yes	c.d.	Yes	c.d.	Yes	No	No	No	No	No	No
Permanent joint committee(s)	c.d.	Yes	c.d.	Yes	c.d.	Yes	No	No	No	No	No	No
Temporary joint committee(s)	c.d.	Yes	c.d.	Yes	c.d.	Yes	No	No	No	No	No	No
Formal agreements about regular meetings between party and organization	No	No	No	No	No	No	No	No	No	No	No	No
Tacit agreements about regular meetings between party and organization	c.d.	Yes	c.d.	Yes	c.d.	Yes	c.d.	Yes	No	No	No	No
Joint conferences	c.d.	Yes	c.d.	Yes	c.d.	Yes	No	No	No	No	No	No
Joint campaigns	c.d.	Yes	c.d.	Yes	c.d.	No	No	No	No	No	No	No

Party-confederation dyad—LPG	SDP-SAK		SDP-STTK		SDP-AKAVA		VAS-SAK		VAS-STTK		VAS-AKAVA	
	P/U	CJ	P/U	CJ	P/U	CJ	P/U	CJ	P/U	CJ	P/U	CJ
Tacit agreements about one-sided/mutual representation in national decision-making bodies	No	No	No	No	No	No	c.d.	Yes	No	No	No	No
Permanent joint committee(s)	No	No	No	No	No	No	No	No	No	No	No	No
Temporary joint committee(s)	c.d.	Yes	c.d.	Yes	No	No	No	No	No	No	No	No
Formal agreements about regular meetings between party and organization	No	No	No	No	No	No	No	No	No	No	No	No
Tacit agreements about regular meetings between party and organization	No	No	No	No	No	No	No	No	No	No	No	No
Joint conferences	c.d.	Yes	No	No	No	No	c.d.	Yes	No	No	No	No
Joint campaigns	No	No	No	No	No	No	c.d.	Yes	No	No	No	No

[1] 'P/U' indicates responses from party/trade union questionnaires, 'CJ' signifies the authors' 'coded judgment' based on alternative sources in cases of diverging or missing P/U answers. 'c.d.' means contradictory data (diverging P/U answers), 'n.d.' means no data (informant didn't know/missing/unclear), and 'n.a.' means not applicable in this case.

conferences, and regular meetings between party and the blue-collar confederation. These tacit relationships draw on decades of experience of working together: in place of statutory links there are shared understandings and unwritten yet *de facto* codified practices. SAK representatives take part in the various working groups of Social Democrats (in late 2014 there were thirty such groups), and the various personnel from both sides, from the level of party and trade union leaders to their youth organizations, meet regularly. SDP representatives take part in SAK meetings, although here it is important to remember that Social Democrats are in any case the dominant party in the confederation. While such routine daily exchange of ideas is the cornerstone of the relationship, interviewees from both sides agreed that cooperation intensifies, or at least becomes more important, during election campaigns. Geographical proximity is also relevant here. Both the SDP and SAK headquarters are located in Hakaniemi in central Helsinki, roughly 200–300 metres from one another. In fact, almost all of the individual unions of SAK have their offices in the blocks next to the SDP's HQ, adjacent to which is a pub called *Juttutupa* that is a regular meeting place for SDP and SAK staff. The two organizations also carry out study trips abroad, for example to the other Nordic countries, to examine how party–union links are operating elsewhere.[3]

Interestingly, according to the survey the SDP also has similar ties with STTK and AKAVA, both of which also often take part in SDP working groups. However, a crucial difference became evident in the interviews: given the changes in occupational structures and in the trade union movement, the Social Democrats have needed to invest resources in contacts with other confederations; however, these links are still much less institutionalized and regular than are ties to SAK. The relationship between the SDP's legislative group and trade unions appears much weaker. Yet, especially at the level of individual MPs, contacts are numerous and regular, particularly among 'trade union MPs'. In marked contrast, the Left Alliance and the confederation report hardly any durable links between them—another sign of the dwindling role of the party inside SAK, even if it does wield influence inside individual unions.

Inter-organizational Links: One-way and Occasional

Largely the same situation applies to occasional ties (Table 5.2). We can again see the Social Democrats, this time including their legislative group, sending invitations to all three confederations. Unfortunately we have no exact data on how often those invitations are taken up, but there is a vast difference between SAK and STTK/AKAVA. Representatives from the Social Democrats attend the conferences and seminars and other meetings of SAK as a rule, and vice versa. Cooperation with STTK and AKAVA is much less frequent, although

Table 5.2. One-way, occasional links at the organizational level between party central organization/legislative group and union confederation, last five years (c.2008–13)[1,2]

Party-confederation dyad—CPO	SDP-SAK		SDP-STTK		SDP-AKAVA		VAS-SAK		VAS-STTK		VAS-AKAVA	
	P/U	CJ	P/U	CJ	P/U	CJ	P/U	CJ	P/U	CJ	P/U	CJ
Invitation to party to participate in the organization's national congress	Yes	Yes	Yes	Yes	c.d.	Yes	c.d.	Yes	No	No	No	No
Invitation to organization to participate in the party's national congress/conference	Yes	Yes	Yes	Yes	c.d.	Yes	c.d.	No	c.d.	No	No	No
Invitations to organization to participate in the party's ordinary meetings, seminars, and conferences	Yes	Yes	Yes	Yes	c.d.	Yes	Yes	Yes	Yes	Yes	c.d.	Yes
Invitations to party to participate in ordinary organization meetings, seminars, and conferences	Yes	Yes	Yes	Yes	c.d.	Yes	Yes	Yes	c.d.	Yes	No	No
Invitations to organization to special consultative arrangements initiated by the party	Yes	Yes	Yes	Yes	Yes	Yes	c.d.	No	c.d.	No	No	No
Invitations to party to special consultative arrangements initiated by the organization	Yes	Yes	c.d.	Yes	Yes	Yes	c.d.	Yes	No	No	No	No

Party-confederation dyad—LPG	SDP-SAK		SDP-STTK		SDP-AKAVA		VAS-SAK		VAS-STTK		VAS-AKAVA	
	P/U	CJ	P/U	CJ	P/U	CJ	P/U	CJ	P/U	CJ	P/U	CJ
Invitation to party to participate in the organization's national congress	Yes	Yes	Yes	Yes	c.d.	No	Yes	Yes	No	No	No	No
Invitation to organization to participate in the party's national congress/conference	n.a.	n.a.	n.a.	n.a.	n.a.	n.a.	n.a.	n.a.	n.a.	n.a.	c.d.	n.a.
Invitations to organization to participate in the party's ordinary meetings, seminars, and conferences	Yes	Yes	Yes	Yes	No	No	Yes	Yes	Yes	Yes	c.d.	Yes
Invitations to party to participate in ordinary organization meetings, seminars, and conferences	c.d.	Yes	Yes	Yes	No	No	Yes	Yes	Yes	Yes	c.d.	No
Invitations to organization to special consultative arrangements initiated by the party	Yes	Yes	Yes	Yes	c.d.	Yes	Yes	Yes	Yes	Yes	c.d.	Yes
Invitations to party to special consultative arrangements initiated by the organization	c.d.	Yes	No	No	c.d.	Yes	Yes	Yes	Yes	Yes	Yes	Yes

[1] 'P/U' indicates responses from party/trade union questionnaires, 'CJ' signifies the authors' 'coded judgment' based on alternative sources in cases of diverging or missing P/U answers. 'c.d.' means contradictory data (diverging P/U answers), 'n.d.' means no data (informant didn't know/missing/unclear), and 'n.a.' means not applicable in this case. The coded judgement in all these cases is based primarily on interviews. Again, the reason for these differing answers is that the SDP reported not having direct connections to the trade unions but to the SDP groups inside SAK and its unions. There were more differing answers between trade unions and Left Alliance's CPO. The coded judgement in these cases is derived from the answer given by the side sending the invitation at each claim. For example, if the claim is that the trade union has sent invitations to the party's CPO and the answers differ, the coded judgement is based on the answer given by the trade union. The same logic applies if the claim says that the party is the one that invites the trade unions. This method has been used in connections between parties' LPGs and trade unions.

[2] SDP CPO's and AKAVA's answers differ four times in Table 5.2. Also SDP CPO's and STTK's answers differ once.

(especially inside STTK) the Social Democrats have strong ties with some of the individual unions.

The Left Alliance is more active regarding the one-way occasional links. In particular, its legislative group invites all three confederations to its meetings, though how often trade union representatives actually attend is unknown. It is natural that VAS personnel attend the meetings and conferences of SAK, since the Left Alliance is still strongly present inside many individual unions. Overall, it is probable that the three confederations often send invitations to all of the parties represented in Eduskunta, including the Finns Party.

Individual-level Links: Personnel Overlaps and Transfers

The individual-level data supports the findings on organizational links. Social Democrats and SAK display strong personnel overlap, and it is very common for SDP officials to have worked previously in SAK, and vice versa. Hence it is not surprising to find that individual-level contacts are numerous and take place on a daily basis. For example, two of the three most recent SDP party chairs are experienced trade union leaders. Personnel overlap and individual contacts also exist between Social Democrats and the STTK, and to a certain extent with AKAVA too, although these links are again considerably weaker than those with SAK. The Left Alliance also enjoys individual-level contacts, and some personnel overlap, with SAK and its individual unions, but despite all this, members of trade union executive committees have only occasionally held seats in the executive organs of VAS or particularly of the SDP (Sundberg 2003, 110–12).

Figure 5.1 reports the share of SDP and VAS MPs in 2013/14 that work or have worked as officials in the national-level bodies of the three confederations. Perhaps surprisingly, Social Democratic MPs have less experience of trade union work than Left Alliance representatives (but, of course, the total size of the latter's party group is also much smaller). In order to get a fuller picture of such individual level ties, we also compiled a data set of all 200 MPs elected to the Eduskunta in the 2011 elections. This data examines all possible positions held by MPs inside trade unions, including at the local level.[4] Some 4 per cent of National Coalition MPs, 31 per cent of Social Democratic MPs, 3 per cent of the Finns Party MPs, 23 per cent of Centre Party MPs, 50 per cent of Left Alliance MPs, 20 per cent of Swedish People's Party MPs, 20 per cent of Green League MPs, and 17 per cent of Christian Democrat MPs had held positions in trade unions at some point during their career. Clearly, the share is much higher in the legislative groups of the two leftist parties than in the others—a finding consistent with earlier studies (Venho 2008, 236). Moreover, in the Centre Party all the MPs with trade union ties had links to the Central Union of Agricultural Producers and Forest Owners (MTK), with whom the

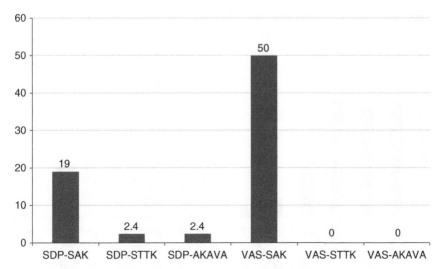

Figure 5.1. Share of SDP and VAS MPs in 2013/14 that hold or have held positions as officials or staff in the confederations of unions at the national level.[1]

[1] Only permanent representatives and deputy representatives who attend the entire term are included. 'n.d.' means no data (missing). N of MPs is 42 for SDP and 14 for VAS.

party has always enjoyed close ties. Meanwhile, the two Swedish People's Party representatives with trade union background had in turn been affiliated with the Swedish-speaking union of farmers, the Central Union of Swedish-Speaking Agricultural Producers in Finland (SLC).

Overall Degree of Closeness and Range

Turning to overall closeness and range of relationships, we see that the total organizational scores echo what we have already picked up (see Figure 5.2a and 5.2b). SDP-SAK, SDP-STTK, and SPD-AKAVA all obtain a scale value of 12 (out of 20) as far as links between the central party organization and the confederations go. However, we would argue that the closest relationship is still that between the SDP and SAK: while not an integrated relationship, the two sides are working together at all levels on a regular, if not daily or at least weekly, basis. This dyad also obtains a higher score than the two other relationships in which the SDP's parliamentary group is involved (7 out of 12). The Left Alliance and SAK are also close, but this applies more to the level of those individual unions where VAS is in a strong position. Yet we see that the scale value for VAS's legislative group and SAK is 8 (out of 12).

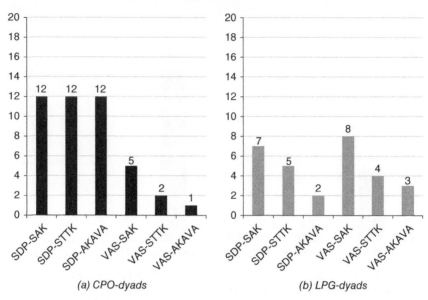

(a) CPO-dyads   *(b) LPG-dyads*

Figure 5.2. Total link scores of central party organization–trade union relationships and legislative party–trade union relationships (0–20/0–12).[1]

[1] The theoretical maximum link score is 20 for the CPO-dyads and 12 for LPG-dyads since some link items are unlikely to apply to the legislative party group and were thus not included in this part of the survey. However, when comparing dyads involving CPOs with those involving LPGs, one should still keep in mind that the latter's maximum involves fewer links than the former's top scores.

The contacts between the two leftist parties and in particular VAS and STTK and AKAVA are more ad hoc and sporadic: sending invitations, visiting each other occasionally, or distributing information. The most distant confederation is AKAVA, whose representative stressed that they do not have any kind of contact with the parties in question.

The party–union informants' rating of the overall degree of closeness/ distance echoes the organizational scores, but not completely (Figure 5.3). VAS and SAK are presented as 'fairly close', just as SDP-SAK and SDP-STTK. Probably, this reflects the fact that the Social Democrats have needed to react to the growing size and influence of the STTK. But given the less partisan nature of that confederation, the links are mainly between the SDP and some of the individual unions inside the STTK. There has thus been a change over time, since previously Social Democrats were almost exclusively focused on working with their 'natural' partner, SAK. Nonetheless, the interviews indicate that the links between the SDP and SAK have remained remarkably stable during recent decades, regardless of the economic situation or the personalities leading either the confederation or the party.

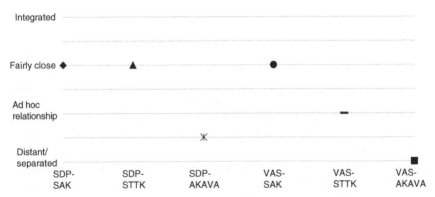

Figure 5.3. Rating of overall degree of closeness/distance (average score) between the party and union confederation, last five years (*c*.2008–13).[1]

[1] Ratings in-between two categories reflect that the party and union responses to the survey question differed. None of the ratings differed with more than one category.

From the trade union side, the decline of the left and the fragmented party system present a challenge. SAK is increasingly casting its net wider, talking to all political parties represented in the Eduskunta. Towards the end of the 1980s there was a feeling inside SAK that they could manage without too close a link to any of the parties, and in 1991, the year when the SDP lost the elections and ended up in opposition, SAK went so far as to remove from its statutes a clause about the confederation forming a part of the international workers' movement. And ever since it has realized that it might be disadvantageous to rely too much on links with leftist parties alone (Sundberg 2003, 159).

However, the interviews suggest that despite the decline of the electoral strength of the left, the SDP and to a lesser extent VAS are still seen as the logical companions of SAK—as people who listen and understand. The National Coalition is the most distant party from the blue-collar confederation, as it is closely linked to the EK. The Centre Party is in turn strongly connected to the MTK. The Greens are in many ways sympathetic towards SAK and its objectives, particularly when it comes to workers' rights; but the party is obviously rooted in the environmental movement and associated interest groups whose policies often are at odds with trade union interests. Greens perhaps also view trade unions as old-fashioned and too hierarchical. The Finns Party make much of its desire to defend the 'common man', and in the 2011 and 2015 Eduskunta elections the party certainly attracted large numbers of working class voters, many of whom defected from the SDP. But the party also includes a lot of small entrepreneurs that are highly critical of unions, and, while defending the welfare state, the party often distances itself from leftist values and also from the trade union movement.

A FAIR EXCHANGE?

What might explain these patterns? This section provides data on two possible drivers of party–union relationships: funding of parties by trade unions and the political loyalties of trade union members. The focus here is on links between SAK, the Social Democrats, and the Left Alliance.

Traditionally the size of SAK donations to either the SDP or VAS has been very low, as it is not the confederation that funds the parties and particularly their individual candidates. Most of the income parties receive comes from public funding: this applies to all Finnish parties regardless of their ideological orientation (Venho 2008). Between 1983 and 2012, public funding contributed between 64 per cent and 87 per cent of the annual income of the SDP, with membership fees accounting for around 7–10 per cent of the income in recent years. The share of SDP income accounted for by 'fundraising', including donations from SAK and individual unions, was on average 8.7 per cent between 1983 and 2010, with peaks in election years (for example, 23 per cent in 2006 when presidential elections were held, and 20 per cent in 2007, the year of Eduskunta elections).[5] The role of SAK becomes more important during election campaigns, but even then not through funding but mainly through organizing seminars and campaign events, producing and distributing information, and just in general through supporting the campaigns of parties. For example, in the 2011 elections SAK donated only 2,000 euros to the SDP while the total sum of trade union funding for Social Democrats in the elections was 39,000 euros. The Left Alliance in turn received 36,500 euros from trade unions, with none of that money coming directly from SAK. While we have no longitudinal data about SAK donations, it appears that the 2011 elections are representative of elections held in recent decades.

Moreover, very active campaigning by SAK can sometimes prove counterproductive. For example, in the 2007 elections SAK financed a TV advert that caused a lot of negative publicity for the confederation and the leftist parties by featuring a wealthy businessman enjoying a table full of fine food, taking pleasure in his ability to decide issues because of the working class's failure to vote.[6] Overall, whereas back in the 1979 elections SAK and its member unions were explicitly telling people to vote for leftist parties, in recent decades it has refrained from giving such recommendations. However, in the 2006 presidential elections SAK openly supported the re-election of the incumbent SDP candidate Tarja Halonen (Venho 2008, 236).

The main donors are instead the individual unions of SAK that fund the left-wing parties and actively support 'their' candidates in all Eduskunta elections.[7] As became evident from the analysis of individual-level contacts, around one-third of SDP and half of VAS MPs elected in 2011 had trade union connections. Individual unions offer direct funding to their candidates. Examining the funding of MPs elected in 2011, we can see again clear differences between the parties: 7 per cent of National Coalition MPs, 57 per cent of Social Democrat MPs, 13 per cent of the Finns Party MPs, 23 per cent of Centre Party MPs, 64 per cent of Left Alliance MPs, 30 per cent of Swedish People's Party MPs, 20 per cent of Green League MPs, and 17 per cent of Christian Democrat MPs received campaign funding from unions. Again the MTK and SLC were active in funding the MPs of the Centre Party and the Swedish People's Party, whereas the two leftist parties clearly stand out in terms of getting money from the unions, mainly the individual unions of SAK.[8] With the exception of some individual representatives, the sums were not significant— ranging from a few hundred euros to around 10,000 euros. However, the Social Democratic MP Lauri Ihalainen, who served as the SAK leader from 1990 to 2009 and was subsequently minister for labour in the 2011–15 coalition, received 28,600 from the unions. Overall, it must be emphasized that direct funding may not be the most important form of campaign help (Venho 2008, 235–44). Union activists at all levels provide a variety of help to SDP and VAS candidates that cannot be captured through funding data. Moreover, SAK as a whole is committed to increasing turnout among its members, a long-term strategy that might be expected to favour those same parties.

Class dealignment and the entry of new issues to the political agenda has, since the 1960s, contributed to increasing electoral instability, both in terms of party system fragmentation and electoral volatility. The three core parties of recent decades—Social Democrats, the Centre Party, and the National Coalition—largely held on to their vote shares for some time, suggesting that the three-front model proposed by Lipset and Rokkan (1967), where the relationship between trade unions and parties reflects underlying social cleavages, was still relevant, with the SDP and VAS representing working class interests (SAK), the Centre Party agrarian or rural interests (MTK), and the National Coalition the interests of the bourgeoisie or capital (EK) (Sundberg 2003; 2008). However, the breakthrough of the Finns Party in 2011 and 2015 now means that the Finnish party system has four almost equally sized large parties (Arter 2009a; Borg 2012; Karvonen 2014).

Structural transformation has contributed to increased unpredictability. More precisely, there is no party that would offer a logical home to the people employed in the large services sector, since it includes such a wide variety of occupational groups ranging from waitresses, teachers, and sales personnel to nurses (Grönlund and Westinen 2012, 157–8). Drawing on surveys carried out in connection with Eduskunta elections, Table 5.3 reports the party choices of trade union members. MTK is unsurprisingly dominated by Centre voters, whereas inside AKAVA the National Coalition is the largest party. With the exception of 1991 and 2015, the SDP has been the biggest party inside STTK, but overall the distribution of party support among STTK members mirrors rather well the distribution of party support among the population as a whole. As for SAK, around 43 per cent of its members voted for the Social Democrats

Table 5.3. The party choice of trade union members in Eduskunta elections, 1991–2015 (%)[1]

		SDP	KESK	KOK	RKP	KD	VIHR	VAS	PS	Others	Total
2015	SAK	27.7	15.0	5.2	1.4	0.9	6.1	11.3	28.2	4.2	100.0
	STTK	16.5	29.6	16.5	7.0	3.5	6.1	5.2	15.7	0.0	100.0
	AKAVA	6.3	16.8	28.8	4.2	4.7	19.4	11.0	7.9	1.0	100.0
	MTK	20.0	80.0	0.0	0.0	0.0	0.0	0.0	0.0	0.0	100.0
2011	SAK	38.2	5.6	6.0	1.3	3.9	7.7	13.3	22.7	1.3	100.0
	STTK	25.6	15.6	15.6	3.3	4.4	5.6	10.0	16.7	3.3	100.0
	AKAVA	10.4	12.5	27.1	8.3	2.8	20.1	8.3	10.4	0.0	100.0
	MTK	0.0	69.2	0.0	15.4	7.7	0.0	0.0	7.7	0.0	100.0
2007	SAK	31.2	15.8	8.5	9.4	5.1	6.0	17.5	4.3	2.1	100.0
	STTK	22.8	19.3	18.4	14.9	7.0	10.5	4.4	1.8	0.9	100.0
	AKAVA	10.2	14.8	18.8	25.8	4.7	18.8	6.3	0.8	0.0	100.0
	MTK	0.0	66.7	16.7	8.3	8.3	0.0	0.0	0.0	0.0	100.0
2003	SAK	42.9	15.3	7.9	4.8	4.8	7.9	15.3	1.1	–	100.0
	STTK	36.2	16.2	18.1	9.5	7.6	8.6	2.9	1.0	–	100.0
	AKAVA	12.9	21.8	25.7	16.8	6.9	10.9	5.0	0.0	–	100.0
	MTK	0.0	81.5	7.4	3.7	7.4	0.0	0.0	0.0	–	100.0
1991	SAK	42.9	17.2	7.1	3.4	3.4	5.0	17.6	1.7	1.6	100.0
	AKAVA	8.2	16.5	39.2	8.2	3.1	17.5	5.2	0.0	2.0	100.0
	STTK	24.5	20.4	30.6	10.2	4.1	2.0	0.0	4.1	2.0	100.0
	MTK	2.0	78.4	13.7	0.0	0.0	3.9	0.0	0.0	2.0	100.0

[1] SDP = Social Democratic Party; KESK = the Centre Party; KOK = National Coalition; RKP = Swedish People's Party; KD = Christian Democrats; VIHR = Green League; VAS = Left Alliance; PS = The Finns Party/Rural Party which fought the 1991 election as SMP.

Source: FNES 1991, 2003, 2007, 2011, 2015. See: <http://www.vaalitutkimus.fi/en/>.

in 1991 and 2003, and the support of VAS seems stable among SAK members. However, the 2015 data show significant differences, with the Finns Party the most popular single party among SAK members. There is thus a firm connection between SDP/VAS and SAK among the voters, but it is possible that the Finns Party will undermine that relationship (see Tiihonen 2015).

Our analysis of organizational links, funding, and voting behaviour indicates that both sides—SAK and leftist parties—see cooperation as mutually beneficial. In terms of exchanging resources, the SDP gets valuable support from SAK (and to a lesser extent from STTK) in terms of votes and campaign support, whereas SAK has party-political allies for achieving its policy goals. In the interviews SAK personnel underlined strongly the importance of Social Democrats joining the government, as the party has managed to do almost uninterruptedly since the late 1930s, with the exception of years 1957–66 when the party suffered from internal splits and then the three more recent periods of rule by centre-right cabinets (1991–5, 2007–11, 2015–). In fact, during these later periods the role of the trade unions has declined, particularly in 2007–11 when the EK unilaterally refused to enter into comprehensive incomes policy agreements—a decision that was reversed when the SDP entered the cabinet after the 2011 elections. In terms of policy, both sides benefit, with the SDP present in political institutions while SAK influences primarily through corporatist channels.

CONCLUSION

The contemporary history of Finland cannot be understood without acknowledging the role of trade unions, primarily those organized by SAK, which, together with their leftist party-political allies, have introduced over the decades reforms that form the backbone of the current welfare state. Trade unions are of course criticized repeatedly, especially by centre-right political actors, but they continue to enjoy a high level of legitimacy. In terms of policies, trade unions are even asked to lay the basis for reforms should the government find itself in deadlock due to lack of unity—something that happens quite often as Finnish cabinets have traditionally been broad coalitions bringing together parties from the left and the right. Corporatist practices are still very much the norm, from centralized wage agreements to more regular cooperation between the trade unions, the employers' federations, and the state.

Despite the drastic decline of the political left in Finland—down to under one-third of Eduskunta seats since the 2007 elections—SAK is still dependent on the Social Democrats, and to a lesser extent on the Left Alliance. The links between trade unions and left-of-centre parties are solid and fairly well institutionalized: they are based on unwritten yet routinized arrangements that draw on decades of experience of working together for mutual benefit: when the Social Democrats are in government 'it makes life so much easier', declared one SAK official interviewed. But even when the SDP is in the cabinet, SAK has needed to reach beyond its core partners, needing to lobby more, to invest more resources in direct contacts with ministries and MPs, and the cabinet and the prime minister's office, and to talk to all parties represented in the Eduskunta.

The recent global and European financial uncertainty, not to mention the current domestic economic challenges, has obviously brought about increasing debate about trade unions. Especially from the right, they are seen as obstacles to much-needed economic reforms, while the left stresses their role in providing macroeconomic stability and peaceful industrial relations. Whereas from the 1960s onwards trade unions were often behind major (and popular) socio-economic reforms, today they mainly focus on defending the status quo, with the initiatives coming from the employers' side or from the centre-right parties (Ruostetsaari 2014, 283–6). Whether trade unions can survive the next few years with their influence and legitimacy intact remains to be seen, but at least for now their role remains strong. The bigger question marks perhaps concern the changes inside the trade union movement brought about by the structural transformation of the economy. The analysis in this chapter has suggested that union confederations are often internally quite heterogeneous and thus 'speaking with one voice' or articulating clear preferences is increasingly challenging for them. This is also one of the reasons why the left-of-centre parties nowadays often deal directly with individual unions as opposed to the actual confederations. Moreover, parties of the left in Finland have experienced a dramatic decline in support over recent decades, in the light of which the Social Democrats in particular may start reconsidering whether strong public links with the trade unions are doing them more harm than good.

NOTES

1. For a very useful timeline of the history of SAK and the Finnish trade union movement, see <http://www.sak.fi/this-is-sak/history/timeline>.
2. A table is not presented as there were no 'yes values' (coded judgments).
3. In Table 5.1, differences between the answers of trade unions and the SDP are explained by the fact that the CPO replied in the survey that it does not have connections to the trade union confederation but to the SDP groups inside SAK and its unions.
4. A note of caution: the data was compiled from various sources: MPs' homepages, their pages at the Eduskunta website, personal CVs found online and written sources, but unfortunately there is considerable variation between representatives in terms of how much information they provide about their work careers or other positions of trust.

5. Based on data kindly provided by Vesa Koskimaa.
6. <https://www.youtube.com/watch?v=gLx-xnBEswo>.
7. Interestingly, while trade union donations are often seen as 'dirty money', the leftist parties escaped the party finance scandal of 2008–9 (which led to more stringent reporting requirements on campaign funding) relatively unscathed. The scandal was particularly troubling for the leading government parties, the Centre and the National Coalition (Arter 2009b).
8. These figures are based on funding disclosures of the elected MPs. For information on the legal provisions, see <http://www.vaalit.fi/en/index/generalinformation/electionfunding.html>. The reports of the MPs and political parties are available at <http://www.vaalirahoitus.fi/fi/index.html>.

6

Left-wing Parties and Trade Unions in France

Nick Parsons

This chapter aims to examine and explain change and continuity in party–union relations in France since the 1970s. To do this it argues that these relationships can be seen in terms of a cost–benefit exchange, but that this exchange is historically and ideationally conditioned as well as subject to political contingencies. Indeed, the early development of trade unions in France set an ideational template of independence for party–union relations. The anarcho-syndicalist origins of the early trade union movement saw it reject any organizational links with parties, a position that was given concrete expression in the founding statutes of the *Confédération générale du travail* (CGT) in 1895, and again in the same organization's 1906 Charter of Amiens. However, while all unions have always paid lip-service to the principles of the Charter, in reality the notion of union independence from political parties has been a myth since the creation of the French Communist Party (PCF) in 1920. The link between the CGT and the PCF was cemented by participation in the wartime resistance movement, with communists taking over the levers of power within the trade union.

PARTY–UNION RELATIONS IN THE POST-WAR PERIOD

After the Second World War, the main cleavage on the left in France appeared to be between the communists, with tight links between the CGT and PCF on the one hand, and parties and unions with weak links on the non-communist left. In reality, unions and parties formed distinct 'political families' based on ideological affinity while maintaining the 'fiction of strict independence'

(Daley 1993, 53). In 1947, with the backdrop of the Cold War, the *Force Ouvrière* (FO) current within the CGT protested at the communist takeover of the confederation before setting itself up as a rival anti-communist confederation in 1948. Other divisions among trade unions centred on religion, with the French Confederation of Christian Workers (CFTC) being established in 1919 as a moderate Catholic alternative to the radical CGT. Later, the Democratic French Confederation of Labour (CFDT) was created in 1964 when the majority of the CFTC decided to deconfessionalize and pursue a 'third way' between the reformist FO and CFTC on the one hand, and the bureaucratic state socialism of the CGT-PCF tandem on the other (Parsons 2013).

Despite the clear call for trade union independence in the CGT's statutes, it was customary during the period from the end of the Second World War to the mid-1990s for the general secretary of the CGT to be a member of the Political Bureau of the PCF, although there were no formal links between the two organizations. In general terms, although the CGT gained some 'relative autonomy' from the 1960s to the mid-1970s, the CGT acted as a 'transmission belt' (Reynaud 1975, 209–10) for the PCF. Relations became more problematic from the late 1970s onwards, as critical voices from within the CGT began to demand 'modernization', and with it greater autonomy. The result was that, whereas previous post-war elections were always marked by CGT calls for a vote for the PCF, from 1988 the CGT did not give any guidance to members on how to vote in either parliamentary or presidential elections.

In 1995, Louis Viannet, the then general secretary, announced that he no longer needed to be an 'organic liaison' between the Party and trade union, and that he was resigning from the National Bureau (now Executive Committee) of the PCF, signifying the end of the 'transmission belt' between the party and the masses (Courtois and Andolfatto 2008, 107). Since then, none of his successors have been members of the National Bureau. CGT General Secretary Bernard Thibault's resignation from the PCF National Council in 2001 appeared to cement the 'gradual disassociation of the CGT from the PCF' (Courtois and Andolfatto 2008, 107). For some, however, ideological affinity and overlapping memberships meant that the union remained the 'hard core' of the party at the turn of the twenty-first century (Andolfatto and Labbé 2000, 185–6).

Among the non-communist trade unions and the PS, relations were looser, being 'more characterized by personal affinities than by organizational linkages' (Daley 1993, 57). Thus, FO had 'discreet' (Reynaud 1975, 210) relations with the SFIO and its successor, the Socialist Party. In the 1980s, as the Trotskyist Workers' Party increased its influence within the confederation, relations with the PS became increasingly tense (Andolfatto and Sabot 2004, 37).

In the 1960s, the other main left-wing non-communist union, the CFDT, formed, with the Unified Socialist Party (PSU), part of the 'second left', rejecting the Soviet-influenced bureaucratic centralism of the CGT-PCF tandem and the welfare reformism inherent in the FO's approach to political and social change. In 1974, however, the PSU merged with the PS and many CFDT members and leaders, wishing to build up a unified non-communist left, followed, despite strong criticism from the left of the confederation (Daley 1993, 57). From the mid-1970s, in the context of economic crisis, the CFDT embarked on a process of 'resyndicalization'—or focussing on trade union action, notably through collective bargaining, rather than seeking national-level political and social transformation, resulting in more difficult relations with the political left. Nevertheless, the CFDT called for a vote in favour of the socialist François Mitterrand in the 1981 presidential elections. Following the latter's victory, high-ranking CFDT (and CGT) members were recruited as advisors in ministerial cabinets, although this was in a personal rather than organizational capacity (Labbé and Croisat 1992, 140–1). By the 1980s, CFDT influence on PS policy could be seen in the field of industrial relations, with the passing of the Auroux Laws in 1982 (Howell 1992). Even austerity policies from 1982 onwards received broad, if not always unqualified, CFDT support (Howell 1992, 161–4; Pernot 2010, 213). However, relations soon soured in a context of persistently high unemployment, unpopular austerity policies, and a rapidly declining membership base. The CFDT, for the first time since 1970, did not call for a vote for the left in the 1986 parliamentary elections. This distancing from the political left continued with no call to vote for Mitterrand in the 1988 presidential elections (Bevort 2004, 57), although certain individuals maintained close ties with the government following Mitterrand's second presidential election victory (Landré 2013).

As the CGT has, since the 1980s, attempted to distance itself from the declining PCF by moving—albeit hesitatingly—towards the social-democratic middle ground, this has opened up space on the left for the so-called 'autonomous' unions, unattached to any confederation, to grow. Thus, *Solidaires, unitaires, démocratiques* (SUD) movements developed in many public sector organizations from 1989 onwards as members defected from established confederations. The SUD unions joined, and radicalized, the 'Group of 10' unions unaffiliated to any confederation, which was created in 1981 and became the *Union syndicale solidaire* (USS) in 1998. Furthermore, the far left *Fédération des syndicats unifiée* (FSU) and the social-democratic *Union nationale des syndicats autonomes* (UNSA) grew out of a split in the National Education Federation (FEN), a teachers' union, in 1992. The overall result, then, is increased union fragmentation (Parsons 2005, 59–62) that weakens unions and reduces incentives for stable party–union relations. Less than 8 per cent of wage earners are unionized in France—the lowest of any OECD country—and French unions have lost two-thirds of their members since the 1970s (Parsons 2013, 190–1, see also Table 2.1a in this volume).

Thus, structural conditions militated against the development of close organizational links between parties and unions in France. Among the non-communist unions and the Socialist Party, relationships from the end of the Second World War to the turn of the twenty-first century can be said to be characterized by individual-level links. In terms of the classification used in this volume, the presence of CFDT officials in ministerial cabinets in the early 1980s represents links with state rather than party actors. Nevertheless, since such developments only occurred when the PS was in power, they can be considered to reflect the existence of individual-level links, at least on an ad hoc basis. The major change in party–union links over the period is the weakening of the PCF-CGT dyad.

RELATIONSHIPS TODAY: MAPPING OF LINKS

The Charter of Amiens has become the iconic text of the French trade union movement and one to which all unions in France still make implicit or explicit reference in their contemporary statutes. In formal terms, independence is enshrined as a principle. For parties, while the independence of the trade union movement is respected, things are more nuanced. Partnership with (in the case of the PCF) and membership of (in the case of the PS) unions is encouraged in statutes, but no guidance is given as to membership of any particular trade union, or indeed of trade unions as opposed to other interest groups. Formal statutes therefore suggest a complete separation of parties and unions.

To test whether this formal independence is reflected in current practice or whether there has been any change over time, questionnaires on party–union links were sent to key informants in the PS and the PCF, as well as all the national union confederations mentioned earlier. Unfortunately, neither political party responded. On the union side, however, responses were received from the CGT, CFDT, UNSA, USS, and FSU, meaning that the two largest French confederations and those with the closest ties historically to the parties of the left—the CGT and CFDT—are represented in these responses, as are the three new autonomous organizations. This allows for extrapolation from these responses to produce informed judgements about current party–union relations across the board.

Inter-organizational Links: Durable and Reciprocal

In line with proclamations of political independence in statutes, no key informant reported any overlapping organizational structures or statutory links.[1] For reciprocal and durable inter-organizational links, only the USS key informant reported engaging in any joint campaigns with both the PS and the PCF (Tables 6.1a and 6.1b). As the key informant also states that the union

Table 6.1a. Reciprocal, durable inter-organizational links between party central organization/legislative group and union confederation, last five years (c.2008–13)[1]

Party-confederation dyad—CPO	PS-FSU		PS-CGT		PS-USS		PS-CFDT		PS-UNSA		PS-FO		PS-CFTC	
	P/U	CJ	P/U	CJ	P/U	CJ	P/U	CJ	P/U	CJ	P/U	CJ	P/U	CJ
Tacit agreements about one-sided/mutual representation in national decision-making bodies	No	No	No	No	No	No	Yes	No	No	No	n.d.	No	n.d.	No
Permanent joint committee(s)	No	No	No	No	No	No	No	No	No	No	n.d.	No	n.d.	No
Temporary joint committee(s)	No	No	No	No	No	No	No	No	No	No	n.d.	No	n.d.	No
Formal agreements about regular meetings between party and organization	No	No	No	No	No	No	No	No	No	No	n.d.	No	n.d.	No
Tacit agreements about regular meetings between party and organization	No	No	No	No	No	No	No	Yes	No	Yes	n.d.	No	n.d.	No
Joint conferences	No	No	No	No	No	No	No	No	No	No	n.d.	No	n.d.	No
Joint campaigns	No	No	No	No	Yes	No	No	No	No	No	n.d.	No	n.d.	No

Party-confederation dyad—LPG	PS-FSU		PS-CGT		PS-USS		PS-CFDT		PS-UNSA		PS-FO		PS-CFTC	
	P/U	CJ	P/U	CJ	P/U	CJ	P/U	CJ	P/U	CJ	P/U	CJ	P/U	CJ
Tacit agreements about one-sided/mutual representation in national decision-making bodies	No	No	No	No	No	No	Yes	No	No	No	n.d.	No	n.d.	No
Permanent joint committee(s)	No	No	No	No	No	No	No	No	No	No	n.d.	No	n.d.	No
Temporary joint committee(s)	No	No	No	No	No	No	No	No	No	No	n.d.	No	n.d.	No
Formal agreements about regular meetings between party and organization	No	No	No	No	No	No	No	No	No	No	n.d.	No	n.d.	No
Tacit agreements about regular meetings between party and organization	No	No	No	No	No	No	No	No	No	No	n.d.	No	n.d.	No
Joint conferences	No	No	No	No	No	No	No	No	No	No	n.d.	No	n.d.	No
Joint campaigns	No	No	No	No	No	No	No	No	No	No	n.d.	No	n.d.	No

[1] 'P/U' indicates responses from party/trade union questionnaires, 'CJ' signifies the authors' 'coded judgment' based on alternative sources in cases of diverging or missing P/U answers, 'c.d.' means contradictory data (diverging P/U answers), 'n.d.' means no data (informant didn't know/missing/unclear), and 'n.a.' means not applicable in this case.

Table 6.1b. Reciprocal, durable inter-organizational links between party central organization/legislative group and union confederation, last five years (c.2008–13)[1]

Party-confederation dyad—CPO	PCF-FSU		PCF-CGT		PCF-USS		PCF-CFDT		PCF-UNSA		PCF-FO		PCF-CFTC	
	P/U	CJ	P/U	CJ	P/U	CJ	P/U	CJ	P/U	CJ	P/U	CJ	P/U	CJ
Tacit agreements about one-sided/mutual representation in national decision-making bodies	No	No	No	No	No	No	Yes	No	No	No	n.d.	No	n.d.	No
Permanent joint committee(s)	No	No	No	No	No	No	No	No	No	No	n.d.	No	n.d.	No
Temporary joint committee(s)	No	No	No	No	No	No	No	No	No	No	n.d.	No	n.d.	No
Formal agreements about regular meetings between party and organization	No	No	No	No	No	No	No	No	No	No	n.d.	No	n.d.	No
Tacit agreements about regular meetings between party and organization	No	No	No	No	No	No	No	No	No	No	n.d.	No	n.d.	No
Joint conferences	No	No	No	No	Yes	No	No	No	No	No	n.d.	No	n.d.	No
Joint campaigns	No	No	No	No	Yes	Yes	No	No	No	No	n.d.	No	n.d.	No

Party-confederation dyad—LPG	PCF-FSU		PCF-CGT		PCF-USS		PCF-CFDT		PCF-UNSA		PCF-FO		PCF-CFTC	
	P/U	CJ	P/U	CJ	P/U	CJ	P/U	CJ	P/U	CJ	P/U	CJ	P/U	CJ
Tacit agreements about one-sided/mutual representation in national decision-making bodies	No	No	No	No	No	No	Yes	No	No	No	n.d.	No	n.d.	No
Permanent joint committee(s)	No	No	No	No	No	No	No	No	No	No	n.d.	No	n.d.	No
Temporary joint committee(s)	No	No	No	No	No	No	No	No	No	No	n.d.	No	n.d.	No
Formal agreements about regular meetings between party and organization	No	No	No	No	No	No	No	No	No	No	n.d.	No	n.d.	No
Tacit agreements about regular meetings between party and organization	No	No	No	No	No	No	No	No	No	No	n.d.	No	n.d.	No
Joint conferences	No	No	No	No	No	No	No	No	No	No	n.d.	No	n.d.	No
Joint campaigns	No	No	No	No	No	No	No	No	No	No	n.d.	No	n.d.	No

[1] 'P/U' indicates responses from party/trade union questionnaires, 'CJ' signifies the authors' 'coded judgment' based on alternative sources in cases of diverging or missing P/U answers. 'c.d.' means contradictory data (diverging P/U answers), 'n.d.' means no data (informant didn't know/missing/unclear), and 'n.a.' means not applicable in this case.

has links with several other parties including the Left Party, the Greens, and the New Anti-capitalist Party, this should not be taken as an indication of organizational closeness, as such campaigns may be general coalitions around issues such as anti-racism.

Inter-organizational Links: One-way and Occasional

In terms of one-way and occasional inter-organizational links (Table 6.2a and 6.2b), apart from the CGT, which reports that it invites the Socialist Party but not the Communist Party, no union invites any party to its congress. Likewise, no union confederation reported that their organization invites any party to participate in its ordinary meetings, seminars, and conferences.

On the other hand, in line with their encouragement of trade union membership, both parties invite union confederations to their national congresses. While the USS and CGT reported being invited to the PCF but not the PS congress, the CFDT, UNSA, and FSU reported that they are invited to both party congresses. The PS would seem to be concentrating on its appeal to the traditionally reformist unions, whereas the PCF appeals to all. The implications of this will be discussed later. However, only the UNSA reported that it was invited to the ordinary meetings, seminars, and conferences of the political parties—in this case both of them. Without further research, this finding is difficult to explain.

When it comes to more ad hoc arrangements, relationships appear to be closer. All unions apart from the CGT reported being invited by central party organizations and legislative parties to special consultative arrangements. In line with notions of trade union independence, the CGT, UNSA, and USS report that such invitations are not reciprocated. On the other hand, the FSU and CFDT extend invitations to special consultative arrangements to both the PS and the PCF. For the CFDT, this is in line with the confederation's shift towards a non-partisan orientation aimed at bargaining for economic and social modernization since the 1970s. In the case of the FSU, this could reflect its strength within the public sector, particularly the teaching profession, and a desire to influence public policy in this sphere. The coded judgement that these invitations are not reciprocated by the FO reflects the avowedly 'apolitical' stance of the confederation. These results and interpretations need confirmation through further research. Finally, the results show no variation at central party and legislative party levels.

Overall, party–union relations in France appear to be based upon occasional links, but these links are weak and multi-directional—the CFDT and the FSU appear to have the strongest ad hoc links with both parties, with invitations to special consultative arrangements reported as being reciprocal. The

Table 6.2a. One-way, occasional links at the organizational level between party central organization/legislative group and union confederation, last five years (c.2008–13)[1]

Party-confederation dyad—CPO

	PS-FSU		PS-CGT		PS-USS		PS-CFDT		PS-UNSA		PS-FO		PS-CFTC	
	P/U	CJ	P/U	CJ	P/U	CJ	P/U	CJ	P/U	CJ	P/U	CJ	P/U	CJ
Invitation to party to participate in the organization's national congress	No	No	Yes	No	No	No	No	No	No	No	n.d.	No	n.d.	No
Invitation to organization to participate in the party's national congress/conference	Yes	Yes	No	No	No	No	Yes	Yes	Yes	Yes	n.d.	Yes	n.d.	Yes
Invitations to organization to participate in the party's ordinary meetings, seminars, and conferences	No	No	No	No	No	No	No	No	Yes	No	n.d.	No	n.d.	No
Invitations to party to participate in ordinary organization meetings, seminars, and conferences	No	No	No	No	No	No	No	No	No	No	n.d.	No	n.d.	No
Invitations to organization to special consultative arrangements initiated by the party	Yes	Yes	No	No	Yes	No	Yes	Yes	Yes	Yes	n.d.	Yes	n.d.	Yes
Invitations to party to special consultative arrangements initiated by the organization	Yes	Yes	No	No	No	No	Yes	Yes	No	No	n.d.	No	n.d.	Yes

Party-confederation dyad—LPG

	PS-FSU		PS-CGT		PS-USS		PS-CFDT		PS-UNSA		PS-FO		PS-CFTC	
	P/U	CJ	P/U	CJ	P/U	CJ	P/U	CJ	P/U	CJ	P/U	CJ	P/U	CJ
Invitation to party to participate in the organization's national congress	No	No	No	No	No	No	No	No	No	No	n.d.	No	n.d.	No
Invitation to organization to participate in the party's national congress/conference	n.a.	n.a.	n.a.	n.a.	n.a.	n.a.	n.a.	n.a.	n.a.	n.a.	n.a.	n.a.	n.a.	n.a.
Invitations to organization to participate in the party's ordinary meetings, seminars, and conferences	No	No	No	No	No	No	No	No	Yes	No	n.d.	No	n.d.	No
Invitations to party to participate in ordinary organization meetings, seminars, and conferences	No	No	No	No	No	No	No	No	No	No	n.d.	No	n.d.	No
Invitations to organization to special consultative arrangements initiated by the party	Yes	Yes	No	No	Yes	No	Yes	Yes	Yes	Yes	n.d.	Yes	n.d.	Yes
Invitations to party to special consultative arrangements initiated by the organization	Yes	Yes	No	No	No	No	Yes	Yes	No	No	n.d.	No	n.d.	No

[1] 'P/U' indicates responses from party/trade union questionnaires, 'CJ' signifies the authors' 'coded judgment' based on alternative sources in cases of diverging or missing P/U answers. 'c.d.' means contradictory data (diverging P/U answers), 'n.d.' means no data (informant didn't know/missing/unclear), and 'n.a.' means not applicable in this case.

Table 6.2b. One-way, occasional links at the organizational level between party central organization/legislative group and union confederation, last five years (c.2008–13)[1]

Party-confederation dyad—CPO	PCF-FSU		PCF-CGT		PCF-USS		PCF-CFDT		PCF-UNSA		PCF-FO		PCF-CFTC	
	P/U	CJ	P/U	CJ	P/U	CJ	P/U	CJ	P/U	CJ	P/U	CJ	P/U	CJ
Invitation to party to participate in the organization's national congress	No	No	No	No	No	No	No	No	No	No	n.d.	No	n.d.	No
Invitation to organization to participate in the party's national congress/conference	Yes	Yes	Yes	Yes	Yes	Yes	Yes	Yes	Yes	Yes	n.d.	No	n.d.	No
Invitations to organization to participate in the party's ordinary meetings, seminars, and conferences	No	No	No	No	No	No	No	No	Yes	No	n.d.	No	n.d.	No
Invitations to party to participate in ordinary organization meetings, seminars, and conferences	No	No	No	No	No	No	No	No	No	No	n.d.	No	n.d.	No
Invitations to organization to special consultative arrangements initiated by the party	Yes	Yes	No	Yes	Yes	Yes	Yes	Yes	Yes	Yes	n.d.	No	n.d.	No
Invitations to party to special consultative arrangements initiated by the organization	Yes	Yes	No	No	No	No	Yes	No	No	No	n.d.	No	n.d.	No

Party-confederation dyad—LPG	PCF-FSU		PCF-CGT		PCF-USS		PCF-CFDT		PCF-UNSA		PCF-FO		PCF-CFTC	
	P/U	CJ	P/U	CJ	P/U	CJ	P/U	CJ	P/U	CJ	P/U	CJ	P/U	CJ
Invitation to party to participate in the organization's national congress	No	No	No	No	No	No	No	No	No	No	n.d.	No	n.d.	No
Invitation to organization to participate in the party's national congress/conference	n.a.	n.a.	n.a.	n.a.	n.a.	n.a.	n.a.	n.a.	n.a.	n.a.	n.a.	n.a.	n.a.	n.a.
Invitations to organization to participate in the party's ordinary meetings, seminars, and conferences	No	No	No	No	No	No	No	No	No	No	n.d.	No	n.d.	No
Invitations to party to participate in ordinary organization meetings, seminars, and conferences	No	No	No	No	No	No	No	No	No	No	n.d.	No	n.d.	No
Invitations to organization to special consultative arrangements initiated by the party	Yes	Yes	No	Yes	Yes	Yes	Yes	Yes	Yes	Yes	n.d.	No	n.d.	Yes
Invitations to party to special consultative arrangements initiated by the organization	Yes	No	No	No	No	No	Yes	No	No	No	n.d.	No	n.d.	No

[1] 'P/U' indicates responses from party/trade union questionnaires, 'CJ' signifies the authors' 'coded judgment' based on alternative sources in cases of diverging or missing P/U answers. 'c.d.' means contradictory data (diverging P/U answers), 'n.d.' means no data (informant didn't know/missing/unclear), and 'n.a.' means not applicable in this case.

CGT and USS report not inviting a party to any event and stand out as the unions with the weakest ties with both the PS and PCF. Parties, on the other hand, are reported as being more likely to invite union confederations to their congresses and meetings. Generally, however, no actor, on either the union or party side, is able to claim exclusivity in any relationship.

In terms of dyads, these results would appear to show the constitution of two blocs. The first is what could broadly be defined as a social-democratic or reformist bloc, with the least distant relations forming between reformist unions and parties: the CFDT, UNSA, and FSU all report the strongest links with the PS in terms of invitations extended and received. To this one can add CFDT-PCF, UNSA-PCF, and FSU-PCF dyads, indicating that these unions wish to preserve their non-partisan status. On the other hand, among the radical unions, both the CGT and USS report much weaker links with both the PS and PCF. Surprisingly, the CGT claims complete separation from the PCF. For the USS, such results reflect its orientation as a militant, far-left union.

For the CGT the surprising assertion that the confederation invites the PS but not the PCF to its congress, and indeed has complete separation from the PCF, has two possible explanations. The first is possible bias in the reporting, with the respondent attempting to portray the CGT as a confederation loosening its ties with the PCF, following criticism of its close alliance with the party during the post-war era, in line with the recent evolution of the confederation. The second, which does not exclude the first, is that the CGT is attempting to tighten links with the PS. Given that this is the major change in party–union relations in the past few decades, we will return to this question when explaining change.

Individual-level Links: Individual Contacts and Personnel Overlaps and Transfers

Only four of our key informants answered questions on contact at the individual level between representatives of parties and unions, with the USS not responding to the questions. Nevertheless, some observations can be made on the basis of the answers given. The most frequently cited form of contact was through 'informal face-to-face meetings and/or conversations by telephone, Skype, etc.', which were most frequently used by the CGT and FSU, and, after them, UNSA. The CGT did not give any second most frequent form of contact. The next most frequently cited forms of contact were official letters, sometimes emailed, cited as the most frequent form of communication by UNSA and the CFDT.[2] As well as official letters, the CFDT reported contact through official meetings or teleconferences and informal written communication through SMS, email, and social media such as Facebook and Twitter. Finally, the FSU was the only one to report contact through conference participation as being one of the most frequent forms of contact with parties.

The data here invite two conclusions, albeit with a note of caution. The first is that contact is mostly informal, with letters, rather than formal meetings, the main form of formal contact. The second is that, for the unions, no privileged relationship appears to exist between any union on the one hand and the PCF or PS on the other. When asked to give the first and second most frequent form of contact between the union organization and each party, all four respondents answered in exactly the same way for contacts with both parties.

Any comparisons across dyads must be treated with care due to the limited number of responses and the different ways in which responses were recorded. However, some observations can be made which would seem to support those made in the previous section. The reformist unions all reported using both formal and informal channels of communication with some degree of frequency. While no conclusions can be drawn from the non-response of the USS to these questions, the CGT's citing of only one informal channel of communication between the union and both the PS and PCF—that of informal meetings and conversations—appears to confirm the separation reported by the union from both parties with respect to one-way/occasional inter-organizational links. Once again, the more reformist unions appear to have the least distant relations with both parties, but these links are not exclusive to one or other of them.

What, then, of our main concern here—the extent of personnel overlaps and transfers between party and union bodies? With the formal independence of unions from parties enshrined in union statutes, not surprisingly, nobody exercising any national level of responsibility in a party exercises any similar level of responsibility in a union. Nevertheless this does not preclude past trade union activity among political elites, which could be seen as an indication of union closeness. To test this, the biographies of the 295 members of the Socialist group in the National Assembly elected in 2012 were examined through their official websites. The same exercise was conducted for the ten members of the Democratic and Republican Left group, to which the PCF *deputés* belong, and for the thirty-two ministers and secretaries of state of Socialist Prime Minister Emmanuel Valls' government, named on 2 April 2014.

While several current members of the Socialist parliamentary party were active in the French student union movement, few reported continuing into their professional lives. Of the 295 Socialist MPs only fourteen referred to any previous trade union membership or activity. Of these, only four made reference to a trade union mandate—two as CFDT workplace trade union delegates, while two claimed to have been active within the FO, one at local and branch level and one as a national secretary. Among the thirty-two ministers and secretaries of state, none mentioned any past union responsibility. Among the nine PCF members of the Democratic and Republican Left group, only one made any reference to any trade union activity in the past. In this case, the activity was workplace CGT representation.

Thus at national level, personnel overlaps appear to be weak, bordering on the non-existent in France, in line with the supposed independence of unions from parties. Where they do appear, they tend to confirm the existence of a 'political family' of reformist unions close in thinking to the PS. An examination of recent events attests to closer informal links between the CFDT and PS than those suggested above. Thus Jacky Bontems, the former deputy general secretary of the CFDT, was recruited to François Hollande's 2012 presidential campaign team along with members of UNSA (Laurent 2012). Following Hollande's victory, François Chérèque, the general secretary of the confederation until November 2012, was named 'inspector for social affairs' in early January 2013. In addition, Bontems was recruited to the government's strategic planning office, the *Commissariat général à la stratégie et à la prospective*, while the former national secretary for relations with political parties, Laurence Laigo was recruited to the ministerial cabinet of Najat Vallaud-Belkacem, the minister for women's rights (Landré 2013; Mariaucourt 2013). Finally, former CFDT General Secretary of the Steelworkers' Federation in the North-Lorraine Region, Edouard Martin, was designated to lead the PS list for the East France constituency in the 2014 European elections (Bourmaud 2013).

This—as well as the presence of CFDT officials in ministerial cabinets in the 1980s—suggests that CFDT–PS relations are closer than suggested by organizational linkages and personnel overlaps. However, with the exception of the last case cited above, these links are not direct or public in the sense that trade unionists are recruited to 'backroom' political functions—essentially acting as political advisers—or they are recruited indirectly to serve the party through state appointments.

Overall Closeness and Range

Turning to the overall closeness and range of relationships, we see that the total organizational scores underline the relatively low level of institutionalization described in the previous section, not least between the parties' parliamentary groups and trade unions (see Figures 6.1a and 6.1b). The maximum score is only 4 (out of 20), obtained by the relationship between the PS's central organization and CFDT. The additive score for PCF-CGT is 2, as is the case for other PCF–union relationships.

The informants' rating of the overall degree of closeness/distance is more or less in line with these results. Again, we only have trade union judgements as to the closeness of the relationship within the various dyads (Figure 6.2). However, all unions classified relations with both the PS and PCF as 'ad

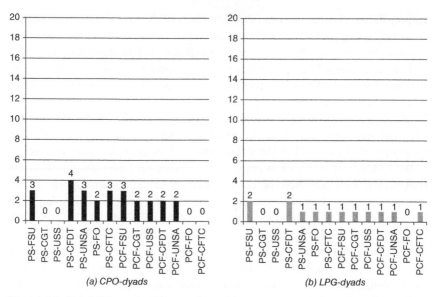

(a) CPO-dyads   *(b) LPG-dyads*

Figure 6.1. Total link scores of central party organization–trade union relationships and legislative party–trade union relationships (0–20/0–12).[1]

[1] The theoretical maximum link score is 20 for the CPO-dyads and 12 for LPG-dyads since some link items are unlikely to apply to the legislative party group and were thus not included in this part of the survey. However, when comparing dyads involving CPOs with those involving LPGs, one should still keep in mind that the latter's maximum involves fewer links than the former's top scores.

hoc' with one exception: the far-left USS characterized its relationship with the PS as 'distant/separate'. Once again, these findings support earlier judgements that the relations between parties and unions in France reflect the formal independence of unions from parties enshrined in their statutes. Furthermore, there is no exclusivity in any relationship, with unions and parties entertaining a multiplicity and broad range of relationships, although a radical union bloc with weaker relationships to both parties and a social-democratic union bloc with less distant ties to the PS can be detected (Figures 6.1a and 6.1b). Again, this is consistent with earlier findings.

The lack of exclusivity in party–union relations is further evidenced by other answers in the questionnaires. When asked what other parties they had relations with, the USS cited Europe Ecology/the Greens, the Left Party (which campaigned with the PCF in the 2012 presidential and legislative elections and sits in the same group in parliament with them), and the New Anti-capitalist Party, thus confirming its far-left orientation; while UNSA cited the right-wing UMP (now the Republicans) and the centre-right Union of Democrats and Independents. Furthermore, in open-ended questions, all respondents were clear that no inter-organizational relations existed with any other

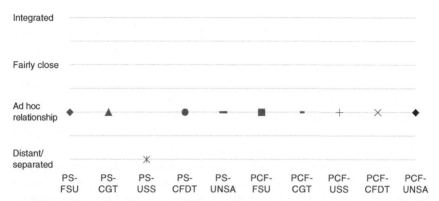

Figure 6.2. Rating of overall degree of closeness/distance (average score) between the party and union confederation, last five years (*c*.2008–13).[1]

[1] The ratings reflect the union's rating only since PS and PCF did not answer the survey.

party, but that such relations were ad hoc and respected the formal independence of unions from parties. The only party that no trade union will enter into discussion with is the far-right Front National.

When asked whether their relations with parties had changed over the last ten years, all key informants bar the respondent for UNSA reported no great change in relations with either the PS or the PCF. For UNSA, although no great change was reported in its relationship with the Socialists, relations were reported to have become more distant with the Communists. This was explained by 'the political orientation of this party on the one hand (UNSA is reformist, the PCF not really…), and on the other by its loss of influence in the country'.

However, longer-term change has been profound. While the ad hoc relationships between the PS and the national union confederations show a large degree of continuity, this change has particularly affected the PCF-CGT dyad. As seen earlier, in the post-war era, relations between the PCF and CGT were close despite the formal independence of the latter from the party. Nowadays, however, the relationship is described by the CGT key informant as far less close and as ad hoc, thereby being little or no different from relationships between the CGT and other political parties. The reasons for this change, as well as for continuing weak and ad hoc relationships elsewhere, will be explored in the following section.

EXPLAINING CONTINUITY AND CHANGE

As the PCF went into decline from the 1980s onwards, the PS emerged as the only credible party of government on the left, finally ending twenty-three years of right-wing hegemony in 1981. These changes could have led to unions seeking greater organizational links with the PS to influence policy. That this has not happened is due to long-run historical and structural factors that mitigate against close party–union relations in France.

In terms of cost–benefit exchange, the ad hoc relationship between parties and unions can be explained by several factors. First, the major potential benefit for parties—the capacity of unions to deliver votes at election-time— is weak in France. The main unions historically close to the PS—the CFDT and FO—have seen a large proportion, and at times the majority, of their sympathizers abandon the left altogether for centrist, Gaullist, and even Front National candidates in presidential elections in the twenty-first century. Nevertheless, CFDT, UNSA, and FSU sympathizers tend to support the PS, although only in the last case does support appear to be stable and strong. Thus, while the PS is the main electoral beneficiary of trade unionists' votes, this support is volatile, with only sympathizers of the FSU voting in a majority for the PS candidate in more than one of the first three presidential elections of the twenty-first century. The exception to this is the USS, whose sympathizers tend to vote for the extreme left (Parsons 2015).[3]

Furthermore, from the party perspective, the most obvious long-term structural barrier to close party–union links in France is fragmentation. The PS has little incentive to form close organizational links with one trade union for fear of pushing away voters sympathetic to other unions. As a potential party of government, it also means that deals with one or more unions may not be acceptable to others, so may not mobilize members to vote for the PS or mobilize them around any political project once in government. Such considerations apply less to the PCF, which until the 1980s acted as an anti-system party and was successful in mobilizing workers' votes through close ties with the CGT (Parsons 2005, 49).

More widely, the agrarian base of the French economy until after the Second World War meant that the working class has always been in a minority. This, along with a highly fragmented union movement, has contributed to generally low levels of unionization throughout the history of the French labour movement, reducing the appeal of close relations for parties (Parsons 2005, 50). As parties are publicly financed in France and unions are prohibited from contributing to their funds, neither have they been able to deliver financial support, although for many years the CGT secretly contributed to PCF finances (Courtois and Andolfatto 2008, 28). As noted earlier, this does not prevent them from contributing to election campaigns through, for example, the secondment of personnel, but it does reduce incentives for a closer relationship, and union influence over policy programmes, on the part of parties.

Politically, the presidency emerged as the key political office following a referendum in 1962 which allowed for the election of the president by universal suffrage. With the two-ballot system, involving a run-off between the two best-placed candidates after the first round of voting, any party seeking office needs to appeal to the broadest possible spectrum of opinion, so any potential governing party has no incentive in being tied to vested interests such as unions. The semi-presidential system put in place after 1962 resulted in the presence of a strong executive, supported by cohesive parties in a weak parliament. This translated into a relative isolation of ministers from interest group activities, and by the predominance of a techno-cratic approach to decision making. These political structures are under-pinned by a political culture that sees the government as the emanation of the 'general will' of the people and strong interest groups as harmful to it (Parsons 2013). Trade union involvement in policymaking, and hence strong party–union links, were thus never considered important by governing elites.

However, unions are consulted over policy in exchange for material and non-material benefits (Parsons 2013). These include the financial resources and political legitimacy associated with participating in state-sponsored con-sultative fora. As some of these positions, for example seats of the governing bodies of social security funds, are dependent upon votes in elections, unions need to have as broad an appeal as possible to attract resources, particularly as unionization rates have always been low in France. On the union side, then, there is again a disincentive for close relations with one party.

From the point of view of unions, with the exception of the CGT in the post-war period, the historical and ideational constraints of the Charter of Amiens are also important in explaining the lack of organizational links with parties, as can be seen from the questionnaire responses. Ideationally, this feeds into a rejection of close party–union links in France. Previous studies and opinion polls regularly show that, while French unions have a generally positive image among French workers, the main criticism of them is that they are too politicized (Labbé and Croisat 1992, 129–31; Parsons 2013). Main-taining, in public, at least, a distance from political parties therefore serves union interests in a situation where membership is already extremely low and inter-union rivalry fierce.

For their part, left-wing parties have been unable consistently to deliver access to government for trade unions. The Fourth Republic (1946–58), under which governments were elected by proportional representation, was generally governed by SFIO-centre right coalitions, although the SFIO was a declining force during this time, following which right-wing governments dominated the Fifth Republic until François Mitterrand's election to the presidency in 1981. While the PS was in government for most of the 1980s, after 1993 it was out of office for most of the time thereafter, with Lionel Jospin's 1997–2002 administration its only time in power until François Hollande's victory in the 2012 presidential elections. Furthermore, the state still retains a major role in labour market regulation, which would elsewhere be devolved to social actors, as well as in welfare and pension reform (Hyman and Gumbrell-McCormick

2010, 326). Unions therefore have an incentive to retain the option of dealing with all potential parties of government, including those on the right, rather than dealing with any of them on an exclusive basis.

The CGT-PCF dyad of the post-war era does not fit with the above explanations. While cost–benefit exchange can explain the ad hoc relations described here, it cannot fully explain the strong post-war PCF-CGT dyad of the post-war era. While for the PCF, the CGT could deliver voters at election time, for the CGT it could not deliver access to power. The explanation here has to be sought in the ideational realm, in terms of ideological affinity, as well as in the deep class cleavages apparent in France at the time. This dyad was able to draw upon deep class cleavages to shore up its position as an opposition, rather than potential governing, force in French politics and society, with the PCF, until the 1970s, garnering the lion's share of working class votes.

However, the major change noted here—the disintegration of the PCF-CGT dyad—can be explained by a cost–benefit analysis rooted in the electoral decline of the communists. From the 1980s onwards, industrial and political change deprived the CGT and PCF of their membership bases and ideological resources, with the result that the PCF was an increasingly marginal force in French politics at the national level, gaining less than 2 per cent of the vote in the 2007 presidential elections, while one in five voters voted for PCF candidates in presidential and parliamentary elections in the 1960s and 1970s (france-politique n.d.). While the CGT's search for greater autonomy from the PCF reflects the battle between orthodox and modernizing currents within both organizations, strategic considerations related to the decline of the PCF also seem to be important. Faced with the near-terminal decline of its ally, the CGT has, in effect, sought to broaden its appeal so as not to suffer the same fate. Hence, CGT relationships have become less exclusive and increasingly oriented towards ad hoc ones with the PS. In terms of a cost–benefit exchange, it is not a case of the party failing to provide the union with policy benefits, but a case of wishing to avoid the reputational costs of closeness to a declining, and increasingly discredited, political force.

CONCLUSION

Structural and ideational factors are important in explaining party–union links in France in terms of a cost–benefit analysis, but so too are political contingencies. The PS–CFDT relationship would appear to be the most durable, but even this suffered under the weight of austerity politics in the 1980s. More recently, in 2012 the CFDT, CGT, FSU, and USS directly or indirectly supported Hollande's presidential campaign, but by 2014 only the CFTC and CFDT still lent any support to his government as austerity policies were implemented in response to crisis (Parsons 2015), suggesting that without formalized links, unions have little impact upon government policy in the face of external macroeconomic pressures.

Overall, party–union relations in France show both continuity and change. The Socialist Party's emergence as a catch–all party since the 1970s largely explains the continuity, as already loose ad hoc relationships have not needed loosening from the party's point of view, while weak and divided unions have not been able to push their concerns to the top of the party's political agenda. The closest relations are maintained by the PS-CFDT dyad on the basis of ideological affinity, but these have not required any loosening as they have always been informal and not based on any durable organizational underpinning. The major change of the weakening of the PCF-CGT dyad can be explained by the decline of the union's political ally.

As a result, party–union relations in France are multi-directional, with no exclusivity in any relationship, on either the union or the party side. While these elements of continuity and change can be explained by cost–benefit exchange, they are also historically and ideationally conditioned. With the decline of the PCF and emergence of the PS as the only credible party of government on the left, the structural conditions for closer links between the PS and the reformist trade unions would appear to have improved, at least from the union standpoint. That this is not occurring is partly due to parties having little incentive to forge close links with fragmented unions that can deliver neither financial resources nor voters. It is also, however, a consequence of trade union culture and history. The notion of independence was not always adhered to, but it has remained a powerful prevailing idea, with public opinion still hostile to the notion of 'politicized' unions, reducing the incentive for partisan alliances for fear of alienating current and potential members. As our respondents made clear in the questionnaires, unions see themselves as independent and wish to remain so, while seeking political influence. The first objective would seem to be achieved more than, and perhaps to the detriment of, the second.

NOTES

1. A table is not presented as there were no 'yes values' (coded judgments).
2. The responses of the latter are difficult to categorize as the respondent put down three most used and three second most frequent from the list of six options. Only those cited as most frequently used are used here.
3. French opinion polls ask voters whether they feel close to a particular union, hence we talk here about 'sympathizers', not just members.

7

Growing Apart?

Trade Unions and Centre-left Parties in Germany

Tim Spier

INTRODUCTION

In a long-term post-war perspective, the relationship between the German Social Democrats (*Sozialdemokratische Partei Deutschlands*, SPD) and the major trade union confederation, the *Deutscher Gewerkschaftsbund* (DGB), seems to be a good example of close relations between a centre-left party and trade unions (Padgett and Paterson 1991, 180–2). They were seen as 'two pillars' of the German labour movement (Merkel 1993, 102), with the unions often referring to the party as their 'political arm' and the Social Democrats calling the unions their 'boot camp'. Certainly, the four decades of the Bonn Republic from 1949 to 1989/90 saw significant political cooperation and personnel overlap, and 60 to 70 per cent of German union members voted for the Social Democrats in federal elections (Schoen 2014, 201). In 1980, 82 per cent of the higher level officials of the trade union confederation were members of the SPD, while 92 per cent of the members of the SPD caucus in the German Bundestag were organized in at least one of the member unions of the DGB (Wehler 2008, 11). Up to 2002, it was quite common for a chairman of a DGB member union to hold a seat in the German Parliament on the ticket of the SPD (Hönigsberger and Osterberg 2014, 100–1).

Historically, however, party–trade union links were not always confined to the Social Democrats. Most German trade unions were established by the political parties of the 1860s (Schönhoven 2014, 63–4), with a separate confederation founded by the social liberal party, by both predecessor parties of the SPD, and by the early organizations of political Catholicism (Wehler 1995, 160–3). Still, the relative strength and importance of social democratic unions meant that by 1920 some 8 million out of 9.2 million union members were organized in the united social democratic confederation (Wehler 2003, 378–9).

After the Second World War, there was a broad consensus in the German trade union movement to end partisanship and establish a common confederation. The doctrine of 'unitary unionism' (*Einheitsgewerkschaft*) became the founding myth of the DGB, with union officials arguing that if the unions had stood together in the early 1930s, they could have prevented the Nazis' rise to power (Silvia 2013, 107). While officially claiming to be non-partisan, and despite the informal rule that one of the members of every executive committee of the DGB and its member unions had to be from the labour wing of the centre-right Christian Democrats (CDU and CSU), the vast majority of union officials, including the chairmen, were members of the SPD (Hassels 2007, 175; Silvia 2013, 109–10). Today, as we will show, the relationship between the SPD and the unions is much less close.

BACKGROUND AND CONTEXT

Although, in comparison to other Western economies, Germany's industrial sector is still a very important employer (30.7 per cent in 2009), deindustrialization has weakened blue-collar unionism, triggering a rapid decline in union membership, with union density falling from 33.7 per cent in the early 1960s to 18.5 per cent in 2010 (see Table 2.1a). Moreover, German labour law prohibits many forms of selective incentives for unionists, such as wage benefits or closed-shop arrangements, therefore promoting free-riding by employees (Ebbinghaus and Göbel 2014, 229–31). That said, density is much higher in blue-collar jobs in the private sector and especially among civil servants in the public sector (Schnabel and Wagner 2007, 121–5).

The post-war doctrine of 'unitary unionism' meant that the German trade union movement was significantly less fragmented than many of its counterparts. The DGB was founded as a unified, officially non-partisan confederation in 1949 and the white-collar union *Deutsche Angestellten-Gewerkschaft* (DAG) merged with the DGB in 2001. The civil servants' union, *Deutscher Beamten-Bund* (DBB), however, stayed separate, with 1.3 million members in 2014, most of whom belong to the special status group of *Beamte*—civil servants with no freedom to strike, but several privileges like tenure for life, special health plans, and state pensions. Another trade union confederation, the *Christlicher Gewerkschaftsbund* (CGB), founded in 1959, claims to be the continuation of Christian trade unionism. However, its claim to have 280,000 members is disputed by the DGB, while some of its member unions are deemed by labour courts to be 'yellow' unions-organizations heavily influenced by the employer side, denying them the right to take part in collective bargaining. In 2014, the DGB unions had more than 6.1 million members, which is roughly three quarters of all unionists in Germany.

Two organizational principles characterized post-war trade unionism in Germany (Silvia 2013, 111–13): The DGB unions are industrial unions (*Industriegewerkschaften*), as they organize all employees of a specific sector irrespective of their individual crafts and trades. Additionally, the main economic activity of each company decides which union is responsible for it, resulting in unitary collective bargaining (*Tarifeinheit*). Originally, there were sixteen sectoral unions organized under the umbrella of the DGB, but mergers in the 1990s reduced this number to eight, most of which span multiple sectors. Here, we evaluate the party–union relations of the DGB as well as four of its member unions: the *Industriegewerkschaft Metall* (IG Metall), responsible for mechanical engineering, steel, textiles, and wood; the *Vereinte Dienstleistungsgewerkschaft* (Ver.di), organizing public and private services; the *Industriegewerkschaft Bergbau, Chemie, Energie* (IG BCE), active in in mining, chemicals, and energy; and the teachers' union *Gewerkschaft Erziehung und Wissenschaft* (GEW). All these organizations, especially the two 'giants' the IG Metall and Ver.di, with more than 2 million members each, display considerable internal plurality, but most scholars of German trade unions would probably agree that the IG BCE is a rather conservative union, while the GEW is much more to the left of the union mainstream. While the DGB is the public voice of its member unions, especially in social policy and other more general issues, the individual unions are responsible for collective bargaining and co-determination through work councils (Silvia 2013, 113). This, and the fact that member unions decide upon the allocation of funds to the DGB, clearly limits the authority of the umbrella organization and boosts the political significance of its member unions.

The German system of industrial relations leaves collective bargaining to employers' associations and unions, while the state sets the legal framework, generally not intervening in this process itself (Silvia 2013, 18–30). Therefore the bread-and-butter work of trade unions—bargaining as well as participation in companies' decisions through work councils—does not require the support of political parties. Changing the legal framework—or preventing a change to the status quo—does, however, require trade unions to lobby political parties, with most of that lobbying being undertaken by the DGB. There have been major initiatives on legal amendments addressing the erosion of coverage of collective agreements, minimum working conditions, or—most recently—the problem of small occupational associations (e.g. pilots, flight attendants, or train-drivers) trying to get much better agreements than the sectoral unions for their clientele by waging very effective strikes.

The primary incentive for political parties in Germany to maintain good relations with trade unions is the fact that they constitute a large and comparatively coherent bloc of voters. Membership in all German trade unions rose from 6 million in 1950 to 13.7 million shortly after German unification in 1990, before shrinking back to 8 million in 2012 (Greef 2014, 703). With most union members eligible to vote and exerting additional influence on family, friends, and non-organized co-workers, this is arguably one of the most important electoral target groups in Germany. Another incentive for good relations is the ability of trade unions to organize or support both electoral as well as issue campaigns. While officially non-partisan, DGB unions support specific campaigns on a case-by-case basis if they seem to be in their interest (Friedrich et al. 2009, 80–3). In contrast to other countries, unions in Germany generally provide no direct financial support to parties, however. Although German party law allows party funding by interest groups via donations, all substantial sums have to be made public. Since this would constitute a breach of 'unitary unionism', unions cannot afford to reveal such an explicit preference for a particular party.

Historically, unionized blue-collar workers and church-going Catholics each formed the core group of the two long-term political cleavages in Germany, with the SPD representing workers in the class conflict, and the *Zentrumspartei*, whose mantle was effectively inherited by CDU/CSU, organizing the sizable Catholic minority in the denominational conflict (Gluchowski and Wilamowitz-Moellendorff 1998, 15–17). Together with the much smaller liberal party the FDP, the CDU/CSU and SPD formed the classic 'two-and-a-half party system' of the first decades of the Bonn Republic, with the two major parties alternating in power, while the FDP was able to tip the scales in favour of one or the other. The post-war SPD was an archetypal mass party, mobilizing a huge proportion of its working-class target groups both as members and voters, but with no particular appeal beyond this *classe gardée*. This was problematic, since this was enough to secure around 30 per cent of the votes in the late 1940s and early 1950s, but not enough to end the electoral asymmetry in favour of the ruling CDU/CSU. Consequently, in an attempt to broaden its electoral appeal beyond blue-collar workers, the SPD removed Marxist ideas from its Bad Godesberg programme in 1959, becoming what Kirchheimer (1966) famously called a 'catch-all party'. Fortunately for the SPD, this process did not affect the voting behaviour of trade unionists—at least initially: 60 to 70 per cent of them regularly voted for the Social Democrats in elections up to 1980 (Schoen 2014, 201). Indeed, it helped to expand their electorate sufficiently to earn the SPD, in 1966, a place in government for the first time since the Second World War and allowed them to remain in power until 1982.

In the years of the Berlin Republic after German unification, relations between the SPD and DGB unions cooled markedly. While the support of the unions remained an important factor in the SPD's successful electoral campaign in 1998, the resulting 'red-green' coalition of the SPD and the Green party under Chancellor Gerhard Schröder launched a series of market-liberal reforms dubbed 'Agenda 2010'. These reforms were heavily opposed by parts of the union movement, leading to a massive protest campaign in 2003 and ultimately the formation of the splinter party, the *Wahlalternative Arbeit & Soziale Gerechtigkeit* (WASG), in 2005, which later merged with the remnants of the former Communist Party of Eastern Germany (Nachtwey and Spier 2007). This new party, called *Die Linke* ('The Left'), successfully established itself as the third strongest political party in Germany. With its left-wing socialist agenda and pro-labour policies, this party is a potential ally to unions, although its opposition status limits its use in governmental lobbying.

RELATIONSHIPS TODAY: MAPPING OF LINKS

What, then, characterizes the organizational relationships between the German left-of-centre parties and trade unions today? As already mentioned, we concentrated on the DGB as well as four of its member unions (IG Metall, Ver.di, IG BCE, and GEW) on the union side and on the SPD and Die Linke on the party side. Their sometimes contradictory survey responses were reviewed by the author using additional information and sources, with a 'coded judgement' presented in all the tables below.

Overlapping Organizational Structures: Statutory Links

The organizational structures of centre-left parties and trade unions in Germany do not overlap through statutory links.[1] As German party law requires members of political parties to join these organizations individually, there is no collective membership in German parties at all (Spier and Klein 2015, 88) and, in as much as it ever existed, it ended in 1906 with the 'Mannheim agreement', in which the SPD recognized the trade unions as independent representatives of the German labour movement (Schönhoven 2014, 65).

Inter-organizational Links: Reciprocal and Durable

The links shown in Table 7.1 are found quite frequently. However, there is some variance between parties. Based on their historic connection the DGB unions maintain stronger inter-organizational ties to the SPD than to Die Linke. Irrespective of party differences, these kinds of links are much more salient in the case of central party organizations than in legislative party groups.

The most institutionalized forms of links are to be found between the DGB unions and the SPD. First, there is a tacit understanding that both sides should

Table 7.1. Reciprocal, durable inter-organizational links between party central organization/legislative group and union confederation, last five years (c.2008–13)[1]

Party-confederation dyad—CPO	SPD-DGB		SPD-IG Metall		SPD-Ver.di		SPD-IG BCE		SPD-GEW		Linke-DGB		Linke-IG Metall		Linke-Ver.di		Linke-IG BCE		Linke-GEW	
	P/U	CJ	P/U	CJ	P/U	CJ	P/U	CJ	P/U	CJ	P/U	CJ	P/U	CJ	P/U	CJ	P/U	CJ	P/U	CJ
Tacit agreements about one-sided/mutual representation in national decision-making bodies	Yes	Yes	c.d.	Yes	Yes	Yes	c.d.	Yes	c.d.	Yes	No	No	c.d.	No	c.d.	No	No	No	No	No
Permanent joint committee(s)	c.d.	Yes	Yes	Yes	c.d.	Yes	c.d.	Yes	c.d.	Yes	Yes	c.d.	No	No	No	No	No	No	No	No
Temporary joint committee(s)	Yes	No	c.d.	No	c.d.	No	c.d.	No	c.d.	No	No	No	c.d.	No	No	No	No	No	No	No
Formal agreements about regular meetings between party and organization	No	No	No	No	No	No	c.d.	No	No	No	No	c.d.	No	No	No	No	c.d.	No	No	No
Tacit agreements about regular meetings between party and organization	Yes	Yes	Yes	Yes	Yes	Yes	Yes	Yes	c.d.	Yes	Yes	Yes	Yes	Yes	c.d.	Yes	No	No	No	No
Joint conferences	No	No	c.d.	Yes	No	No	c.d.	Yes	No	No	c.d.	Yes	c.d.	Yes	No	No	No	No	No	No
Joint campaigns	c.d.	No	No	No	No	No	No	No	No	No	c.d.	No	No	No	No	No	No	No	No	No

(continued)

Table 7.1. Continued

Party-confederation dyad—LPG	SPD-DGB		SPD-IG Metall		SPD-Ver.di		SPD-IG BCE		SPD-GEW		Linke-DGB		Linke-IG Metall		Linke-Ver.di		Linke-IG BCE		Linke-GEW	
	P/U	CJ	P/U	CJ	P/U	CJ	P/U	CJ	P/U	CJ	P/U	CJ	P/U	CJ	P/U	CJ	P/U	CJ	P/U	CJ
Tacit agreements about one-sided/mutual representation in national decision-making bodies	No	No	No	No	No	No	No	No	No	No	No	No	c.d.	No	c.d.	No	No	No	No	No
Permanent joint committee(s)	No	Yes	No	Yes	No	No	No	Yes	No	Yes	c.d.	No	No	No	No	No	No	No	No	No
Temporary joint committee(s)	No	No	No	No	No	No	No	No	No	No	No	No	No	No	No	No	No	No	No	No
Formal agreements about regular meetings between party and organization	No	No	No	No	No	No	No	No	No	No	No	No	No	No	No	No	No	No	No	No
Tacit agreements about regular meetings between party and organization	Yes	Yes	No	No	No	No	Yes	Yes	No	No	Yes	Yes	c.d.	Yes	c.d.	Yes	No	No	c.d.	Yes
Joint conferences	No	No	Yes	Yes	No	No	No	No	No	No	No	No	No	No	No	No	No	No	No	No
Joint campaigns	No	No	No	No	No	No	No	No	No	No	No	No	No	No	No	No	No	No	No	No

¹ 'P/U' indicates responses from party/trade union questionnaires, 'CJ' signifies the authors 'coded judgment' based on alternative sources in cases of diverging or missing P/U answers. 'c.d.' means contradictory data (diverging P/U answers), 'n.d.' means no data (informant didn't know/missing), and 'n.a.' means not applicable in this case.

be represented in each other's decision-making bodies, and most of our respondents acknowledged as much. It is very obvious in the case of the DGB and its three member unions the IG Metall, Ver.di, and the IG BCE: for decades, at least a relative majority of the members of each union's national executive board belonged to the SPD, often including the chair (Hassels 2006, 207–10). Only the teacher's union GEW lays great emphasis on not disclosing any party affiliation of their board members. Nearly all leading Social Democrats, including people represented in the boards of the party organization and the legislative caucus, are at least members of one DGB union, sometimes even two.

Second, the SPD has a permanent advisory body, the *Gewerkschaftsrat* ('union council'), which consists of important people from the SPD central and legislative party organization as well as all DGB union chairs, as long as they are members of the SPD. The influence of this joint committee heavily depends on the current state of relations between the SPD and the DGB unions (Neusser 2013, 121–32). Especially after the turbulent years of welfare cuts under SPD-chancellor Schröder, the *Gewerkschaftsrat* was an important attempt to reconcile relations with the unions. Third, there is the *Arbeitgemeinschaft für Arbeitnehmerfragen* (AfA), a SPD sub-organization for unionized party members with approximately 100,000 supporters. In many cases, the AfA is commensurate with the left wing of the party (Grunden 2012, 113).

On the other side, the left-wing socialist party Die Linke lays great emphasis on good relations with trade unions, but this is not matched by similar efforts on the part of the DGB unions, at least not in an institutionalized sense. Although nearly all members of Die Linke's national executive body are union members, the party is still not part of the political quota system used by most DGB unions to fill their executive bodies: with the majority of board members of the DGB and its member unions coming from the SPD, there should always be at least one person from the Christian Democrats, nowadays even comple- mented by some Green party members. Not a single executive position in any of the unions studied is occupied by anyone who is openly a member of Die Linke. Moreover, there is no permanent joint committee like the SPD's Gewerkschaftsrat within Die Linke's party organization. Similar to the SPD's AfA, Die Linke has a sub-organization for unionized party members, the *Arbeitgemeinschaft Betrieb & Gewerkschaft*, but it seems to be less important.

Although there are generally no formal agreements about meetings between each party and the unions, consultations are so frequent that most sides rate this as a tacit agreement. All of the unions studied here meet regularly with the SPD, and most of them with Die Linke too. Only the IG BCE and GEW avoid regular contacts with Die Linke. There have been some joint conferences between some of the unions and the two parties, but there seems to be no systematic pattern. As mentioned earlier, regular contacts between unions and the legislative party group are less frequent than they are with the central party organization.

Inter-organizational Links: One-way and Occasional

Table 7.2 presents the event-based links that exist. Overall, links involving, for example, invitations to events like congresses, conferences, meetings, or hearings, are very frequent. Unions in particular tend to have speakers from all the parties represented in the German Bundestag at their conferences, so this is no sign of a special relationship. Again, invitations between unions and the legislative party organization are a little rarer than between unions and the central party organization, but every union studied had at least contact with one of the two 'faces of party organization'. There is no obvious case of two organizations shunning each other.

Individual-level Links: Personnel Overlaps and Transfers

The relationship between parties and trade unions is not only a question of official inter-organizational cooperation, but also operates on the individual level. When it comes to the unions, the political quota system employed by DGB unions leaves nearly all the unions studied here with a sizeable number of SPD members in their executive committees. The DGB board has four out of six, the IG Metall four out of seven, Ver.di six out of fourteen, and the IG BCE four out of six seats filled by Social Democrats. With the exception of Ver. di's, all union chairs are members of the SPD. The GEW does not disclose the party memberships of their executive committee. Yet, while DGB, Ver.di, and the IG BCE have a member of the CDU in their executive, there seems to be no member of Die Linke on any of the boards of the unions studied here.

On the side of the central party organizations, ten out of thirteen members of the SPD's national executive body are members of a DGB union—four are in Ver.di, two—including the SPD's chair Sigmar Gabriel—in the IG Metall, two in the GEW, and one in the food and catering union NGG. The general secretary of the SPD, Yasmin Fahimi, who also belongs to this body used to be a department head in the IG BCE's national administration. The SPD's appointment of a senior union staff member to this position in 2014 was seen as a further attempt by the party to repair its relations with DGB unions (Spier and Alemann 2015, 65). While this leaves the SPD with a huge personal overlap of nearly 78 per cent in this category, the same is also true for the national executive of Die Linke: seven out of eight board members (86 per cent) are members of a DGB union—in fact all are members of services union Ver.di. Union membership in the steering committees of both legislative party groups is also high, with 71 per cent in the case of the SPD and even 92 per cent in the case of Die Linke. Two prominent members of Die Linke's legislative party steering committee, Klaus Ernst and Sabine Zimmermann, are (former) mid-level union officers.

Table 7.2. One-way, occasional links at the organizational level between party central organization/legislative group and union confederation, last five years (c.2008–13)[1]

Party-confederation dyad—CPO	SPD-DGB		SPD-IG Metall		SPD-Ver.di		SPD-IG BCE		SPD-GEW		Linke-DGB		Linke-IG Metall		Linke-Ver.di		Linke-IG BCE		Linke-GEW	
	P/U	CJ	P/U	CJ	P/U	CJ	P/U	CJ	P/U	CJ	P/U	CJ	P/U	CJ	P/U	CJ	P/U	CJ	P/U	CJ
Invitation to party to participate in the organization's national congress	Yes	Yes	Yes	Yes	Yes	Yes	Yes	Yes	Yes	Yes	Yes	Yes	Yes	Yes	Yes	Yes	Yes	Yes	Yes	Yes
Invitation to organization to participate in the party's national congress/conference	Yes	Yes	Yes	Yes	Yes	Yes	Yes	Yes	Yes	Yes	Yes	Yes	Yes	Yes	Yes	Yes	Yes	Yes	Yes	Yes
Invitations to organization to participate in the party's ordinary meetings, seminars, and conferences	Yes	Yes	Yes	Yes	Yes	Yes	Yes	c.d.	c.d.	Yes	Yes	Yes	Yes	Yes	Yes	Yes	Yes	c.d.	c.d.	Yes
Invitations to party to participate in ordinary organization meetings, seminars, and conferences	Yes	Yes	Yes	Yes	Yes	Yes	Yes	c.d.	c.d.	Yes	Yes	Yes	Yes	Yes	Yes	Yes	Yes	c.d.	c.d.	Yes
Invitations to organization to special consultative arrangements initiated by the party	Yes	Yes	Yes	Yes	Yes	Yes	Yes	Yes	Yes	Yes	Yes	Yes	Yes	Yes	Yes	Yes	No	Yes	Yes	Yes
Invitations to party to special consultative arrangements initiated by the organization	Yes	Yes	Yes	Yes	Yes	Yes	Yes	c.d.	c.d.	Yes	Yes	Yes	Yes	Yes	Yes	Yes	No	No	c.d.	Yes

(continued)

Table 7.2. Continued

Party-confederation dyad—LPG	SPD-DGB		SPD-IG Metall		SPD-Ver.di		SPD-IG BCE		SPD-GEW		Linke-DGB		Linke-IG Metall		Linke-Ver.di		Linke-IG BCE		Linke-GEW	
	P/U	CJ	P/U	CJ	P/U	CJ	P/U	CJ	P/U	CJ	P/U	CJ	P/U	CJ	P/U	CJ	P/U	CJ	P/U	CJ
Invitation to party to participate in the organization's national congress	Yes	Yes	No	No	Yes	Yes	Yes	Yes	Yes	Yes	Yes	Yes	c.d.	Yes	Yes	Yes	Yes	Yes	Yes	Yes
Invitation to organization to participate in the party's national congress/conference	n.a.	n.a.	n.a.	n.a.	n.a.	n.a.	n.a.	n.a.	n.a.	n.a.	n.a.	n.a.	n.a.	n.a.	n.a.	n.a.	n.a.	n.a.	n.a.	n.a.
Invitations to organization to participate in the party's ordinary meetings, seminars, and conferences	Yes	Yes	Yes	Yes	Yes	Yes	Yes	Yes	Yes	No	Yes	Yes	Yes	Yes	Yes	Yes	c.d.	Yes	c.d.	Yes
Invitations to party to participate in ordinary organization meetings, seminars, and conferences	Yes	Yes	No	Yes	Yes	Yes	Yes	Yes	Yes	No	Yes	Yes	c.d.	Yes	Yes	Yes	c.d.	Yes	c.d.	Yes
Invitations to organization to special consultative arrangements initiated by the party	Yes	Yes	Yes	Yes	Yes	Yes	Yes	Yes	Yes	Yes	Yes	Yes	Yes	Yes	Yes	Yes	c.d.	Yes	Yes	Yes
Invitations to party to special consultative arrangements initiated by the organization	Yes	Yes	Yes	Yes	Yes	Yes	No	No	No	No	Yes	Yes	Yes	Yes	Yes	Yes	No	No	c.d.	Yes

[1] 'P/U' indicates responses from party/trade union questionnaires, 'CJ' signifies the authors' 'coded judgment' based on alternative sources in cases of diverging or missing P/U answers. 'c.d.' means contradictory data (diverging P/U answers), 'n.d.' means no data (informant didn't know/missing), and 'n.a.' means not applicable in this case.

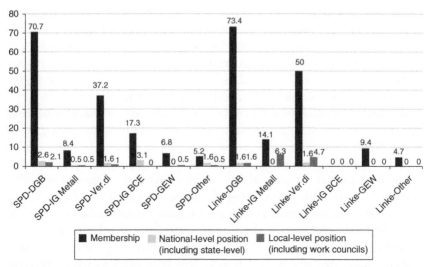

Figure 7.1. Share of SPD and Die Linke MPs in 2014 with union membership or current/former positions as officials or staff in the unions at the national or local level.[1]

[1] DGB 'membership' is that of all member unions; DGB national or local positions are only those MPs directly working for the confederation. Only permanent representatives and deputy representatives who attend the entire term are included. 'n.d.' means no data (missing). N of MPs is 191 for SPD and 64 for Linke.

Source: Author's own calculations based on the online biographies of MPs of the German Bundestag <http://www.bundestag.de/bundestag/abgeordnete18/listeFraktionen>.

Turning to all members of these two legislative party organizations, Figure 7.1 shows significant personnel overlap with the DGB unions as well: 70.7 per cent of the MPs of the SPD caucus are members of at least one of the DGB unions. Since many MPs have white-collar jobs, often coming from the public services sector, Ver.di membership with 37.2 per cent of all caucus members is quite common. It seems a little surprising at first that 17.3 per cent of the SPD's MPs are member of the IG BCE, a union with only one-third of the membership of the IG Metall and Ver.di. But the IG BCE organizes industrial sectors particularly subject to government intervention, especially mining and energy. The political culture of this union therefore is rather conservative, prefers social partnership to open conflict, and cultivates very close ties to the SPD—a long-term governing party in many states with mining and energy-producing industries like North Rhine-Westphalia or the Saarland. Many MPs belonging to the conservative wing of the party are actually members of the IG BCE, even if they haven't had jobs in the sectors organized by this union. Compared to this, the IG Metall, Germany's largest union, has only 8.4 per cent of the SPD's MPs as members. Since many MPs have an occupational background in the education sector, the small education and science worker's union GEW is also heavily overrepresented among the Social Democrats in the Bundestag. The SPD's strong personnel overlap with the unions is surpassed, however, by the legislative party group of Die Linke: 73.4 per cent of their 64 MPs are organized in at least one DGB union. Thirty-two of them are members of Ver.di alone—50 per cent of all the caucus' MPs— followed by the IG Metall (14.1 per cent) and the GEW (9.4 per cent).

Membership alone is probably not the best indicator for union influence in parliament. As many MPs come from jobs which are typically not organized by any union, such as the legal profession, membership may be just a symbol of their claim to represent the interests of working people. We get a better picture if we look at the share of MPs who have worked for the unions, either as officials or as staff, before being elected to parliament. In Figure 7.1 we further distinguished between union positions on the national level, including the state level, which is of the utmost importance in the organizational structure of German unions, and the local level, including members of work councils. Some eighteen of the 191 SPD MPs have previously held national-level union positions. Generally, they are not from the highest ranks of union administration, but regional chairs or members of the national staff. This is an important change, as it was previously quite common for a DGB union chair to sit in the Bundestag on the ticket of the SPD (Hönigsberger 2008, 61–6). Nine MPs have previously held local positions in the DGB unions, suggesting national-level positions in DGB unions remain a better stepping-stone to a parliamentary career in the SPD than their local equivalents. On the other hand, Die Linke has two members of its caucus who have held national-level positions in union administration, but eight from the local level. These party differences are no coincidence: in the years of the highly controversial social reforms by the SPD's Chancellor Schröder from 2003 to 2005, national-level union officers protested vigorously but nevertheless tried to stay in contact with the SPD. At the same time, a significant number of middle-level union secretaries left the party, some of them founding the splinter WASG, later joining Die Linke in 2007.

Overall Degree of Closeness and Range

Figures 7.2a and 7.2b suggest that, following the general trend discussed above, relations between central party organizations and trade unions are generally closer than those which the latter enjoy with parties' legislative groups, although it should be noted that the maximum score is lower for the relationships in the parliamentary arena. Additionally, the relationships between any union and the SPD are always a little closer than those the union has with Die Linke—this is especially the case with the IG BCE but does not in any case exceed the medium level.

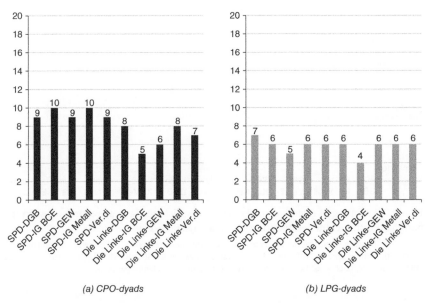

(a) CPO-dyads (b) LPG-dyads

Figure 7.2. Total link scores of central party organization–trade union relationships and legislative party–trade union relationships (0–20/0–12).[1]

[1] The theoretical maximum link score is 20 for the CPO-dyads and 12 for LPG-dyads since some link items are unlikely to apply to the legislative party group and were thus not included in this part of the survey. However, when comparing dyads involving CPOs with those involving LPGs, one should still keep in mind that the latter's maximum involves fewer links than the former's top scores.

We can contrast these 'objective' scores with the subjective perception of links in the view of the organizations themselves (Figure 7.3). One thing that stands out is that the relationship is seen to be closer by the parties than it is by the unions. This is especially pronounced in case of the SPD: our informant rated the degree of closeness to all DGB member unions as 'integrated', while the union side judged the same relations from 'fairly close' (DGB, IG BCE) and even 'distant/separated' (GEW). This is also the case with Die Linke—with two exceptions: both Die Linke and Ver.di agree that their relationship is 'fairly close', while our respondent from Die Linke's CPO rated its links to the IG BCE as even more distant than did the union side. Overall, the relations between the unions and the SPD are judged to be a little closer than those between them and Die Linke.

The DGB and all of its member unions studied here display a broad range of relationships with all parties represented in the Bundestag. In addition to their links to the SPD and Die Linke, all unions emphasized their contacts with *Bündnis 90/Die Grünen* and CDU/CSU, too. DGB and GEW even mentioned having contacts with the now extra-parliamentary FDP, a liberal party with strong pro-business policies. But these relationships vary greatly in intensity.

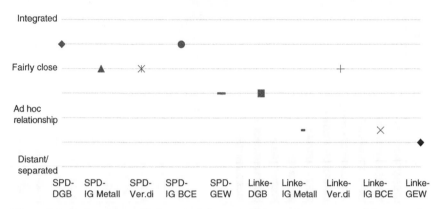

Figure 7.3. Rating of overall degree of closeness/distance (average score) between the party and union confederation, last five years (*c*.2008–13).[1]

[1] Ratings in-between two categories reflect that the party and union responses to the survey question differed. None of the ratings differed with more than one category, except for SPD-IG Metall (integrated vs ad hoc), SPD-Ver.di (integrated vs ad hoc), and SPD-GEW (integrated vs distant/separated).

Owing to historic connections with the SPD, the majority of unions maintain their most institutionalized links with that party, but there are also strong ties to Die Linke. Nearly all unions reported distant relations with Bündnis 90/Die Grünen and CDU/CSU.

Unions and parties also reported on recent changes in the relationship to each other in the last ten years. Most union respondents surveyed here point to a decline. Only the IG Metall reports a rapprochement with the SPD following serious conflicts over Agenda 2010. Additionally, Ver.di mentions better relations with Die Linke. Nearly all respondents blame the social cuts triggered by Agenda 2010 for distancing them from the SPD. The DGB informant even spoke of a split in labour movement due to Agenda 2010, resulting in two competing pro-labour parties, SPD and Die Linke. It is possible that the DGB, unwilling to take sides in this intra-labour conflict, has since then distanced itself from both parties in order to stay neutral.

EXPLAINING CHANGE AND CONTEMPORARY VARIATION

How can we explain the current state of, and recent changes in, relations between the two centre-left parties and the five trade unions examined in this chapter? The starting point of the analysis of the current state of links between centre-left parties and trade unions has to be the historic 'privileged partnership' (Schroeder 2005; 2008) between the SPD and the DGB and its member unions. Although officially non-partisan, the DGB was dominated by social democratic trade unionists during most of the post-war Bonn Republic. This was not only a legacy of the past, but an active exchange of resources that were valuable to both sides.

For the DGB unions, this meant privileged access to parliamentary and sometimes even governmental power. This was, as we have noted, not so much help in the day-to-day activities of trade unions but it was very important in general lobbying, for example in the labour-related fields of economic and social policy, as well as in preventing any changes in the legal framework of industrial relations itself. Up to the 1990s, senior union officials often had a seat in the Bundestag on the ticket of the SPD. They were members of important parliamentary committees, had privileged access to party, government, and bureaucracy, and were prime candidates for government positions like the Federal Minister of Labour and Social Affairs (Hönigsberger 2008, 61–6). The influence of the DGB unions reached its peak in the time of the social-liberal coalition under Chancellors Brandt and Schmidt in the 1970s and early 1980s. The lobbying efforts of the unions succeeded in the introduction of co-determination through work councils, early retirement options, better protection against dismissal, and improved welfare provisions (Hassels 2006, 210–11).

For the SPD, the support of the DGB unions was crucial, especially in elections, and union members formed a substantial share of the membership base of the SPD, with 61 per cent in 1983 (Greven 1987, 20). Although there were no direct financial contributions made by the DGB unions to any party, the membership fee of the unionized SPD members alone made up a good proportion of the party's finances. Historically, these organizations were from the same milieu. The problem was that same milieu was crumbling: by the 1980s, younger SPD members were much less rooted in it than their older counterparts (Greven 1987, 124–51). A new well-to-do and academically trained generation without a working-class background became dominant in the party. Matters were not helped by the economic downturn in the late 1970s and 1980s and the tightened public finances which resulted, even if the SPD's loss of office in 1983 prevented the party from being blamed for downsizing the welfare state or for labour market liberalization. Instead, the SPD in opposition stood shoulder to shoulder with the unions in their fight against reductions and deregulation in the labour market, health, and pension policies proposed by the CDU/CSU-led government under Chancellor Kohl (Trampusch 2011, 111–22; Neusser 2013, 59–61). In 1998, the DGB nearly gave up its official non-partisanship by starting a multi-million dollar electoral campaign, which was directed at voting out the governing conservative-liberal coalition—the main slogan of the DGB campaign ('Arbeit und soziale Gerechtigkeit') was only one word different from the SPD's ('Innovation und soziale Gerechtigkeit'). The electoral campaign was successful and a red-green coalition was formed under Chancellor Schröder.

The campaign of 1998, however, was the turning point in SPD–union relations. During the red-green coalition from 1998 to 2005 the cost–benefit calculus for the SPD of having the DGB unions as allies seems to have changed. Structural factors mattered. The core clientele of trade unions is in secular decline in Germany (Schroeder 2005, 15–16): from 1953 to the late 1990s, the share of blue-collar workers in the electorate shrank from 36 to 20 per cent, while the proportion of unionists dropped from 18 to 10 per cent, meaning that the electoral significance of these two groups for the Social Democrats diminished. Over the same period, the proportion of blue-collar workers among their voters sunk from more than 50 to 25 per cent, and the share of union members from 30 to 17 per cent. While the support of DGB unions was probably crucial for winning the 1998 election, the SPD tried to reach new target groups with an economically much more liberal profile in the years that followed. As with the 'New Labour' strategy of Tony Blair in the United Kingdom, SPD party strategists developed a 'Third Way' position—the *Neue Mitte*—through which they hoped to attract middle-class voters with a white-collar or self-employed background (Nachtwey 2009, 177–84).

A connected, but independent, reason for the change in SPD–union relations is the dominant position of the moderate-conservative factions within the Social Democrats. The SPD has always been divided between strong intra-party factions, but the years of the Schröder cabinet saw a near-complete takeover of all important positions in party, legislative caucus, and government by the two moderate and conservative factions, that is the *Seeheimer Kreis* and the *Netzwerker*, while the union-friendly left-wing *Parlamentarische Linke* struggled (Reinhardt 2009, 53–112; Grunden 2012, 112–13). The German media dubbed this as a conflict between 'reformers' and 'traditionalists'. Gerhard Schröder became a candidate for chancellor in 1998 as the exponent of the reformist factions, promising to be an economically liberal and pro-business chancellor. To keep the factional balance, the SPD put Oskar Lafontaine, party chairman, former chancellor candidate, and most prominent member of the left wing, by Schröder's side as 'super minister' for economy and finances. However, the conflict over economic policy between Schröder and Lafontaine resulted in the resignation of the latter from all offices in 1999, effectively decapitating the left wing of the party.

This meant Schröder was able to push through Agenda 2010, but it also meant that DGB unions, especially those with a clientele particularly prone to unemployment like the services union Ver.di, attacked its measures vigorously, to the point of intra-party resistance, the refusal of unionist members of the SPD caucus to vote for the reform package, public criticism by union officials, one of the largest protest campaigns in recent decades with hundreds of thousands of protesters, and eventually large numbers of union activists leaving the SPD for the WASG. Agenda 2010 had in effect created a political opportunity structure for the establishment of a new party of the left in both Western as well as Eastern Germany—a role that the former Communist Party, the *Partei des Demokratischen Sozialismus* (PDS), was clearly unable to play as it was then constituted (Nachtwey and Spier 2007). Under Lafontaine's leadership, the new party, Die Linke, made its electoral breakthrough with 8.7 per cent in 2005 and 11.9 per cent in 2009, winning at least a million voters directly from the SPD in each federal election (Alemann and Spier 2008; 2011).

That many middle-ranking union officials supported the new party was no coincidence: Die Linke is strongly pro-labour and imported many union positions into its electoral platforms. Although there is no official confirmation, it is quite obvious that the DGB unions profit from having a union-friendly party to the left of Social Democracy: while Die Linke as an opposition party with no realistic chance of participating in government in the near future has no opportunity to implement union policies directly, it is an electoral threat to the SPD if Social Democrats position themselves too close to the middle of the road. Indirectly, the existence of Die Linke increases the electoral costs of the SPD adopting positions unfavourable to the unions and provides it with an incentive to embrace union-friendly positions in the hope of winning back some leftist voters. An example of this indirect policy influence could be seen in the electoral campaign of 2013, in which the SPD adopted some DGB and Die Linke policies, including a federal minimum wage and an early retirement option, and succeeded in stemming its electoral losses to the left. In this sense, the former 'privileged partnership' of SPD and DGB unions has transformed into a 'pluralized partnership' (Neusser 2013), in which the unions try to build situational coalitions with any partner willing to cooperate—and not only with the SPD and Die Linke, but also with the CDU/CSU and Bündnis 90/Die Grünen—in order to maximize their direct or indirect influence on policymaking.

CONCLUSION

Although the privileged partnership between the SPD and the unions in Germany is well and truly over, remnants of it admittedly still exist: many leaders of DGB unions are SPD members, and the Gewerkschaftsrat, a permanent advisory body of the SPD and trade unions, still exists. Yet when it comes to day-to-day contacts and the overall degree of closeness to the unions, there are in truth differences between the SPD and Die Linke. It is telling, too, that both parties rate their relations to the unions better than the respective unions rate theirs to the parties—an indication, perhaps, of an improved bargaining position for the union side. There are, of course, some differences between individual DGB unions: while the rather conservative IG BCE remains very loyal to the SPD, the services union Ver.di has significantly improved its relations with Die Linke. But generally, the union movement's relations with the Social Democrats are only slightly better than its relations with their electoral competitor on the left.

What, then, is the political significance of these links? Clearly, since Die Linke is an opposition party, links between it and the unions only have indirect effects on the political process. The SPD, on the other hand, has only been out of government for four years since 1998, making it very valuable for influencing governmental decisions. Two examples: to get back into power after the conservative-liberal coalition under Chancellor Merkel between 2009 and 2013, the SPD adopted union demands for a federal minimum wage and an early retirement option, and made those two demands a *sine qua non* for participation in a second 'Grand Coalition'. Another significant example of the impact of union lobbying on Social Democrats in power was the unitary collective bargaining act (*Tarifeinheitsgesetz*) of 2015: to avoid increasing competition from small occupational associations like pilots, flight attendants, or tain-drivers, this law re-established the principle of one collective agreement in one company, effectively limiting the ability to negotiate to the union with most members—which is nearly always a DGB union. The DGB unions may have failed to prevent the social cuts in the 'Agenda 2010' years, but they now seem to have regained some influence.

So are parties and trade unions really growing apart in Germany? While the days of a privileged partnership between the SPD and the unions are over, a new pluralized set of relationships came into existence, replacing some of the ties to Social Democracy with connections to other parties, most notably to Die Linke. On the one hand, this leaves the DGB unions in a good bargaining position: at least the two centre-left parties compete with each other for union support in elections. On the other, this turns the trade unions into 'normal' interest groups, working with every party willing to promote their positions and interests.

NOTE

1. A table is not presented as there were no 'yes values' (coded judgments).

8

Parties and Labour Federations in Israel

Ronen Mandelkern and Gideon Rahat

INTRODUCTION

This chapter examines the relationship between two old left-of-centre parties and a centre-right party with trade unions federations in Israel, as well as the political and economic changes that led to the current state of affairs. For many years, there were very close ties between the old left parties and the main labour federation. In recent decades these ties have significantly diminished. A symbiotic organizational linkage has been replaced by mainly ad hoc links between unions and parties and personal links between union leaders and national politicians.

HISTORICAL BACKGROUND

The State of Israel was established in 1948 but the formation of its political system began decades before that, in the framework of the World Zionist Organization and the Jewish community that lived in Palestine, first under Ottoman rule, then under British rule. Workers' parties (especially Mapai) dominated the Israeli political scene from the early 1930s until the late 1970s. It was these parties that established the main federation of workers' unions (the Histadrut) in 1920.

The Histadrut was formed as an exclusively Jewish organization which operated in a context of national conflict with the Arab-Palestinian population. During its pre-state days the Histadrut aimed to protect Jewish immigrant workers from competition from Arab workers (who could be paid cheaper salaries). This was achieved, among other things, through the formation of enterprises owned by the Histadrut itself, which employed only Jewish workers as well as by providing a wide array of welfare services which limited the dependency of Jewish workers on their market wages. For this reason the Histadrut was much more than a Labour federation. It was a central vehicle for the development of the Jewish economy in Palestine and thus functioned as both employer and as a trade union. It was also a central supplier of various social services, including education and health. In short, it was a major player in the establishment of the infrastructure of the state of Israel. And even after Israel was established, it took decades until the Histadrut gave up on most of its economic corporations, its management of large pension funds, and its link with Israel's largest health provider.

Until the 1990s, the traditional workers' parties won all elections to the Histadrut, although other parties also joined the Histadrut over the years and, by participating in its internal elections, won an increasing share of representation and positions in its institutions. The close relations between the Histadrut and the workers' parties, Mapai/Labour in particular, were also based on joint decision-making arrangements in which national economic policies were determined. As the evidence in this chapter demonstrates, however, these strong ties between Labour and the Histadrut have weakened, up to the point that when one looks at current relationships one can hardly trace their glorious past. That weakening was a two-way street: Labour lost its status in Israeli politics as a possible governing alternative, and while Histadrut kept its position as the dominant federation of trade unions, it lost many of its assets and its influence on economic policies declined substantially. It is also worth noting the relationship between the main Israeli centre-right party, the Likud, and the Israeli unions. Likud has special relations with Histadrut Ha'ovdim Ha'le'umit (the National Labour Federation) (HL), the alternative workers federation that was established by its ancestor—the Revisionist party—in 1934. Moreover, since the 1960s, the Likud has also participated in the Histadrut.

CONTEMPORARY POLITICAL AND INSTITUTIONAL CONTEXT

The main characteristics of the Israeli democratic polity, its being parliamentary and unitary, made it likely that there would be relatively strong links between left-wing parties and trade unions (see Chapter 1). Yet these links weakened while Israel stayed unitary and, for most of the time (1948–96, 2003–), parliamentary. It can, though, be argued that the adoption of direct elections for the prime minister (1996–2003) encouraged the Histadrut to adopt direct elections for its chair, and contributed, in turn, to significant changes in its internal party system, namely fragmentation and the rapid weakening of 'catch-all' parties similar to those that occurred following the adoption of direct elections for the prime minister (Kenig et al. 2005) and city mayors (Brichta 2001).

Yishai (1999) described the Israeli interest group system as one that moved from being elitist (that is, symbiotic links between parties and interest groups) to being corporatist and then to a pluralist interest group system. In other words, over the years Israeli interest groups became more and more autonomous. In a similar vein, Cohen et al. (2007) characterize industrial relations in Israel as shifting from an extreme version of the German-style corporatist system towards an American-style pluralist one. They point to a decline of both union density—from some 80–85 per cent in 1980 to 34 per cent in 2006 (Haberfeld et al. 2010)—and coverage, as well as decentralization of collective bargaining and workers' representation. At the same time, we see decentralization and even decline on the side of the employers' organizations (Cohen et al. 2007; Kristal and Cohen 2007) and a parallel increase in the role of state organs—parliament, government, and courts—in industrial relations (Mundlak 2007). This gradual weakening of corporatist arrangements and the decline in union density in Israel went along with the weakening of party–unions ties (see Chapter 1 in this volume).

WORKERS' FEDERATIONS IN ISRAEL: HISTRADRUT, HL, AND KL

Our study examines the three politically and economically most active labour federations out of thirteen workers organizations that are currently registered in Israel, eight of which are independent professional workers associations (Ziloni 2010). These are the Histadrut (*Histadrut Ha'Ovdim Ha'Hadasha*—the New Labour Federation), HL (*Histadrut Ha'Ovdim Ha'Le'umit*—the National Labour Federation), which date back to the pre-state period, and KL (*Ko'ach La'Ovdim*—Power to the Workers). The Histadrut is by far the most important, both politically and economically, of the three.

The late 1980s and early 1990s should be seen as the watershed for union politics. There were significant changes in the Histadrut structure and its political-economic influence. It had to cope with an economic crisis and a political legitimacy crisis. During the early 1990s it was restructured and began focusing only on its trade union functions: it sold its vast array of business enterprises (*Hevrat Ha'Ovdim*—the Workers' Company) and ended its role as one of the main employers in the Israeli economy. It also gave up its control of major pension funds and withdrew its position as owner of the main Israeli health services provider and insurer (Nathanson 2002; Harpaz 2007; Weinblum 2010). To signal these changes its name changed to *Histadrut Ha'Ovdim Ha'Hadasha*—the New Labour Federation—in 1994.

Since its establishment, the Histadrut leadership has been determined through elections in which all of its members are eligible to participate. Up until the 1990s, Mapai/Labour won a majority of the vote and thus dominated its governing bodies. Since 1994 Labour lost that dominance, but other national parties did not replace it. Instead a separate party system, with loose links to national parties, was created, mainly based on ad hoc coalitions between powerful unions and prominent individuals.

Despite its relative decline, the Histadrut is still the dominant federation of unions in Israel. Unlike the past, when a large proportion of its members were non-unionized people whose membership was based on their health services eligibility, most of its current members are unionized (Mundlak et al. 2013). Recent years have seen some revitalization of the Histadrut in terms of industrial relations, such as the 'package deal' signed during the 2008–9 global economic crisis, and legislative influence, like the introduction of a general pension law and the increased protection of union rights (Weinblum 2010).

Although detailed data on unionization in Israel are missing, we can observe a moderate rise in the share of non-Histadrut federations, which might testify to modest fragmentation. First, though the HL's political-economic role was and still is much less significant than that of the Histadrut, it currently claims some 60,000 workers, a higher share than in the past. Still, this is only about a tenth of the Histadrut's unionized workers and even lower than the membership of the teachers' autonomous professional union.

Fragmentation is also evident when we turn to KL. It was established in 2007 as an alternative to the Histadrut, particularly to its centralized top-down structure and its neglect of the increasing sector of marginalized workers. Indeed, KL has only about 15,000 members, yet its challenge to the larger veteran federations of unions through media and legal actions seems to have encouraged them to react and to renew efforts to increase unionization, particularly among marginalized workers (Weinblum 2010). KL's presence also seems to have contributed to the growing distance between the Histadrut and Meretz, one of the traditional left-wing parties (see next section), exemplifying, perhaps, how fragmentation can have this effect (see Chapter 1).

THE POLITICAL PARTIES: LABOUR, LIKUD, AND MERETZ

Two of the parties that are included in our study, Labour (and its predecessor Mapai) and Meretz (and especially its predecessor Mapam), are left-of-centre parties. Both have (or rather had) strong historical links with the Histadrut. The third party is the (centre) right-wing Likud, which has its 'own' federation of unions (HL) as well as links with the Histadrut since its decision to join it and compete in its elections in the 1960s.

The Israeli Labour Party was established in 1968 as a unification of several labour-affiliated parties which were descendants of pre-state workers' parties, among which Mapai was the strongest. Mapai dominated the party system from the mid-1930s and continued to do so after the establishment of Israel in 1948. Labour lost its dominant position in the 1977 general elections, but kept its hold on the Histadrut until the latter's 1994 elections, since when its links with it as a party have weakened. However, Labour politicians continued to play a central role in the Histadrut, and all its chairpersons until 2014 were Labour Party members.

Likud was established in 1973 as an electoral alliance between several parties, mainly two centre-right parties that created an alliance in 1965. It became a unified party in 1988. The links between one of Likud's ancestor parties and the HL go as far back as the 1930s, and since 1965 its representatives have also taken part in Histadrut politics. Thus Likud has an exclusive link with the rather weak HL and links shared by other parties with the dominant Histadrut.

Meretz was established in 1997 primarily to unite two left-wing parties, Ratz (The Movement for Civil Rights) and Mapam (United Workers Party). Ratz, which was established in 1973, took part in the elections for the Histadrut but never won more than a few percentage points. Mapam is a socialist party that was established in 1948 and was based on the more socialist forces within the Zionist labour movement. As a workers' party, being in alliance with Labour in the years 1969–84 meant it had some power and influence within the Histadrut, usually as the third-largest force.

RELATIONSHIPS TODAY: MAPPING ALMOST EXTINCT LINKS

Analysing three labour federations and three parties produces nine possible dyads. Yet we report on only six of these in detail because in three cases there are no links whatsoever: the HL has no affiliation with parties other than Likud, while Likud and the KL have no connections at any level.

Overlapping Organizational Structures: Statutory Links

As shown in Table 8.1, there is no collective affiliation of union members to any party. This has to do, mainly, with the Histadrut's multi-partisan structure. Yet collective affiliation from the other side was the rule for the

Table 8.1. Overlapping organizational structures between party central organization and union confederation, as of 2013–14[1]

Party-confederation dyad—CPO	Labour-Histadrut		Meretz-Histadrut		Likud-Histadrut		Likud-HL		Labour-KL		Meretz-KL	
	P/U	CJ	P/U	CJ	P/U	CJ	P/U	CJ	P/U	CJ	P/U	CJ
National/local collective affiliation (membership) of a union	No	No	No	No	No	No	No	No	No	No	No	No
The party enjoys representation rights in at least one of the union's national decision-making bodies[2]	Yes	No	Yes	No	Yes	No	No	No	No	No	No	No
The union enjoys representation rights in at least one of the party's national decision-making bodies[2]	Yes	No	Yes	No	n.d.	No	n.d.	Yes	No	No	No	No

[1] There are no LPG cells in this table as we assumed the questions (link types) do not apply to the legislative party group and they were thus not asked. We report only six of the nine dyads because there are no links whatsoever between KL and Likud and between KL and Meretz, and HL and Labour. 'P/U' indicates responses from party/trade union questionnaires and 'CJ' signifies the authors' 'coded judgment' based on alternative sources in cases of diverging or missing P/U answers. 'c.d.' means contradictory data (diverging P/U answers), 'n.d.' means no data (informant didn't know/missing/unclear), and 'n.a.' means not applicable in this case.

[2] See Chapter 2 for a description of the specific rights/bodies that have been mapped.

Labour and Mapam (Meretz's ancestor) parties. They obliged virtually all their members to be members of the Histadrut until 1990 (Labour) and 1994 (Mapam), and, according to the chairperson of Labour's Knesset faction and to its general secretary, party members are still officially recommended to join the Histadrut.

Labour and Likud, as well as Meretz, report that they give their representatives in the Histadrut *ex officio* positions in their party institutions. However, further research revealed that these positions are reserved for people who have been selected to the Histadrut institutions as party representatives. The number of seats depends on their parties' electoral fortunes in Histadrut elections. All this means, we think, that the Histadrut is not represented in the parties and parties are not represented in the Histradrut in a guaranteed *ex officio* manner. Our three parties are connected to the Histadrut through their representatives in its national, regional, and locally elected institutions and governing bodies, depending on the electoral success of the party-affiliated lists (and increasingly on the electoral fate of individual politicians that are affiliated with these parties) in the Histadrut elections. This is the reason why our coded judgments in Table 8.1 differ from the P/U responses: there is no formal affiliation of unions and guaranteed *ex officio* representation in these party–union cases, with one exception: Likud reserves positions for HL seniors in its party institutions.

Table 8.2 demonstrates the development over time of Histadrut–party relations by presenting the election results for the Histadrut convention. It is about selecting delegates that have some decision-making power of their own but more importantly serve as a coalitional base for the smaller governing bodies. For the purpose of our analysis, what is important is what we might call the Histadrut party system created after each election.

The old left-wing parties enjoyed a majority until the mid-1990s and formed the Histadrut's ruling coalition during that time. The parliamentary majority these parties enjoyed until 1977 further strengthened the ties between the Mapai/Labour-government-Histadrut 'iron triangle' (Zalmanovitch 1998). The change began in 1994, when Labour lost its majority in the Histradrut and never gained it back except as a member within a coalition of parties. Likud and Meretz also became part of alliances. These alliances started as mainly multiparty alliances, which brought together parties that would never cooperate at the national level due to their differences on foreign affairs, security matters, and state and religious issues. Later on, the partisan element in these alliances declined, and they became based, more and more, on the personal and non-partisan level.

This trend should be put in the context of general differentiation between national and trade union politics. As can be seen, until 1990 the national parties were the sole actors on the scene. Since the mid-1990s a non-partisan trend developed, in the sense that trade union politicians who were affiliated with a national party created personal alliances up to the point that they

Table 8.2. Results of Elections to the Histadrut conference, 1956–2012 (%)[1]

Year	No. of members	Largest list	Second-largest list	Third-largest list
1956	261,410	**Mapai** (57.7)	**Achdut Haavoda** (14.6)	**Mapam** (12.5)
1960	504,539	**Mapai** (55.4)	**Achdut Haavoda** (17.0)	**Mapam** (14.0)
1966	669,720	**Alignment** (50.9)	Gachal (15.2)	**Mapam** (14.5)
1969	620,850	**Alignment** (62.1)	Gachal (16.9)	Independent Liberals (5.7)
1974	797,419	**Alignment** (58.3)	Likud (22.7)	Independent Liberals (6.0)
1977	934,044	**Alignment** (55.3)	Likud (28.2)	DMC (8.0)
1981	829,484	**Alignment** (63.1)	Likud (26.8)	Hadash (3.6)
1985	840,634	**Alignment** (69.4)	Likud (23.5)	Hadash (4.4)
1990	829,000	**Alignment** (55.1)	Likud (27.4)	Mapam (9.0)
1994	n.d.	Haim Hadashim (46.0)	**Labour** (32.5)	Likud (14)
1998	627,405	Am Echad (58.6)	Haver (18.6)	Oz (15.6)
2002	552,362	Am Echad (62.3)	Oz (18.1)	**Labour** (13.5)
2007	459,918	Oganim (83.2)	Ofek (16.7)	Hadash (4.7)
2012	503,233	Oganim (65)	Habayit Hahevrati (29.3)	Temura (5.7)

[1] **Bold** denotes lists that are directly affiliated with national parties. Achdut Haavoda is a workers' party that joined Mapai and established the Labour Party in 1968. Alignment in 1969–85 includes Labour and Mapam. In 1966 and 1990 it includes Labour and smaller parties. Gahal is a parties' alignment that was the basis for the establishment of Likud in 1973. Hadash is based on the Communist party. 'n.d.' means no data (missing).

Sources: up to 1990, Bartal 1991; official records of the Histadrut for 1998, 2002, 2007, 2012; for 1994 elections various sources.

competed in alliance with people from other parties against people from their own party. In some cases, trade union politicians now lack any partisan affiliation. Indeed, at the time of writing, a non-partisan Histadrut functionary replaced the Labour-affiliated chairperson, who, in any case, never ran for his post under the Labour Party label.

Table 8.3 reveals another important part of the story, focussing attention on the trend towards personalization that has weakened Israeli parties. After a revolt from within Labour (in cooperation with other parties) put an end to its hold on the Histadrut in 1994, it came back with the victory of Amir Peretz in the first direct elections for the chairmanship in 1998. Peretz, who was one of the defectors from Labour in 1994, returned to it for a short period. In 1999 he left Labour, however, and established a national party (Am Echad) that was based on his faction in the Histadrut. Peretz held the post of leader in the Histadrut until he decided to return and compete for the Labour chairmanship. A Labour Perty member, Ofer Eini, replaced him and played the same game in the Histadrut arena, that of creating large coalitions and running under a non-partisan label.

The 2012 elections for the Histadrut further exemplify the movement towards non-partisanship and personalization. First, the two competing candidates for chairmanship were from Labour: the incumbent chairman and his

Table 8.3. Elections to the Histadrut Chair (%)[1]

Year	Winner	Other candidates
1998	Amir Peretz (**Labour**) 77.7	Maksim Levi (**Gesher**) 22.3
2002	Amir Peretz (Am Echad) (no race)	
2007	Ofer Eini (Oganim) 92.5	Leon Ben Lulu (**Likud**) 7.4
2012	Ofer Eini (Oganim) 66.6	Eitan Kabel (Social House) 33.3

[1] **Bold** denotes candidates directly affiliated to national parties.

Sources: Official records of the Histadrut 1998, 2002, 2007, 2012.

rival who was a Member of Knesset. Second, the results of the elections for the 171 seat Histadrut House of Representatives were even more confusing, involving four 'lists' that included within them factions. One was headed by the re-elected chairman and included fifty-three representatives of a non-partisan list (including himself), twenty-five representatives of another non-partisan list (closely affiliated to a Likud MK), and additional representatives under labels of national political parties: Labour (fourteen), Likud (eleven), and the ultra-orthodox Shas (eight). The second largest candidate list (forty-one seats), which was headed by the losing candidate, included two non-partisan and two partisan factions. The two additional lists were based on a single faction, one partisan (Meretz, nine seats) and the other not. To make things even more complicated, many rival non-partisan lists included figures who were members of the same national party. It is not the case, then, that the Histadrut has its own ideologically divided party system, but that politics there is now personalized and based on ad hoc alliances.

Accordingly, two main developments are evident: first the decline of the left-of-centre parties' hold on the major federation of trade unions, and second the weakening of the links between the Histadrut and the national parties *qua* parties. These two developments parallel the decline of Israel's left-wing parties from their status as the country's main political forces to, at best, junior partners in centre- or right-led governing coalitions (Kenig and Knafelman 2013). The growing differentiation between the national party system and the Histadrut party system testifies to the weakening of these links. It should be remembered, however, that in the context of personalized politics the Histadrut is still an important stronghold for some national-level politicians, especially in intra- as opposed to inter-party politics.

Inter-organizational Links: Hardly any Reciprocal and Durable Links

Most officials reported that there were no reciprocal, durable links at the organizational level between parties and union confederations in the last five years and, even when such links were reported (for example by Labour's general secretary), such reports were almost certainly based on a misunderstanding.[1] Indeed, we identified only one viable link, namely tacit agreement on the representation of the HL in Likud's national decision-making bodies.[2]

Inter-organizational Links: One-way and Occasional

Contradictions between left-wing parties' respondents and Histadrut respondents are also evident in Table 8.4. According to Labour respondents it has many one-way occasional links with the Histadrut, especially but not exclusively through its party institutions. According to the reports of its officials, Meretz also seems to have some one-way occasional links to the Histadrut, though less than Labour, notwithstanding the fact that Meretz's representative in the Histadrut claimed in an interview that its relations with the Histadrut are closer than those of Labour. Furthermore, the links to the Histadrut reported by parties' representatives were not confirmed by the descriptions of Histadrut representatives with whom we met. In our judgement, therefore, the Histadrut and the left parties have no organizational links as such; rather, the connections they do have are based on the Histadrut parties' factions and hence are electorally conditioned. That is, the members of the Histadrut parties' factions invite to their activities both the leaders of the national party to which they are affiliated but also Histadrut representatives (who are not necessarily members of their Histadrut faction or national party). Furthermore, most of these occasional and one-way links are personal.

Unlike Labour, Meretz also has some links with KL. Meretz's secretary general testified that 'many of Meretz's Knesset Members are invited to take part in various activities of KL, such as demonstrations and workers meetings. Additionally, KL is assisted by the party parliamentary group to initiate deliberations or put KL's struggles on the agenda.' Obviously, neither left-wing party has anything to do with HL, which is affiliated only with Likud.

Table 8.4 reveals that the only linkage between Likud's party organization and federations of unions, even its exclusively affiliated HL, is through its institutions, not its Knesset faction. While we were unable to collect responses from the Likud director general and members of its Histadrut faction, we could discover no such links. This makes sense because while Likud has been taking part in Histadrut politics since its historical decision to join it in the 1960s, and while it probably has as much power as Labour these days, its leader (Netanyahu) holds neoliberal views that do not encourage closer relationships. In a way, the Likud party and the Likud in the Histadrut try 'to leave each other alone', and the main expression for their connection is in intra-party politics, where the Histadrut serves as one of various power bases.

Table 8.4. One-way, occasional links at the organizational level between party central organization/legislative group and union confederation, last five years (c.2008–13)[1]

Party-confederation dyad—CPO	Labour-Histadrut		Meretz-Histadrut		Likud-Histadrut		Likud-HL		Labour-KL		Meretz-KL	
	P/U	CJ	P/U	CJ	P/U	CJ	P/U	CJ	P/U	CJ	P/U	CJ
Invitation to party to participate in the organization's national congress	c.d.	No	c.d.	No	No	No	Yes	Yes	No	No	No	No
Invitation to organization to participate in the party's national congress/conference	c.d.	No	No	No	No	No	No	Yes	No	No	c.d.	No
Invitations to organization to participate in the party's ordinary meetings, seminars, and conferences	c.d.	No	No	No	No	No	Yes	Yes	No	No	No	No
Invitations to party to participate in ordinary organization meetings, seminars, and conferences	c.d.	No	No	No	No	No	No	No	No	No	No	No
Invitations to organization to special consultative arrangements initiated by the party	c.d.	No	No	No	No	No	No	No	Yes	Yes	c.d.	Yes
Invitations to party to special consultative arrangements initiated by the organization	c.d.	No	No	No	No	No	No	No	No	No	No	No

Party-confederation dyad—LPG	Labour-Histadrut		Meretz-Histadrut		Likud-Histadrut		Likud-HL		Labour-KL		Meretz-KL	
	P/U	CJ	P/U	CJ	P/U	CJ	P/U	CJ	P/U	CJ	P/U	CJ
Invitation to party to participate in the organization's national congress	c.d.	No	No	No	No	No	No	No	No	No	c.d.	No
Invitation to organization to participate in the party's national congress/conference	n.a.	n.a.	n.a.	n.a.	n.a.	n.a.	n.a.	n.a.	n.a.	n.a.	n.a.	n.a.
Invitations to organization to participate in the party's ordinary meetings, seminars, and conferences	c.d.	No	c.d.	No	No	No	No	No	No	No	c.d.	No

(*continued*)

Table 8.4. Continued

Party-confederation dyad—CPO	Labour-Histadrut		Meretz-Histadrut		Likud-Histadrut		Likud-HL		Labour-KL		Meretz-KL	
	P/U	CJ	P/U	CJ	P/U	CJ	P/U	CJ	P/U	CJ	P/U	CJ
Invitations to party to participate in ordinary organization meetings, seminars, and conferences	No	No	c.d.	No	No	No	No	No	No	No	c.d.	No
Invitations to organization to special consultative arrangements initiated by the party	No	No	c.d.	No	No	No	No	No	No	No	c.d.	Yes
Invitations to party to special consultative arrangements initiated by the organization	No	No	c.d.	No	No	No	No	No	No	No	c.d.	No

[1] We report only six of the nine dyads because there are no links whatsoever between KL and Likud and between HL and Meretz, and HL and Labour. 'P/U' indicates responses from party/trade union questionnaires, 'CJ' signifies the authors' 'coded judgment' based on alternative sources in cases of diverging or missing P/U answers. 'c.d.' means contradictory data (diverging P/U answers), 'n.d.' means no data (informant didn't know/missing/unclear), and 'n.a.' means not applicable in this case.

Individual-level Links: Individual Contacts
and Personnel Overlaps and Transfers

All parties reported that there are personal links between politicians and representatives of the Histadrut. Only Meretz reported that there are personal connections with KL and only Likud reported that there are personal connections with HL. The most common personal interactions reported are informal face-to-face meetings and telephone conversations. Some of the responses indicated additional contacts through appearances at each other's seminars and conferences, sending of formal written letters (including electronic), informal written communication via SMS, e-mail, and social media. Formal meetings or teleconferences and informal written communications were hardly reported.

HL personal contacts are only with Likud, as expected from their partisan affiliation. The nonpartisan KL reported that it has personal connection with politicians—mainly MKs rather than Central Office people—from all parties. These are described by one of their leaders as 'Close connections on policy matters with parliament members. Organization members are active in several parties and influence their agenda.' He also testified that KL have 'connection with parliament members—especially with Haim Katz [a Likud Member of Knesset with a powerbase within the Histadrut], who's the Chair of Parliament's Labour and Welfare Committee, in policy issues and concrete struggles.'

Formally, there are no reserved positions for union representatives in the parties' legislative candidate lists. As for the past, we can recall only one instance in which a seat on the Knesset list was reserved on this basis—in 1988 the fourth position on Labour's candidate list was reserved for the Histadrut general secretary. Yet union affiliation used to be a political asset, whether the selection was conducted by small nomination committees that thought it was important to have such representatives, or by more inclusive selectorates for which this affiliation was an important power base.

The data presented in Figure 8.1 demonstrate that there was a decline in the linkage between unions and the legislative faces of the parties. Looking at the totals, the overall picture is one of very small decline between the 1970s and the 1990s, and of an almost total disappearance of representatives with union past or present affiliation by 2013. In Likud, the decline is already evident in the 1990s, while in Labour and Meretz there is no significant difference between the 1970s and 1990s. In fact, in 1992 many Labour MKs enjoyed their affiliation with the Histadrut as a source of membership support in party primaries. Then came the revolt from within Labour against the old guard that dominated the Histadrut (1994 elections for the Histadrut). The revolution succeeded. The Young Turks took over. This ignited a process of separation between the parties and the Histadrut. After 2005, neither the chairs of the Histadrut or HL were Knesset members. The culmination of this separation

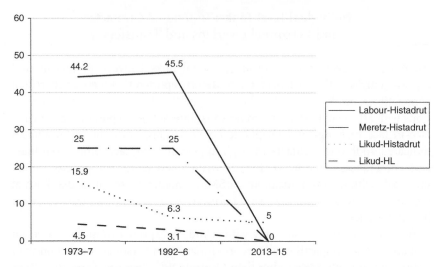

Figure 8.1. Share of Labour, Likud, and Meretz MKs that hold or have held positions as officials or staff in the confederations of unions at the national level.[1]

[1] N of MKs is 52 for Labour, 8 for Ratz and Mapam, and 44 for Likud between 1973 and 1977, 44 for Labour, 12 for Meretz, and 32 for Likud between 1992 and 1996, and 15 for Labour, 6 for Meretz, and 20 for Likud between 2013 and 2015.

Source: Authors' own calculations based on the online biographies of Members of the Knesset: <http://knesset.gov.il/mk/eng/mkdetails_eng.asp>.

was evident in 2013 when there was no representative with a union background in either of the two old left parties. And when one member of the Knesset challenged the incumbent Histadrut chair in the 2012 Histadrut elections, he lost and returned to the Knesset. The only remaining union man was a Likud MK who headed the union of Israel Aerospace Industries and the OZ faction in the Histadrut.

Overall Degree of Closeness and Range

Figures 8.2a and 8.2b summarize the total organizational scores of the party–union relationships in Israel. We have identified no organizational links between Labour's central organization and the Histradrut today. The Likud and HL obtains a score of 7 (out of 20) since Likud reserves positions for HL seniors in several party bodies and also relies on some other organized links. Apart from that, there is only one link between Meretz and KL. In the legislative arena, there are barely any organizational links at all.

However, we have seen that there are connections indirectly through the Histradrut elections, and that the decline of formal and organizational links at the level of the party-confederation at large have given way to informal, ad

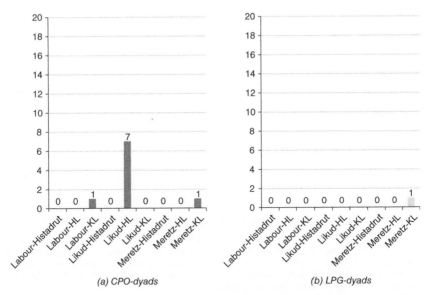

Figure 8.2. Total link scores of central party organization–trade union relationships and legislative party–trade union relationships (0–20/0–12).[1]

[1] The theoretical maximum link score is 20 for the CPO-dyads and 12 for LPG-dyads since some link items are unlikely to apply to the legislative party group and were thus not included in this part of the survey. However, when comparing dyads involving CPOs with those involving LPGs, one should still keep in mind that the latter's maximum involves fewer links than the former's top scores.

hoc, personal links between politicians and unions. These are based on shared power and policy interests and reflect the personalization of Israeli politics (Rahat and Sheafer 2007; Balmas et al. 2014). We should also remember that partisanship in Israel is mainly based on views regarding matters of foreign affairs and security; it is therefore not too surprising to find union-friendly politicians 'even' in right-wing parties. That said, we have also documented the decline—even the disappearance—of Knesset representatives with past or present affiliation to a union.

Figure 8.3 presents assessments of union and party officials of the overall degree of closeness/distance between the parties and union confederations in the last five years. Several points should be made. First, as already noted, the table presents only six out of nine possible dyads because we did not report the non-existing organizational links between HL and the left-of-centre parties and KL and Likud. Note, too, that while HL seems to lack any links with non-Likud politicians, non-partisan KL has personal relationships with Likud politicians. In general, the scores reflect the patterns described earlier: on average, the parties' and unions' ratings are clearly not close to rating the relationships as 'integrated' and tend towards 'ad hoc relations'.

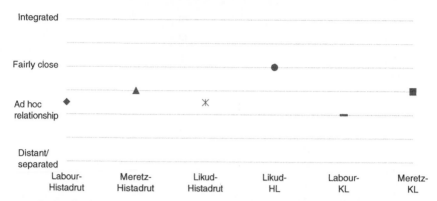

Figure 8.3. Rating of overall degree of closeness/distance (average score) between the party and union confederation, last five years (*c*.2008–13).[1]

[1] We report only six of the nine dyads because there are no links whatsoever between KL and Likud and between HL and Meretz, and HL and Labour. Ratings in-between two categories reflect that the party and union responses to the survey question differed. None of the ratings differed with more than one category, except for Labour-Histadrut (fairly close vs between ad hoc and distant/separated) and Likud-Histadrut (fairly close vs between ad hoc and distant/separated).

Second, the two sides' evaluations tend to differ. Respondents of all three parties actually report similarly 'fairly close' relations with Histadrut. This is of course noteworthy, since it indicates no distinction between left-wing and centre-right parties due to the mismatch with the organizational scores. It probably reflects the fact that relations between the Histadrut and the parties were and still are electorally conditioned. The 'fairly close' relations between the parties and the Histadrut reflect the limited and relatively similar influence their factions have within the Histadrut. In the past, when the power balance was different and Labour dominated the Histadrut, the definition of closeness/distance was probably 'fully integrated'.

Third, the Histadrut's assessment of its relationship with the parties is more moderate than their assessment of their relationship with the Histadrut. This seems to reflect a reality in which the national parties became secondary actors in comparison to the personalized and union-based Histadrut factions. The parties seem to be less sensitive to this reality, maybe because many of those who play the 'non-partisan' game within the Histadrut are, at the end of the day, affiliated with them.

It is also noteworthy that despite the historical special and exclusive relationship between HL and Likud, Likud perceived its relationship with 'its own' labour federation (HL) and its relationship with the Histadrut as being similar in their intensity. This reflects the status of the Histadrut in comparison to the HL. In short, a share of Histadrut power is worth at least as much as dominance in the HL.

Regarding change over time, the key informants themselves identified no significant changes in the relationship between the parties and the Histadrut in the last decade, with one exception (an ex-member of the Histadrut executive committee). Yet even the one that identified change (a weakening, incidentally) was keen to stress that 1994—with the loss of Labour hegemony and the beginning of the creation of the cross-partisan and non-partisan Histadrut party system—was the watershed in Histadrut/political party relationships. Indeed, there was a decline in the status of national political parties within the Histadrut over time and a decline of the status of the Histadrut within the parties as evident from the analysis of MKs' (lack of) union background (Figure 8.1). As we pointed out, the links of parties with the Histadrut are electorally conditioned and their strength is mainly a consequence of their electoral power within it. Labour's previous electoral dominance meant much closer links between it and the Histadrut. National parties' exclusive status as competitors in Histadrut elections until 1994 meant that national parties as such had closer relationships with the Histadrut.

No respondent identified any significant changes in the relationships between the parties and HL. It is still exclusively tied to Likud. Although the HL chairman identified no change in relationships with Likud, it is notable that, in contrast with the past (up to 2005), the HL's chair is not a Likud MK, signifying the weakening of these ties.

Some respondents (significantly KL's) claimed that KL's relationship with parties had become closer. It is of course natural that an organization that was established in 2007 and started from zero improved its relationships over time. In addition, these relationships are mainly with individual politicians rather than parties.

The Histadrut, Israel's main union federation, is indeed making every effort to distance itself from political parties in general and the left parties in particular. The tension between the unions—especially the powerful among them—and the partisan-controlled Histadrut was indeed always evident (Grinberg 1991). Recent decades have seen union leaders form non-partisan lists and win election to the Histadrut. Limited partisan influence and constrained ties between the national parties and their Histadrut factions are evident. The implications of this process are obviously most significant for the links between the Histadrut and the left-of-centre parties.

The left-wing parties, and Labour in particular, have also made efforts, especially during the 1990s and early 2000s, to distance themselves from the Histadrut. Indeed, it was Labour politicians who led the struggle to weaken the Histadrut's political-economic power during the 1990s. They aimed to minimize the party's dependence on the Histadrut, which at the time was suffering a financial and budgetary crisis as well as a very bad public reputation. Current links are mainly ad hoc and personal, based on the ideology and interests of individual politicians.

EXPLAINING DECLINE OF LINKS

The weakening of the links between the Histadrut and the left-of-centre parties in Israel should be set in the context of macro political-economic transformations. Since the mid-1980s, and following a severe 'stagflation' experience, Israel's political economy went through dramatic liberalization (Shalev 1999; Mandelkern and Shalev 2010). As in many other countries, this meant a decline in the influence of both the unions and the left-wing parties on socio-economic policies. The willingness and/or ability of the Labour Party to advocate economic intervention that would support the interests of the Histadrut and the unions became more limited (Shalev 1992). In fact, changes of macroeconomic governance and the increased power of the Central Bank and the Ministry of Finance led every government since the late 1980s to adopt fiscal restraint and promote privatization, even if such policies were more enthusiastically promoted by Likud-led coalitions (Mandelkern 2015). Clearly, this substantially limited the policies and achievements that cooperation between the Histadrut and the left-wing parties could have produced.

A cost–benefit analysis of the relations between Labour and the Histadrut can account for their parallel weakening and distancing. The ability of Labour to provide the Histadrut with policy and legislation has substantially eroded over time. Thus it makes more sense for the Histadrut to be less interested in Labour and more interested in those parties (plural) and politicians that may promote its interests. At the same time, Labour also had weaker incentives for maintaining close relations with the Histadrut, which suffered severe economic and legitimacy crises in the 1980s and 1990s. At that point, the Histadrut could no longer serve the party with economic resources but rather became an economic burden—and one which the party had to take on when in government. The decline in its membership (see Table 8.2), means that the Histadrut's role as a potential electoral resource had also weakened. At the same time, the Histadrut was regarded as mainly representing the interests of the powerful public sector 'insider' unions, rather than the 'outsider' secondary labour-market workers. Furthermore, it was perceived as a corrupted body that could hurt rather than help strengthen Labour's legitimacy.

The decline in the links between the Histadrut and the centre-left parties is also related to changes in the Israeli political system, namely the decline of Israeli parties and the personalization of politics. In the past, political parties were the main actors in the Israeli political system and played a central part in state-building (Galnoor 1982). Yet recent decades witnessed the decline of Israel's main political parties—a decline which was sharper than that of their counterparts in other established democracies (Kenig and Knafelman 2013). At the same time, and unlike some other democracies (Karvonen 2010), clear signs of the personalization of politics are apparent (Balmas et al. 2014). In such a context, maintaining links to politicians from various parties and avoiding dependence on specific parties might be a more worthwhile strategy for any interest group. In addition, politicians from various parties may also prefer, in such a context, to connect to unions on a personal level in the hope of gaining, in return, personal support in party primaries.

Note that when it comes to the relations of the Histadrut and the parties, variation between dyads is very small. Figure 8.3 shows that there is generally a similar degree of distance/closeness between the Histadrut and all the parties examined. The ideological differences between the more pro-market Likud and more social-democratic Labour and Meretz seem to play a minor role in this context, as do historical roots and relationships—contrary to what some of the hypotheses laid out in Chapter 1 suggest.

We have so far focused on a cost–benefit analysis at the national level, that is, on the declining incentives of (left-wing) parties to cooperate with unions for greater electoral gains, and on the declining incentives for the Histadrut to cooperate with parties for greater policy gains. Yet the links that still exist between Israeli national parties and unions (the Histadrut in particular) seem to fit with the idea of a cost–benefit calculus at the intra-party level, and also at the intra-union level. On the one hand, Histadrut members serve as an electoral power base for some politicians, especially in Labour and Likud, both of which hold party primaries. On the other hand, party organization and party members provide political support for the competition within the Histadrut's political institutions.

While a cost–benefit analysis makes sense (both at the national and intra-party and intra-Histadrut levels), we should nevertheless recall some of its limits—and note that history, tradition, and ideology slow and constrain change. Labour declined, yet Labour politicians headed the Histadrut until 2014. Right-wing Likud did not attempt to take over the Histadrut even though it might have been able to do so. Even though the Histadrut faces renewed (HL) and new (KL) competition, it is still by far the largest federation of labour unions. In addition, and as already stressed, the nature of the actors playing the cost–benefit game has changed. It is much less about parties and their electoral gains and much more about individual union politicians and some national party politicians and their personal gains.

CONCLUSION

The change that occurred in the relationship between labour federations and political parties in Israel was dramatic. The main significant linkage was between Mapai/Labour and the Histadrut. It was a very strong connection that was central in political, societal, and economic terms to the establishment of the state of Israel. Later on, these same links were central to the preservation of Mapai/Labour dominance. With the decline of Labour and then the decline of political parties, the linkage has dramatically weakened. If in the past the Histadrut party system was composed of national parties with a clear bias towards the left, now one can hardly trace the national parties. In addition, the representatives of these parties behave differently and create alliances that cannot be imagined at the national level, often even cutting through parties.

This state of affairs is not unique to the Histadrut. Similar party systems also developed at the local level, where unstable local lists that are based on both partisan and non-partisan politicians developed. Power was clearly decentralized over time, going from being concentrated in the hands of the iron triangle of government-Mapai/Labour-Histadrut to being diffused between and within these institutions. Power diffusion may be almost intuitively interpreted as good news for a liberal democratic polity. Yet a price is paid when national parties, especially the large aggregative ones, lose their links with civil society (Mair 2013), among them the important link with union federations. It is also the case that personalized politics, with its enhancement of charismatic authority, can be a threat to liberal democracy, which is based on legal rational authority.

A central question in the study of political parties is whether parties have declined or adapted to changing circumstances. In Israel, Labour, the parties in general, and the Histadrut have declined in comparison to their respective golden ages. Yet the Histadrut as an organization (while losing its role in welfare and the economy) has adapted and kept its hegemonic status as a federation of unions vis-à-vis its tiny competitors (HL and KL), while parties in general and Labour in particular have declined.

While the links between unions and parties have weakened, the links between unions and politicians continue to play a role. Moreover, when the personal links are between senior leaders from both sides, then the organization and the party can be mobilized. The chairperson of the Histadrut was perceived to be a key actor in bringing Labour into the 2009 Likud-led coalition government, in designing and signing a package deal with the government and the employees in the face of the economic crisis, and in promoting legislation that protected unionization rights. In short, the Histadrut chairman played a central role in Israeli politics, both in the power domain and the policy domain. The personal links are also significant for less senior politicians, who express pro-Labour viewpoints and at least sometimes gain, in return, union members' support in party primaries when they campaign for reselection. In other words, workers' federations and specific unions are part of Israel's personalized politics. Some unions' chairs register their members to parties and use that to promote themselves and/or candidates that support their interests. This is not a partisan but a personal game and an organized-interests game, and a union member may find him or herself a member of Labour one day and Likud the next. Historical links may matter, but only residually.

NOTES

1. For example, Labour's general secretary testified that Labour has a variety of reciprocal and durable links with the Histadrut. However, when we rechecked and examined these claims on behalf of the groom from the perspective of the bride, the Histadrut, it seems that he had confused guaranteed reciprocal and durable links with the electorally conditioned links mentioned earlier.
2. A table is not presented as our coded judgments resulted in only one 'yes value'.

9

Left-of-Centre Parties and Trade Unions in Italy

From Party Dominance to a Dialogue of the Deaf

Liborio Mattina and Mimmo Carrieri

The links between trade unions and left parties in Italy have traditionally been less structured than in the countries of northern Europe and Scandinavia (Duverger 1972; Morlino 1998; Thomas 2001c; Allern 2010). In Italy, as in France, the religious cleavage and the divisions within the labour movement have made the formation of an exclusive relationship between the trade-unions and a single party of the left impossible. However, the links between the *Confederazione italiana generale del lavoro* (Italian General Confederation of Labour—CGIL)—the most important Italian trade union—and the Communist Party (PCI) were numerous and durable. These ties were reinforced during the Second World War by strong ideological glue. But they weakened in the first fifteen years of the twenty-first century as a consequence of the dissolution of the Communist Party and its transformation into the Democratic Party (PD)—the sole heir of parties like the Christian Democrats (DC), the Socialist Party (PSI), and the smaller parties that in different ways had established links with unions but then disappeared when, between 1991 and 1994, scandals and judicial investigations forced their dissolution. This change paved the way for a gradual deterioration in relations that has greatly reduced the trade unions' capacity to influence major public policy decisions.

This chapter will examine the political factors that promoted both the strong alliance between the PCI/PD and the CGIL and the permanent frag-mentation of the trade union movement. It will then describe the number and variety of organizational links that exist today between the PD and the three major Italian trade unions, CISL, UIL, and CGIL, and suggest that the weakening of this relationship has had a significant impact on public policy, particularly when it comes to employment laws. The chapter concludes by looking at the likely further evolution of the relationship between the PD and the CGIL.

COMMUNISTS AND UNIONS

In Italy, as in many European countries, the Socialist Party was set up before the unions. The PSI was founded in 1892 while the General Confederation of Labour (CGL) was established in 1906. The formation of the Socialist Party was hampered by ideological divisions and internal fragmentation which remained endemic until the beginning of the First World War. Because of its internal divisions, the PSI was unable to control the CGL, which also suffered similar ideological divisions and was hampered in its development by the creation of the Catholic workers' organizations (Bartolini 2000, 243–60). These internal divisions led to organizational weaknesses in the labour movement that, in the years preceding the birth of Fascism, provided only a very limited boost to the PSI's electoral growth. Though sharing the same political vision, the PSI and CGL lacked strong organizational, ideo-logical, and personal overlaps (Bartolini 2000, 248). Although the climate of political mobilization after the First World War fostered the organizational growth of the CGL, the establishment of the fascist regime meant it was forced to dissolve in 1927.

After the end of the Second World War, the Communist Party exploited its organizational strength, penetrating the major relevant organizations that had existed under fascism and creating new associations. The PCI's primary objective was to assume the control of the former CGL, which, on the initiative of the PSI (the then PSIUP—*Partito socialista italiano di unità proletaria* (Italian Socialist Party of Proletarian Unity)), the DC and the PCI itself (Cattaneo 1968, 35), was refounded in Rome in June 1944 and renamed the 'Confederazione italiana generale del lavoro'. The first national CGIL Con-gress in June 1947 saw a clear victory for the Communists, who won 57 per cent of the congressional votes against the 22 per cent of the Socialists, while 13 per cent of the delegates voted in favour of the Christian component. These results established the basis for the long-term control of the Communists over the left-wing union (Bartolini 2000, 37–8).

With the onset of the Cold War, the major influence acquired by the PCI within the CGIL allowed the Communists to mobilize the Confederation into a series of political strikes against the government from which they had been removed. This action resulted in the abandonment of the CGIL by the other political currents represented in the Union (Christian Democrats, Repub-licans, Social Democrats, and some Socialists). In July 1948, the CGIL suffered its first split when the Christian component broke away, forming the Italian

Confederation of Union Workers (CISL), which immediately established a special relationship with the Christian Democrats (DC), the largest centre party which would lead all Italy's governing coalitions until the early 1990s. Soon after, the CGIL suffered another split following the formation of the Union of Italian Workers (UIL), which linked itself to the Social Democrats and other smaller parties before eventually establishing a permanent relationship with the PSI. The CGIL remained, therefore, under the control of Communist leaders who shared power with a group of Socialist leaders who remained politically subordinate to the Communists.

Among the main social and political factors that came together to shape the links between the PCI and CGIL, the class cleavage had only a moderate weight, even if that weight was initially greater than it is today. This was evident during electoral campaigns, where the political importance of the religious cleavage, and of the ideological fractures generated by the reformist and revolutionary versions of Marxism, characterized inter-party competition and stoked competition among a fragmented trade union movement, each component part of which was mobilized in support of its 'brother' party.

Another factor that helps to explain the relationships between the PCI and the CGIL was the *conventio ad excludendum* on the part of the government parties towards the PCI that precluded any possibility of the Communists entering government. Freezing the Communist Party in this position led to a reaction in the leftist camp that resulted in the creation of an alliance between the Communists and their allies in the labour movement based on ideological cohesion as well as on a common organizational effort. Such alliances were never in danger of being compromised by corporatism, which, with the exception of a brief experiment by the 'technocratic' governments which held office in the early 1990s, never took hold in Italy (Regini 1997). And only in the wake of dramatic changes in the Italian party and electoral systems that occurred from the early 1990s onwards did Italy's biggest left-wing party begin to cultivate more pluralistic relationships with the unions.

Today the CGIL, CISL, and UIL continue to represent the bulk of Italy's unionized workers, claiming a membership of more than 12 million people, representing 30 per cent of both blue- and white-collar workers. They are, however, rivals—their rivalry fuelled by inter-organizational competition rather than ideology, differences over the latter having dissipated with the dissolution of the parties previously allied to the unions.

RELATIONSHIPS TODAY: MAPPING OF LINKS

The current statutes of the trade unions and the Democratic Party do not provide for overlapping structures—which is not surprising, perhaps, because the latter never really existed in the past. It is true that in the early 1950s, when the relationship between the two organizations was particularly intense, the statutes of the Communist Party implied its members must join the CGIL. But this requirement was removed in the mid-1950s. The Democratic Party does not encourage—either explicitly or tacitly—its members to join a trade union.

Inter-organizational Links: Reciprocal and Durable

Our party–union relationship survey confirms that there are no lasting and mutual links between the unions and the main left-of-centre party in Italy between PD, CGIL, and CISL[1]—a finding which, while expected when it came to the Democratic Party and the CISL and UIL, was slightly surprising given the CGIL's historical links with both the Communist Party, ancestor of the Democratic Party, and with the Socialist Party. It is common knowledge among Italian scholars that in the late 1980s tacit inter-organizational agreements were still operating at the top level, and that these allowed the two main left parties to share the leadership positions in the CGIL, those positions apportioned as roughly two-thirds to the Communists and one-third to the Socialists, with a few given over to the 'third component' which collected unionists belonging to some small radical left parties. Until the beginning of the 1990s, the general secretary of the CGIL elected by the CGIL congress always came from the PCI, reflecting the balance of power existing among the two main currents. After the disappearance of the allied parties, the selection of the general secretary took place exclusively within the CGIL. The last two general secretaries ruling the Confederation (from 2000 to 2018) have been PSI members but have been chosen independently from within the CGIL.

The current absence of any inter-organizational durable links between the CGIL and the Democratic Party confirms, therefore, a separation that occurred even before the formation of the Democratic Party. On the other hand, the PD-CPO reports that there are still tacit agreements between the Democratic Party and the CGIL aimed at ensuring the representation of CGIL and CISL leaders in the central organs of the party (Table 9.1). However, this claim has been contradicted by the two unions' respondents and by the available data, which confirm the absence of union representatives in the national secretariat and show that they account for only two out of 210 members of the national executive of the Democratic Party.[2] The two former CGIL representatives that currently sit on the national executive of the Democratic Party do not feel accountable towards the Union for their individual choices, and were co-opted by the party leadership before the changes of December 2013 that carried

Table 9.1. One-way, occasional links at the organizational level between party central organization/legislative group and union confederation, last five years (*c.*2008–13)[1]

Party-confederation dyad—CPO	PD-CGIL		PD-CISL		PD-UIL	
	P/U	CJ	P/U	CJ	P/U	CJ
Invitation to party to participate in the organization's national congress	Yes	Yes	c.d.	Yes	Yes	Yes
Invitation to organization to participate in the party's national congress/conference	Yes	Yes	Yes	Yes	c.d.	n.d.
Invitations to organization to participate in the party's ordinary meetings, seminars, and conferences	Yes	Yes	Yes	Yes	Yes	Yes
Invitations to party to participate in ordinary organization meetings, seminars, and conferences	Yes	Yes	c.d.	No	Yes	No
Invitations to organization to special consultative arrangements initiated by the party	Yes	Yes	Yes	Yes	Yes	Yes
Invitations to party to special consultative arrangements initiated by the organization	Yes	Yes	c.d.	Yes	Yes	Yes

Party-confederation dyad—LPG	PD-CGIL		PD-CISL		PD-UIL	
	P/U	CJ	P/U	CJ	P/U	CJ
Invitation to party to participate in the organization's national congress	Yes	Yes	c.d.	Yes	Yes	Yes
Invitation to organization to participate in the party's national congress/conference	n.a.	n.a.	n.a.	n.a.	n.a.	n.a.
Invitations to organization to participate in the party's ordinary meetings, seminars, and conferences	c.d.	n.d.	c.d.	n.d.	c.d.	n.d.
Invitations to party to participate in ordinary organization meetings, seminars, and conferences	c.d.	n.d.	c.d.	No	c.d.	n.d.
Invitations to organization to special consultative arrangements initiated by the party	Yes	Yes	Yes	Yes	Yes	Yes
Invitations to party to special consultative arrangements initiated by the organization	Yes	Yes	Yes	n.d.	c.d.	n.d.

[1] 'P/U' indicates responses from party/trade union questionnaires, 'CJ' signifies the authors' 'coded judgment' based on alternative sources in cases of diverging or missing P/U answers. 'c.d.' means contradictory data (diverging P/U answers), 'n.d.' means no data (informant didn't know/missing/unclear), and 'n.a.' means not applicable in this case.

a new generation of leaders to the top of the PD who are prepared to go against the unions (see section on 'Why Have Party–Union Links Weakened?'). Those changes, moreover, made the possibility of a tacit interorganizational agreement between the Democratic Party and trade union leaders highly unlikely.

Inter-organizational Links: One-way and Occasional

While overlapping structures and lasting links are non-existent, the PD and the three unions have established numerous one-way and occasional links. As shown in Table 9.1, the Democratic Party and the three unions, and in particular the PD and CGIL, have established a variety of links that covers practically the entire range of possible options listed. Some links, of course, may be more important than others. For example, invitations to the leaders of the party and the trade union to participate in their respective national congresses should not be overstated: such invitations are often addressed to a very wide audience of political actors and are mostly to do with institutional courtesy. On those occasions the interchange takes a predominantly cere-monial character, devoid of material content. More important seem to be the mutual invitations to attend seminars and conferences at which issues of common interest are discussed, or to participate in special consultative arrangements when the sponsoring organization of the meeting wants to present its position on a given matter in order to gauge the opinion of the representatives of the invited organization.

Unfortunately it is with regard to meetings which are more than merely symbolic that the questionnaires revealed the highest number of contradictory answers. That said, the PD respondents were keen to stress the importance of this type of link saying that, when it seems necessary, the party activates a channel of 'formal consultation' with the CGIL, CISL, and UIL on major issues, and that those meetings are more frequent with the CGIL representatives, then with CISL, and least with UIL. In other words, the data reported in Table 9.1, and the additional answers of informants in the Democratic Party, suggest the links that unite the Democratic Party with the CGIL are the most important.

Individual-level Links: Individual Contacts and Personnel Overlaps and Transfers

When it comes to individual contacts with members of the Democratic Party, union representatives do not distinguish between a first and a second more common form of contact. Uniformly they attribute the same importance to the opportunities arising from 'speakers at each other's seminars/conferences' and the opportunities arising from 'informal face-to-face meetings, telephone conversations/Skype conversations, etc.' Respondents from the PD confirm their relevance but suggest there are differences between the central office and the parliamentary group in this respect: for the party's central office the most common form of individual contact is generated from seminars and confer-ences promoted by both organizations, while for the party's parliamentary group the most frequent contacts are via face-to-face informal meetings. This makes sense, since the central organizations of both party and union confederation are precisely the bodies likely to generate official and (semi-)public meetings, while it is the individual initiative of a deputy or of a union representative—or both—which generates informal contact between two individuals in the lobby of the Parliament, or encourages a phone conversation. The two party representatives are, in our judgement, probably more accurate than the union representatives when they suggest that the second most common form of individual contact is the sending of formal written letters (PD-CPO) and informal written communication (PD-LPG).

It is interesting to note that all respondents indicate the existence of mutual contacts between the PD and the trade union federations. There are no privileged or exclusive relationships. The PD is open to contacts with all unions: none of these are excluded from the possibility of getting in touch with members of the main party of the left. That said, the data relating to MPs who were former trade unionists, and the different degree of organizational closeness/distance that the trade unions representatives perceive when it comes to the PD, suggest the persistence of certain links between the PD with the CGIL that, in the case of the CISL and UIL, are tenuous or non-existent.

Before going into detail in this respect, however, it is worth remembering that in the early 1970s the three confederations wanted to stress their independence by making the holding of trade union office positions and leading political party positions incompatible—a decision which led to all the main union leaders refusing to stand as candidates in elections (Cesos CISL-Ires CGIL 1982). Previously, the main union leaders had been inserted in their respective party's electoral lists and often been elected to parliament. Subsequently, only ex-unionists have been elected to parliament and their total number has always been limited.

The elections of February 2013 showed, however, that it is mainly the PD that hosts former union leaders on its electoral lists, and that they come mainly from the CGIL. From parliamentary sources and the media we know that in the seventeenth legislature (2013–18) the PD has seven parliamentarians who held national offices in the CGIL (five) and in the CISL (two). As a proportion of the total number of deputies and senators (415) belonging to the parliamentary groups of the PD in both houses of Italian Parliament this constitutes just 1.7 per cent, and the percentage only rises to 3.3 per cent if the parliamentarians who held offices (seven) in the CGIL at the provincial level (six), and in the UIL at company level (one), are included. Among the parliamentarians who held important positions at national level in the CGIL and CISL, we find representatives of the federations of metalworkers, textiles, telecommunications, and credit. The most important former unionists are the former general secretary of the National Federation of Metalworkers (FIM) of

CISL, who was also appointed under-secretary for the budget in the government, the former national representative of the employees within the Federation of Employees and Metal Workers (FIOM), affiliated to the CGIL, who became the chairman of the Parliament's Standing Committee on 'Labour private and public', and Guglielmo Epifani the former general secretary of the CGIL from 2002 to 2010.

However, even if among the former trade unionists in parliament there are some influential personalities, the CGIL and CISL cannot place a great deal of reliance on them to influence the PD on social and labour policies. This is because the former union leaders are few in number and because they have never attempted to form a faction—and because their loyalty to the party is stronger than any link they maintain with their union. The electoral law under which the elections were held in 2013, and the one under which the next election will be fought, promotes the election of candidates selected by the national leaders of the party, in consultation with the local leadership. Those elected therefore owe something of a debt of gratitude to the national leadership of the party, and realize that their loyalty to the party is essential for the continuation of their political career.

Overall Degree of Closeness and Range

As we have noted, there are no overlapping organizational structures between the unions and the Democratic Party, or any mutual and durable links. Figures 9.1a and 9.1b show that the result is a maximum additive organizational score of 6 (out of 20) for PD's central organization and CGIL, but nearly as many for PD-CISL. We are not able to calculate a total score for PD-UIL. As we cannot assign a total score for more than PD's parliamentary group and CISL, it is hard to tell if the links in the parliamentary arena are generally weaker than outside public office. In any case, the relationships between PD and the confederations are characterized by a relatively low degree of institutionalization in general.

This situation is confirmed by the answers given by the respondents of the PD and the representatives of the three confederations (Figure 9.2). All respondents declare that there are no integrated relations. Most of the responses indicate that ad hoc links prevail—with two exceptions. The first is indicated by the UIL respondent who sees his union as distant from the Democratic Party. This declaration is supported by the PD-LPG respondent who signals a lower frequency of contacts between his party and the UIL. The second is made by the CGIL respondent who says that relations between his organization and the Democratic Party are fairly close.

This statement, together with the presence of former CGIL trade unionists among the PD parliamentarians, suggests the existence of a greater number of

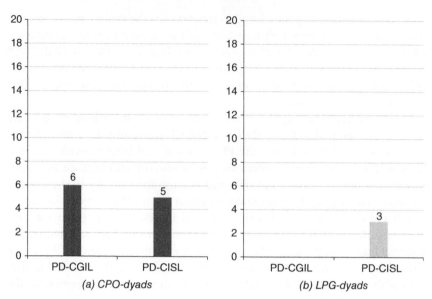

Figure 9.1. Total link scores of central party organization–trade union relationships and legislative party–trade union relationships (0–20/0–12).[1]

[1] The theoretical maximum link score is 20 for the CPO-dyads and 12 for LPG-dyads since some link items are unlikely to apply to the legislative party group and were thus not included in this part of the survey. However, when comparing dyads involving CPOs with those involving LPGs, one should still keep in mind that the latter's maximum involves fewer links than the former's top scores.

Figure 9.2. Rating of overall degree of closeness/distance (average score) between the party and union confederation, last five years (*c*.2008–13).[1]

[1] Ratings in-between two categories reflect that the party and union responses to the survey question differed. None of the ratings differed with more than one category.

links between the PD and the CGIL (Figure 9.1a and 9.1b). These links—however weak in comparative terms (see Chapter 2 and Chapter 15)—are more numerous if we keep in mind the existence of a hundred or more former trade unionists active at the local level of the party organization who often become candidates on the lists of the PD and are regularly elected to provincial and regional councils, while, as we have seen, a few of them are also elected to parliament.

When it comes to the relations that the PD has cultivated with the unions in the last decade or so, it is worth recalling that the PD-CPO respondent emphasizes the value of his party involving all the confederations in a relationship of 'formal consultation on major issues'. Actually, that involvement was more intense during the experience of governments led by the centre-left Democratic Party between 1996 and 2000 and for two years (2006–8) in the first decade of the twenty-first century. Not coincidentally, the PD-CPO attributes to those governments the credit for having 'developed an intense phase of consultation with the social partners'. For the rest, the first decade of the 2000s was politically characterized by governments led by the centre-right parties that shelved consultation and tried to divide the trade union movement, triggering the effective isolation of the CGIL by the other two federations. This strategy had some success: the CISL, followed by the UIL, was available to maintain dialogue with the governments of the centre-right while the CGIL assumed an uncompromising position, in tune with the attitude taken by the PD, which became the largest opposition party. The new political situation helped to maintain some links between the CGIL and the PD during the first decade of the twenty-first century, while those with the CISL became, as the PD-LPG respondent put it, 'thinned out'.

An apparently contradictory perception of the relationship between the PD and the largest confederation was expressed by the CGIL respondent when he declared that the relationship of his organization with the PD is quite narrow and at the same time became more distant over the past decade. This did not, however, prevent him from affirming the special rapport his organization enjoys with the Democratic Party—so much so that he still cited the Democratic Party, along with SEL (a small radical leftist party), as the party with which the CGIL in the past five years had the largest number of *political* but not organizational contacts. Indeed, the CGIL respondent acknowledged the existence of a special relationship between his union and the heir of the PCI. At the same time the CGIL respondent considered that relationship to be threatened by some of the directions in which the PD now seemed to be headed. In particular, the CGIL respondent complained that the PD sometimes forgets it is a leftist party because 'the Democratic Party tends to not put the social value of work at the centre of its own initiatives. This approach makes for rather unfriendly relations.' Such concerns express a real problem that complicates current relations between the PD and the CGIL. Throughout the course of the first decade of the new millennium and beyond, until the beginning of 2013, the CGIL maintained a closer relationship with the PD than the relationships it cultivated with the other two confederations, which in turn seem to be less enthusiastic themselves about such relationships.

Compared to 1945, then, there has been a significant change in the relationship between the main party of the left and the unions. The heir of the PCI significantly expanded the range of unstructured links with unions, extending them to the CISL and UIL. At the same time, the Democratic Party loosened the links cultivated in the past by the PCI with the CGIL. However, they remain more robust than those which the PD has recently managed to forge with the other two union confederations.

WHY HAVE PARTY–UNION LINKS WEAKENED?

The two main factors that help to explain the weakening of the links between the CGIL and the PD are to be found, first, in the ideological and programmatic transformation of the main left-wing party, which now has very little in common with the Communist Party from which it originated, and, second, in the reduced capacity of the largest union to influence the votes of its membership and to support the PD in its electoral campaigns. These changes challenge the maintenance of the exchange relationship between the left-wing party and CGIL prevailing in the past.

The long transformation of the PCI into a reformist party began in 1989, after the collapse of the Soviet Union, and finished in October of 2012 when the party's National Assembly definitively introduced primary elections for both the selection of the PD leaders and candidates to public offices. With the introduction of primaries the PD opened itself up to society and obliged its leadership to engage in a real competition, with challengers who did not traditionally belong to the party establishment. The results of internal competition through the primaries promoted a radical generational turnover inside the party, opening the way to the leadership of Matteo Renzi, a former mayor of Florence, who was elected as general secretary of the party in December 2013, and then became prime minister in February 2014 after overthrowing the left-right governmental coalition of *larghe intese* (broad agreements) led by Enrico Letta, a Democratic Party leader to some extent associated with the PD old guard. The radical generational shift in the PD ruling class began to extend to the intermediate and local party levels. As the new prime minister of the same *larghe intese* coalition, Renzi shifted the party to the centre of the political spectrum. He also assumed a critical position towards the unions, accusing them of hindering the changes needed to revive the country's economy, barricaded as they were into exclusively defending only those workers who are permanently employed and organized.

Meanwhile the CGIL, together with CISL and UIL, is losing its capacity to maintain a fruitful relationship with the Democratic Party. Indeed, the three confederations are increasingly weak in terms of social embeddedness, negotiating skills, and public credibility. The economic crisis has severely tested unions' capacity for social representation. Between 2007 and 2014, more than a million jobs were lost in Italy. The unemployment rate more than doubled, reaching 13.2 per cent of the working population and 43.7 per cent among those aged between 15 and 24 years old, inevitably impacting negatively on the membership of trade unions. Membership has continued to decline among active workers, while pensioners now make up 50 per cent of all union members.[3] Recruiting new members in the most dynamic sectors of employment linked to the international economy has been difficult, too. Moreover, the unions have also failed to translate into negotiable proposals the protests of millions of workers affected by austerity measures launched by Italian governments in recent years, especially those affecting pensions and the labour market. And their bargaining power significantly decreased as a result of the centre-right government's decision to abandon corporatist-style concertation during the first decade of the 2000s—a policy continued by Renzi's Democratic Party.

Finally, the three confederations do not enjoy a good reputation among broad segments of the public, which consider the unions among those responsible for Italy's ongoing hard times (Demos and Pi 2014).[4] The unions also face serious internal problems. For instance, the CGIL, according to the CGIL National Pensioners Union' (SPI) secretary, is almost absent in the workplace, where it is no longer able to recruit the delegates needed to represent the union in the factories. This makes it difficult to renew the leadership and to maintain a satisfactory level of participation among workers in basic union activities (Cantone and Franchi 2014).[5] Moreover, many of the members the CGIL does recruit seem to believe that its leaders are relatively uninterested in being involved on the shop floor, preferring instead to carve out a comfortable space in the union's organizational structure (Cerri and Soli 2008, 43).

As far as financial support to the Democratic Party goes, there is no evidence of union donations that might promote a closer relationship between the three confederations and the PD or other parties. None of the official available information shows that the trade unions currently finance, or have financed, political parties, which have so far benefited from generous public funding, as well as from private contributions, both legal and illegal, rendering them financially independent.[6] This is backed up by responses to our questionnaire.

The other relevant currency of exchange that could reinforce collaboration between the CGIL and the Democratic Party is the electoral support that the former could give to the latter. Certainly, such support seems to have been forthcoming at the beginning of the 1980s.[7] CGIL respondents to our questionnaire, however, did not give any answer to the questions related to their electoral support to the PD, although both the PD respondents seem to suggest that the unions still mobilize in favour of the PD at list by offering labour, material resources, and union premises during election campaigns. The CGIL contribution helps to explain the success of former trade unionists in national elections. It also helps to explain the electoral success of the former trade unionists who are frequently elected to the municipal, provincial, or regional assemblies. Their success derives from an electoral base consisting of consensus networks created thanks to the services provided by the trade unions' local affiliated branches, which offer tax assistance to union members, keep members' working days registers, calculate the members' social security contributions, and assist them with their pension arrangements.

The available data (for the 2008 national elections) show that the CGIL members who vote most reliably for the PD are public employees and pensioners (Feltrin 2010, 101–3). But the effectiveness of the CGIL support to PD electoral campaigns has been declining in recent years and has led the main Italian left-of-centre party to distance itself from its ally. Indeed, the positive correlation between the party's vote and CGIL membership has weakened because the majority of Italian manual workers in the last two decades have mostly voted for centre-right political parties. Moreover, in the same period a reduction of electoral support for left-wing parties has been registered in central Italy—an area of the country that was a traditional reservoir of votes for the left and where the CGIL is still particularly strong (Feltrin 2010, 103). CGIL members feel less bound to the policy guidelines of the organization and instead take into consideration the general political climate or the situation of the area in which they live and work. At the elections for the House of Deputies of February 2013, some 40 per cent of manual workers voted in favour of the protest movement *Cinque stelle* (Five Stars), which won 25.5 per cent of the popular vote. The PD won 29.5 per cent of the popular vote but only 21.7 per cent of the workers vote—less than the share of the workers' vote won by *Popolo delle libertà* (People of Freedoms) led by Silvio Berlusconi (Demos and Pi 2013).

Traditionally the CGIL offered electoral and organizational support to the main Italian left party, receiving in return politically educated activists, access via union leaders to parliamentary positions, and worker-friendly policies passed in parliament. But its reduced ability to represent workers, and its reduced bargaining power, public reputation, and electoral support, has led the new leadership of the Democratic Party to believe that the maintenance of the traditional exchange with the unions, in particular with the CGIL, is no longer profitable. This belief resulted in a clear electoral choice before the European elections of May 2014, at which the Democratic Party distanced itself sharply from the unions, correctly calculating that any losses in terms of trade union electoral support would be largely compensated by the benefits flowing from positioning the party at the centre of the electoral spectrum and as responsive to the demands of the moderate electorate—a stance consistent with its vision of a rapid 'modernization' of the country. The PD won 40.8 per cent of the vote—the best performance by a party of the left in Italy since the introduction of parliamentary democracy.

THE DECLINING POLITICAL INFLUENCE OF UNIONS

The party–union relationship survey suggests that the PD is nevertheless interested in consulting all three unions whenever it is studying economic and social issues of general importance. Such consultation has, apparently, been more frequent with the CGIL representatives than with the other two unions. However, the already low level of institutionalization in the relations between the main party of the left and unions tends to reduce the influence of the CGIL over PD's labour and welfare policies. This trend has become more evident after recent changes at the top of the party, which have ushered in a new political class that evidently has far less time for the unions than its predecessors (Carrieri 2014).

During the 1990s and the first decade of the twenty-first century, the CGIL's influence on public policies was greater when the governments were composed of centre-left coalitions (Cella and Treu 2009). Even when the Democratic Party was forced into opposition, the influence of CGIL on social policies had some relevance, because it was able to count on the support provided in parliament and in the country by the largest party of the left (Mania and Sateriale 2002). Particularly significant was the battle that the CGIL led in early 2002 against the planned reform of the labour market by the centre-right governments of that period, and which included a liberalization of individual and collective procedures for workers' dismissal. This project was bitterly opposed by unions and they gained the support of the Democratic Party (then 'Democrats of the Left') and other minor parties of the left. At the height of the protests in Rome the CGIL mounted a demonstration attended, according to the union's official sources, by 3 million workers, prompting the government to back down and shelve the project.

The economic and financial crisis that began in 2007 further worsened in Italy in 2011 following the so-called sovereign debt crisis. This situation caused a rise in unemployment that weakened the unions, while the Democratic Party shrank its social policy promises in the light of external constraints resulting from the economic and financial crisis. This did not initially affect the maintenance of links between the unions and the PD, nor prevent a certain symmetry on social policy. However, the severity of the economic-industrial situation and the duration of the crisis have put on the agenda drastic reforms to improve the functioning of public administration and education, a relaunch of the industrial system, and a reconsideration of social policies.

On all these issues the unions have argued that nothing must be done which increases unemployment (Mania 2013). But, while the Democratic Party initially supported this approach, inside the party a heated debate raged over the need to meet the expectations and demands of European institutions and international investors. This debate began to have a negative impact on the maintenance of links, especially after the appointment of the PD's Matteo Renzi as Italy's premier. The new prime minister immediately expressed a more liberal vision of public policy and made no secret of his dislike for the intermediary institutions, in particular for the unions. This significantly reduced the unions' opportunity to influence public policy, because the prime minister wanted to avoid any form of dialogue that would put the unions in a position to block the government's reform projects. Among the measures taken by the Renzi government aimed at reviving the economy is the almost complete liberalization of dismissals in the industrial sector. This proposal, with essentially the same goals that fourteen years earlier had aroused mass protests organized by the CGIL, was included in a legislative package called the Jobs Act, which also provided a more flexible system of recruitment (Trivellato 2015). The Jobs Act aroused protests from the three confeder-ations, which considered the measure detrimental to the rights of workers legally to contest redundancies deriving from presumed disciplinary action. The national secretary of the CGIL also accused the prime minister of being the man 'of the strong powers' (La Repubblica 2014)—in other words, a puppet of industrial conglomerates—and proclaimed a national protest rally that was held in Rome on 25 October 2014. In spite of this, the Jobs Act was passed in parliament in December that year by a large majority, and one which included nearly all the former trade unionists in the ranks of the Democratic Party.

The links that the CGIL has cultivated with the main left party throughout the existence of the Italian Republic are now undergoing a sharp deterioration, and one which could escalate further because the PD's new national secretary is trying to replace the party's local leaders with people loyal to the new generation of national leaders. This replacement may well lead to the margin-alization of the officials and staff who have been the traditional partners of CGIL and who have helped to maintain the links between the two organiza-tions. If the new PD leadership is able to establish lasting control of the party—something which looks likely but is not of course guaranteed—it is probable that the (already limited) influence of the CGIL (and also of the other unions) on public policy will decline even further.

CONCLUSIONS

The fragmentation of the union movement and the divisions between Italy's left-wing parties have prevented one party establishing exclusive links with unions based on overlapping structures or mutual and lasting organizational links. However, the links between the CGIL and the PCI were numerous and durable, although not formalized at the organizational level. Such links then faded and became, after the transformation of the PCI into the PD, mainly ad hoc relations. Recently, the relationship between the CGIL and the PD has badly deteriorated, following the generational change which has occurred within the Democratic Party and the electoral success of Matteo Renzi. Two major factors contributed to the success of the Democratic Party in the recent European elections—a new, more liberal consensus on economic policy and the declared impatience of the new party leader with the trade unions. If all this means that the new Democratic Party becomes something of a cartel party (Katz and Mair 1995), then its relationship with the CGIL, already severely tested in recent years, will be reduced simply to one between a ruling party and one of the many and varied interest groups with which a party with governmental ambitions is obviously obliged to communicate.

NOTES

1. A table is not presented as there were no 'yes values' (coded judgments).
2. Direzione nazionale PD. Indice alfabetico dei membri (PD National Direction, Alphabetical index of members), in <http://www.partitodemocratico.it/utenti/direzione.htm>.
3. In 2013, 52.5 per cent of members registered to the CGIL and 47 per cent to the CISL were pensioners. Our calculations from official data published on CGIL and CISL web sites.
4. See the survey on 7,687 cases realized by Demos and Pi (2014): <http://www.demos.it/2014/pdf/3301itasta2014_20141229.pdf>.
5. See also <http://www.huffingtonpost.it/2014/04/29/carla-cantone-libro-_n_5232261.html > (accessed June 2014).
6. However, a government decree was issued at the end of 2013 providing for the abolition of public funding of political parties. But the new law will not come into effect until 2017.
7. Shortly before the general elections of 26 June 1983, the CGIL General Secretary Luciano Lama, in a speech given at the conclusion of the organization's Steering Committee meeting, reminded those present of the need for the union to support the allied parties: 'what counts is to bar the way to the old guard's attack using the ballot to prevent those political forces aiming at restoring the old social relations from prevailing. Even more so, because these are the terms of the political struggle, we invite all workers, women and young people, to vote' (CGIL 1983: 8–9).

10

The Legacy of Pillarization

Trade Union Confederations and Political Parties in the Netherlands

Simon Otjes and Anne Rasmussen

The Netherlands may look like a Scandinavian country, with political institutions that provide a fertile breeding ground for strong trade union–political party relationships. It has a large welfare state and a strong corporatist tradition. However, the relationship between the trade unions and the party political left has been rather different. Most importantly, there are strong divisions within the Dutch trade union movement reflecting the fact that Dutch society has traditionally been pillarized—divided into four subcultures with their own integrated network of societal organizations, including trade unions and parties. During this period, major parties and ideologically aligned trade unions had strong personal, organizational, and ideological ties. Trade unionism was not, therefore, exclusive to the left. In addition, Christian Democratic parties had ties with trade unions—ties which we examine in this chapter. Indeed, current Dutch trade union confederations have (part of their) roots in Christian Democratic trade unionism. In the mid-1960s these pillarized ties weakened at the mass and elite level, but the legacy of pillarization is nevertheless reflected in the fragmentation of today's party and trade union systems in the Netherlands in which trade unions interact with parties of many different political colours.

The divisions within both trade unions and political parties lead to two questions in our analysis. With which kind of trade union confederations does the Dutch social-democratic Labour Party have relationships? And do Dutch trade union confederations chose to link themselves to one party or to several?

A PILLARIZED PAST

We examine three parties and three trade union confederations. Our analysis focuses on the three government-recognized, trade union confederations: the Dutch Federation Trade Union Movement (*Federatie Nederlandse Vakbeweging*, FNV), with over a million members, is by far the largest trade union confederation; the Christian National Trade Union Confederation (*Christelijk Nationaal Vakverbond*, CNV) has a Christian-social profile and 300,000 members; and the small, white-collar Confederation for Middle and Higher Personnel (*Vakcentrale voor Middelbaar en Hoger Personeel*, MHP) with over 100,000 members, which in April 2014 reconfigured itself as the Trade Union Confederation for Professionals (*Vakcentrale voor Professionals*, VCP). On the party side, we focus on the large, centre-left Labour Party (*Partij van de Arbeid*, PvdA), which has been the main social-democratic party since 1946; the mid-sized Christian Democratic Appeal (*Christen-Democratisch Appèl*, CDA), which was formed as a merger of three Christian Democratic parties, all of which had trade union wings; and the old-left, mid-sized Socialist Party (*Socialistische Partij*, SP), which has rapidly grown since the mid-1990s.

Pillarization had its heyday between 1918 and 1967. During this period the directorates of the different pillarized organizations were interlocked. As an example, the leader of the Dutch Catholic Trade Union Confederation (*Nederlands Katholiek Vakverbond*, NKV) was a member of parliament for the Catholic People's Party (*Katholieke Volkspartij*, KVP). The Catholics represented the largest and best-organized pillar: in 1964, 80 per cent of NKV members voted KVP (Lijphart 1968a, 43). However, the links between pillarized organizations began to weaken in the 1960s. In the Catholic pillar, the NKV severed its bonds with the KVP and oriented itself more towards the PvdA (Bank 1985, 315). In less than fifteen years, the Catholic family grew apart: the KVP formed the non-denominational CDA together with two Protestant parties, and the NKV merged with the secular Dutch Trade Union Confederation (*Nederlands Verbond van Vakverenigingen*, NVV) to form the FNV.

Other pillars were weaker: the social-democrats shared some institutions (e.g. schools) with the liberals, but the relationship between the secular trade union NVV and the Labour Party was as strong as the relationship between the Catholic federation and party, the NKV and the KVP. The tacit agreement was that one NVV board member could serve as an MP and another on the national executive (Hueting et al. 1983, 157). Overlap between the two was visible at the mass-level: in 1964, 80 per cent of the NVV members voted for the PvdA and, in 1968, 44 per cent of PvdA members were members of the NVV (Lijphart 1968a, 43; Mulder 2012, 141). The links at the elite level began to weaken in the early 1970s when the agreement about mutual representation in decision-making bodies was cancelled by the PvdA. To replace these formal ties, the PvdA founded a working group of trade unionists consisting of all unions and party activists (Koole 1986, 190). However, this group was never able to fulfil its role and was dissolved in the late 1980s.

The Protestant parties and trade unions kept more of a distance from each other. The two Protestant parties, the Christian Historical Union (*Christelijk-Historische Unie*, CHU) and the Anti-Revolutionary Party (*Anti-Revolutionaire Partij*, ARP) cooperated with the CNV: it had representatives in both parliamentary parties until the early 1970s (Hazenbosch 2009, 410). After the formation of the CDA, the CNV established links with this party (Hazenbosch 2009, 521). At the voter level, 35 per cent of CNV members voted for CHU and 33 per cent voted for ARP in 1964 (Lijphart 1968a, 43). However, the conservative economic course of the Christian Democrats estranged the two (Hazenbosch 2009, 516). A formal committee of the CDA and the CNV meant for regular consultation was formed in 1981, but it was short-lived (Hazenbosch 2009, 517). Since the 1980s, CNV members have no longer voted exclusively for Christian Democratic parties (Hazenbosch 2009, 524).

Eventually, the pillarized structure started to weaken due to organizations merging across subcultural lines. The largest Dutch trade union confederation FNV was founded in 1982 as a merger of the social-democratic trade union confederation NVV and the Catholic NKV, although one Catholic trade union for higher personnel did not agree with the formation of the FNV and broke away to form the core of the white-collar MHP, the third-largest Dutch trade union confederation (van der Velden 2005, 151)—one with a right-wing economic orientation and no formal ties to parties. The FNV, meanwhile, was politically and religiously neutral (van der Velden 2005, 152). Its members were not exclusively oriented to one party: in 1986, half of FNV members voted PvdA and one-fifth CDA (van Praag 1987). According to FNV chair Wim Kok (1984, 258), the relationship between the leader of the Labour Party and the chair of the FNV was informal and irregular. Still the relationship between the two was different from other relationships: in 1986, for instance, Kok, then a trade unionist, became PvdA leader without having any previous political function. He is not the only one: five of the six FNV chairs had positions in the Labour Party before or after they left the trade union.[1] This did not, however, prevent unions and party coming into conflict when the PvdA was in government during troubled economic times, notably over sick leave in 1982, disability benefit in 1991, and the pension age in 2009 (Otjes 2016).

Depillarization also meant the development of new political parties, such as the Socialist Party. It was formed in 1971 as a Maoist split from the Communist Party, but has distanced itself from its Maoist roots and adopted a socialist course. It entered parliament in 1994, and its electoral support, especially among FNV members, grew considerably between 2000 and 2010. The SP often criticized the FNV for neglecting the interests of its members in tripartite negotiations (*Tribune* 2002). It also began to support the activist wing of the FNV. It has a special platform, *Solidair*, for SP-members who are active within the FNV and for trade unionists who share the party's vision of an activist trade union (*Tribune* 1997). Here, SP MPs and FNV activists meet to discuss agreements the FNV has made with employers or the government. In these meetings, the SP disseminates its arguments within the FNV. In this way, the SP became a potent force within it: by 2007, the SP polled better among FNV members than the PvdA (Interview NSS 2007). The SP's support of the trade union activist wing was likewise successful. The FNV now has two wings: a consensual wing oriented towards the Labour Party, willing to make compromises with employers and government, and an activist wing oriented towards the SP, unwilling to make compromises. The activist wing has become more vocal and is an important part of the trade union confederation's base. However, the consensual wing is strongest in the federation's leadership (Otjes 2016).

Pillarization left its legacy in a fragmented system of trade unions and parties. This kind of fragmentation may be less conducive to party–trade union relations because unions have to deal with many parties and vice versa. In general, there is a limited potential for exchange relationships between Dutch trade unions and political parties. Trade unions cannot offer Dutch parties a reliable constituency. Even if Dutch citizens tend to have very positive views of trade unions compared to political parties (van der Velden 2005, 1), the Netherlands has moderate levels of trade union density in comparative terms: by 2013 less than one fifth of the Dutch workers were unionized. Moreover, even in the 1960s the Netherlands scored among the lowest levels of class voting in comparative perspective: despite the fact that the Netherlands did have a sizeable working class, it was divided between religious groups. Depillarization did not increase the levels of class voting: although the religious working class increasingly voted for the PvdA, the social-democrats lost their control over the secular working class (Nieuwbeerta 1996, 356). At the same time, the size of the working class dwindled to a fifth of the population. Finally, trade unions do not now offer parties finance, since the Dutch parties primarily rely on state subventions and membership fees (Andeweg and Irwin 2008, 78).[2] The main asset trade union confederations can offer parties is therefore public support: their relative popularity can be used by political parties to boost legitimacy. However, the exchange of general support between the government and the trade unions is typically much more important than trade union support of an individual party's proposal.

Corporatism has been a key feature of Dutch politics since the Second World War. The most important corporatist body is the Social-Economic Council (*Sociaal-Economische Raad*, SER), which advises the government on social-economic policy. A third of its members are appointed by the three recognized trade union confederations. Some argue (see Chapter 1 in this volume) that corporatism fosters strong relationships between left-wing parties and trade unions, but the Dutch case may show that things are more complex. The institutionalized dialogue between the government and trade union confederations undermines the need for a privileged relationship between specific trade union confederations and specific parties. Instead, trade union confederations have a direct connection to the government, independent of its composition (Poppe 1980; Kok 1984). As left-wing parties have only been in government in the Netherlands for less than half of the last fifty years, left-wing parties do not offer trade unions an instant pathway to power. Corporatist structures, however, do so. Dutch trade unions have to deal with right-wing coalitions more often than not. In this way, associating too closely with the Labour Party means associating closely with an opposition party, which potentially weakens the ability of trade unions to make deals with the government.

Dutch governments are formed by a system of partially altering coalition governments: each coalition is formed by two out of three core parties: the Labour Party, the Liberal Party, and the major Christian Democratic party (until 1977 it was the KVP and afterwards the CDA). This makes coalition negotiations unpredictable: as every combination of two of these three parties is possible, it is unclear after elections which government will take office. Arguably, the pattern of coalition governance affects interest group–party collaboration: insecurity regarding future coalition formation means that interest groups cannot afford to lobby ideologically close parties exclusively, but need to lobby all three major parties (Otjes and Rasmussen 2015).

RELATIONSHIPS TODAY: MAPPING OF LINKS

Our empirical evidence on the nature of the relationship between the social-democratic Labour Party, the Christian Democratic CDA, the Socialist Party, and the three recognized trade union federations (the large FNV, Christian-social CNV, and white-collar MHP) is derived from the party–union relationship survey, i.e. structured interviews conducted with leading members of these organizations in late 2013.[3]

One thing emerged immediately: trade unions did not have overlapping organizational structures with parties. Moreover, collective membership has never existed. Guaranteed access to decision-making bodies used to exist within the context of pillarization but disappeared in the early 1970s.[4]

The Absence of Durable Links

As Table 10.1 shows, durable links are also quite rare. The PvdA has the strongest durable ties with the largest confederation, the FNV. Two out of

Table 10.1. Reciprocal, durable inter-organizational links between party central organization/legislative group and union confederation, last five years (c.2008–13)[1]

Party-confederation dyad—CPO	PvdA-FNV		PvdA-CNV		PvdA-MHP		SP-FNV		SP-CNV		SP-MHP		CDA-FNV		CDA-CNV		CDA-MHP	
	P/U	CJ	P/U	CJ	P/U	CJ	P/U	CJ	P/U	CJ	P/U	CJ	P/U	CJ	P/U	CJ	P/U	CJ
Tacit agreements about one-sided/ mutual representation in national decision-making bodies	No	No	No	No	No	No	No	No	No	No	No	No	No	No	No	No	No	No
Permanent joint committee(s)	No	No	No	No	No	No	No	No	No	No	No	No	No	No	No	No	No	No
Temporary joint committee(s)	No	No	No	No	No	No	No	No	No	No	No	No	No	No	c.d.	No	Yes	Yes
Formal agreements about regular meetings between party and organization	No	No	No	No	No	No	No	No	No	No	No	No	No	No	No	No	No	No
Tacit agreements about regular meetings between party and organization	c.d.	Yes	No	No	No	No	c.d.	Yes	No	No	No	No	No	No	No	No	No	No
Joint conferences	No	No	No	No	No	No	No	No	No	No	No	No	No	No	No	No	No	No
Joint campaigns	Yes	Yes	No	No	No	No	c.d.	Yes	No	No	No	No	No	No	No	No	No	No

Party-confederation dyad—LPG	PvdA-FNV		PvdA-CNV		PvdA-MHP		SP-FNV		SP-CNV		SP-MHP		CDA-FNV		CDA-CNV		CDA-MHP	
	P/U	CJ	P/U	CJ	P/U	CJ	P/U	CJ	P/U	CJ	P/U	CJ	P/U	CJ	P/U	CJ	P/U	CJ
Tacit agreements about one-sided/ mutual representation in national decision-making bodies	No	No	No	No	No	No	No	No	No	No	No	No	No	No	No	No	No	No
Permanent joint committee(s)	No	No	No	No	No	No	No	No	No	No	No	No	No	No	No	No	No	No
Temporary joint committee(s)	No	No	No	No	No	No	No	No	No	No	No	No	No	No	No	No	c.d.	No

(continued)

Table 10.1. Continued

Party-confederation dyad—CPO	PvdA-FNV		PvdA-CNV		PvdA-MHP		SP-FNV		SP-CNV		SP-MHP		CDA-FNV		CDA-CNV		CDA-MHP	
	P/U	CJ	P/U	CJ	P/U	CJ	P/U	CJ	P/U	CJ	P/U	CJ	P/U	CJ	P/U	CJ	P/U	CJ
Formal agreements about regular meetings between party and organization	No	No	No	No	No	No	No	No	No	No	No	No	No	No	No	No	No	No
Tacit agreements about regular meetings between party and organization	c.d.	Yes	c.d.	Yes	No	No	c.d.	Yes	No	No	No	No	c.d.	Yes	c.d.	Yes	No	No
Joint conferences	c.d.	No	No	No	No	No	No	No	No	No	No	No	No	No	No	No	No	No
Joint campaigns	Yes	Yes	No	No	No	No	Yes	Yes	No	No	No	No	No	No	No	No	No	No

[1] 'P/U' indicates responses from party/trade union questionnaires, 'CJ' signifies the authors' 'coded judgment' based on alternative sources in cases of diverging or missing P/U answers. 'c.d.' means contradictory data (diverging P/U answers), 'n.d.' means no data (informant didn't know/missing/unclear), and 'n.a.' means not applicable in this case.

three informants reported a tacit agreement regarding an informal discussion group between the chair of the FNV, its parliamentary lobbyists and its policy advisors, the PvdA chair, PvdA MPs, and their policy advisors. It was set up in 2012 and meets two to four times a year. The goal of this group is to provide an opportunity for the FNV to give input to the Labour Party, and it was formed as a reaction to the growing influence of the Socialist Party on the FNV.

The range of the FNV's political network goes beyond the PvdA, since its chair meets with the chairs of all parliamentary parties in a yearly round in September. Both FNV and PvdA representatives refer to the existence of joint campaigns by the PvdA and the FNV, such as a joint campaign by the Labour Party, the small left-wing party GreenLeft, and the FNV about childcare facilities around 2005. When the PvdA was in opposition, the social-democrats (but also the SP and GreenLeft) regularly supported FNV demonstrations. One interviewee pointed, as an example, to the campaign 'Poverty Does Not Work', which the FNV organized against the budget cuts of the first Rutte cabinet. The representative of the Labour Party's parliamentary party also mentioned joint conferences, but we found no specific examples of such conferences within the last ten years. The PvdA has weaker durable ties with the Christian-social CNV. The trade union representative mentioned the existence of a tacit agreement with the parliamentary party group to meet regularly. In contrast, there are no durable links between the Labour Party and the white-collar MHP.

The Socialist Party is linked exclusively to the FNV. The representative of the SP board (but not the FNV representative him or herself) mentioned a tacit agreement between the party and the FNV to meet regularly; there is at least one regular meeting in the September round. As mentioned earlier, the SP regularly organizes meetings where trade union activists and MPs discuss current affairs. However, unlike the regular talks between the PvdA and the FNV, these meetings focus on the trade union base, not its leadership, and the emphasis is on what the SP feels the FNV should do. Both sides mentioned joint campaigns: the SP is often active at FNV demonstrations and strikes, where it supports the unionists with soup, sandwiches, and leaflets. The SP has no durable links with the CNV or the MHP.

As the main Christian Democratic party, the CDA has historic ties with all three recognized trade unions or their predecessors. This is reflected in limited durable ties between the Christian Democrats and the FNV and CNV respectively. At least one side reports a tacit agreement regarding regular meetings between the Christian Democratic legislative party group and the leadership of the FNV and the CNV respectively. The leaders of the FNV and the Christian Democrats meet at least during the September round. The respondents from the CDA and MHP also mentioned the existence of temporary joint committees between the CDA and the CNV and the MHP respectively. However, the existence of such joint committees was neither supported by the CNV nor by additional written sources.[5]

The Ubiquity of Occasional Links

Occasional links are far more prevalent than durable links and they encompass a broader range of actors, as can be seen in Table 10.2.

All possible forms of occasional links between the Labour Party and the FNV were mentioned by at least one of the three respondents. As a principle, the FNV invites all national political parties to its conference. All three trade union confederations are also invited to the party conference of the PvdA. The occasional links between the Labour Party and the CNV are also relatively tight, although they are almost completely focused on the legislative party group. The only activities between trade unions and parties not mentioned by either side are special consultative arrangements of the parliamentary party.

The two trade unions approach the PvdA differently. Whereas the FNV is more focused on the Labour Party as a whole, the Christian-social CNV focuses on the political decision-makers in The Hague—perhaps a remnant of the special relationship between the PvdA and the FNV. Finally, links between the Labour Party and the white-collar MHP are limited to party and trade federation conferences and ordinary meetings initiated by the party.

As with the PvdA, all forms of occasional links between the Socialist Party and the FNV were mentioned by at least by one side. In contrast, there are no occasional links at all between the SP and the CNV and MHP. The SP is a party single-mindedly focused on the FNV; the CNV and the MHP appear to take no interest in the SP. Given the ideological difference between them, this is not surprising.

The Christian Democrats appear to have the most ubiquitous, occasional links with trade unions: almost every kind of link was mentioned by at least one side for every trade union. The only exception is that the CDA has not been invited to any special consultative meeting initiated by the MHP. The Christian Democratic central party organization is more active than the legislative party group, as it is invited to and invites trade unions to special consultative meetings, to which the legislative party group is not invited.

Individual-level Links: Individual Contacts and Personnel Overlaps and Transfers

Personal links between trade union confederations and parties can contribute to the smooth running of a corporatist democratic system. Here, we will look

Table 10.2. One-way, occasional links at the organizational level between party central organization/legislative group and union confederation, last five years (c.2008–13)[1]

Party-confederation dyad—CPO	PvdA-FNV		PvdA-CNV		PvdA-MHP		SP-FNV		SP-CNV		SP-MHP		CDA-FNV		CDA-CNV		CDA-MHP	
	P/U	CJ	P/U	CJ	P/U	CJ	P/U	CJ	P/U	CJ	P/U	CJ	P/U	CJ	P/U	CJ	P/U	CJ
Invitation to party to participate in the organization's national congress	Yes	Yes	No	No	c.d.	Yes	Yes	Yes	No	No	No	No	c.d.	Yes	Yes	Yes	Yes	Yes
Invitation to organization to participate in the party's national congress/conference	Yes	Yes	c.d.	Yes	c.d.	Yes	Yes	Yes	No	No	No	No	Yes	Yes	c.d.	Yes	Yes	Yes
Invitations to organization to participate in the party's ordinary meetings, seminars, and conferences	Yes	Yes	No	No	c.d.	Yes	Yes	Yes	No	No	No	No	c.d.	Yes	c.d.	Yes	Yes	Yes
Invitations to party to participate in ordinary organization meetings, seminars, and conferences	c.d.	Yes	No	No	No	No	Yes	Yes	No	No	No	No	c.d.	Yes	c.d.	Yes	Yes	Yes
Invitations to organization to special consultative arrangements initiated by the party	c.d.	Yes	No	No	No	No	Yes	Yes	No	No	No	No	Yes	Yes	c.d.	Yes	c.d.	Yes
Invitations to party to special consultative arrangements initiated by the organization	c.d.	Yes	No	No	No	No	Yes	Yes	No	No	No	No	c.d.	Yes	c.d.	Yes	No	No

Party-confederation dyad—LPG	PvdA-FNV		PvdA-CNV		PvdA-MHP		SP-FNV		SP-CNV		SP-MHP		CDA-FNV		CDA-CNV		CDA-MHP	
	P/U	CJ	P/U	CJ	P/U	CJ	P/U	CJ	P/U	CJ	P/U	CJ	P/U	CJ	P/U	CJ	P/U	CJ
Invitation to party to participate in the organization's national congress	Yes	Yes	c.d.	Yes	c.d.	Yes	Yes	Yes	No	No	No	No	c.d.	Yes	c.d.	Yes	c.d.	Yes

(continued)

Table 10.2. Continued

Party-confederation dyad—CPO	PvdA-FNV		PvdA-CNV		PvdA-MHP		SP-FNV		SP-CNV		SP-MHP		CDA-FNV		CDA-CNV		CDA-MHP	
	P/U	CJ	P/U	CJ	P/U	CJ	P/U	CJ	P/U	CJ	P/U	CJ	P/U	CJ	P/U	CJ	P/U	CJ
Invitation to organization to participate in the party's national congress/conference	n.a.	n.a.	n.a.	n.a.	n.a.	n.a.	n.a.	n.a.	n.a.	n.a.	n.a.	n.a.	n.a.	n.a.	n.a.	n.a.	n.a.	n.a.
Invitations to organization to participate in the party's ordinary meetings, seminars, and conferences	Yes	Yes	c.d.	Yes	c.d.	Yes	Yes	Yes	No	No	No	No	c.d.	Yes	c.d.	Yes	c.d.	Yes
Invitations to party to participate in ordinary organization meetings, seminars, and conferences	Yes	Yes	Yes	Yes	No	No	Yes	Yes	No	No	No	No	c.d.	Yes	c.d.	Yes	c.d.	Yes
Invitations to organization to special consultative arrangements initiated by the party	Yes	Yes	No	No	No	No	Yes	Yes	No	No	No	No	c.d.	Yes	No	No	No	No
Invitations to party to special consultative arrangements initiated by the organization	Yes	Yes	c.d.	Yes	No	No	Yes	Yes	No	No	No	No	c.d.	Yes	No	No	No	No

1 'P/U' indicates responses from party/trade union questionnaires, 'CJ' signifies the authors' 'coded judgment' based on alternative sources in cases of diverging or missing P/U answers. 'c.d.' means contradictory data (diverging P/U answers), 'n.d.' means no data (informant didn't know/missing/unclear), and 'n.a.' means not applicable in this case.

at the nature of the communication between trade unionists and political parties, and whether MPs have roots in the trade union movement.

The PvdA and the SP on the one hand and the FNV on the other communicate through informal channels primarily, such as face-to-face conversations. There appears to be less communication between the CNV and the MHP, on the one hand, and the Labour Party, on the other hand. The CNV and the SP communicate through formal letters and informal face-to-face meetings. The CDA's communication with all three trade union confederations takes place via formal letters, and informal written and oral communication.

Informal communication works best if MPs and trade unionists have a shared background. Figure 10.1 shows the share of PvdA, SP, and CDA members of parliament that hold or have held positions as officials and staff in the confederations of trade unions at the national level (including both the lower and the upper house).[6] In 2013, SP, the Labour Party, and the Liberal Party, as well as the GreenLeft, had one representative of the FNV in their lower house group. Similarly, the CDA and the GreenLeft had one representative of the CNV in its lower house group. One of the PvdA MPs has worked for a MHP affiliated union. In the upper house, there are four representatives of trade union confederations: two representatives of the FNV (for the PvdA and the SP) and two of the CNV (for the PvdA and the CDA).

We have also examined the extent to which there are union-affiliated MPs in the Social-Economic Council, which is the pinnacle of the Dutch corporatist system. Eleven members of this official advisory body of the government are appointed by trade union confederations. In 2013, six of the eleven had public ties to parties. Three of the eight FNV councillors were members of the Labour Party, whereas one was a member of the social-liberal D66. One of the two CNV representatives and the sole MHP-member were Christian Democrats.

Overall Degree of Closeness and Range

We have discussed a number of different ways to assess the closeness of the trade union confederations and parties. We looked at durable and occasional links between parties and unions. Figures 10.2a and 10.2b present the total organizational scores of each possible pair of party and union confederation. Here we see that PvdA-FNV and the SP-FNV obtain the highest scores in both party spheres, approaching a medium level of strength. The scores for CDA and CNV are also worth noting, although somewhat lower, while in the other cases we see that links are generally weaker or non-existent.

If we also take account of the other data available, our results indicate that we can distinguish between four levels of intensity. First there are dyads between parties and trade unions, with a limited number of durable links

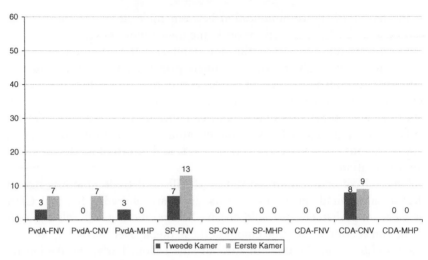

Figure 10.1. Share of PvdA, SP, and CDA MPs in 2013/14 that hold or have held positions as officials or staff in the confederations of unions at the national level.[1]

[1] Composition of both houses on 1 January 2014. N of MPs is 38 for PvdA, 15 for SP, and 13 for CDA in the Tweede Kamer, 14 for PvdA, 8 for SP, and 11 for CDA in the Eerste Kamer.

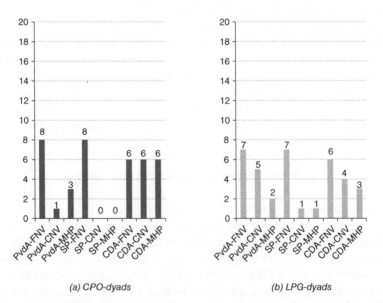

Figure 10.2. Total link scores of central party organization–trade union relationships and legislative party–trade union relationships (0–20/0–12).[1]

[1] The theoretical maximum link score is 20 for the CPO-dyads and 12 for LPG-dyads since some link items are unlikely to apply to the legislative party group and were thus not included in this part of the survey. However, when comparing dyads involving CPOs with those involving LPGs, one should still keep in mind that the latter's maximum involves fewer links than the former's top scores.

but with a high number of occasional and personal links: the relationships between the FNV and PvdA and Socialist Party respectively. Even if the relationship of the FNV with the former is somewhat stronger than the relationship with the latter, there are a number of signs that the relationship between the FNV and the Labour Party and the SP respectively are different from the other relationships analysed here. Our study may downplay the character of the 'special relationship' between the two somewhat, since the only indicator that taps the special relationship is the tacit agreement to meet regularly. The FNV reports meeting regularly with all parties, but the question is what is discussed during these meetings? As one FNV-chair put it: the PvdA is one of a number of parties with which the FNV is in dialogue, 'but it is one with which we try to think a bit more about strategy' (Godfroid 1995). In contrast, the SP primarily has an intensive working relationship with the activist wing of the FNV, but not its consensual wing. The SP has pursued a strategy of mobilizing activists within the FNV. By organizing the activist wing of the base level of the trade union, the SP has become a major player *within* the trade union.

The second group of relations involves occasional links of a less intensive nature than the first category. Such links exist between the CDA and the Christian-social CNV and the white collar MHP respectively, as well as between the Labour Party and the CNV. Third, we have a group of dyads characterized by distant relationships. Examples include the links between the FNV and the Christian Democrats, and between the MHP and the PvdA. As a neutral trade union confederation, the FNV formally treats the Christian Democrats in an equal manner to other parties, but there is little love lost between them. The same is true of the relationship between the MHP and the Labour Party. Finally, and at the other end of the scale, we find examples of no collaboration. The relationships between the SP and the MHP and the CNV respectively are examples of dyads which involve no collaboration at all.

We also asked the trade union confederations and party representatives to assess the strength of these relationships themselves (shown in Figure 10.3).

Most of the relationships do not exceed the level of an 'ad hoc relationship', notwithstanding a few durable links. This is how the PvdA and the largest trade union confederation FNV both describe their relationship, and how the PvdA, CDA, and SP representatives describe their relationship with the Christian-social CNV. Parties and the trade union confederations tend to work together when they have a shared interest. The respondent from the SP describes the relationship between the party and the union as 'fairly' close, whereas the FNV representative describes it as 'ad hoc'. It is perhaps most appropriate to say that the SP has a fairly close relationship with the activist wing of the federation. The relationships between the white-collar MHP and the SP and PvdA respectively are weaker than their relationship with the Christian Democrats. The left-wing parties feel distant from this white-collar

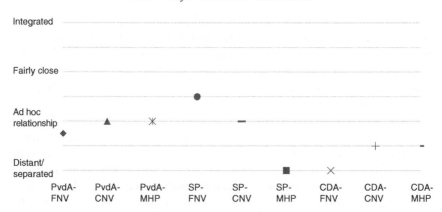

Figure 10.3. Rating of overall degree of closeness/distance (average score) between the party and union confederation, last five years (*c*.2008–13).[1]

[1] Ratings in-between two categories reflect that the party and union responses to the survey question differed. None of the ratings differed with more than one category. The PvdA-CNV, SP-CNV, and CDA-CNV ratings reflect the party's rating only since CNV answered the survey question with 'Not applicable.'

trade union confederation and the MHP itself thinks that its relationship to these parties is ad hoc. Finally, the relationship between the CDA and the FNV is more distant than the FNV's relationship with the SP and the Labour Party. Both the CDA and the PvdA have a broad range of links to each of the three trade union confederations, although these are weaker as the ideological distance between the union confederations and the parties increases. The SP is focused single-mindedly on the FNV.

In order to discuss the range of these relationships from the unions' point of view, it is necessary to also consider the other parties in the Dutch multiparty system. Officially the FNV is neutral, which means that it invites all political parties to its congresses and meetings. When it comes to more durable links, such as common campaigns, the party is more focused on the Labour Party and SP, as well as the smaller left-wing party GreenLeft. The CNV also mentions GreenLeft as a cooperative partner. Finally, the MHP reports that it has some links with the social-liberal D66 and the Liberal Party.

The overall image is one in which the FNV has a broad network of links to different parties but a special relationship with the PvdA and a somewhat more complex one with the SP. In contrast, the CNV focuses on the Christian Democrats and the Labour Party. The MHP has weaker links with parties but focuses on the political right rather than the political left.

Compared to the period of pillarization, party–union relationships have changed in terms of intensity and range. During pillarization, there were close, exclusive relationships in each pillar where directorates of trade unions and political parties interlocked and their support bases overlapped. Such links have now disappeared. The merger of Catholic and socialist trade union confederations into the FNV meant the end of pillarized relationships. As a politically neutral trade union confederation, the FNV talks to and invites all parties. However, there are remnants of a special relationship between some trade unions and the PvdA, but it has weakened over time. All three respondents report a growing distance from the FNV. One reason is that tensions between the Labour Party and FNV have grown on specific political issues. All respondents mention problems related to the rise of the pension age (discussed in greater detail later in the chapter). Recently, a communication structure between the leadership of the PvdA and the FNV has been set up to ease the relationship between the two. At the same time, we see 'a new kid on the bloc': the Socialist Party. The party itself reports increasing closeness to all confederations, although only the FNV respondent reciprocates this view. The SP has been active within the FNV since the mid-1990s and has gained ground in the mid-2000s in particular. The orientation of the FNV to both the SP and the Labour Party reflects a tension within its base. It has a growing 'radical' wing oriented towards the SP (which is stronger in the confederation's base), and a 'consensual' wing with strong ties to the PvdA (which is stronger in the confederation's leadership).

The relationship between the CNV and the new CDA was never as close as its relationship to the Protestant parties had been. Currently, the CNV appears to have as close a link to the Labour Party as it has to the Christian Democrats. As the MHP was formed after pillarization, it has always operated independently.

CUTTING LINKS, CORPORATISM, AND COALITION GOVERNMENT

The intimate relationships between particular political parties and trade unions that used to exist under pillarization have disappeared. Why did this happen? Depillarization, but also continuing patterns of corporatism and coalition government, are possible explanations. First, depillarization itself meant that parties and trade union confederations cut their ties and reorganized along new lines: the FNV was meant to unite all workers, religious or secular. Therefore it was set up to be politically neutral. After the CDA was formed in the late 1970s it pursued more conservative economic policies, estranging the Christian-social CNV. Close relationships between parties and trade unions were no longer appropriate in an era in which citizens no longer identified themselves as Catholic, Protestant, social-democratic, or liberal. At the same time, trade unions had relatively little to offer parties in terms of a traditional, direct exchange relationship. Pillarization had resulted in low levels of class voting in the Netherlands, which continue today.

Moreover, the size of the working class has been shrinking and the level of union membership is low.

Second, the context in which the parties and trade union confederations acted undermined the need for cooperation with specific parties. Corporatism means that trade unions have the attention of the government irrespective of who is in power. This goes against the standard hypothesis that corporatism would foster close relationships between parties and trade unions. If the trade union confederations act in too partisan a manner they lose the ability to work with right-wing governments. Instead, trade unions must have good relations with all political parties that are likely to get into government in the fragmented Dutch party system. With frequent changes in government composition and the fragmented party system, there is no guarantee that the PvdA will be in government. This also means that the direct exchange of votes for policy influence is unlikely to play a major role in the relationship between trade union confederations and parties. In corporatist structures, this exchange of policy influence for support occurs between political parties of any colour, trade union confederations, and employers.

What may account for differences in the closeness between different pairs of parties and unions today? More specifically: why are the relationships between certain pairs of unions and parties (such as the FNV and the PvdA, or the MHP and the CDA) closer than between others (such as the CNV and the SP)? First, the extent to which unions and parties hold similar policy positions plays a role. Trade union confederations and parties have their own agendas. However, the left-wing agenda of the FNV comes closer to the agenda of the SP and the Labour Party. In contrast, the MHP and CNV are much more open to welfare state reform. Whereas the centrist CNV still shares some positions with the PvdA it is much further away from the SP than from the Christian Democrats. The white-collar MHP (and its successor) is close to the political right.

Second, resources play a role in the closeness of the relationship that develops. Although trade unions are unlikely to deliver votes directly, the trade union confederations can give public support to governments or they can organize public protests against government policy. Trade union confederations can be a useful ally for both government *and* opposition parties. The exchange between the government and trade unions occurs outside of partisan politics in corporatist structures: government parties trade influence on policy for public support. Trade union support for welfare state reforms is particularly important for the Labour Party. Its left-wing credentials have been under threat, which has led to the rise of the SP. Trade union confederations focus on collaborating with larger parties that are in government or had a history of government participation. Moreover, one of the reasons that the relationships between the SP and the trade union confederations improved is the increased size of the SP.

Finally, agency plays a role in understanding differences in closeness between unions and parties. It would be a mistake to consider trade union confederations as unitary organizations that are able to set a completely collective course. Skilful parties can make use of the fact that Dutch trade union confederations are organized democratically and participate in union politics. The SP has used this opportunity to support the radical *wing* of the FNV. In this way it has been able to ensure that the FNV is much closer to the SP than it is likely to have been without its involvement.

RELEVANCE: COMPARING THE PENSION AGE AND LABOUR MARKET REFORMS

Even though the relationships between Dutch political parties and trade unions are not institutionalized, they are of political significance. The existing party–union links contribute to the smooth running of a corporatist demo-cratic system and also to the ability of governments to implement changes with broad support. One can see this in how the governments and trade unions cooperated during two major reforms after the financial crisis in the Netherlands: the rise of the pension age (2009–11) and the reform of the labour market (2013). There are important differences in the closeness of the links between trade unions and politicians in the two cases, with important implications for the speed of decision making and policy outcomes.

The first case is the proposal of a centre-left cabinet of Christian Democrats and social-democrats to raise the retirement age in 2009. The largest trade union confederation, the FNV, opposed this reform. The FNV-chair announced that she would make a deal with anyone (including 'the devil and his mother') in order to save the pension age. At the same time, informal contacts between the FNV and Labour Party were under pressure, as there were no FNV represen-tatives in the PvdA's legislative party group (Otjes 2016). Due to the FNV's resistance, decisions on the reform measures were postponed. New elections were held and the FNV had to accept the reform when it was proposed again by a centre-right government. The agreement passed through parlia-ment with the support of the Labour Party. The SP had been opposed to the reform and chastised the FNV for having acted against the interests of its supporters. The two largest unions in the FNV voted against the pension agreement, plunging the organization into an internal crisis. The case was one in which the weakened relationship between the PvdA and the FNV hurt both: they had to accept the pension age reform on the terms put forward by the centre-right.

The second case is the reform of the dismissal law and unemployment benefits presented by the Liberal/Labour government in 2013. Plans for this reform dated back to the late 2000s, but had faced opposition. After the pension crisis, the FNV appointed a former Labour Party MP as its chair and the PvdA put a former trade unionist high on its list of candidates, with the two organizations intensifying their contacts. This allowed the new government to put forward its proposal for major reform of labour market policies with support from the FNV. The return of corporatist politics helped the government ensure broad approval for its policies, while allowing the trade unions to exert more influence on decision making.

The difference between the two cases underlines the value of contacts between politicians and trade unionists for both sides: politicians can adopt reforms more quickly and with greater support; trade union confederations get more influence on policy. Both reforms took place within the same, formal corporatist structure, but resulted in very different outcomes as a result of the decision by the Labour Party to improve its relationship with the FNV. Contacts between the two improved both the smoothness and the speed of decision making.

CONCLUSION: POST-PILLARIZED RELATIONSHIPS

In the Netherlands today, political parties and trade union confederations operate independently of each other and mainly decide to cooperate when they have a common interest. The relationships between Dutch parties and trade union confederations are comparatively and historically weak: the strong ties that existed between Dutch political parties and trade unions during pillarization have disappeared and are weaker than they are in some other countries (see Chapter 15 in this volume).

Among the few formal durable links that exist between parties and trade unions, the strongest ones consist of support for each other's campaigns. Such links exist especially between the largest trade union confederation, the FNV, and the social-democratic PvdA and Socialist Party respectively. Occasional links are in place between the Labour Party and the Christian-social CNV, whereas the Christian Democrats have instead had weak ties to the white-collar MHP and the Christian-social CNV. Overall, the different trade union confederations chose to have weaker relationships with many political parties rather than an intensive relationship with one party only.

There are a number of explanations for the decline and lack of highly institutionalized links between parties and trade union confederations. First, the process of depillarization loosened the bonds between parties and unions so that specific trade union members no longer exclusively vote for one party. Second, corporatism means that trade unions do not need to have exclusive links with specific parties, as they have a direct link to the government no matter who is in power. When it comes to explaining variation in links between parties and trade unions at the individual level, it matters whether the actors involved have shared policy preferences. As an example, we found that the SP has better ties with the left-wing FNV than with the centrist CNV and MHP, while the Christian Democrats also have ties to these centrist organizations.

Despite the relatively weak links between trade unions and parties in the Netherlands, there is evidence that such links can play an important role in smoothing decision-making in practice. This was illustrated in a comparison between the reforms of the pension age (2009–11) and the labour market (2013–14). In the former, the lack of collaboration between the FNV and the PvdA resulted in controversial and difficult decision-making. In the latter, intensified contacts between the two led to a smoother decision-making process and resulted in broader support for the chosen policy. In this way, the special relationship between the Labour Party and the largest trade union confederation in the Netherlands can still be useful, not least as a means of greasing the wheels of the country's democratic corporatist system.

NOTES

1. Johan Stekelenburg (FNV chair 1988–97) was a PvdA-senator; Lodewijk de Waal (FNV chair 1997–2005) was a symbolic candidate on the PvdA list in 2010; Agnes Jongerius (FNV chair 2005–12) is currently a PvdA MEP; Ton Heerts (FNV chair 2012–current) was a PvdA MP before becoming FNV chair.
2. The only example of a financial link between a party and a trade union we could find concerned the NKV and the KVP in the 1950s (Bank 1985, 310).
3. The GreenLeft is included in the study at large, but not in this country chapter due to space constraints. Our key informants in the other cases were:
   (1) the chief of staff of the PvdA parliamentary party;
   (2) the chief of staff of the CDA parliamentary party;
   (3) the secretary-general of the SP executive;
   (4) the chair of the CDA;
   (5) a member of the executive of the PvdA;
   (6) the parliamentary lobbyist of the FNV;
   (7) one of the two co-chairs of the MHP; and
   (8) an advisor to the board of the CNV.
4. A table is not presented as there were no 'yes values' (coded judgments).
5. Moreover, because our MHP respondent sat on the CDA board *à titre personnel*, the nature of the committees may have been blurred.
6. Data were obtained from the Parliamentary Documentation Centre (2014).

11

Two Branches of the Same Tree?

Party–Union Links in Sweden in the Twenty-First Century

Jenny Jansson

The relationship between the Swedish Social Democrats and trade unions has traditionally been an intimate one, at least in comparative terms (Epstein 1967, 149–50). The social democratic party SAP (*Socialdemokratiska arbetar-partiet*) and the Trade Union Confederation LO (*Landsorganisationen*) were powerful organizations, and they constitute the prototype of a successful historical cooperation between parties and unions. SAP, founded in 1889, was the driving force behind the establishment of an umbrella organization for trade unions in Sweden. Ever since, the two organizations have been seen as 'two branches of the same tree'. When the labour movement fragmented in many other countries in the 1910s and 1920s, LO ensured its members remained well-behaved social democrats (Jansson 2012, 2013). Collective affiliation to the party was practiced for local union sections. National unions made large grants to the national party and, as in Britain, furnished much of the campaign apparatus at election time.

Social democracy did extremely well in Sweden during most of the twentieth century: union density was high; SAP governed Sweden for forty-four years in a row (1932–76); and the corporatist system introduced during the first half of the twentieth century gave extensive powers to the union movement and the employers' organization. The 1950s and 1960s was the 'golden age' of social democracy: Sweden experienced full employment, the welfare state system expanded, comprehensive all-inclusive social insurance schemes were introduced, and wage inequality was actively combatted. Cooperation ran smoothly between the party and the trade union movement.

Since the 1970s, however, this happy marriage has undergone several crises due to economic, social, and political changes. The corporatist system has declined. As in other Western European countries, the working class has shrunk in size. Voting patterns among union members have changed. Although union density is comparatively high in Sweden, union density has declined in the working class. These structural changes challenge the traditional cooperation between SAP and LO and call for a re-examination of party–union links.

FROM SUCCESSFUL COOPERATION TO 'THE WAR OF THE ROSES'

An important component of SAP's traditional success was its cooperation with LO. Institutional settings in Sweden have also worked in favour of such cooperation: Sweden is a unitary state, and has parliamentary governments and a proportional election system. SAP's and LO's common history has been considered a successful exchange of resources (Allern et al. 2007; Öberg 1994): SAP has been able to offer access to government and could thus implement social and labour market policies favoured by LO. LO, on the other hand, had the resources to mobilize its members to vote for SAP; it also had financial resources to contribute to the party.

One key component for the social democratic dominance, and possibly an effect of party–union alignment (Padgett and Paterson 1991, 178), was the cooperation between LO and the employers' organization that began in the 1930s and ensured peaceful labour market relations. The 1920s had been chaotic, with innumerable labour market conflicts which affected the whole economy. When SAP won the elections in the 1930s, the government threatened both sides that it would legislate on wages unless they could agree on a model for solving labour market conflicts. As a result, LO, which had previously advocated free collective bargaining—wages should not be dependent on the will of parliament or the state but decided solely by agreements between unions and employers—concluded a labour market agreement with the employers' organization in 1938 which became the start of a very long period of peace. During this time, the corporatist system was developed. The institutionalized cooperation between interest groups and the state resulted in representation on government agencies' boards for both LO and the employers' organization.

Cooperation ran smoothly until the 1970s and especially the 1980s. LO radicalized and pressured the party to legislate both on workplace democracy (increasing employees' impact on working conditions) and on wage-earner funds (meant to distribute the profits of Swedish industry between employers and employees). The funds came to be very controversial, even among social democrats (Johansson and Magnusson 2012, chapter 6; Lewin 2002, chapter 9). These internal disagreements, known as 'the war of the roses'—a reference to the party symbol, the rose (Englund 1984)—continued into the next decade.

But if LO was the dominant partner in the relationship in the 1970s and 1980s, this changed in the wake of the economic crisis in the 1990s. The crisis has been compared to the depression in the 1920s and struck Sweden very hard (Magnusson 2006, 24). Not only was the union movement, like the party, shocked by the unemployment rate (the highest since the 1920s), the employers' organization had decided only a few years earlier to leave the corporatist system, forcing the union movement to do the same (Johansson 2000). Moreover, SAP was in opposition when the economic crisis started and this probably gave LO unrealistic expectations about what a social democratic government actually could and would do. When, then, the party won the 1994 general election, cracks in party–union cooperation became more and more visible. Ever since SAP adopted Keynesianism in the 1930s, the primary goal had been to fight unemployment (often at the expense of inflation), and this is almost certainly what LO assumed that SAP would continue doing. Instead, SAP abandoned Keynesianism and unemployment became secondary to fighting inflation, as Minister of Finance Göran Persson (who in 1995 was elected party leader) became the engineer of the social democrats' new policy. As a consequence the relationship between the party and the union movement grew decidedly chilly (Persson and Kask 1997; Johansson and Magnusson 2012, chapter 11).

For many years, LO members were collectively affiliated to SAP. In 1908 a decision was made to affiliate local union sections to the party (Casparsson 1947, 144–55). It required an active act from the member to renounce his or her party membership. The SAP's opponents tried their best to make an issue of its collective affiliation with LO, with both the right-wing parties and the left-wing VP (*Vänsterpartiet*) party questioning the system. From VP's perspective, the formalized relationship between SAP and LO was an obstacle to its own closer cooperation with LO. When VP and the right-wing parties threatened to legislate against collective affiliation in 1985, SAP decided to abolish the system from 31 December 1990 onwards (RD 1990/91:KU40; Socialdemokraterna 1986; Vänsterpartiet-kommunisterna 1988). Abolition triggered profound changes in the SAP membership. Following it, the proportion of party members coming from LO has decreased, which has had two possible impacts on party–union relations. First, research suggests that LO members' involvement in the party's 'ordinary' party work in local party associations is no longer as common. Second, the party is not impacted by LO to the extent that it used to be when LO members were active in the party and could use their membership to make the party engage in issues important to LO. Research has suggested that 'a newer generation' of party members with higher education, and white rather than blue collars, is changing the party (Aylott 2003).

It is not only the party's membership structure which has changed since the 1990s. So, too, has LO's. As is the case elsewhere, the working class has become a shrinking proportion of all employees, which further undermines LO's position. Traditionally strong industries like mining and the metal industry are not major employers anymore. Instead working-class occupations are now found in the service sector in jobs that are often insecure and part time, which makes it harder for the unions to organize them (Magnusson 2000; Allern et al. 2007). And while union density has been comparatively high in Sweden, it has nevertheless dropped: in 1993 it reached 85 per cent, but has, especially after the centre-right government entered office in 2006, rapidly decreased and today stands at just 70 per cent (Medlingsinstitutet 2016, 46). High density has been explained by unions' presence at workplace level, and the structure of the unemployment insurance. The latter has been administered by unions, and up to 1998 union membership was necessary in order to receive insurance (Rothstein 1992; Kjellberg 2001, 26–38). This is not the case today, and the trend is that workers are less eager to join unions. White-collar unions, on the other hand, are experiencing the opposite pattern: union density among white-collar workers and professional employees has increased in recent years. Today these groups are organized by two organizations—TCO and Saco—but neither of these organizations has had any formalized cooperation with a political party. Indeed, claiming neutrality and maintaining some distance from the labour movement, especially LO, has been a strategy for member recruitment (Nilsson 1985, 121ff.; Bergstrand 2003; Strand 2013).

Despite some changes in the links between SAP and LO, research on party–union relations in Sweden has shown that the ties between the two branches persisted during the first years of the new millennium (Aylott 2003; Allern et al. 2007). What is the state of affairs some ten years later?

LINKS BETWEEN PARTIES AND UNIONS TODAY

Sweden has two traditional left parties represented in the parliament: the social democrats, SAP and the left party, VP. Because VP did not respond to our survey, the information on its relationship with the unions is solely based on the latters' answers. Parties' groups in the Riksdag do not have independence from the central party organizations. Indeed, SAP is known for its disciplined MPs (Barrling Hermansson 2004; Davidsson 2006). There have always been personnel overlaps between the parliamentary party group and the central party organization, and in 2010 a decision was made to collapse the two units into one.[1] The union movement in Sweden is strictly divided into three different umbrella organizations: the trade union confederation for blue-collar workers, LO, currently has 1.5 million members (Landsorganisationen 2014b), TCO (*Tjänstemännens centralorganization*), the Swedish Confederation for Professional Employees, organizes white-collar workers and has 1.2 million members (TCO 2013), and Saco (*Sveriges akademikers centralorganisation*), the Swedish Confederation of Professional Associations, organizes professional employees with a college degree and has 650,000 members (Saco 2013b). Apart from LO, TCO, and Saco there is yet another union organization in Sweden, the syndicalist union SAC (*Sveriges arbetares centralorganisation*), which organizes anyone but which has been very small and marginalized since the 1940s.

Overlapping Organizational Structures

After the abolition of collective affiliation in 1990 there are no longer any statutory links between parties and unions in Sweden.[2] Local union associations still *can* affiliate with the local party organization, if an active decision to do so is taken, but this is not very common (Landsorganisationen 2013). That said, one important statutory link—not covered by framework for the comparative study—still exists. The Social Democratic Youth League (SSU, *Sveriges Socialdemokratiska Ungdomsförbund*), which is social democracy's political youth organization in Sweden, is LO's and SAP's *common* political youth organization (Landsorganisationen 2014a). Thus young party members are socialized into an organizational culture in which cooperation between the union movement and the party is a natural part.

Reciprocal and Durable Inter-organizational Links

There are multiple durable and reciprocal inter-organizational links between SAP and LO, and overall they suggest a high degree of institutionalization and something close to an integrated relationship. First and foremost, we see that there is a tacit agreement about representation in decision-making bodies, the most important one being LO's representation in the party's executive committee and the board. The president of LO is and has always been one of the ordinary members of SAP's national executive committee (VU, *verkställande utskottet*) and the party board (*partistyrelsen*). This order is not formally established in the party's statues. The party board is elected by the party congress and is the decision-making body between the congresses. Aside from the LO president, a number of union chairmen (at the moment three) also have seats on the party board (Landsorganisationen 2013; Socialdemokraterna 2013a, 14f.). These practices of representation in the party give LO great insight into and influence over how the party is run. The link is however not reciprocal: the party has no such representation in LO. Historically, the party board has had members with posts in TCO as well.

Moreover, SAP and LO have frequent day-to-day contacts, both through formal committees (see Table 11.1) and informal contacts. The party's *Socialdemokraternas Fackliga Utskott* (SFU), the Trade Union Committee, is one of the formal committees where representatives from LO and the party meet on a regular basis. The party secretary (in charge of organizational issues) and the second in command from LO are represented in the SFU. In addition to the SFU, there are several other party committees in which LO has representation, for instance the permanent committees on social insurance, economy, EU-related issues, and the metal and mining industries (Socialdemokraterna 2009b, 106; Landsorganisationen 2013; Thörn 2013; Socialdemokraterna 2014, 128). Besides the permanent committees there are temporary committees for handling current political issues, and LO is usually represented in these as well (Socialdemokraterna 2009b, 106; Socialdemokraterna 2014, 128). Permanent Trade Union Committees also exist at the regional and local level in the party organization (Aylott 2003; Socialdemokraterna 2013a). Another permanent forum where both organizations meet is the so-called workplace party–union associations set up by SAP to compensate for membership losses due to the abolition of collective affiliation, of which there were 515 in 2008 (Socialdemokraterna 1970, 25; Socialdemokraterna 2009a, 7). Joint campaigns as well as joint conferences are also common, especially during election years.

The inter-organizational links between SAP and the other unions, TCO and Saco, have different characteristics. The white-collar unions and the professionals are very eager to stress that they are independent from all political parties. Because of this, contacts through joint campaigns or joint committees are unthinkable. TCO has pointed out a number of times that it would welcome increased cooperation with LO, but LO's relationship with SAP prevents such mobilization of members in joint campaigns (Martos Nilsson 2012). From SAP's point of view, however, the white-collar workers and the upper middle class are important groups for the party, and have been since as far back as the 1940s (Przeworski and Sprague 1986). Attempts to tie these groups to the party resulted in *Tjänstemannarådet*, a council for input from these groups. The main aim was to encourage formation of white-collar party associations (Svensson 1994, 102f.). Because of the structural changes to the labour market from the 1960s onwards, SAP has repeatedly tried to improve relations with the service sector employees, with TCO the main target for such strategies. Different measures have been taken: SAP tried to establish workplace party associations; courses for white-collar workers were arranged at the LO school in Brunnsvik; representatives from the white-collar trade unions were invited to different meetings with the party, both formal and informal; and conferences were arranged.

Table 11.1. Reciprocal, durable inter-organizational links between party central organization/legislative group and union confederation, last five years (c.2008–13)[1]

Party-confederation dyad—CPO	SAP-LO		SAP-TCO		SAP-Saco		SAP-SAC		VP-LO		VP-TCO		VP-Saco		VP-SAC	
	P/U	CJ	P/U	CJ	P/U	CJ	P/U	CJ	P/U	CJ	P/U	CJ	P/U	CJ	P/U	CJ
Tacit agreements about one-sided/ mutual representation in national decision-making bodies	Yes	Yes	No	No	No	No	No	No	No	No	No	No	No	No	No	No
Permanent joint committee(s)	Yes	Yes	No	No	No	No	No	No	No	No	No	No	No	No	No	No
Temporary joint committee(s)	Yes	Yes	No	No	No	No	No	No	No	No	No	No	No	No	No	No
Formal agreements about regular meetings between party and organization	Yes	Yes	No	No	No	No	No	No	No	No	No	No	No	No	No	No
Tacit agreements about regular meetings between party and organization	Yes	Yes	No	No	No	No	No	No	No	No	No	No	No	No	No	No
Joint conferences	Yes	Yes	No	No	No	No	No	No	No	No	No	No	No	No	No	No
Joint campaigns	Yes	Yes	No	No	No	No	No	No	No	No	No	No	No	No	No	No

Party-confederation dyad—LPG	SAP-LO		SAP-TCO		SAP-Saco		SAP-SAC		VP-LO		VP-TCO		VP-Saco		VP-SAC	
	P/U	CJ	P/U	CJ	P/U	CJ	P/U	CJ	P/U	CJ	P/U	CJ	P/U	CJ	P/U	CJ
Tacit agreements about one-sided/ mutual representation in national decision-making bodies	c.d.	No	No	No	No	No	No	No	No	No	No	No	No	No	No	No
Permanent joint committee(s)	Yes	Yes	No	No	No	No	No	No	No	No	No	No	No	No	No	No
Temporary joint committee(s)	Yes	Yes	No	No	No	No	No	No	No	No	No	No	No	No	No	No

Formal agreements about regular meetings between party and organization	Yes	Yes	No	No	No	No	No	No	No	No	No	No	No	No	No
Tacit agreements about regular meetings between party and organization	Yes	Yes	No	No	No	No	Yes	Yes	No	No	No	No	No	No	No
Joint conferences	Yes	No	Yes	No	No	No	No	No	No	No	No	No	No	No	No
Joint campaigns	Yes	No	No	No	No	No	No	No	No	No	No	No	No	No	No

[1] 'P/U' indicates responses from party/trade union questionnaires, 'CJ' signifies the authors' 'coded judgment' based on alternative sources in cases of diverging or missing P/U answers. 'c.d.' means contradictory data (diverging P/U answers), 'n.d.' means no data (informant didn't know/missing/unclear), and 'n.a.' means not applicable in this case.

None of the union confederations currently cooperates with the left party. Nevertheless, VP considers unions important, and the strategy towards unions has been to influence the union movement through encouraging its members to become active union members (Vänsterpartiet 2004; Jansson 2012; Vänsterpartiet 2012).

One-way and Occasional Inter-organizational Links

As was the case with the formal, institutionalized links, there are multiple one-way, occasional links between LO and SAP (see Table 11.2a and 11.2b). In fact, both organizations have claimed that they are cooperating in every possible way listed in the survey. LO is always invited to SAP's congress and SAP is also invited to LO's congress. SAP is also invited to all LO affiliates' congresses, and the party seems to take part in as many congresses as possible (Olofsson 1979, 162ff.; Socialdemokraterna 2014, 121f.).

Informal one-way and occasional links between TCO and SAP as well as between Saco and SAP are, however, also quite common. The most common form of links between the party and TCO are meetings arranged by either SAP or TCO for information exchange. SAP has a TCO network which aims at increasing contacts between TCO and SAP's members of parliament. Until 2013 these forms of cooperation were mainly information exchange between SAP and TCO through meetings. In 2013 a different strategy for cooperation was developed by SAP, which now directs its efforts towards TCO affiliates instead of TCO. Eleven SAP MPs are responsible for contacts with one TCO-union each (Socialdemokraterna 2014, 65).

Invitations to the SAP congress are also sent to TCO and Saco. Because of the lack of formal positions in the party, TCO and Saco have no mandate to influence its debates and discussions. One should bear in mind, though, that even if the congress takes decisions on the overall policy orientation of the party and its programme, this is not a closed forum: the debates are always broadcast on national TV. Thus, attending the congress does not imply support for SAP on the part of TCO or Saco but it is a good forum for networking. TCO and Saco also invite SAP to their congresses, but they invite other political parties too (Saco 2013a).

All the unions have stressed that they invite other political parties to meetings for information exchange and cooperation, and the four centre-right parties that formed the Swedish government in 2006–14 were a natural target for all unions' attempts to impact politics. Some of the respondents emphasized, however, that they do not cooperate with the xenophobic party, Sweden Democrats. Among the unions, SAC stands out, having declared that it does not believe in or support political parties; consequently it is completely isolated from them.

Table 11.2a. One-way, occasional links at the organizational level between party central organization and union confederation, last five years (c.2008–13)[1]

Party-confederation dyad—CPO	SAP-LO		SAP-TCO		SAP-Saco		SAP-SAC		VP-LO		VP-TCO		VP-Saco		VP-SAC	
	P/U	CJ	P/U	CJ	P/U	CJ	P/U	CJ	P/U	CJ	P/U	CJ	P/U	CJ	P/U	CJ
Invitation to party to participate in the organization's national congress	Yes	Yes	c.d.	Yes	Yes	Yes	No	No	No	No	n.d.	Yes	No	No	No	No
Invitation to organization to participate in the party's national congress/conference	Yes	Yes	Yes	Yes	Yes	Yes	No	No	No	No	n.d.	n.d.	No	No	No	No
Invitations to organization to participate in the party's ordinary meetings, seminars, and conferences	Yes	Yes	Yes	Yes	Yes	Yes	No	No	Yes	Yes	Yes	Yes	Yes	Yes	No	No
Invitations to party to participate in ordinary organization meetings, seminars, and conferences	Yes	Yes	Yes	Yes	Yes	Yes	No	No	Yes	Yes	Yes	Yes	Yes	Yes	No	No
Invitations to organization to special consultative arrangements initiated by the party	Yes	Yes	Yes	Yes	Yes	Yes	No	No	Yes	Yes	Yes	Yes	Yes	Yes	No	No
Invitations to party to special consultative arrangements initiated by the organization	Yes	Yes	Yes	Yes	Yes	Yes	No	No	Yes	Yes	Yes	Yes	No	No	No	No

[1] 'P/U' indicates responses from party/trade union questionnaires, 'CJ' signifies the authors' 'coded judgment' based on alternative sources in cases of diverging or missing P/U answers. 'c.d.' means contradictory data (diverging P/U answers), 'n.d.' means no data (informant didn't know/missing/unclear), and 'n.a.' means not applicable in this case.

Table 11.2b. One-way, occasional links at the organizational level between legislative group and union confederation, last five years (c.2008–13)[1]

Party-confederation dyad—LPG	SAP-LO		SAP-TCO		SAP-Saco		SAP-SAC		VP-LO		VP-TCO		VP-Saco		VP-SAC	
	P/U	CJ	P/U	CJ	P/U	CJ	P/U	CJ	P/U	CJ	P/U	CJ	P/U	CJ	P/U	CJ
Invitation to party to participate in the organization's national congress	Yes	Yes	c.d.	Yes	Yes	Yes	No	No	No	No	Yes	Yes	No	No	No	No
Invitation to organization to participate in the party's national congress/conference	n.a.	n.a.	n.a.	n.a.	n.a.	n.a.	n.a.	n.a.	n.a.	n.a.	n.a.	n.a.	n.a.	n.a.	n.a.	n.a.
Invitation to organization to participate in the party's ordinary meetings, seminars, and conferences	Yes	Yes	Yes	Yes	Yes	Yes	No	No	n.d.	Yes	Yes	Yes	No	No	No	No
Invitations to party to participate in ordinary organization meetings, seminars, and conferences	Yes	Yes	Yes	Yes	c.d.	Yes	No	No	Yes	Yes	Yes	Yes	Yes	Yes	No	No
Invitations to organization to special consultative arrangements initiated by the party	Yes	Yes	Yes	Yes	Yes	Yes	No	No	Yes	Yes	Yes	Yes	Yes	Yes	No	No
Invitations to party to special consultative arrangements initiated by the organization	Yes	Yes	Yes	Yes	Yes	Yes	No	No	Yes	Yes	Yes	Yes	Yes	Yes	No	No

[1] 'P/U' indicates responses from party/trade union questionnaires, 'CJ' signifies the authors' 'coded judgment' based on alternative sources in cases of diverging or missing P/U answers. 'c.d.' means contradictory data (diverging P/U answers), 'n.d.' means no data (informant didn't know/missing/unclear), and 'n.a.' means not applicable in this case.

Individual-level Links: Personnel Overlaps and Transfers

Sweden's political elite is small, and so is the elite in the labour movement, and we can find both personnel overlaps and personal ties between the different organizations. Although there has never been a formalized procedure in which the party has earmarked a certain number of seats in the parliament, it is a fact that a large proportion of SAP MPs has had a background in the union movement. With one exception (August Lindberg 1936–47) LO's president was an MP for SAP until 1983 when LO President Stig Malm refused to enter parliament despite pressure from the party (Hansson 1936–9; Norberg et al. 1985–92; Pauli 2012, 60).

Figures 11.1a and 11.1b present an estimate of SAP MPs' and VP MPs' connections to the union movement.[3] In 2010, 8 per cent of SAP MPs had a background in LO or one of LO's affiliates on the national level—a share which, compared to 1970, has decreased. Moreover, in 1970 the LO president, three LO union chairmen, and three former chairmen (of which one came from TCO) were MPs. There are no SAP MPs that have worked for either TCO or Saco in 2010, neither do we find any chairmen among the MPs. Among the left party's MPs, 10 per cent (two people) have held positions in unions at the national level in 2010; in both cases the unions have been white-collar and upper middle class unions.

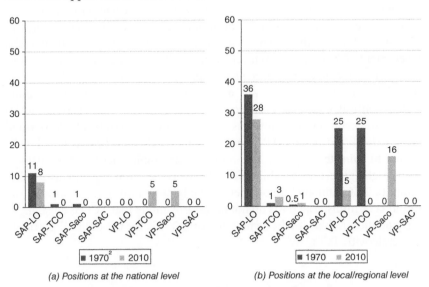

(a) Positions at the national level   (b) Positions at the local/regional level

Figure 11.1. Share of SAP and VP MPs that hold or have held positions as officials or staff in the confederations of unions at the national or local level.[1]

[1] Only permanent representatives and deputy representatives who attend the entire term are included. 'n.d.' means no data (missing). N of MPs is 204 for SAP and 4 for VP in 1970, 112 for SAP and 19 for VP in 2010.
[2] The figures from 1970 are from 1 January 1970, hence before the abolition of the bicameral system.

Sources: Norberg et al. (1985–92); Riksdagen (2011); SCB (1970), <http://www.riksdagen.se>.

If we look at the regional and local level, the figures are higher for both SAP and VP. The trend is the same as on the national level; SAP MPs have backgrounds in LO whereas VP MPs have a background in Saco. The share of MPs with an LO background has somewhat decreased over time. VP's engagement in the professional and white-collar unions is hardly surprising: out of the nineteen MPs VP had between 2010 and 2014, fourteen MPs had a university degree, two of the MPs were students, and the remaining three MPs had working-class occupations (and two of those three held, or had held, the position of party leader).

Other kinds of personal overlaps and transfers between the parties and the unions also exist. In 2012, Stefan Löfven was elected party leader of SAP. Löfven, who at the time was the president of the Metal Workers' Union, became the first LO leader to become party leader in the history of the party. Not even during the heyday of the union movement was the party leader recruited from LO. The career path to the party's top job has, with few exceptions, been through the youth organization SSU. The same year, LO also elected a new president: Karl-Petter Thorwaldsson, who not only had a background in the Metal Workers' Union but was also the leader of the SSU in the 1990s. The appointments of Löfven and Thorwaldsson indicate how intertwined LO and SAP still are.

Although TCO's links to SAP have not been formal, there have been links through personnel—all TCO presidents except two have had positions in SAP, either at the national level or at the municipal level (including the present president). Two of them have had ministerial posts in social democratic governments (Björn Rosengren and Lennart Bodström). After the elections 2014, Löfven formed a government and appointed Annika Strandhäll minister of social security. Strandhäll was at the time chairman of the TCO union *Vision*. Political 'neutrality' has been a contested issue in TCO throughout its history, and claiming neutrality has at some points been difficult (Westerlund 2011, 191–6). However, SAP is not the only party that has recruited TCO leaders to ministerial posts. The minister for employment in the 2010–14 centre-right government, Hillevi Engström, came from the Swedish Police Union (a TCO-affiliated union) before she became minister. Engström's and Strandhäll's ministerial posts do not necessarily imply that TCO is engaging in party politics; rather, it tells us how important it is for the political parties to cooperate with TCO.

Overall Degree of Closeness and Range

From the analysis we can distinguish between three sets of dyads regarding the degree of closeness: one dyad where the party and the union has an intimate relationship (SAP-LO), a group of dyads with a number of occasional links

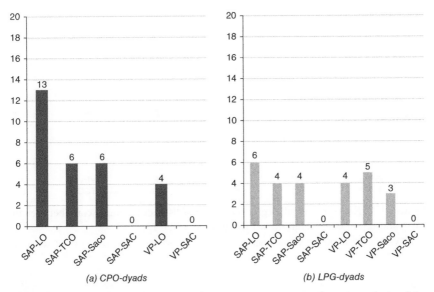

(a) CPO-dyads   *(b) LPG-dyads*

Figure 11.2. Total link scores of central party organization–trade union relationships and legislative party–trade union relationships (0–20/0–12).[1]

[1] The theoretical maximum link score is 20 for the CPO-dyads and 12 for LPG-dyads since some link items are unlikely to apply to the legislative party group and were thus not included in this part of the survey. However, when comparing dyads involving CPOs with those involving LPGs, one should still keep in mind that the latter's maximum involves fewer links than the former's top scores.

(SAP-TCO, SAP-Saco, and VP's relation to the unions), and two dyads where there are no contacts between parties and union, namely SAP-SAC and VP-SAC. Figures 11.2a and 11.2b illustrate all this, and shows that the SAP-LO extra-parliamentary relationship obtain a high total organizational score, yet a few points lower than the theoretical maximum due to no statutory links as defined here.

These results conform fairly well to the organizations' own evaluations of the degree of closeness (see Figure 11.3). Both SAP and LO describe their relationship as integrated despite the important changes that have taken place over the years, and the total link scores indicate a close relationship, although not a completely integrated one; there are no formal overlapping structures any more. However, LO still has representation in SAP's national executive committee, which gives it privileged access to the party leadership and thereby a great opportunity to influence party decision-making. The internal disputes in the party between 2008 and 2012 highlight the difficulties for any SAP leader trying to act without support from LO. After being in office for twelve years in a row, SAP lost the elections in 2006. In the election campaign of 2010 the social-democratic party leader Mona Sahlin declared that, if victorious, SAP would govern together with the Green Party. Choosing to cooperate with

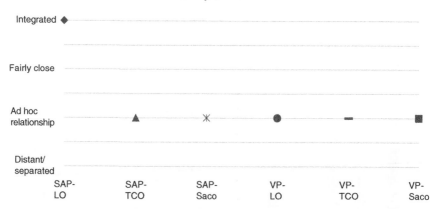

Figure 11.3. Rating of overall degree of closeness/distance (average score) between the party and union confederation, last five years (*c*.2008–13).[1]

[1] The VP-LO, VP-TCO, and VP-Saco ratings reflect the union's rating only since VP did not answer the survey.

the Green Party was an attempt to win the well-educated middle class, but it did not appeal to LO members. On the contrary, some of the Greens' goals, such as taxes on emissions and gas, were not compatible with the goals of the industrial sector, and were even considered a direct threat to employment in them. Several of the LO-affiliated unions' chairmen and retired chairmen openly declared that they preferred cooperation with VP. So did one of the party's most influential districts. A few days after the announcement, Sahlin had to invite VP into government too, suggesting to many that the SAP had given in to pressure from LO (Andersson 2008; DN 2008a; DN 2008b; Rudén and Häggström 2008; Johansson and Pettersson 2009; SVT 2014).

In the end SAP lost the 2010 election anyway. Indeed, the result was the worst result for SAP since the introduction of universal suffrage. According to the party's own analysis, giving in to the wishes of LO to include VP in the government was a fatal mistake; the voters did not want the left party in the government (Socialdemokraterna 2010; Oscarsson and Holmberg 2011; SVT 2014; Sydsvenskan 2014). Sahlin resigned as party leader, triggering a period of extreme turbulence. The left faction and the right faction in the party more or less publicly fought each other. In a party that had a tradition of leaders staying in office for between one and three decades, Sahlin's replacement, Håkan Juholt, managed less than a year in office, with meddling by LO cited by some as a factor in his resignation (Loberg 2012; Suhonen 2014). The chaotic situation ended in 2012 when Löfven was elected party leader with the support of LO even though he was considered something of a conservative—a stance which therefore made him something of a compromise candidate. Even if we have seen the end of statutory links—overlapping organizational structures—the crisis in the party revealed LO's influence over it. In light of this, it is not surprising that both SAP and LO have rated the relationship as integrated.

EXPLAINING CONSTRAINED DECLINE AND TODAY'S PARTY–UNION LINKS

How can we understand contemporary links between left-of-centre parties and unions? To some researchers, party–union relations can be seen as a game between actors that exchange resources (see Chapter 1 in this volume). Accordingly, party–union relations can be explained by actors' access to resources that the other actors covet (Öberg et al. 2011). In order to explain SAP's relation to LO we therefore need to examine what resources SAP and LO hold and what resources they want.

The resources offered by the unions to parties have traditionally been mobilization of voters and financial contributions. Sweden has a system of state subventions to political parties, and these subventions form the largest source of income for the country's political parties (Riksdagen 2015). But Sweden also lacks transparency regarding private contributions to parties. There are no regulations regarding private contributions, and the parties were until very recently not even obliged to record where their funding came from. SAP received between 20–25 million SEK (2–2.6 million euros) a year in 2008–12 (Socialdemokraterna 2013b; 2013c). The left party received less than 1 million SEK (100,000 euros) during 2013, the whole of it coming from individual sympathizers (Vänsterpartiet 2013).

Among the Swedish unions, LO and its affiliated unions are the only organizations that provide financial resources to a political party. LO donates 0.33 SEK per member/month to SAP which amounts to 6 million SEK/year (approximately 690,000 euros). During election years the party receives more. The affiliates have traditionally also paid an annual sum per member to SAP. LO strongly recommends that its affiliates give to the party, and the recommended sum is 6 SEK (0.6 euros) per member per year (Landsorganisationen 2013). It is however unclear if and how many of the affiliates actually pay, since most of the unions do not share such information. Ten out of fourteen LO affiliates have budget lines in their accounts which would suggest contributions to the party; the remaining four have not published their annual reports (Elektrikerna 2010; Handels 2010; Kommunal 2011; Byggnads 2012; Fastighets 2012; HRF 2012; Livs 2013; Seko 2013; Transport 2013; Metall 2014).

Mobilizing members to vote for the party is claimed to be one of the most important resources in a resource exchange model. Historically, class voting

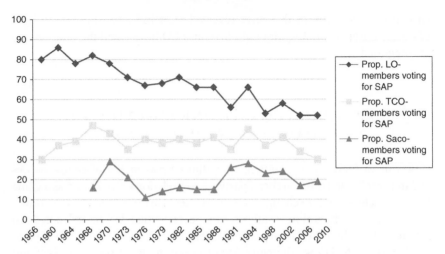

Figure 11.4. LO, TCO, and Saco members voting for SAP (%).
Sources: Oscarsson and Holmberg (2011: 93); SCB (2008: 312 f.)

has been strong in Sweden. As in other Western countries it has, however, declined over time due to structural changes: the working class has declined rapidly (Oscarsson and Holmberg 2011, 87).

In the 2010 and the 2014 elections support for the xenophobic right-wing populist party Sweden Democrats (*Sverigedemokraterna*) increased among LO members (Oscarsson 2016). Altogether, approximately 60 per cent of the LO members vote for SAP or VP (Figure 11.4). Compared to the 1950s and 1960 this is far from impressive, and LO members are no longer the reliable constituency they once were. There are several explanations put forward for this, among them the perception that the ideological differences between the parties are smaller and that SAP is no longer a 'working-class party'. But whatever the true cause, and given how the working class is shrinking, SAP's share of its voters is not sufficient to win elections any more.

Joint activities such as campaigns and conferences were unproblematic for the union movement as long as a larger majority of union members voted for SAP. However, the changes among the union members' political preferences make these arrangements more difficult. Surveys on LO members' attitudes towards cooperation with SAP indicate two contradictory trends (see Figure 11.5): on the one hand, the number of LO members critical of trade union–party cooperation has increased over time; on the other hand, so has the number of LO members who feel positive about cooperation with SAP.

All of the LO-affiliated unions (except the Musicians Union, but this could be due to sparse material) claim that they support and cooperate with SAP, but very few of them have such declarations in their statues anymore. Only one LO affiliate, the Transport Workers' Union, mentions cooperation with VP. In the

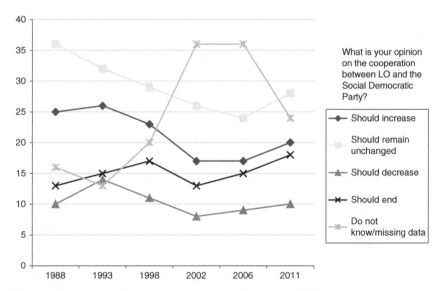

Figure 11.5. Support for union–party cooperation among LO members, 1988–2011.

Sources: Landsorganisationen (2011). *Röster om facket och jobbet* (RoF) is a survey on attitudes towards the union movement, the membership, working conditions etc. conducted every fifth year by LO.

annual report from 2013 the union declared that it has 'a wide political cooperation' with the SAP, the Green Party, and the Left Party (Transport 2013, 5). Traditionally, cooperation with the former Communist Party has been very controversial. Lately, however, more LO affiliates have softened their stance towards VP, and in 2009 VP's party leader was invited for the first time ever to speak at the congress of an LO union, the Union of Service and Communication Employees (SEKOväst 2009). VP has also sided with LO on high-profile issues where SAP and LO have been in disagreement.

On the other side of the exchange-model's ledger, political parties can offer unions access to government. SAP has historically been very successful in Swedish elections. Consequently, close cooperation with the party has been useful to LO. However, in the past twenty years the scene has changed. SAP has steadily won a smaller and smaller proportion of votes. The party was in opposition between 2006 and 2014—in its experience, anyway, an unusually long time. Even though the party formed a coalition government with the Green Party after the elections of 2014, the election was far from a triumph for SAP, which received only 31 per cent of the votes.

How well, then, does the exchange model explain the party–union relationship? Access to resources has changed for both actors the past thirty years, which could be an explanation for the changes in the links that have taken place. But despite these changes the organizations still cooperate and the links are multifarious. The troublesome years 2010–12 indicate that, even though resources have decreased, the organizations are still integrated, which suggests that party–union relations are not *only* based on an exchange of resources: common history and shared organizational culture also play a part.

CONCLUSION

No one questions the importance of the links between SAP and LO for Swedish politics during the twentieth century, and according to this study the relationship seems to be fairly stable over time, and is without doubt still of great political significance. One important party–union link has disappeared the past thirty years, namely collective affiliation. The impact of its abolition on SAP's membership has been profound. Yet the relationship appears to be vital despite changes in social, economic, and institutional settings. Moreover, there are still personnel overlaps between LO and SAP, and LO still has representation on the party's board and executive committee. The support from LO, in terms of financial resources and manpower during election campaigns, is very important for SAP. There are, then, precious few signs that the links between SAP and LO are about to end any time soon.

But the party also needs to win voters among white-collar workers and employees with a college degree. As in other countries, the working class in Sweden is shrinking due to changes in the economy. Consequently it has become increasingly important for political parties to cooperate with white-collar unions. White-collar workers are well organized in Sweden; union density among these groups exceeds that achieved by LO. In the past, SAP has successfully formulated a political agenda that appealed to both the working class and the middle class, but since the 1990s it has struggled to do so. One measure taken by the Löfven government was to recruit ministers and staff to the government's office from TCO after the SAP's election victory in 2014. Considering the volatility of Swedish voters, and the size of the white-collar unions, links to these unions will be increasingly important for any political party in Sweden. It remains to be seen whether the SAP's continuing close connection to LO will constitute an obstacle to the party's pursuit of politics that appeal to these groups.

NOTES

1. The decision to collapse the CPO and LPG into one unit took place in 2010 after the party lost the elections, and the CPO physically moved to the parliament building in

late 2013/beginning of 2014. Note, however, that our questionnaire was sent to two different respondents who replied on behalf of the CPO and Riksdagsgrupp respectively, and that it covers the period 2006–13.

2. A table is not presented as there were no 'yes values' (coded judgments).

3. I collected the data from the personal webpages of the 112 SAP MPs and the twenty-nine VP MPs during the term 2010–14. I have also used the book published by the Swedish parliament every new mandate period in which every single MP is presented. In some cases I have also checked personal blogs. That said, there are several caveats. First, there is no systematic information on all members of parliament, only whatever information the MPs themselves deem interesting to share. Thus, while some have presented extensive information, others have presented very little. Second, some have indicated that they have had positions or worked for the unions but without specifying where. In such cases I have assumed that these persons have worked on a regional or local level since this is the most common form of union work. Overall, the figures are likely to be an underestimate rather than an overestimate—especially the figures on local union work. The data for 1970 were collected from the biographical encyclopaedias of Swedish MPs, 1867–1970.

12

Strong Ties between Independent Organizations

Unions and Political Parties in Switzerland

Roland Erne and Sebastian Schief

INTRODUCTION

Relationships between Swiss unions and Swiss political parties are rather informal but not necessarily weak. According to their rulebooks, all unions are politically independent and none is affiliated to a political party. Nevertheless, we shall argue that the centre-left MPs still retain very strong ties to the Swiss trade union movement. In April 2014, every third social democratic or Green MP was or has been working as a union official.

The liberal and Protestant founders of the Swiss federation in 1848 were heavily influenced by the socio-economic and political tradition of the USA. Accordingly, the federal Swiss system of interest politics initially developed along the pluralist lines described by Tocqueville, rather than according to the unitarist thoughts of Rousseau (Hutson 1991; Erne 2014). Early industrialization and Switzerland's liberal political system also led to an early rise of workers' associations from the 1860s onwards. These associations not only assumed union and mutual insurance functions, but also stood candidates in elections and conducted referendum campaigns. In 1880, however, the first Swiss Workers' Federation dissolved itself, leading to the creation of two formally independent successor organizations, the SGB (*Schweizerischer Gewerkschaftsbund/Union Syndicale Suisse*) and the SP (*Sozialdemokratische Partei/Parti Socialiste*) (Degen 2012).

In Switzerland, then, the major party of the left was not founded by the unions (as in Britain), but nor was the major union confederation founded by political parties (as in Italy). Rather, the SP and SGB are both formally independent offspring of the same socialist political family. At the same time, linguistic, regional, and religious differences militated against the political mobilization of the Swiss population along the class cleavage (Bartolini 2000). The early politicization of Catholic minorities provided the SGB and the SP with a powerful competitor for working-class support. Although Catholic unions never surpassed the SGB, Catholic social teaching and the union movement played a significant role in the Catholic cantons governed by the CVP (*Christlichdemokratische Volkspartei/Parti démocrate-chrétien*). Following the secularization of Swiss society, the relationship between the Christian union confederation, *Travail.Suisse*, and the CVP lost a lot of its intensity. Autonomous employee associations also play a significant role in Swiss industrial relations and interest politics. Of these, the KV (*Kaufmännischer Verband/ Société des employés de commerce*) is the biggest and most important. Although initially founded in 1873 to manage a vocational training system for administrative employees, the politically non-aligned KV has also taken up union functions in the area of collective bargaining (König 2009).

BACKGROUND AND CONTEXT

The world economic crisis of the 1930s shattered liberal economic beliefs in Switzerland. Even so, in 1935, 57 per cent of Swiss voters rejected a popular initiative by the labour movement which called for the inclusion of an anticyclical, anti-crisis article in the Swiss Constitution. Nonetheless, a majority of the country's liberal leaders subsequently agreed to integrate organized labour into the policymaking process. In 1937, employers and unions in the engineering sector signed a peace accord, which started Switzerland's ongoing commitment to social partnership (Fluder and Hotz-Hart 1998; Crouch 1993). At the beginning of the Second World War, the federal government appointed leading socialists to reorganize the economy by way of a compromise between market and plan (Wenger 2010). And in 1943, liberal and Catholic MPs elected a social democrat government minister for the first time.

Although the inclusion of organized labour was also a product of the promotion of Swiss 'values'—such as social partnership—in response to the threat from Nazi Germany, labour continued to be seen as a social interest that must be integrated in the policymaking process even after the war, not least given the rise of the Soviet Union. In 1947, Swiss voters narrowly accepted a constitutional amendment that not only enshrined pre-existing corporatist mechanisms for the legal extension of collective agreements in the Swiss constitution, but also obliged the government to organize a consultation process with all socially relevant interests before submitting legislative proposals to the two chambers of parliament (Tanner 2015, 314). In addition, in 1959, the unwritten 'magic formula', which aims to ensure the proportional representation of all major parties in the government, became part of Switzerland's governance regime.

Comparative research usually classifies the Swiss system of industrial relations as neo-corporatist (Katzenstein 1985; 1987; Crouch 1993). Yet the categorization of this global hub of capitalism as a democratic corporatist country has also met with vociferous disapproval from scholars with social democratic leanings, for whom Scandinavia provides a better model. The Swiss balance of class power has certainly been less favourable for labour than the Scandinavian one, although unions and left-wing parties have at times also been successful in using the country's particular direct democratic institutions to their advantage: for example, by making their support for Swiss affiliation to the EU's single market conditional upon labour-friendly accompanying measures (Afonso 2010; Wyler 2012). Hence, corporatist politics is said to remain strong in Switzerland—at least formally (Armingeon 1997; Mach 2006; Oesch 2007; Kriesi and Trechsel 2008)—even though the nature of corporatist arrangements differs substantially across policy areas and economic sectors. Whereas equal pay by nationality—i.e. the fight against social dumping—is, for instance, enforced by a strong corporatist regime, equal pay by gender is governed by a much weaker, liberal policy regime (Erne and Imboden 2015).

The core of the problem in classifying Switzerland in terms of corporatism lies in the following interconnected aspects: the centralization and monopolization of interest groups; the balance of class power between them; their incorporation in policy formation and implementation; and the interaction between political parties in Switzerland's consociational democracy (Lijphart 1969). Switzerland's classification depends on the weighting of these dimensions. Those analyses that emphasize the limited power of the union movement or the decentralized system of wage bargaining (Fluder and Hotz-Hart 1998) emphasize the weakness of Swiss corporatism. Conversely, studies that emphasize the incorporation of organized interest groups in Switzerland's concordance democracy (Nollert 1995) conclude that Switzerland is a corporatist country, even if Swiss corporatism differs from Schmitter's ideal type (Erne 2008, 55). Any analysis of the relationship between unions and political parties has to take this into account, since the specific framework of Swiss corporatism leads to different implementations and interpretations of this relationship.

In contrast to its (labour) policymaking regime however, other aspects of Swiss interest politics very much follow Tocqueville's classical pluralist philosophy (Erne 2014). Political campaigns and their funding, for example, are not regulated by law. There are no limits on corporate or individual donations or payments for consultancy activities to parties or individual politicians. Swiss law does not even include a provision that would oblige politicians to disclose the origins of the financial payments they receive. The parliament only publishes an annual list of MPs' self-declared, permanent, extra-parliamentary professional and consulting activities (Nationalrat 2015a; Ständerat 2015a) and a register of external persons who obtained one of the two additional passes ('access keys') allocated to each MP (Nationalrat 2015b; Ständerat 2015b). The access key register contains the names of the representatives of leading Swiss interests, namely, those representing individual corporations, specialized lobbying firms, organized capital, and organized labour, and the names of the parliamentarian who acted as the gate-opener in each case. As corporations and interest groups can employ Switzerland's semi-professional, part-time MPs directly without having to declare what they pay them, they do not depend on paid lobbyists as much as their counterparts elsewhere. It is therefore hardly surprising that the Group of States against Corruption of the Council of Europe (GRECO) has repeatedly urged Switzerland to introduce appropriate legislation to guarantee transparency in the funding of parties and individual MPs by private donors. So far, however, the Swiss government and the centre-right parliamentary majority have ignored its recommendations (GRECO 2013).

Neither is there public funding for political parties in Switzerland, in contrast to most other modern democracies. This explains why centre-left Swiss parties have far fewer financial resources at their disposal than their sister parties in almost all other Western democracies. The corruption of liberal political and economic elites, however, has nevertheless been an issue. In the late nineteenth century, the progressive democratic movement successfully challenged the concentration of political and economic power in the hands of the urban upper bourgeoisie. However, instead of introducing public funding for political parties or limits on campaign contributions, the democratic movement fought for the introduction of extensive direct democratic citizens' rights, free public education, progressive taxation, and active social policies (Erne 2003; Bürgi 2014). Consequently, two new direct democratic instruments were introduced into the Swiss constitution: the referendum, which entitles 50,000 citizens (1 per cent of the population) to call for a popular vote on recently adopted laws; and the popular initiative, which entitles 100,000 citizens to propose a new constitutional amendment and to demand a binding popular vote on it. In addition, Swiss voters not only determine the number of seats a party will get in parliament, but also choose the individual candidates. The two seats per canton in the Senate (*Ständerat*) are distributed according to a majoritarian, 'first-two-past-the-two-posts' system. In contrast, the seats in the House (*Nationalrat*) are distributed according to a proportional electoral system, in which voters can radically alter party lists through double preference votes for candidates on the same list (*Kumulieren*) but also for candidates of another party (*Panaschieren*).

Whereas these direct democratic rights have given citizens direct access to the political decision-making process, they have also further weakened the relative power of parties in comparison to interest groups. Swiss parties, indeed, are much more dependent on active citizens than are parties in other countries. This resonates well with classic democratic theory; it may also be more difficult to corrupt an entire people in a direct democracy than to corrupt an individual official in a representative democracy. Yet Swiss political parties are also much less independent of interest groups, notably organized capital but also organized labour, especially given the latter's ability to access the political process directly through people's initiatives and referendums as well as targeted electoral campaigns for individual candidates using the personal preference voting system. Given the lack of public funding, Swiss politics also heavily depends on private campaign contributions. As a result, financial contributions from business interests to their political allies far exceed the political campaign spending of unions (Hermann 2013). The lack of public funding for political parties, however, also makes centre-left parties that do not attract a lot of business support even more dependent on trade union resources.

Swiss democracy, then, strengthens the power of interest groups and social movements in relation to political parties: hence the relative stability of corporatist arrangements and interest group–party relations across time (Kriesi and Trechsel 2008). Trade union density has also been declining in Switzerland—from 31 per cent in 1960 to 16.2 per cent[1] in 2013. Nevertheless, Swiss trade unions continue to be important political players, mainly due to their capacity to derail or deter unwelcome laws through the use of direct democratic instruments.[2] Essentially, 'as long as there is no broad agreement on reform' (Armingeon 1997, 176), there is no policy change.

WHICH PARTIES AND TRADE UNIONS?

Since we are concerned with the relationship between trade unions and the *traditional* parties of the centre-left, ties with the new-left Greens (*Grüne Partei/Les Verts*, GP) are not examined, notwithstanding the very high proportion of current and former union officials in the Green parliamentary party (Ackermann 2011). We have also excluded the former communists (*Partei der Arbeit/Parti suisse du Travail*, PdA) because they do not have enduring representation in parliament. Given the relative importance of the Catholic labour movement in some parts of Switzerland, however, we also look at unions' ties with the CVP. In 2011, the SP obtained 18.7 per cent of the popular vote and two of the seven seats in Switzerland's power-sharing executive, whereas the CVP obtained 12.3 per cent and one seat in the government. Given its strong position in the Catholic cantons however, the CVP has more deputies in the Swiss Senate (*Ständerat/Conseil des États*) than the SP.

On the other side of the equation, we focus on Switzerland's two trade union confederations, the SGB and Travail.Suisse, as well as the biggest autonomous union, the KV. The SGB is Switzerland's biggest trade union confederation. It is composed of sixteen affiliated unions, which organize around 370,000 members, i.e. roughly 50 per cent of all unionized employees in Switzerland (SGB 2014). The SGB is denominationally neutral and notionally independent from partisan politics (SGB 2010, Article 3), even though, as already explained, it is an offspring of the socialist political family. Travail. Suisse is Switzerland's second union confederation. It is composed of eleven affiliates representing 150,000 workers (Travail.Suisse 2013a; 2013b) and was formed in 2002 by the merger of the Christian confederation (*Christlichnationaler Gewerkschaftsbund/Confédération des syndicats chrétiens*) and the non-denominational Federation of Swiss Employee Associations (*Vereinigung Schweizerischer Angestelltenverbände/Fédération des sociétés suisses d'employés, VSA*). This merger was not a merger between equals, since VSA's biggest affiliate, the office workers' employee association KV, had already left the VSA in 2000 (König 2009). In 2012, another former VSA affiliate, *Angestellte Schweiz*, also left Travail.Suisse, as it wanted to be seen as an agent of the *Mittelstand* (the upper middle-class) rather than as a labour union (Angestellte Schweiz 2013). Travail.Suisse's constitution still refers to Christian social ethics. At the same time, it stipulates that the confederation shall act independently from religious denominations and political parties (Travail.Suisse 2009, Article 2). Most of its affiliates also explicitly refer to Christian social ethics, including the Hotel and Gastro Union (22,000 members), which is now Travail.Suisse's biggest former VSA affiliate (Hotel and Gastro Union 2012).

As 30 per cent of Switzerland's unionized workforce is not affiliated to any national overarching organization (SGB 2014), we also decided to include the most relevant autonomous union in our study. With 55,000 members, the KV is Switzerland's biggest non-affiliated employee association. The organization is denominationally neutral and independent from partisan politics (KV 2013a). Although the KV avoids calling itself a *Gewerkschaft* (trade union)—probably because of the workerist and left-wing connotations of this term in Switzerland—and defines itself as an organization of the employees and apprentices of all professions in commerce and related sectors, the organization acts as a union in the area of collective bargaining. The KV also runs one of Switzerland's most popular vocational education programmes, namely the *KV-Lehre* (KV-Apprenticeship) for administrative employees. The KV-owned business schools are also Switzerland's biggest operator in the field of commercial vocational and further (college-level) education.

RELATIONSHIPS TODAY: MAPPING THE LINKS

The following sections discuss the current relationship of the SP and the CVP, which historically were linked to the socialist and the Catholic labour movement respectively, with three union organizations—the Red trade union confederation, SGB, the Christian union confederation, Travail.Suisse, and the white-collar employees' association, KV.

The responses to our survey confirm that Swiss union organizations get opportunities to exercise considerable political influence. At the same time, the respondents from the SGB, Travail.Suisse, and the KV declare unanimously that they are non-partisan. Accordingly, there are hardly any statutory links between the political parties and the trade unions. Unions are not collectively affiliated to a particular party, nor are there any provisions in party or union rulebooks that would guarantee one-sided or mutual representation in national decision-making bodies (see Table 12.1). The closest we get is the SGB delegates' statutory right to attend the SP congress, albeit without voting rights.

Conversely however, the responses of party and union officials with regard to the very same party–union relationship repeatedly contradict each other. As shown by the recurrent appearance of contradictory data (c.d.) in Table 12.2 and even more in Table 12.3, the party and union respondents often disagree on whether there is durable (Table 12.2) or occasional (Table 12.3) party–union cooperation.

Fortunately, however, we were able to cut through this confusion and provide our own judgements (CJ in the tables) by consulting alternative written sources, namely, party and union documents, by conducting informal conversations with leading SP and SGB officials, and by falling back on our long-term engagement with the Swiss trade union movement from a comparative European perspective. In what follows, we will summarize the main findings, discussing each party–union relationship in turn.

SP: Organized Labour's Political Party

Both the SP and the SGB are heirs of the socialist labour movement. Although the SP no longer sees itself as a party that represents a particular social group, the replies of its federal secretariat and parliamentary party to our questionnaire confirm close and ongoing cooperation with the SGB. In addition, the SP secretariat acknowledges material campaign contributions (including office space) from the SGB and its affiliates. The SGB secretariat, in turn, confirms durable links with the SP too, although it judges that the SP–SGB connections at organizational level are less intense.

Table 12.1. Overlapping organizational structures between party central organization and union confederation, as of 2013–14[1]

Party-confederation dyad—CPO	SP-SGB		SP-TS		SP-KV		CVP-SGB		CVP-TS		CVP-KV	
	P/U	CJ	P/U	CJ	P/U	CJ	P/U	CJ	P/U	CJ	P/U	CJ
National/local collective affiliation (membership) of a union	n.a.	No	n.a.	No	n.a.	No	n.a.	No	n.a.	No	n.a.	No
The party enjoys representation rights in at least one of the union's national decision-making bodies[2]	No	No	No	No	No	No	No	No	No	No	No	No
The union enjoys representation rights in at least one of the party's national decision-making bodies[2,3]	Yes	Yes	No	No	No	No	No	No	No	No	No	No

[1] There are no LPG cells in this table as we assumed the questions (link types) do not apply to the legislative party group and they were thus not asked. 'P/U' indicates responses from party/trade union questionnaires and 'CJ' signifies the authors' 'coded judgment' based on alternative sources in cases of diverging or missing P/U answers. 'c.d.' means contradictory data (diverging P/U answers), 'n.d.' means no data (informant didn't know/missing/unclear), and 'n.a.' means not applicable in this case. Note that the KV is not a union confederation but Switzerland's biggest autonomous union organization.

[2] See Chapter 2 for a description of the specific rights/bodies that have been mapped.

[3] SGB delegates have the statutory right to attend the SP congress, although without voting rights.

Table 12.2. Reciprocal, durable inter-organizational links between party central organization/legislative group and union confederation, last five years (c.2008–13)[1]

Party-confederation dyad—CPO	SP-SGB		SP-TS		SP-KV		CVP-SGB		CVP-TS		CVP-KV	
	P/U	CJ	P/U	CJ	P/U	CJ	P/U	CJ	P/U	CJ	P/U	CJ
Tacit agreements about one-sided/mutual representation in national decision-making bodies	Yes	Yes	No	No	No	No	c.d.	No	c.d.	No	c.d.	No
Permanent joint committee(s)	No	No	No	No	No	No	No	No	No	No	No	No
Temporary joint committee(s)	c.d.	Yes	No	No	No	No	c.d.	No	c.d.	Yes	c.d.	Yes
Formal agreements about regular meetings between party and organization	No	No	No	No	No	No	No	No	No	No	No	No
Tacit agreements about regular meetings between party and organization	Yes	Yes	Yes	Yes	No	No	c.d.	No	Yes	Yes	c.d.	No
Joint conferences	Yes	Yes	Yes	Yes	No	No	No	No	Yes	Yes	No	No
Joint campaigns	Yes	Yes	Yes	Yes	c.d.	No	c.d.	No	Yes	Yes	No	No

Party-confederation dyad—LPG	SP-SGB		SP-TS		SP-KV		CVP-SGB		CVP-TS		CVP-KV	
	P/U	CJ	P/U	CJ	P/U	CJ	P/U	CJ	P/U	CJ	P/U	CJ
Tacit agreements about one-sided/mutual representation in national decision-making bodies	Yes	Yes	No	No	No	No	No	No	No	No	c.d.	No
Permanent joint committee(s)	No	No	No	No	No	No	No	No	No	No	No	No
Temporary joint committee(s)	c.d.	Yes	No	No	No	No	No	No	c.d.	No	c.d.	Yes
Formal agreements about regular meetings between party and organization	No	No	No	No	No	No	No	No	No	No	No	No
Tacit agreements about regular meetings between party and organization	Yes	Yes	c.d.	Yes	No	No	No	No	c.d.	Yes	c.d.	No
Joint conferences	c.d.	Yes	c.d.	Yes	No	No	No	No	No	No	No	No
Joint campaigns	c.d.	Yes	c.d.	Yes	c.d.	Yes	c.d.	Yes	No	No	No	No

[1] 'P/U' indicates responses from party/trade union questionnaires, 'CJ' signifies the authors' 'coded judgment' based on alternative sources in cases of diverging or missing P/U answers. 'c.d.' means contradictory data (diverging P/U answers), 'n.d.' means no data (informant didn't know/missing/unclear), and 'n.a.' means not applicable in this case. Note that the KV is not a union confederation but Switzerland's biggest autonomous union organization.

Table 12.3. One-way, occasional links at the organizational level between party central organization/legislative group and union confederation, last five years (c.2008–13)[1]

Party-confederation dyad—CPO

	SP-SGB		SP-TS		SP-KV		CVP-SGB		CVP-TS		CVP-KV	
	P/U	CJ	P/U	CJ	P/U	CJ	P/U	CJ	P/U	CJ	P/U	CJ
Invitation to party to participate in the organization's national congress	Yes	Yes	Yes	Yes	c.d.	No	c.d.	No	Yes	Yes	No	No
Invitation to organization to participate in the party's national congress/conference	Yes	Yes	c.d.	No	Yes	Yes	c.d.	Yes	c.d.	No	c.d.	No
Invitations to organization to participate in the party's ordinary meetings, seminars, and conferences	Yes	Yes	Yes	Yes	c.d.	No	c.d.	No	Yes	Yes	c.d.	No
Invitations to party to participate in ordinary organization meetings, seminars, and conferences	Yes	Yes	No	No	c.d.	No	c.d.	No	c.d.	Yes	c.d.	No
Invitations to organization to special consultative arrangements initiated by the party	Yes	Yes	Yes	Yes	c.d.	Yes	c.d.	Yes	Yes	Yes	c.d.	No
Invitations to party to special consultative arrangements initiated by the organization	Yes	Yes	Yes	Yes	c.d.	No	c.d.	No	c.d.	Yes	No	No

Party-confederation dyad—LPG

	SP-SGB		SP-TS		SP-KV		CVP-SGB		CVP-TS		CVP-KV	
	P/U	CJ	P/U	CJ	P/U	CJ	P/U	CJ	P/U	CJ	P/U	CJ
Invitation to party to participate in the organization's national congress	c.d.	n.d.	Yes	Yes	c.d.	No	c.d.	No	Yes	Yes	No	No
Invitation to organization to participate in the party's national congress/conference	n.a.	n.a.	n.a.	n.a.	n.a.	n.a.	n.a.	n.a.	n.a.	n.a.	n.a.	n.a.
Invitations to organization to participate in the party's ordinary meetings, seminars, and conferences	Yes	Yes	c.d.	No	c.d.	Yes	c.d.	No	c.d.	Yes	c.d.	No
Invitations to party to participate in ordinary organization meetings, seminars, and conferences	Yes	Yes	Yes	Yes	c.d.	No	c.d.	No	c.d.	Yes	c.d.	No
Invitations to organization to special consultative arrangements initiated by the party	Yes	Yes	c.d.	Yes	c.d.	Yes	c.d.	Yes	c.d.	Yes	c.d.	No
Invitations to party to special consultative arrangements initiated by the organization	Yes	Yes	c.d.	Yes	c.d.	No	c.d.	No	Yes	Yes	c.d.	No

1 'P/U' indicates responses from party/trade union questionnaires, 'CJ' signifies the authors' 'coded judgment' based on alternative sources in cases of diverging or missing P/U answers. 'c.d.' means contradictory data (diverging P/U answers), 'n.d.' means no data (informant didn't know/missing/unclear), and 'n.a.' means not applicable in this case. Note that the KV is not a union confederation but Switzerland's biggest autonomous union organization.

There is only one, rather weak, statutory link between the SP and the SGB, as mentioned earlier. However, both organizations report well-organized interaction involving, for example, joint referendum campaigns, and a tacit norm of mutual representation in national decision-making bodies. Interestingly, the SP again sees stronger and more durable links on an organizational level with the SGB than vice versa (see Table 12.2). Nevertheless, the two organizations do not differ in the assessment of their mutual occasional links (see Table 12.3).

There is also tacit agreement about mutual representation in national decision-making bodies and about regular meetings of the party and the union organization. It is, however, difficult to distinguish leading SGB from SP officials analytically, since many of them have leadership roles in both organizations. SP President and Senator Christian Levrat, for example, was, like four of nine SP leaders since 1919 before him, a union leader. He also continues to play an important role in the SGB, for example, as regular discussion partner and gate-opener—in the very literal sense—for his successor as leader of the SGB's communications sector union *Syndicom*, as well as for the SGB's central secretary in charge of legal affairs (Ständerat 2015b).[3] In turn, SGB President and SP Senator Paul Rechsteiner, like all his predecessors (with one exception) since 1919, is a leading figure in the SP's parliamentary party. The SP and the SGB also organize joint conferences and campaigns on a regular basis. These are usually of a temporary nature, for example in relation to a referendum campaign on a particular topic. These committees often also include other organizations, namely, other parties, interest groups, and social movements that share the campaign's objectives. As there are nationwide votes almost every three months, such joint campaign committees assume very significant functions in the Swiss system of direct democracy.

Both the federal SP secretariat and the SP parliamentary party also regularly invite the SGB to participate in parliamentary party events; this confirms that strong *inter-organizational links* exist between the two organizations. The SGB also cooperates fairly closely with the Green Party (GP). This cooperation, however, is less intensive than the SP–SGB relationship. Although the proportion of SGB union officials in the GP parliamentary party is actually higher than it is in the SP (Ackermann 2011), former and current officials of SGB unions also play a leading role in the SP's parliamentary party. The share of full-time career politicians in the social democratic parliamentary party increased from 0 per cent in 1957 to 27.9 per cent in 2008, and this professionalization of the Swiss parliament led to a decline of full-time interest group officials within the ranks of the parliamentary party from 28.3 per cent in 1957 to 14.0 per cent in 2008 (Mazzoleni et al. 2010, 344). That said, fifteen of the forty-six members of the SP parliamentary party in the lower chamber are, or have been, union officials at national or regional level.[4] In the Senate, the proportion amounts to three out of eleven, as indicated in Figures 12.1a and 12.1b.

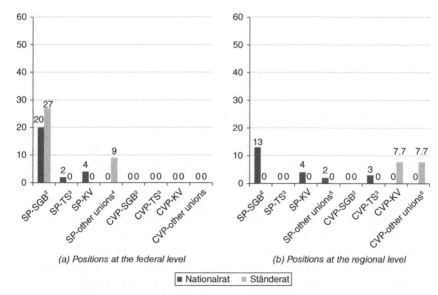

(a) Positions at the federal level   *(b) Positions at the regional level*

■ Nationalrat   ▨ Ständerat

Figure 12.1. Share of SP and CVP MPs in 2013/14 that hold or have held positions as officials or staff in unions at the federal or regional level.[1]

[1] Only permanent representatives and deputy representatives who attend the entire term are included. 'n.d.' means no data (missing). N of MPs is 46 for SP and 29 for CVP in the Nationalrat, 11 for SP, and 13 for CVP in the Ständerat.
[2] SGB unions; [3] Travail.Suisse unions; [4] Midwives' Association (SHV/FSSF); [5] Teachers' Association (LCH); [6] Solothurn State Employees' Association (SSV).

Sources: Nationalrat (2015a); Ständerat (2015a); Ackermann (2011); MPs' personal web sites; communication with A. Pelizzari (president, *Communauté genevoise d'action syndicale*), 17 April 2015, and R. Zimmermann (former general secretary, SGB), 18 April 2015.

The traditional bonds between the SP and the SGB unions remain very strong; but the federal SP secretariat and its parliamentary party also confirm improving cooperation with the Christian union confederation Travail.Suisse. Even though there are no overlapping organizational structures, Travail.Suisse reports a remarkable improvement in its relations with the SP following the election of SP MP Josiane Aubert as Travail.Suisse deputy president in 2009, and her replacement with another SP MP, Jacques-André Maire, when she resigned from both posts in 2014. In contrast to the SGB–SP relationship, however, Travail.Suisse seems to be more interested in getting access to the SP than vice versa. In its answers regarding organizational links with the SP, the SGB indicates that the SP proactively seeks cooperation with it, whereas Travail.Suisse states that it initiates cooperation with the SP. Even so, the SP's answers do not indicate any difference in treatment regarding any particular trade union organizations. At the same time, the SP acknowledges material campaign contributions from Travail.Suisse.

In its response to our questionnaire, the biggest autonomous trade union, KV, portrays itself as a non-partisan organization that represents the interests of middle- and higher-ranking employees. In contrast to the SGB and Travail. Suisse, it describes its relationship to all parties as distant. This, however, does not mean that the KV is apolitical. On the contrary, the KV publishes the political affiliations of all members of its executive. Of the nine members on its central committee, three are members of the right-wing Liberal Party (FDP), two of the left-wing SP (including KV president Jositsch), and one of the centrist CVP (KV 2014). Likewise, the KV actively supports candidates across the political spectrum. As already mentioned, the specificities of the Swiss electoral system, and in particular people's ability to influence the composition of parties' parliamentary groups through the use of individual preference votes, allows non-aligned organizations to exercise significant political influence. The KV's targeted support for KV-friendly candidates across the entire political spectrum may be as effective as the SGB's traditional alliance with the SP, as indicated by the contradictory answers of the SP and KV to our questions.

In their responses on durable and occasional organizational links, the SP reports close (but informal) cooperation between the two organizations, whereas the KV denies any cooperation. What we find instead are a few one-way and occasional inter-organizational links. The SP invites the KV to its national congress on a regular basis, and consults KV leaders in other situations. Moreover, the SP's parliamentary group invites the KV to ordinary meetings or seminars. Those inter-organizational links appear to be initiated by the party. At the same time, the formal distinction between the SP and the KV should not be overstated, considering, for example, that the KV's president, Daniel Jositsch, is also a leading figure within its parliamentary party, as is another local KV official (see Figure 12.1b). In addition, the SP also acknowledges receipt of material campaign contributions from the KV, despite the KV's statement to the contrary in the questionnaire. However, neither the SP secretariat nor its parliamentary group is aware of any contributions to individual SP politicians, which the KV mentioned in its response on that topic. In addition to personal campaign contributions, KV-related MPs may also be in receipt of a considerable extra income if appointed to any KV-related position. Since the SP MP, Daniel Jositsch, became KV president and board member of several KV companies for example, he is entitled to receive substantial additional remuneration (KV 2013b) on top of his remuneration as an MP and his salary as law professor at the University of Zürich.[5]

CVP: A Catholic Party that is Losing its Traditional Trade Union Links

In their responses,[6] both organizations confirm that there are no joint SGB–CVP structures (Table 12.1), and that reciprocal, durable inter-organizational links between the SGB and the CVP are largely non-existent (Table 12.2). Nor are any former or current SGB officials members of the CVP parliamentary party (Figures 12.1a and 12.1b). These results are hardly surprising, if one considers the distinct ideological legacies of the two organizations. Incidentally, the CVP respondent still believes that her party and its parliamentary group represent a particular social group in the Swiss political system, which arguably is Switzerland's Catholic population rather than its working class.

The picture changes somewhat when we compare the answers of the CVP and the SGB in relation to the questions captured by Table 12.3 and Figure 12.3. Whereas the SGB denies any significant cooperation with the CVP or its parliamentary group, the CVP mentions several one-way and occasional inter-organizational links, such as an invitation by the SGB to its national congress. These differences, however, seem to be a result of different understandings of what cooperation might mean rather than of strategic answers by the two organizations. If cooperation means more than an occasional invitation to events, however, there are indeed only loose connections between the CVP and the SGB.

Despite the continuing importance of Christian social values, Travail. Suisse's response to our questionnaire indicates a notable loosening of its

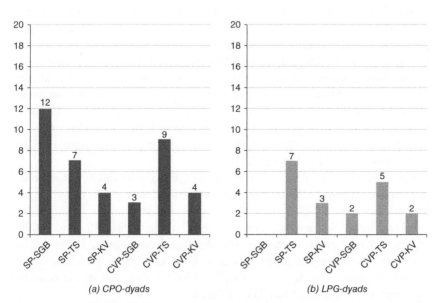

(a) CPO-dyads   *(b) LPG-dyads*

Figure 12.2. Total link scores of central party organization–trade union relationships and legislative party–trade union relationships (0–20/0–12).[1]

[1] The theoretical maximum link score is 20 for the CPO-dyads and 12 for LPG-dyads since some link items are unlikely to apply to the legislative party group and were thus not included in this part of the survey. However, when comparing dyads involving CPOs with those involving LPGs, one should still keep in mind that the latter's maximum involves fewer links than the former's top scores.

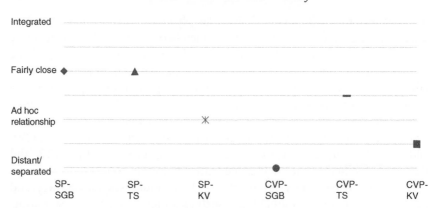

Figure 12.3. Rating of overall degree of closeness/distance (average score) between the party and union confederation, last five years (c.2008–13).[1]

[1] Ratings in-between two categories reflect that the party and union responses to the survey question differed. None of the ratings differed with more than one category, except for SP-KV (fairly close vs distant/separated).

ties with its traditional political allies within the CVP. No member of the CVP parliamentary party replaced the former CVP MP from Canton Tessin and cantonal union official Meinrado Robbiani as deputy president of Travail. Suisse after he decided not to seek a new parliamentary mandate in 2011. As a result, Robbiani also had to hold on to his mandate as Travail.Suisse deputy president during the legislative period (2011–15). As Figure 12.1b shows, only one member of the CVP's parliamentary party is, or has been, an official of a Travail.Suisse union, namely, the Nationalrat member Stefan Müller-Altermatt, who became deputy president of *Transfair*, the Christian public service union in 2014. However, it should also be noted that the Christian union movement always played an inferior role within the CVP. In contrast to the SP, none of the twenty Christian democrat party leaders since 1919 has been a union official (Altermatt 2010).

In contrast to Travail.Suisse, however, the CVP respondent nevertheless did not believe that the relationship between Travail.Suisse and the CVP had become more distant over time. On the contrary, she not only continues to consider Travail.Suisse as a member of the Catholic political family, but also argues that relations towards the confederation have improved over the last ten years. Moreover, the party considers the links to the overarching organization stronger than vice versa. Finally, the CVP does not report receiving campaign contributions from Travail.Suisse.

There are no overlapping organizational structures between the CVP and Travail.Suisse, but we find several durable and reciprocal inter-organizational links, such as joint conferences and campaigns, occurring on a regular basis. The party and the Christian trade union confederation also indicate instances of occasional cooperation on a regular basis. The party is invited to the national congress of Travail.Suisse, and to ordinary meetings, seminars, and conferences, and vice versa. Moreover, the two organizations invite each other on an ad hoc basis to discuss public policy.

As in the case of the SP, the CVP reports durable as well as occasional connections with the KV, whereas the KV denies any cooperation between the two organizations, such as collaboration in joint committees or the presence of informal but implicit cooperation agreements.

There are neither overlapping organizational structures (statutory links) between the CVP and the KV nor durable and reciprocal inter-organizational links between the two, with the exception of occasional cooperation on joint referendum campaign committees. Nevertheless, one CVP senator, Konrad Graber, is (according to his official website) also working as a KV executive (*Beirat*) in Lucerne (Figure 12.1b); this is certainly helpful, as Swiss federal elections are either won or lost at the cantonal level. Even so, the CVP does not seem to be the party with the closest connections to the KV, possibly owing to the white-collar union's geographical strongholds in the urban and Protestant rather than the rural and Catholic parts of Switzerland. As already stated, the KV's federal executive is dominated by FDP and SP members.

The Overall Degree of Closeness and Range

Figures 12.2a and 12.2b present the total organizational link scores of all party-union dyads studied here. We see that the strongest links are between SP's central organization and SGB (12) followed by CVP's CPO and Travail.Suisse (9). Although we lack a total score for the links between SP's legislative party groups and SGB, we see from Tables 12.2 and 12.3 that multiple links also exist in this case. We also notice that the links between the Socialist Left and Travail. Suisse approach a medium-high score, at least in the parliamentary arena.

Hence, the SP and the SGB share enduring, strong bonds of siblings of the same political family. The links between the organizations are of remarkable stability. The SP-Travail.Suisse dyad, on the other hand, developed more recently. There are new ties across traditional political family boundaries. The SP–KV relation is primarily based on personal relationships and mutual interests rather than a broader attachment to shared principles and larger policy frameworks. In fact, the KV's relationships with political parties rather mirror patterns of liberal interest politics than corporatist interest intermediation (Erne 2014).

The traditional weakness of the link between the CVP and SGB is confirmed by our data: the link hardly exists. In contrast, the traditionally stronger relationship between the CVP and Travail.Suisse has weakened over time and may even be in crisis. The CVP-KV dyad is marked by personnel links, as was the case with the SP. The links between the traditional allies, Travail.

Suisse and the CVP, are definitely still stronger than those between SGB and the CVP. At the same time, however, Travail.Suisse now seems to be better connected to the SP than to the CVP.

The organizations were asked to rate the overall degree of closeness and distance between the party and the union confederation during the last five years (see Figure 12.3). The results are broadly in line with our own expectations. The SP and the SGB do not see themselves as parts of an integrated organizational structure, but they do describe their relationship as fairly close. In addition, both organizations state that there have been no changes in their relationship during the past ten years.

More surprisingly, the SP and Travail.Suisse also describe their relationship as fairly close. We would have expected the SGB–SP link to be seen as closer than the SP–Travail.Suisse link, given the organizational scores and different ideological background of the two trade union confederations. Yet, both the SP and Travail.Suisse state that their relationship has changed over the last ten years for the following reasons: first, the election of the first SP MP as vice president of Travail.Suisse, which is seen by both organizations as a fundamental change in their relationship; second, Travail.Suisse also mentioned the growing secularization of its membership base.

Furthermore, the SP describes its links to KV as fairly close, in contrast to the KV. The SP respondent even stated that the SP–KV relationship was as close as the one the party enjoyed with Travail.Suisse and SGB. The KV, however, qualifies the SP–KV relationship as distanced, which seems to be closer to the truth, if one considers the answers captured in earlier tables. Be that as it may, there is consensus between the SP and the KV insofar as both agree that their relationship has not changed over time.

As expected, the relationship between the CVP and the SGB is interpreted as rather distant or ad hoc by both organizations. This is consistent with our earlier findings. Both organizations acknowledge that the fact they come from different political traditions limits the possible range for collaboration. The CVP and the SGB also confirm that there has been no change in their relationship over the last ten years.

The results from Travail.Suisse are even more surprising, as the CVP and the Christian union confederation portray their relationship very differently. Whereas the CVP sees a fairly close relationship, Travail.Suisse understands it as an ad hoc relationship. Likewise, relations between the two organizations, according to the CVP, are closer than they were ten years ago, whereas Travail. Suisse sees, in contrast, a more distant relationship. The reasons given by Travail.Suisse for the changing relationship appear to be more convincing, however. First, the social-Christian wing has indeed lost a lot of ground within the CVP. Second, the political standpoints of the two organizations are increasingly moving apart. Third, even though Travail.Suisse continues to reserve one of its two deputy president positions for a member of the CVP parliamentary party, nobody was appointed to this position during the 2011–15 legislative period.

In turn, both the CVP and the KV attest to a rather distant relationship between each other, which is very much in line with the findings reported earlier, and neither organization sees any change in the relationship over time. Finally, it is also noteworthy that the SGB acknowledges good relations with the GP—mainly because of good interpersonal links with GP leaders and MPs, but also because of shared political standpoints. Travail.Suisse, in turn, named the Protestant People's Party (EVP), the GP, and Green Liberal Party (GLP) as regular dialogue partners, whereas the KV claims to keep an equal distance from all major parties.

EXPLAINING STABILITY AND CHANGE OVER TIME

This chapter demonstrates, first and foremost, that the links between the Swiss unions and the major party of the left, the SP, did not decline over the past decade, despite the ongoing decline in the working-class vote for the SP that began in 1971 (Rennwald 2014).

Swiss voters still use their preferential votes for individual candidates in a way that leads to a very high proportion of union officials in the SP parliamentary party. This pattern may be explained by a higher proportion of employees from higher social classes within the Swiss union movement (Oesch 2006, 168), especially in the public sector. In addition, it is likely that the SP share is higher among SGB unionized working-class voters, although corresponding survey data are not available. Be that as it may, the bonds between the traditional socialist sister organizations, the SP and the SGB, continue to be strong and enduring, even though the class composition of the SP vote has changed over time. At the same time, both the SP and the SGB have made new alliances that go beyond their traditional partners. Whereas the SGB is now almost as well connected with the GP, the SP has significantly strengthened its ties with Christian unions.

Furthermore, the ongoing secularization of Swiss society and the decreasing cohesion among the Catholic community, as well as the increasing role of corporate donations in party politics, have led to a declining influence of the Christian union movement within the CVP. Even though the CVP continues to enjoy broad cross-class support (Rennwald 2014), it is facing increasing difficulties in safeguarding its ties with the Catholic union movement. In 1995 for example, the then Christian-social MP and Travail.Suisse president, Hugo Fasel, caused upheaval when he refused to join the CVP parliamentary party and opted for the Green group instead. The relations between the SP and Travail. Suisse improved significantly in turn, and this also suggests that the role of the

SP in relation to Switzerland's union movement is changing significantly. Instead of just being the traditional partner of the socialist SGB, the SP also became a party of reference for the Catholic labour movement. The SP has also consolidated its relations with the non-aligned white-collar unions, although the KV is keen to reiterate its political independence.

CONCLUSION

Although Swiss unions are notionally independent from political parties, political scientists and industrial relations scholars have distinguished three currents within the Swiss labour movement: a left-wing current around the SGB, related to the social democratic tradition (SP); a Christian current around Travail.Suisse, related to the Christian democratic tradition (CVP); and a non-aligned, politically moderate current, which consists of autonomous white-collar employee associations, such as the KV. At the same time, analysts of social and political change in Western Europe (Crouch 1999; 2004) have suggested that the social relations and political cleavages that shaped the formation of the labour movement, and the corresponding party–union relationships, have been subject to profound changes. Our research confirms an ongoing strong link between the SGB, but moreover a growing relationship between the formerly distant Travail.Suisse and the SP. The link between the CVP and Travail.Suisse, on the other hand, seems to have weakened over time.

The consolidation of unions' influence within the SP during the last two decades has not only foiled regressive social and labour market policies, such as pension age increases and labour market deregulations, but unions have also played an important role in putting equal pay by gender and by nationality on the political agenda (Erne and Imboden 2015). The continuing political influence of unions, however, is as much a result of their own efforts as it is an outcome of Switzerland's particular political system. The parliament is now playing a more important role in social policymaking by comparison to the 1960s and 1970s, when 'the major decisions had usually already been made in preceding negotiations in corporatist and administrative realms' (Häusermann 2010, 192). Nevertheless, the representatives of capital and labour still exercise considerable influence, due not only to their ability to use Switzerland's direct democratic institutions to their advantage but also to the lack of public funding for political parties. This chapter has confirmed intensive ties between the SP and the unions. We claim with Armingeon (1997) that mutual support between parties and interest groups, a necessity in corporatist systems, is still strongest between the SP and the SGB in Switzerland. If one is considering the history of business interests in

Swiss policymaking (Leimgruber 2008), however, a similar project on the impact of moneyed corporate interests on centre-right parties would almost certainly detect an even bigger interest group influence on Swiss party politics.

NOTES

1. ICTWSS database.
2. In 2004, for example, a left-wing coalition coordinated by the SGB triggered and won a referendum campaign against a pension reform proposed by the centre-right majority of the parliament (Häusermann 2010, 166–95). Usually, however, the threat to use direct democratic instruments is more important than its actual use, for example in the case of the 'accompanying measures' against social dumping that the parliament accepted in order to secure union support for the bilateral EU-Switzerland agreements on the free movement of persons (Afonso 2010; Wyler 2012; Erne and Imboden 2015).
3. Until 1990, many SP leaders even continued to be employed as union officials during their tenure at the helm of the SP: Ernst Reinhard (union official 1918–20; SP president 1919–36), Hans Oprecht (union official 1925–63; SP president 1936–52), Helmut Hubacher (union official 1953–63, 1979–91; SP president 1975–90), Christiane Brunner (union official 1982–9, 1992–2000; SP president 2000–4), Christian Levrat (union official 2001–8; SP president 2008–to date) (Degen 2013).
4. The candidates for national elections are designated by autonomous party organizations at cantonal level. The regional level is therefore as important as the national level in Swiss party politics.
5. Swiss MPs are not considered to be full-time employees and are therefore entitled to be employed by other organizations. This possibility is also used extensively by centre-right MPs who work for corporations or other interest groups.
6. It is noteworthy that the questionnaires for the federal CVP party headquarters and its parliamentary group were filled out by the same person. This is hardly surprising given that the same relatively small CVP secretariat is in charge of both the federal party organization and its parliamentary group.

13

No Place Else To Go

The Labour Party and the Trade Unions in the UK

Paul Webb and Tim Bale

The relationship between the Labour Party and trade unions has historically been unusually close, especially in comparative terms (see Rawson 1969). The Labour Representation Committee (LRC) was created in 1900 by various political societies and individual trade unions, with the latter going on to provide the bulk of its organizational and financial resources. Its founding conference had declared among its aims the 'securing of better representation of labour in the House of Commons (and) promoting legislation in the direct interest of labour'. However, the party was from the outset a coalition of different types of actor. Although the Labour Party did eventually adopt socialism as its official ideology in 1918, the more limited and less abstract goals of its affiliated unions continued to influence the party heavily.

None of this means, however, that the organizational and political position of the trade unions within the party has been immune to change—and, indeed, to a significant degree of erosion over time. It used to be the case, particularly in the first three decades after the Second World War when the UK flirted with corporatism, that Labour leaders attempted to trade electorally on the promise that they would be better placed than the Conservatives to guarantee harmony with the unions who, owing largely to full employment, were then at the height of their powers. However, after 1979, and as the unions went from being virtually an estate of the realm to just another pressure group, the Labour Party became increasingly conscious of the need to assert its political independence, notwithstanding the fact that the unions remained formally embedded in its structures. The unions, too, have long since lost whatever illusions they had about their political allies. Indeed, while there has been a revival of mutual affection, at least on left of the party and the union movement, in the wake of Labour electing an old-style socialist leader in September 2015, the relationship between the industrial and political wings of the British labour movement has, at least until very recently, come to rest less on a sense of shared values and identity, and more on limited, instrumental exchanges of resources (from unions to party) and policy commitments (from party to unions).

BACKGROUND AND CONTEXT

The multiple dimensions of the party–union relationship in Britain have often been the subject of controversy and conflict, leading the author of the most comprehensive treatment of its history to dub it *The Contentious Alliance* (Minkin 1991; see also Taylor, 1987). The experience of office has often provided the greatest test of the relationship, since in government the party, obliged to take account of economic constraints and the need to expand its appeal to a growing middle class, has never been able to deliver everything on the unions' policy wish-lists, much to their frustration and disappointment. Throughout the 1960s and 1970s, the party sought to manage the economy through a series of corporatist-style deals involving the Trades Union Congress (the TUC)—the federation to which over fifty UK unions covering almost 6 million workers now belong—and the major employers' peak organization, the Confederation of British Industry (CBI). That it ultimately failed to do so owed much to the decentralized nature of the British trade union movement: the TUC simply could not guarantee the compliance of all its member unions with such deals, and neither could its union affiliates always deliver the support of their own grassroots.

The result was electoral defeat for Labour in 1979. Over the course of a decade in office, Margaret Thatcher's Conservative governments turned their backs on corporatist institutions and procedures, introduced a series of reforms that deprived the unions of many of their legal privileges, oversaw a shift towards deindustrialization and privatization that saw union membership plummet, and vanquished the militant vanguard of the labour movement in the year-long miners' strike of 1984–5. The defeat and demoralization of the unions eventually helped bring them and the Labour Party to a new *modus vivendi*, contributing to consecutive election victories for Labour in 1997, 2001, and 2005. But there were considerable downsides: in 1979 there were 13.2 million trade union members, but by the time that Labour regained office in 1997 there were just 7.8 million, a decline of over 40 per cent. And, although Labour served three consecutive terms in office for the first time in its history, it also lost support over time. The days when, if it performed well, it could hope to win 40 per cent of the electorate now look to be long gone. Its comfortable parliamentary majority in 2005 was won on just 35 per cent of the vote. Facing a revived Conservative Party, and with the rise of nationalist parties in Scotland and Wales, and more recently, the Greens and the populist radical-right United Kingdom Independence Party (UKIP), Labour won just 29 per cent of the vote in 2010, 30 per cent in 2015, and is widely predicted to do poorly at the election scheduled for 2020 (Harrop 2015).

The watchword of the 'New Labour' governments of Tony Blair and Gordon Brown with regard to the unions was 'fairness, not favours'—in other words it was made clear to them, albeit to their chagrin, that there would be no attempt to restore the *status quo ante* of the pre-Thatcher years (McIlroy 1998). True, a legal minimum wage was introduced for the first time, and rights of union recognition were improved through the Employment Relations Act 1999. But there was no return to anything smacking of corporatism, Thatcher's industrial relations legislation was left in place, and her privatizations were not rolled back—all of which ensured that some on the left of the union movement equated, and still equate, New Labour with what, notwithstanding thirteen years of unprecedented rises in public spending, particularly on health and education, they insist on labelling 'neoliberalism'. But New Labour, despite making much of its cleaning up political finance via The Political Parties, Elections and Referendums Act 2000, did not manage to reform the basis of party funding, ensuring that the UK's parties still rely in very large part for their financial resources on private actors and interest groups, which in Labour's case means (and increasingly so) the unions (see Fisher 2015).

With some exceptions (such as Quinn 2004 and Russell 2005, both of whom cover Labour Party (re)organization more generally), the existing work on the relationship between the party and its traditional trade union allies either predates many of these changes or else focuses primarily on union involvement in party leadership elections (see Jobson and Wickham Jones 2011, and Pemberton and Wickham Jones 2013) or finances (see Quinn 2010), rather than on the quotidian institutional links we focus on here.

RELATIONSHIPS TODAY: MAPPING OF LINKS

As of early 2016, total union membership in the UK stood at just 6.5 million (95 per cent of whom are in TUC-affiliated organizations). According to official figures, some 26 per cent of British workers belong to a union, with more and more of them represented by the so-called super-unions formed—partly as a rational, cost-saving reaction to decline—by amalgamating a host of smaller, often craft-based unions. In this chapter, we focus on the relationship not just between Labour and the TUC, the UK's major trade union federation, but also between Labour and two of the biggest trade unions in the UK, Unite and the GMB—the two unions which, out of the five biggest unions we contacted, responded to our survey.[1] The TUC has always resisted any move that might fragment the union movement along ideological lines, meaning that it can claim all-inclusiveness but not political coherence, strength, or leadership. By no means all of the unions that belong to it are affiliated to the Labour Party, and it exerts nowhere near as much influence over them as do federations in some other (mainly Northern European) countries. In the British case, then, it makes much more sense to look as well at individual unions (cf. Chapter 2 in this volume). The unions we cover here represent a diverse group of employees. Unite has 1.4 million members whereas the GMB organizes about 631,000 employees, and their members work in both white- and blue-collar jobs across the public and private sectors (with the boundary between those sectors often a blurred one because of the rise of outsourcing by public agencies).

Overlapping Organizational Structures: Statutory Links

The British Labour Party and trade unions are still connected through over- lapping organizational structures, both due to corporate membership and representation rights in decision-making bodies. Following the planned dis- affiliation of the media and entertainment union, BECTU, in the wake of its decision to merge with a bigger, non-affiliated union (Prospect), there are thirteen unions affiliated to Labour, representing around 3 million members, compared to an individual party membership of 515,000 in July 2016—up from 201,000 at the general election of 2015, mainly as the result of a huge influx of members enthused by the candidacy and the eventual election of left- winger, Jeremy Corbyn. However, as far as Unite and the GMB go, we see that the rights to representation are not reciprocal, nor are they symmetrical (see Table 13.1).

Both the GMB and Unite are affiliated to the Labour Party, with their strongest formal connection being to the extra-parliamentary Labour Party: like other affiliated unions, Unite and the GMB are represented on Labour's National Executive Committee (NEC) and send delegates to Conference. But the Labour Party does not enjoy guaranteed representation on the executives of its affiliated trade unions, nor of the General Council or the Executive Committee of the TUC. Neither the TUC nor the individual unions which affiliate some of their members to the Labour Party has arrangements for collective membership or guaranteed representation in decision-making bod- ies of the Parliamentary Labour Party (the PLP). When it comes to the extra- parliamentary party, the TUC and the Labour Party enjoy no statutory organizational links.

The National Executive Committee (NEC) is the governing body of the Labour Party, which oversees the overall direction of the party and the

Table 13.1. Overlapping organizational structures between party central organization and union confederation, as of 2013–14[1]

Party-confederation dyad—CPO	Labour-TUC		Labour-GMB		Labour-Unite	
	P/U	CJ	P/U	CJ	P/U	CJ
National/local collective affiliation (membership) of a union	No	No	Yes	Yes	n.d.	Yes
The party enjoys representation rights in at least one of the union's national decision-making bodies[2]	No	No	No	Yes	No	Yes
The union enjoys representation rights in at least one of the party's national decision-making bodies[2]	n.d.	No	n.d.	Yes	n.d.	Yes

[1] There are no LPG cells in this table as the questions do not apply to the legislative party group and they were thus not asked. 'P/U' indicates responses from party/trade union questionnaires and 'CJ' signifies the authors' 'coded judgment' based on alternative sources in cases of diverging or missing P/U answers. 'c.d.' means contradictory data (diverging P/U answers), 'n.d.' means no data (informant didn't know/missing/unclear), and 'n.a.' means not applicable in this case.

[2] See Chapter 2 for a description of the specific rights/bodies. 'Yes' refers to party observers to union conferences.

policymaking process. All members of the NEC are members of the National Policy Forum and therefore participate in policy commissions whose reports are presented to and consulted on with the party membership before going to annual conference, which (theoretically at least) has the final say on policy. The NEC is also responsible for upholding the rules of the party and propriety of its selection processes. It is intended to represent all key stakeholders, so that, along with the leader and deputy leader of the party, it has members elected from Labour's parliamentarians, its representatives in local government, its affiliated socialist societies, its constituency parties (CLPs), and the trade unions, who have ten seats (out of thirty-three) reserved for them—a proportion consistent with the historic position throughout the post-war period (Webb 1992, 36). When allowance is made for the fact that some of those sitting on the NEC in non-union representational capacity often have union backgrounds as well, it appears that the unions have frequently been able to play a prominent role at this level of the party structure. Moreover, the NEC has a number of permanent subcommittees upon which the unions have been equally well-represented. Some caveats, however, are in order. First, expert analysis suggests that the number of NEC positions which union votes at party conference are able to determine has declined from over 60 per cent to around 40 per cent since 1990 (Quinn 2010, 374). Second, although this has arguably begun to change under the Corbyn regime (Wintour 2015), the NEC does not hold the power within the party that it did prior to the internal reform of policymaking, which saw the creation under Blair of the National Policy Forum.

Members of the Labour Party are encouraged, but not obliged, to join a trade union, although anyone wishing to be a parliamentary candidate without being a union member now has to be granted the express permission of the full NEC, not simply its Organization Sub-Committee, as was previously the case. Trade union members who are willing to pay the 'political levy' as part of their subscription to their union can be affiliated to the Labour Party if their union has decided to affiliate itself to Labour, although until recently it was up to the union to decide how many of its levy-payers it would affiliate. This has always been an important decision, for two reasons. First, it has governed how much money, outside of any additional voluntary donations that a union might choose to make, that it would hand over every year to Labour in 'affiliation fees', which in total provide the party with around a quarter of its central income (Quinn 2010, 366). Second, the fact that more than 90 per cent of Labour's total membership has typically comprised affiliated members gave the unions massive influence at the party's annual conference through the so-called 'block vote'. Until the 1990s, this afforded the unions voting power at conference in direct proportion to the weight of their affiliated membership. Obviously, as a combined group, this conferred upon their leaders an overwhelming numerical advantage over the delegates from the local con-stituency parties (i.e. the representatives of the individual party members). It is for this reason that both left and right have, over the years, sought so assiduously to court them, the left winning them over in the late 1970s and early 1980s, and then the right winning them back until the end of the New Labour era, after which many of them seem to have swung back to the left. Whether this was due simply to ideological disappointment or was a reac-tion to organizational changes which, for instance, saw them awarded just 16 per cent of the seats in the party's new National Policy Forum and made it impossible for affiliated organizations to hold more than 50 per cent of the weighted voting power at conference (Russell 2005; Quinn 2010, 373–4) is a moot point.

Another way in which affiliated trade unions have enjoyed formal rights of representation in Labour Party organization since the early 1980s—and one not captured by the comparative study's analytical focus on the party's general decision-making bodies—has been through the electoral colleges that have been utilized to choose the party leader, deputy leader, and, for a brief period, parliamentary candidates (see Bale and Webb 2014). The electoral college was a typically idiosyncratic piece of democratic engineering by the Labour Party, which initially gave 40 per cent of the votes to affiliated organizations (mainly unions), 30 per cent of the votes to local CLPs, and 30 per cent to the party's MPs in the parliamentary party, the PLP (who hitherto had been the sole selectorate for the leader). This plainly gave the unions as a bloc a huge influence in the choice of party leader that they had never previously enjoyed. However, the system always had its critics, particularly on the reformist right of the party, and in 1993 the leadership/ deputy leadership electoral college was reformed so that the unions only controlled one-third (instead of 40 per cent) of the votes; moreover, the ability of union leaderships to determine the preferences of their section of the college by the 'block vote' disappeared as votes in the union (and indeed also in the CLP) sections of the college were henceforth cast by individual levy-paying union members and individual party members respectively. At the same time, the local electoral colleges, which since 1987 had given union branches affiliated to CLPs control of up to 40 per cent of the voting power in the choice of parliamentary candidates, were abolished. From this time on, candidates were selected by ballots of individual CLP members on a one-member, one-vote basis. However, voting rights were accorded to those trade unionists who volunteered to pay a further subscription to the party, over and above the basic political levy (Webb 1995).

The electoral college employed to choose the Labour Party's leader continued to attract criticism, especially after the election of 2010 when Ed Miliband prevailed over his brother David primarily because he was preferred in the affiliated organizations section dominated by the unions. Ironically, and in spite (or perhaps because?) of predictable allegations that he was especially beholden to them, Ed Miliband seized on the opportunity provided by a row over union interference in parliamentary selections to call for reforms, one of which was to abolish the college altogether. Despite heavy criticism from some of the affiliated unions, Miliband's proposals gained the approval of a special party conference convened in March 2014. The electoral college was replaced by a simple one-member, one-vote ballot of all individual members of the party. This includes not only individual CLP members and so-called 'registered supporters', but also members of affiliated trade unions who (in an important change to the *status quo ante*) actively choose to 'contract in' to paying the political levy to Labour and to declare themselves 'affiliated supporters' of the party (the 'double opt-in'). It was this change to the selectorate, coupled with the decision of some Labour MPs to nominate Jeremy Corbyn simply to 'broaden the debate' in the leadership election fought after the party's stunning defeat at the general election of 2015, that led eventually to the party electing by far its most left-wing leader since 1935.

Inter-organizational Links: Reciprocal and Durable

The responses from our key informants in the unions and the party in Table 13.2 confirm that, with the exception of the TUC, substantial inter-organizational links continue to exist between Labour and the affiliated trade unions. A great number of reciprocal and durable links are reported across unions, including tacit agreements about mutual or one-sided representation,

Table 13.2. Reciprocal, durable inter-organizational links between party central organization/legislative group and union confederation, last five years (*c*.2008–13)[1]

Party-confederation dyad—CPO	Labour-TUC		Labour-GMB		Labour-Unite	
	P/U	CJ	P/U	CJ	P/U	CJ
Tacit agreements about one-sided/mutual representation in national decision-making bodies	No	No	Yes	Yes	n.d.	Yes
Permanent joint committee(s)	No	No	Yes	Yes	n.d.	Yes
Temporary joint committee(s)	No	No	Yes	Yes	n.d.	Yes
Formal agreements about regular meetings between party and organization	No	No	Yes	Yes	n.d.	Yes
Tacit agreements about regular meetings between party and organization	No	No	Yes	Yes	n.d.	Yes
Joint conferences	No	No	Yes	Yes	n.d.	Yes
Joint campaigns	No	No	Yes	Yes	n.d.	Yes

Party-confederation dyad—LPG	Labour-TUC		Labour-GMB		Labour-Unite	
	P/U	CJ	P/U	CJ[2]	P/U	CJ
Tacit agreements about one-sided/mutual representation in national decision-making bodies	n.d.	No	Yes	No	n.d.	No
Permanent joint committee(s)	No	No	Yes	No	n.d.	No
Temporary joint committee(s)	No	No	Yes	No	n.d.	No
Formal agreements about regular meetings between party and organization	No	No	Yes	No	n.d.	No
Tacit agreements about regular meetings between party and organization	Yes	Yes	Yes	No	n.d.	No
Joint conferences	No	No	No	No	n.d.	No
Joint campaigns	No	No	Yes	No	n.d.	No

[1] 'P/U' indicates responses from party/trade union questionnaires, 'CJ' signifies the authors' 'coded judgment' based on alternative sources in cases of diverging or missing P/U answers. 'c.d.' means contradictory data (diverging P/U answers), 'n.d.' means no data (informant didn't know/missing/unclear), and 'n.a.' means not applicable in this case.

[2] There appears to have been some confusion on the part of the respondent as to whether these questions refer to CPO or LPG links. 'Yes' makes sense if the questions refer to the former, but not the latter; GMB per se has no representation in the PLP, no joint committees, etc. (although there are GMB-sponsored constituency MPs).

permanent and temporary joint committees, as well as formal and tacit agreements about regular meetings. What is also clear, however, is that these links, as far as individual trade unions themselves are concerned, exist mainly (and perhaps a little unexpectedly) with the extra-parliamentary party rather than with the parliamentary party (LPG), although there is some contact with the latter via TULO (the Trade Union and Labour Party Liaison Organization), the liaison body whose *raison d'être* is to foster links between the party and the unions affiliated to it.

TULO is the successor to various bodies set up since the 1970s—among them Trade Unions for Labour Victory (TULV), Trade Unions for Labour (TUFL), the TUC-PLP Liaison Committee, and the Trade Unions Coordinating Committee (TUCC)—with a brief to 'ensure the party and the unions work well together'. Through its National Committee, the general secretaries of all the affiliated unions meet regularly with senior Labour Party officials and ministers/shadow ministers, to discuss policy matters and campaigns of concern to the trade unions. Representatives of the 'Trade Union Group' of sponsored MPs also attend the National Committee of TULO.

The Trade Union Group of MPs originates in the financial sponsoring of individual Labour MPs by trade unions. That sponsorship is, in fact, the oldest form of collaboration between unions and political parties in Britain, beginning with the Liberals, before the unions switched their loyalties to Labour at the beginning of the twentieth century. For many years, local trade union branches were permitted to fund up to 80 per cent of a parliamentary candidate's election expenses, which created the potential for a considerable say—albeit, strictly speaking, an informal one—in the selection of these candidates. The proportion of the PLP sponsored by unions grew from 30 per cent in 1945 to 40 per cent in 1970 and 60 per cent in 1992. However, in 1996 the party abolished this form of sponsoring MPs, although trade unions are still able to sponsor constituency parties, and it is generally assumed that MPs will be members of a union. The Trade Union Group of Labour MPs continues to exist, its main function now being to issue regular bulletins and briefings on any parliamentary business in which there is a union interest. Note that neither the group's members, nor the MPs who have been sponsored by unions over the years, are or have been especially politically cohesive: rather than agreeing a common line, they have been far more likely to be guided by the particular interests of their various union backers.

Inter-organizational Links: One-way and Occasional

What Table 13.3 makes clear is the sheer extent of occasional ad hoc links between individual unions and the party—and that, unlike the statutory and reciprocal, durable links between them, these extend as much to relations with the PLP (the LPG) as they do to relations with the extra-parliamentary party, very probably because they are facilitated by MPs whose constituency parties benefit from union support. Given its desire to retain its position as a comprehensive peak organization open to members of all political persuasions, we would not expect the TUC to be as integrated with the Labour Party; but Table 13.3 shows that this does not preclude occasional ad hoc links with the party, such as the issuing and accepting of invitations to participate in conferences or consultative processes.

Table 13.3. One-way, occasional links at the organizational level between party central organization/legislative group and union confederation, last five years (*c*.2008–13)[1]

Party-confederation dyad—CPO	Labour-TUC		Labour-GMB		Labour-Unite	
	P/U	CJ	P/U	CJ	P/U	CJ
Invitation to party to participate in the organization's national congress	Yes	Yes	Yes	Yes	n.d.	Yes
Invitation to organization to participate in the party's national congress/conference	Yes	Yes	Yes	Yes	n.d.	Yes
Invitations to organization to participate in the party's ordinary meetings, seminars, and conferences	No	No	Yes	Yes	n.d.	Yes
Invitations to party to participate in ordinary organization meetings, seminars, and conferences	No	No	Yes	Yes	n.d.	Yes
Invitations to organization to special consultative arrangements initiated by the party	Yes	Yes	Yes	Yes	n.d.	Yes
Invitations to party to special consultative arrangements initiated by the organization	Yes	Yes	Yes	Yes	n.d.	Yes

Party-confederation dyad—LPG	Labour-TUC		Labour-GMB		Labour-Unite	
	P/U	CJ	P/U	CJ	P/U	CJ
Invitation to party to participate in the organization's national congress	Yes	Yes	Yes	Yes	n.d.	Yes
Invitation to organization to participate in the party's national congress/conference	n.a.	n.a.	n.a.	n.a.	n.a.	n.a.
Invitations to organization to participate in the party's ordinary meetings, seminars, and conferences	Yes	Yes	Yes	Yes	n.d.	Yes
Invitations to party to participate in ordinary organization meetings, seminars, and conferences	No	No	Yes	Yes	n.d.	Yes
Invitations to organization to special consultative arrangements initiated by the party	Yes	Yes	Yes	Yes	n.d.	Yes
Invitations to party to special consultative arrangements initiated by the organization	No	No	Yes	Yes	n.d.	Yes

[1] 'P/U' indicates responses from party/trade union questionnaires, 'CJ' signifies the authors' 'coded judgment' based on alternative sources in cases of diverging or missing P/U answers. 'c.d.' means contradictory data (diverging P/U answers), 'n.d.' means no data (informant didn't know/missing/unclear), and 'n.a.' means not applicable in this case.

Individual-level Links: Personnel Overlaps and Transfers

Our research suggests no particularly clear pattern to informal interactions, although the TUC respondent—understandably, given the lack of formal affiliation—placed the emphasis on them, commenting that 'most connections are informal. These ebb and flow with the political situation and are currently good. But this will not be captured by analysing formal links.' Personnel overlaps are generally thought to be important, in the sense that many Labour MPs work for trade unions—often in campaigning, policy, or communications roles earlier in their career. Without surveying them, however, it is impossible to gauge the precise proportion or even to make an educated guess at it. The alternative would be to look at MPs' biographies, but even this risks running into problems because of the selective presentation involved, especially when the right-wing, anti-trade union titles which dominate the newspaper industry in the UK like to make as much as they can of the number of Labour politicians with union backgrounds—and of union 'interference' in candidate selection—in order to reinforce Conservative claims that 'union bosses' control the party.[2] That said, a trawl of the biographies of the twenty-seven MPs in its 'shadow cabinet' (i.e. the parliamentary leadership in opposition) in December 2014 (just before the following year's general election) revealed that five (in other words just under a fifth of the total) had previously worked for unions in a variety of roles—most often as researchers or political officers—before entering parliament. Under Corbyn (who had himself been a trade union organizer back in the 1970s) the proportion remained the same—at least before the majority of his shadow cabinet resigned in June 2016, declaring they had lost confidence in him in the wake of the shock result of the EU referendum. Whether Labour MPs worked for unions because that was originally the height of their ambition, or because they hoped it might be a useful stepping stone to a political career in the Labour Party, is debatable.

Overall Degree of Closeness and Range

The Labour Party and the trade unions are still closely bound up with each other in the UK. The unions, as individual unions rather than via their federation, the TUC, continue to enjoy formal representation in the extraparliamentary party, continue to enjoy a guaranteed say in policy, and continue to supply the party with members who enjoy the right (among other things) to vote in its leadership contests and parliamentary selections. Thus, the relationship between the Labour Party and some individual unions is still very intimate (formally integrated). The party does not enjoy reciprocal rights. There is more reciprocity, however, when it comes to inter-organizational links (durable and occasional) between the two sides of what, despite some serious disputes, still qualifies as something of 'a special relationship'. And it is clear that those links exist in the parliamentary as well as extra-parliamentary arena in the case of the TUC and the unions mapped here. Figures 13.1a and 13.1b summarize the organizational scores for the dyads we can assign with a total score. We see that the strongest links are between the party and individual unions, not the TUC. Labour's central party organization and GMB

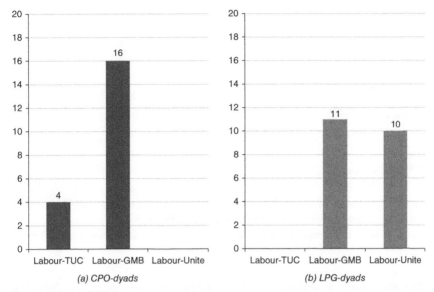

Figure 13.1. Total link scores of central party organization–trade union relationships and legislative party–trade union relationships (0–20/0–12).[1]

[1] The theoretical maximum link score is 20 for the CPO-dyads and 12 for LPG-dyads since some link items are unlikely to apply to the legislative party group and were thus not included in this part of the survey. However, when comparing dyads involving CPOs with those involving LPGs, one should still keep in mind that the latter's maximum involves fewer links than the former's top scores.

together obtain a very high score (16)—close to the maximum of twenty links. We do not have a total score for Labour-CPO and Unite, but can see that any difference in scores between these dyads in the parliamentary arena is insignificant.

Figure 13.2 shows how our informants themselves assess the overall closeness of the relationship. Interestingly, nearly all of them believed their respective organizations were at least 'fairly close', even if the Labour–TUC link was rated slightly less so. The party sees the relationship with affiliated unions which enjoy representation rights as integrated, in line with our conceptualization, but interestingly the unions do not. In terms of qualitative feedback the TUC respondent observed that the 'TUC's relationship with Labour is usually better when Labour is in opposition—and the current leader has moved on from triangulating against unions as an electoral tactic.' The GMB respondent tried to put this in perspective, notwithstanding tensions over Ed Miliband's reforms of the party–union relationship: 'GMB is still a major affiliate to the party and a significant contributor to its finances. GMB sends a delegation to annual LP conferences; always promotes the party in its journal; seeks to encourage membership . . . and has a large political department whose prime business is to liaise with the LP. GMB sponsors Labour

Figure 13.2. Rating of overall degree of closeness/distance (average score) between the party and union confederation, last five years (*c*.2008–13).[1]

[1] Ratings in-between two categories reflect that the party and union responses to the survey question differed. None of the ratings differed with more than one category.

MPs and local councillors.' The Unite respondent said simply, if drily, that 'there are structures in which we are integrated'.

For all that, there has clearly been a change in the relationship over time. The party was established quite explicitly to represent union interests in parliament. Although it continues to do this, it has found, especially in government, that it has to balance this with all sorts of other interests and tasks—sometimes much to the chagrin of the unions, which understandably resent the fact that they are financing an organization which does not always deliver what they want. Partly as a result, but partly, too, as a result of changes in society, in the economy, and in public opinion on unions, the relationship has gradually moved from something like a family one to a working (although more than merely contractual) relationship. Whether it is a healthy one, however, remains a matter of live (and often lively) debate. Our informant from the TUC felt that things had improved owing to Labour's shift from government to opposition. However, the two major unions have publicly expressed concern over aspects of their relationship with the party in recent years. This was reflected by our key informant from the GMB. Despite maintaining that the parties were still fairly close, he noted:

> The cultural shift in the Blair—and post-Blair Labour party—has meant that increasingly Labour politicians/employers have different priorities and speak an entirely different language to GMB officials and members. The union has not 'left' its position in relation to Labour; the party has moved away from us. Union members—in what is still a blue collar/unskilled union—are NOT automatically Labour voters, though they are often taken for granted as such.

This provides an insight into union perceptions of Labour's transformation since New Labour emerged in the mid-1990s. Clearly, this gave rise to a growing sense of distance in the lack of a common 'language' and the hint at a lack of shared values. Equally, there is no mistaking who was to blame for this, at least from the unions' point of view: it was the party that changed, not the unions. What this did not encourage, however, is any attempt on the part of the party to seek a greater range of durable links with other, non-affiliated unions, or (on the part of those affiliated unions) other parties. Our key informant at the TUC reported one-way occasional links with parties other than Labour (Conservatives, Liberal Democrats, and Greens) and indicated that its officers and representatives had received invitations to the meetings, seminars, conferences, and other consultations of other parties over the course of the preceding five years. By contrast—and not surprisingly—neither Unite nor the GMB reported any such contacts.

EXPLAINING CONSTRAINED DECLINE: TIME AND TIDE

There has been erosion over time, but the relationship between the party and the unions in the UK retains features that have long been abandoned in other polities. The explanation for this almost certainly lies, at least in part, in the financial nexus. Indeed, to many observers, especially those who are critical of the Labour Party, the trade unions, or both, 'it's all about the money'.

As the unions became less popular with the public at large from the 1960s onwards, the jibe that Labour effectively did the bidding of its union paymasters became increasingly damaging (Quinn 2010), although their relative weakness from the 1980s onwards means such accusations now enjoy considerably less traction than once they did. Whatever the truth behind them, it is undeniable that the unions remain an important source of funding for Labour, notwithstanding some fluctuation in the party's dependence on them over the past twenty years. The unions contribute financially in one of two ways most of the time: via affiliation fees and via ad hoc donations, which, in an ideal world, go towards the party's election 'war chest'. Historically, the unions have been vital to both of these funds, being responsible for 70 to 80 per cent of what was called the General Fund prior to the emergence of New Labour, and as much as 90 per cent of the so-called General Election Fund (Webb 1992, 20). These figures, we should note, do not take account of the further subsidies-in-kind that the party has derived from the unions by way of unpaid labour from union officials working on election campaigns, or the willingness of the unions to foot extraordinary expenditures from time to time, including the provision of national party head office premises.

However, under Tony Blair, leader between 1994 and 2007, 'New Labour' sought to reduce its financial dependence on the unions by generating greater income from private donors, investments, and trading activity. The party enjoyed partial and temporary success in this strategy. In 1992, trade union affiliation fees accounted for 54 per cent of total central party income, though when one adds in union donations to that year's election fund, the proportion of total central income deriving from the unions rose to 66 per cent. By the following election in 1997, the respective figures had dropped to 27 per cent and 40 per cent. However, the balance gradually shifted back towards financial dependence on the affiliated unions across the course of the following decade, with nearly two-thirds of all donations emanating from the unions by 2009, in addition to the affiliation fees that still constituted a quarter of all central party income (Quinn 2010, 366). The party's financial vulnerability to this continuing dependence on the unions was revealed after 2001 when—for the first time—unions began to use it as a weapon to express their displeasure with party policy. At various times, the Communication Workers' Union, the GMB, and UNISON all cut funding to the party for this reason, while two small unions (the Rail, Maritime and Transport Union, the RMT, and the Fire Brigades Union, the FBU)—one of which (the FBU) has now reaffiliated—disaffiliated altogether. This led to the so-called 'Warwick Agreement' of 2004, when a meeting of the party's National Policy Forum saw an accord through which union funding was guaranteed for the 2005 election in return for a series of policy pledges by the party on workers' rights.

More recently, some unions responded to Ed Miliband's reforms of the electoral college system for choosing Labour's leader by cutting the number of members they affiliate to the party (and therefore, the affiliation fees they pay). In September 2013, the GMB began the process by announcing that it intended to cut its affiliation fees to Labour from £1.2 million annually to just £150,000—an amount calculated by multiplying the £3 membership levy by the approximately 50,000 GMB members who voted in the 2010 Labour leadership contest rather than by the 420,000 it had previously chosen to affiliate. It was swiftly followed by UNISON, which announced it was cutting its affiliation fee by £210,000 per annum. In March 2014, Britain's largest union, Unite, halved its affiliated membership from 1 million to 500,000 (and thus its affiliation fee from £3m to £1.5m). The new rules, which were to apply only to new joiners in the first instance and be phased in over five years for existing members, also mean that the political levy which they pay over and above normal union membership subscriptions can only be passed on to the party in affiliation fees if they give their express consent to this happening—a switch from 'contracting out' to having to 'contract in'.

This change will either mean that Labour's funding from the unions will drop precipitately or, if the unions wish to maintain it, it will afford their executives more discretion and possibly more leverage over the party: after all, a greater proportion of that funding will henceforth have to come from donations that can be denied, rather than from fees which are to some degree automatic. Whether there will be much money available through either channel, however, is now in serious doubt. In 2015 the Conservatives talked about passing legislation which would see union members pay their union's political levy only if they explicitly opted in to do so—a move which, if it ever goes ahead, is widely predicted to have a catastrophic effect on union finances and therefore the financing of the Labour Party.

That said, finance is not the be all and end all. It remains the case, for instance, that voters with a trade union connection are, all other things being equal, significantly more likely to vote Labour than those who do not have one. In 2015, 42.2 per cent of trade union members voted Labour, while just 28.7 per cent of non-members did (p < 0.000). Moreover, it is not just votes, at least in this sense, that the unions can offer. Possibly even more important is their willingness to see their officials work for Labour at general elections—a significant addition to the party's campaigning strength, especially perhaps when its back is against the wall as it was in 2010, when its 'ground game' almost certainly prevented what would (and, given its drop in vote share, should) have been a much bigger loss of parliamentary seats.

Nor is there any doubt that, especially compared to the situation which pertains when the Conservatives are in power, the unions know that they have far better access to ministers and therefore a far bigger input into policy under Labour. While they may no longer enjoy what came in the 1960s and 1970s to be called 'Beer and Sandwiches at Number Ten', this helps to explain why unions have been reluctant to give up on the Labour Party altogether.

CONCLUSION

Britain's first Labour prime minister, Ramsay MacDonald, admitted at the beginning of the twentieth century that 'only by them [the unions] could the party have got mass support and money' at the same time as lamenting the 'terrible incubus' this represented (Sidney Webb, cited in Forester 1976, 96). Since then, the party–union relationship in Britain has been through many trials and tribulations—especially (although not exclusively) when Labour has gone into government. Yet it remains an integrated, organic one insofar as the formal affiliation of some unions continues to exist and continues to carry with it rights of representation and influence in the party's institutions and procedures, its structures, and its processes. When Tony Blair rechristened the party as 'New Labour', however, this sense of a common identity and mission began to seem much less secure, and the links that remained, while far from insubstantial, began to feel residual. Hence, the long-term collaboration between Labour and the unions on shared policy goals seemed to have grown weaker (at least in the years prior to Corbyn's election to the leadership) than it had been at any time in their relationship's hundred-year history, despite the survival of overlapping organizational structures and durable inter-organizational links. The unions did not always trust the goals of the party leadership, while the latter often seemed encumbered by the presence of the unions, to the point that at least one of them may, albeit privately, welcome the autonomy that formal divorce would bring. For their part, the union leaderships became increasingly willing to play hardball as a consequence, especially when it came to funding.

For all this, the two halves of the country's labour movement—a phrase one hears much less these days—have continued to cling to each other for practical and strategic reasons. Affection—save perhaps between left-wing union leaders and their kindred spirits in the newly left-wing leadership—may be missing, but exchange still counts. For the time being at least, the party still needs the money the unions bring with them. And, given the constraining effect of the electoral system on what might otherwise be a much more fragmented party system, the unions simply have nowhere else to go politically. If not Labour, then who? Affiliated unions like Unite and the GMB continue to have a relatively integrated relationship with Labour and there is no realistic prospect of them replicating that relationship with any other party. Even the non-affiliated umbrella organization, the TUC, whose links are not formal, can still be considered relatively close to the party.

Moreover, despite the dismissive attitude displayed by some contemporary trade union leaders to the 'New Labour' era, one can argue that they and their members actually did rather well out of the thirteen years of Labour government between 1997 and 2010. There was a slight, if not huge improvement in the legal framework under which they operated. A minimum wage was legislated for the first time ever in the UK, even if real wages for many began to stagnate after 2003. Labour also managed, at least until the global downturn that began in 2007/8, not only to engineer steady growth but to ensure that its fruits, in terms of tax revenues, were poured into additional spending on health, education, and other public services in which union members were either directly employed or on which the private companies they worked for were deeply reliant. Nor was there any return to attempts by previous Labour governments to control inflation by trying to control wages. And when the crash came, Labour offered the electorate (and therefore the unions) a less austere alternative than did the Conservatives.

Parties make a difference, and getting the Labour Party elected still matters to the UK's trade unions—possibly all the more so after receiving two harsh reminders since 2010 of what can happen when they fail. That did not stop many union leaders, as well as over half of the 30,000 or more trade union members who opted to become affiliated members of the party, plumping for an out-and-out left-winger to lead Labour in 2015. Yet even left-wing unions declined to support that leader's desire to scrap the Trident nuclear submarine programme that guarantees jobs for some of their members (Settle 2016). Meanwhile, one of them (the GMB) decided to endorse his opponent in the 2016 leadership contest following a ballot of its members. This suggests that union support for Corbyn is rather more contingent and therefore short-lived than many of us or, indeed, many of them imagine. That said, there is a serious possibility, should Labour's grassroots members continue to support a leader who has lost the confidence of over three-quarters of his parliamentary colleagues but refuses to resign, that the party might split. Quite what the unions would do in that worst-case scenario is anyone's guess.

NOTES

1. The other unions were UNISON, the National Union of Teachers (NUT), and the Union of Shop, Distributive and Allied Workers (USDAW). We have excluded those unions from the tables in this chapter on purely practical grounds: not to have done so would have meant that indications of 'missing data' would have appeared throughout, doing little or nothing for the reader. They are, though, included in the dataset, where we are of course able to make some judgements based on publicly available information.
2. For more detail on allegations of union 'interference', see Bale (2015).

14

Still So Happy Together?

The Relationship between Labour Unions and the Democratic Party

Christopher Witko

Compared to most other affluent democracies, relationships between labour unions and the traditional centre-left (Democratic) party in America have generally been less institutionalized and, thus, probably weaker (Epstein 1967). The major parties have never been organs of the union movement, nor have unions ever been organized by parties. There have been no statutory links between labour organizations and the Democratic Party. Nevertheless, organized labour and the Democratic Party have a long history of working together to achieve common political goals. In the New Deal and post-Second World War eras, unions and the Democratic Party strengthened one another through the mutual exchange of valuable resources, and together transformed American politics and public policy. But things have changed substantially in recent years. In this chapter, I consider the current state of the relationship between trade unions and the Democratic Party in the United States, and place the contemporary interactions into broader historical and comparative context. As the union movement has weakened, arguably so too have the links between the Democratic Party and organized labour.

BACKGROUND AND CONTEXT

A number of the features of American political institutions and society discourage close, exclusive relationships between external groups and parties in general, and labour unions and parties in particular. The American political system is characterized by a fragmentation of government authority with separated powers and federalism, features that arguably make exclusive relationships with parties less attractive for organized interests (Allern and Bale 2012a). In addition, in a two party system in a large, diverse society it is also less attractive for parties to closely ally themselves with one group, since they need broad support among different social groups (Epstein 1967). In the late nineteenth century, when the labour movement fully emerged, American parties were weak and decentralized and represented a broad range of interests with no true left-wing alternative, so the benefits of close relationships with either party were questionable from labour's perspective. In addition, the system of federalism and separated powers makes it difficult for even programmatic parties to implement their agenda (and American parties were far from programmatic) making strong links with a single party less attractive (see Chapter 1).

Labour decided not to form an independent party, in part due to the electoral system (which makes forming a successful third party difficult), but also because, given that the formation of the party system preceded the growth of the labour movement, often trade union leaders already had deep partisan attachments to either existing party (Archer 2010). From the perspective of the Democratic Party, in the late 1800s and early 1900s when union-party dyads were forming in other countries, the relative weakness of the labour movement in the US meant that it could provide relatively few resources for the party, making unions an unattractive ally.

Despite these obstacles, a robust working relationship between labour and the Democratic Party developed. While both parties still had heterogeneous economic constituencies, after the election of 1896 the Democratic Party was probably the more left-wing alternative (Kazin 2006), making it a more attractive option for unions. However, support for the Republican Party among some union leaders prevented an outright alliance at this early date (Archer 2010). Labour flirted with the idea of aligning itself with the Democratic Party when unions strongly supported the election campaigns of Woodrow Wilson in 1912 and 1916, but it was not until the 1930s and the emergence of Roosevelt's New Deal that unions became consistent supporters of Democratic candidates, albeit remaining officially non-aligned (Greenstone 1969).

In the 1930s, two large labour federations existed. The older American Federation of Labour (AFL) generally represented skilled trades (e.g. carpenters and electricians) in craft-based unions. The Congress of Industrial Organizations (CIO) typically represented lower-skilled workers and organized along an industrial union model (where workers in a single plant would be organized in the same union regardless of their job within the plant). For a number of decades these federations competed, but in the 1950s they merged to form the AFL-CIO, which is the largest, and technically only, labour federation in America (an organization called 'Change to Win', formed in 2005, includes four unions that left the AFL-CIO, but bills itself as a 'coalition').

The merger probably made it easier to coordinate interactions between unions and the Democratic Party (Dark 1999; Klemm 1944; Mergen 1972), which can make it easier to maintain relationships with external organizations (Witko 2009).

Much like the relationships between other interests and parties (Allern and Bale 2012a), because the Democratic Party is not in any way an organ of the labour movement (or vice versa), nor the product of a true left-wing ideology, the strength of the relationship between unions and the Democratic Party is largely dependent on the perception of mutually beneficial resource exchange. In turn, the potential for resource exchange between unions and the Democratic Party to be realized was dependent on the peculiarities of machine politics and the location of industrial development and trade union strength across the country. Democratic Party machines and strong union organizations tended to grow up alongside one another in the industrial cities of the East Coast and Midwest, but in parts of the US where this proximity did not exist, most notably in the South with its later industrial development and weak unions, unions have not played much of a role within local Democratic Party organizations (Witko 2009).

The non-ideological but highly permeable nature of American parties created both opportunities for, and challenges to, organized labour's influence in the Democratic Party. Due to this permeability, it was relatively easy for labour to gain a foothold in the Democratic Party in the 1930s, but it was also fairly easy for other groups to gain a strong position within the party from the 1960s onwards, weakening labour's position. In contrast, unions are typically not very open to outside organizations. Thus, top Democratic officials rarely played an important role in individual unions or the union movement, with the notable exception of some Democratic Party politicians and officials actively encouraging the merger of the AFL-CIO in the 1950s (Mergen 1972).

Nonetheless, the Democratic Party was important to the union movement by providing beneficial legislation in exchange for electorally valuable resources, such as money and campaign workers. From the 1930s through the late 1960s, organized labour became the largest source of electoral resources—money and campaign workers—for the Democrats (Greenstone 1969; Wright 2000). Consequently, unions played a very important role within the Democratic Party, both in terms of winning elections and in shaping the policy agenda when the party was in power (Greenstone 1969; Dark 1999). This agenda included pro-union legislation, a commitment to promoting growth in heavily unionized industries, and legislation beneficial for the working class more broadly (Grant and Wallace 1994; Radcliff and Saiz 1998; Dark 1999). These policies were important to maintaining a strong labour movement.

Because the party–union relationship was built largely on resource exchange, the relationship has changed substantially as union resources have declined. Compared to other countries, the US never had a very high union density rate, and union density has declined much further than in most countries (see Chapter 2). From the 1950s to the present, union density has dropped from about one-third of workers to just over 10 per cent. This reflects the decline of heavy industry, the rise of the service sector, and an unfavourable political environment for unions, among other factors (Tope and Jacobs 2009).

Though American campaigns are not publicly funded, American campaign finance laws make it very difficult for unions to keep pace with businesses and wealthy individuals (Gais 1996). Somewhat remarkably, given the decline in union density, unions have actually increased their campaign contributions even as union membership has declined (Francia 2006), but the increase in labour's contributions has not kept up with the increasing contributions by other entities, especially business and the wealthy. Perhaps more damaging still, the number of votes that labour can turn out has fallen substantially due to a decline in the industrial working class and in union density (as can be seen in the data presented in Chapter 2). As a result, the Democratic Party has increasingly tried to appeal to middle class and affluent voters, weakening the party's traditional emphasis on economic issues (Berry 1999; Witko 2016).

To replace labour union campaign financing, the Democratic Party has courted business interests and firms with the result that organized labour appears to have less access to party leaders and influence over the policies pursued when Democrats hold office (Francia 2010). Accordingly, it is argued that in recent years the relationship between unions and the Democratic Party has shown some signs of weakening as the value of labour union ties to the Democratic Party has declined, and vice versa.

These conclusions about the strains in the relationship between labour and the Democrats have, however, been made based on an analysis of campaign finance and voting data, which are conceptualized as the independent variables that influence the organizational strength of relationships within the theoretical framework set out in this volume. There has been little study of the different links that connect labour organizations to Democratic Party decision-making bodies and/or decision-makers, or whether labour union and party actors share the perceptions of increased distance and how these strains manifest themselves in particular policy issues. In what follows, I discuss the actual strength of links between labour organizations and the Democratic Party using the project's party/union survey data and other publicly available data sources, and analyse changes in the explanatory factors that are thought to influence the strength of links between labour organizations and parties, such as campaign finance and voting data.

Since the merger of the AFL and CIO, most American unions and union members are affiliated with the AFL-CIO. While there is only one major labour federation, large individual unions can and do engage in independent political action. Therefore, in addition to surveying the AFL-CIO, attempts were made to survey the American Federation of Teachers (AFT), the

International Brotherhood of Carpenters and Joiners (the Carpenters), the Service Employees International Union (SEIU), the United Auto Workers (UAW), and the Change-to-Win (CTW) coalition, which for a brief period was attempting to rival the AFL-CIO as a major labour federation. These unions were selected because they are large (the SEIU is the largest union in America) and cover different cleavages within the union movement. These unions represent different sectors (mostly white-collar public sector workers in the AFT and mostly blue-collar private sector workers in the Carpenters and UAW), and represent the traditional craft unions of the AFL (the Carpenters) and the industrial CIO unions (the UAW). Unfortunately only one labour organization completed the questionnaire, but fortunately it was the AFL-CIO. For the other labour organizations, coded judgments have been inserted into the tables when these were possible to make with publicly available sources.

The US has notoriously weak party organizations. Historically the Democratic Party's central party organization—the Democratic National Committee (DNC)—has focused almost exclusively on presidential elections, and did not do much between presidential election cycles, though this has changed somewhat in recent years beginning with DNC Chair Howard Dean. Because the US has a bicameral legislature, the Democratic Party has two legislative party organizations (the House Democratic Caucus (HDC) and the Senate Democratic Caucus (SDC)). Unfortunately, all three of these party organizations stated that they have a strict policy of not completing surveys, so we are left in the position of relying on the AFL-CIO's perspective along with other data in the public domain to understand contemporary labour–Democratic Party relationships.

RELATIONSHIPS TODAY: MAPPING OF LINKS

Unlike some of the other countries studied, the US has two legislative party groups (LPGs) for the major centre-left party: the HDC and the SDC (see previous section). But because the survey responses were the same for each, they are presented in a single column to maintain consistency with other chapters.

Overlapping Organizational Structures: Statutory Links

It should not be surprising, given our earlier discussion, that there are not any clear statutorily defined links between the Democratic Party and unions.[1] This is very apparent for unions and labour organizations that do not generally allow for any external actors to have a formal, statutorily defined role in internal governance.

The Democratic Party does allow for external organizations and actors to have formal representation within the party, but not unions. One way that the Democratic Party does this is by recognizing 'caucuses', which are smaller groups of party members from minority racial, ethnic, gender, or other demographic categories that convene to discuss issues during the DNC convention. The AFL-CIO indicated that there is no guaranteed representation for the organization within either the CPO or LPGs, however, but open-ended comments indicated that there is a 'labour caucus' within the DNC (see also Dark 1999; Bodah et al. 2003). The discrepancy may reflect the fact that this caucus is not exclusively for, nor limited to, the AFL-CIO or its union affiliates. Nevertheless in practice, due to the AFL-CIO's dominant position within the labour movement, AFL-CIO unions would be virtually guaranteed representation in this body.

However, Masket et al. (2014) note that this labour organization within the DNC is actually a 'council' that meets before the Democratic National Convention, rather than an officially recognized party caucus. In practice these two types of organizations are fairly similar and party activists often conflate the two, but for our purposes a key difference is that councils are not officially recognized in party statutes, though they serve similar functions of facilitating communication between groups and party leaders (Masket et al. 2014).

Inter-organizational Links: Reciprocal and Durable

As with formal statutory links, reciprocal and durable links are non-existent.[2] While the AFL-CIO indicated that there are no tacit agreements about one-sided or mutual representation, the labour council just discussed arguably provides for some representation of union members in the DNC, though again this is not restricted to, or guaranteed to be from, the AFL-CIO. Unfortunately only the AFL-CIO completed the survey, but it is safe to assume that other labour organizations would have even fewer institutionalized linkages with the Democratic Party than the AFL-CIO.

Inter-organizational Links: One-way and Occasional

In contrast with statutorily defined or durable and reciprocal links, we see more evidence of occasional links between the labour organizations and the Democratic Party (see Table 14.1). Again, both the HDC and the SDC had the same pattern of interactions with the AFL-CIO, so I report these responses in a single column for both organizations.

Table 14.1. One-way, occasional links at the organizational level between party central organization/legislative group and union confederation, last five years (c.2008–13)[1]

Party-confederation dyad—CPO	Dem-AFL-CIO		Dem-Change to Win	Dem-SEIU	Dem-UAW	Dem-Carpenters	Dem-AFT
	P/U	CJ	CJ	CJ	CJ	CJ	CJ
Invitation to party to participate in the organization's national congress	Yes	Yes	Yes	Yes	Yes	Yes	Yes
Invitation to organization to participate in the party's national congress/conference	Yes	Yes	Yes	Yes	Yes	Yes	Yes
Invitations to organization to participate in the party's ordinary meetings, seminars, and conferences	No	No	No	No	No	No	No
Invitation to party to participate in ordinary organization meetings, seminars, and conferences	Yes	Yes	Yes	Yes	Yes	Yes	Yes
Invitations to organization to special consultative arrangements initiated by the party	No	No	No	No	No	No	No
Invitations to party to special consultative arrangements initiated by the organization	n. d.	n. d.	No	No	No	No	No

Party-confederation dyad—LPG	Dem-AFL-CIO		Dem-Change to Win	Dem-SEIU	Dem-UAW	Dem-Carpenters	Dem-AFT
	P/U	CJ	CJ	CJ	CJ	CJ	CJ
Invitation to party to participate in the organization's national congress	No	No	No	No	No	No	No
Invitation to organization to participate in the party's national congress/conference	n.a.	n.a.	n.a.	n.a.	n.a.	n.a.	n.a.
Invitations to organization to participate in the party's ordinary meetings, seminars, and conferences	No	No	No	No	No	No	No
Invitation to party to participate in ordinary organization meetings, seminars, and conferences	No	No	No	No	No	No	No
Invitations to organization to special consultative arrangements initiated by the party	Yes	Yes	Yes	Yes	Yes	Yes	Yes
Invitations to party to special consultative arrangements initiated by the organization	n.d.	n.d.	No	No	No	No	No

[1] 'P/U' indicates responses from party/trade union questionnaires, 'CJ' signifies the authors' 'coded judgment' based on alternative sources in cases of diverging or missing P/U answers. 'c.d.' means contradictory data (diverging P/U answers), 'n.d.' means no data (informant didn't know/missing/unclear), and 'n.a.' means not applicable in this case. Note that for all organizations except the AFL-CIO it is difficult to be certain about the existence of such informal interactions based on publicly available sources. Therefore, while a coded judgment has been included in the table, the confidence is above 40, but not very high compared to the AFL-CIO cells, which are based on that organization's responses to a survey.

We see here that there are multiple forms of event-based links between the AFL-CIO and the Democratic Party. Representatives of the DNC have been invited to ordinary meetings, seminars, and conferences. The DNC has not reciprocated by inviting the AFL-CIO, however. In contrast, relationships appear closer with the LPGs, which are probably much more important in the context of American politics, where the DNC is a relatively weak organization that is most active around presidential elections and plays a limited role in the policy process. Though the AFL-CIO has not invited LPGs to its meetings, it has been invited to attend some special consultative sessions and annual meetings of the LPGs. Thus, despite the lack of more formal, institutionalized linkages, we do see significant evidence that the Democratic Party and the AFL-CIO work together in a variety of different settings.

Because the other unions did not complete the survey it is not possible to say with complete confidence what the patterns of occasional links would be between these other labour organizations and the Democratic Party organizations. The SEIU is seen as a major ally of President Obama because it announced its support for him early in the primary season against Hillary Clinton in 2008, but whether these close links with the Obama campaign have translated into close links with the DNC remains unclear. Given the dominant position of the AFL-CIO in the American union movement, it is again probable that for the individual unions and Change to Win, occasional links with the Democratic Party would be fewer.

Individual-level Links: Individual Contacts and Personnel Overlaps and Transfers

It is possible that, even without formal institutional arrangements or special meetings that bring together both organizations, personal interactions between party officials and union officials ensure linkage between parties and labour unions. For example, the AFL-CIO reported that they engage party officials in informal meetings or phone conversations, e-mails, SMS, etc.

In addition to these communications among members of different organizations, if individuals often transfer between positions in the party and in labour organizations, this would facilitate cooperation through shared loyalties and operational information. Unlike some other countries, however, where working in the labour movement is a stepping stone to a political career, in the US this is a very unusual career path for members of Congress, and almost unheard of for presidents (ironically, one exception to this was Ronald Reagan, who was president of the Screen Actors Guild but eventually had very anti-union views).

Getting a firm count of which Democrats in Congress have backgrounds in labour unions is difficult because we must rely on how they present themselves in their official biographies, and this 'presentation of self' is very much the result of political calculations (Fenno 1978). Some members (i.e. those from working class districts with a strong union presence) have an incentive to advertise their union background, while others lack such an incentive. But given the upper class and professional bias in the backgrounds of members of Congress (Carnes 2013), the percentage with backgrounds as high-ranking union officials is almost certainly in the single digits. Notable examples include Representative Stephen Lynch of Massachusetts, who served as president of the Ironworkers Union, and Representative Linda Sanchez, who was an official with the electrician's union (IBEW), and also headed the Orange County (California) Central Labour Council before seeking public office. A number of other members have been rank-and-file members of unions at one point or another.

Some unelected party officials also have a background or currently hold leadership positions in labour organizations. For instance, Maria Elena Durazo, the executive-secretary treasurer of the Los Angeles County Federation of Labour (which is a local affiliate of the state of California AFL-CIO, and the national AFL-CIO), is also a vice chair of the DNC. There are also examples of staff and strategists going from the party to work for unions. For example, Mary Beth Cahill worked in a number of positions within and for the party before becoming political director of the United Auto Workers union in 2011, and subsequently worked for a pro-Obama political organization (i.e. a so-called super PAC[3]).

Overall Degree of Closeness and Range

The organizational structures of the Democratic Party and the trade unions do not overlap via statutory links. There are essentially no reciprocal and durable links between unions and Democratic Party organizations either. There are some occasional, one-way links, but even many of these potential linkages are absent. Not surprisingly then, we can see in Figures 14.1a and 14.1b that the score for overall links is very low in an absolute sense, achieving at most 5 out of a possible 20 and 3 out of 12—the total scores obtained by the AFL-CIO-Democrats' central organization and the AFL-CIO-Democrats in the Congress/Senate respectively. In a comparative sense the total link scores are also fairly low. While the US does have links about as strong as France, the link scores are lower than for most other countries, including what may be the best historical comparison, Australia.

Moreover, there is comparatively little personnel overlap. Considering this, one might expect that labour organizations would not feel that they have a very close relationship with the Democratic Party. Somewhat surprisingly then, in response to a question about the organization's closeness to the

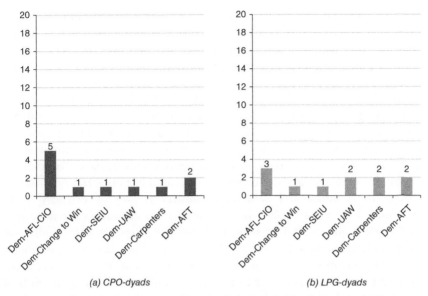

Figure 14.1. Total link scores of central party organization–trade union relationships and legislative party–trade union relationships (0–20/0–12).[1]

[1] The theoretical maximum link score is 20 for the CPO-dyads and 12 for LPG-dyads since some link items are unlikely to apply to the legislative party group and were thus not included in this part of the survey. However, when comparing dyads involving CPOs with those involving LPGs, one should still keep in mind that the latter's maximum involves fewer links than the former's top scores.

Democratic Party, the AFL-CIO reported that it has a 'fairly close' relationship with the Democratic Party organizations, when presented with that option along with 'integrated', 'ad hoc', and 'distant/separated'. Though they did not complete the questionnaire, it is probable that at least some of the other unions would have answered similarly.

How can organizations with so few official links with the Democratic Party consider themselves to be fairly close to the party? Some of this feeling of closeness probably reflects the history of closeness, and also the lack of a viable alternative ally within the party system, since the Republican Party is openly anti-labour. The result is that unions have essentially no relationship with the Republican Party as an organization, or even very many individual Republicans, despite the fact that unions sometimes had close relationships with Republican politicians in the past. The current Republican Party in Congress has more members with backgrounds in business, with less favourable attitudes towards and weaker relationships with unions (Witko and Friedman 2008). Within the union movement there is a very limited range of types of relationships within the two major parties. Virtually all unions and labour organizations have stronger links with the Democratic Party. However, some unions—such as police and firefighter unions—have some sort of relationship with both parties, and the traditional building trade unions (plumbers, carpenters, etc.) probably have more distant relations with the Democratic Party than the public employee or service sector unions, or unions with less-skilled blue-collar workers.

But the perceived closeness also reflects the decentralized nature of American political parties, where interactions with formal party organizations are not as important because these organizations are not as important. Labour's relationships with the Democratic Party are about as institutionalized as those of any other interests. American politics scholars have characterized the collection of official party organizations, candidate organizations, interest groups, think tanks, and even media outlets as part of 'extended party networks' (Koger et al. 2009). Within the Democratic Party's extended network there is quite a bit of movement of staff and resources among individual Democratic candidates, Democratic Party organizations, labour organizations, and other progressive organizations with pro-labour views. And though we focused on contacts between organizational officials in our assessment of the closeness of relations, when considering their closeness with the Democratic Party, labour unions undoubtedly consider this broader organizational context, which still includes the sharing of staff, financial resources, expertise, etc., and helps union leaders and Democratic officials maintain good working relationships, even if direct interactions and organizational overlap are minimal.

In addition, the AFL-CIO reported little change in the relationship with the Democratic Party over the last five years, and this probably reflects the fact that labour has reached a place where it is an important, but not dominant, member of the party coalition as it arguably was in past decades. I discuss some of the factors that have led to a more distant relationship between labour and the Democratic Party, and how this has likely influenced union-related policy, in the following section.

EXPLAINING INCREASED AND RELATIVE DISTANCE

The day after assuming the presidency following Kennedy's assassination, one of the first people that Lyndon Johnson phoned was the head of the AFL-CIO, George Meany (Dark 1999). In 2012, despite union objections, the Democratic National Convention was held in Charlotte, North Carolina, a state with laws that are very unfavourable to union organizing, causing some unionists to boycott the convention (Gardner 2012). These are just anecdotes, of course, but they do capture changes in the relationship between labour and the Democratic Party.

This decline of links and influence for labour likely reflects the fact that unions provide the Democratic Party with relatively fewer resources nowadays. During the heyday of the labour–Democratic Party relationship, labour provided an abundance of finance and votes for the party, while the Democrats aided labour by providing legislation that would allow labour unions to thrive as organizations, providing broader legislation that benefited the working class in general (such as the expansion of the welfare state), and providing access to government leaders that could be used to pursue a number of goals (Dark 1999). Because the Democratic Party controlled Congress almost uninterruptedly from the early 1930s through to the late 1970s, labour had substantial political influence in the government overall, and played a major role in the advancement of labour rights, the expansion of the welfare state, and even civil rights (Greenstone 1969; Dark 1999).

Yet we should not overstate the ability of unions to see their policy preferences enacted, even when Democrats were in control of government and labour was at its pinnacle in the 1950s and 1960s. As is well known, American parties are highly decentralized and greatly lacking in discipline. Democrats from the South, where labour was weak, joined with Republicans to support legislation that seriously weakened unions, such as in the Landrum–Griffin Act, which regulated the internal operations of labour unions, and the Taft–Hartley Act of 1947, which allowed US states to outlaw the practice of making workers join unions as a condition of employment (Ellwood and Fine 1987; Moore 1998). Thus, there were real limits to labour's power within the Democratic Party even when approximately one-third of workers were represented by unions. Nonetheless, there can be little doubt that unions historically benefited from having access to Democratic office-holders when they were in power.

From the standpoint of the Democratic Party, however, unions simply have less to offer than they did in the past. This reflects the dramatic decline of labour union membership that took place during the 1970s and 1980s, translating into fewer union voters than can be mobilized for Democrats. Unions continue to do a good job of marshalling their resources on behalf of Democratic campaigns (Francia 2012), but they have not been able to keep pace with the growing financial mobilization of business interests and wealthy individuals (Hacker and Pierson 2010; Witko 2013; Witko 2016).

Unions never provided very much money to central Democratic Party organizations per se—partly due to campaign finance laws which prohibited unions from making political donations directly from their treasuries and laws limiting the amount that labour PACs could contribute to any single entity (see Chapter 2 in this volume). The AFL-CIO indicated in the survey that they have donated to party committees and individual candidates in recent years (which is easily corroborated using the Federal Election Commission donation database). In recent years, all unions combined provided less than 1 per cent of the contributions received by the DNC ($575,100 out of contributions of approximately $131 million). They do donate substantially more to individual candidate campaigns but, while Wright (2000) reports that unions provided around two-thirds of the contributions to Democratic congressional candidates in the 1960s, between the 1980 and 2012 election cycles the percentage of campaign contributions provided to Democratic candidates from organized labour declined from almost 40 per cent to under 10 per cent (Witko 2013).

In addition to labour organizations providing financial resources, union members and their families have historically provided a higher proportion of votes for Democratic candidates than voters in non-union households (Francia 2012). However, in recent years the gap between union and non-union household support for the Democratic Party has declined. In the 1950s and 1960s the gap in support for Democrats among union and non-union households was around 20 percentage points, but in the last two elections the gap was around 7 percentage points.[4] Rather than any dramatic decline in union support for Democratic candidates, this reflects growing support for the Democrats among non-union households in recent years, probably reflecting successful Democratic appeals for the votes of more affluent professionals. The latter make perfect sense considering that voters from union households comprise a much smaller portion of the vote as union density has declined. Indeed, the unionized share of the presidential electorate has declined from typically over 25 per cent in the 1950s and 1960s to around 15 per cent in recent elections. With higher turnout among union households, labour has arguably managed to maintain more influence than might be expected (Francia 2006), but the decline in resources on offer has probably weakened labour's influence in the party (Francia 2010).

From the standpoint of unions, Democrats also became less willing or able to deliver access or pro-union policies after the 1980s. From 1933 through to 1969, the Democratic Party controlled the executive and both houses of Congress in all but ten years, or over 70 per cent of the time. But since 1980 the Democrats have had unified control of the Congress in only four years, or just over 10 per cent of the time. Thus the Democratic Party has had less of an opportunity to advance its and labour's agenda. And even when the Democrats have controlled institutions of government, there has perhaps been less of a willingness to support union demands or provide unions with access. True, as recently as the late 1990s the head of the DNC would regularly attend major labour union annual conferences, and President Bill Clinton invited major labour union leaders to the White House for individual meetings annually in the 1990s.[5] The president also typically holds an annual 'labour summit' where union leaders are invited to the White House. However, although elected officials have attended union annual conferences in recent years, there is no available evidence that the head of the DNC has done so.

This declining access reflects in part the fact that, with labour's declining resources in the 1980s, many Democrats began openly to question the value of relationships with organized labour, and at the same time began to court business interests and middle class professionals and managers (Hacker and Pierson 2010). This was best exemplified by Bill Clinton, who was known for his embrace of centrist economic positions rather than the more left-leaning economic policies associated with Democrats like Johnson and Franklin Roosevelt. Indeed, the Democratic Leadership Council (a centrist Democratic Party organization once led by Bill Clinton) consciously eschewed relationships with the older Democratic Party constituencies, including organized labour, in support of appeals to the growing ranks of economically moderate white-collar professionals (Bodah et al. 2003). Given the shrinking membership of organized labour, the perceived costs associated with openly supporting unions in terms of a loss of support from non-union constituencies began to outweigh the benefits of such support for many Democrats.

SUMMARY AND CONCLUSION

Trade unions, and especially the major labour federation in America, the AFL-CIO, have long had a relatively close, although mainly informal, relationship with the Democratic Party. The alliance between labour and the Democrats emerged in the 1930s, as unions demanded legal recognition and a Democratic Party moving to the left embraced this, along with other pro-labour policy positions. The relationship was cemented over the decades by large amounts of union campaign contributions and the mobilization of union voters and households. In return, the Democrats provided access to government officials and favourable policy. Even at the height of labour power, union influence within the Democratic Party was limited compared to the power of unions in left-leaning parties in other countries. After all, conservative Southerners comprised a large bloc of Democratic officeholders, who were often vehemently anti-union, and who led the charge on some anti-union policies. On the other hand, labour unions were clearly the most powerful interest within the Democratic Party. Now, the declining importance of union funds and votes means that they are just one of a number of organized interests that can make claims regarding access to Democratic Party leaders, which likely results in fewer links than in previous decades.

This decline of organizational links between unions and the Democratic Party has had an important influence on policy debates and public policy outcomes over the last few decades. For instance, in their compelling work on growing income inequality, Hacker and Pierson (2010) argue that the relative decline of union power within the Democratic Party fuelled economic and tax policy changes that created what those authors call 'the winner takes all economy'. Thus, in general, public policy has become more favourable to the wealthy, and important union priorities do not get much of a hearing, even when the Democratic Party controls government.

While President Obama was perhaps rhetorically a little more leftist than President Clinton, in fact the policies pursued by Democratic governments have probably remained very similar since the 1990s. The Republican grip on Congress after the 1994 election prevented unions successfully advocating for changes to labour law that would have made it easier to form unions and recruit members during the 1990s and early 2000s. For example, so-called 'card check' would have allowed for workers to check cards indicating their support for joining a union, avoiding the need for a protracted union recognition election campaign, which American companies are expert in defeating. However, when the Democrats gained control of Congress in 2007, and then unified control of government in 2009, these ideas were not seriously pursued (Francia 2010).

Union weakness within the Democratic Party also probably contributed to the financial crisis and the federal government's arguably anaemic response to its aftermath. As unions and the working class became weaker within the Democratic coalition, the Democratic Party became less distinguishable from the Republican Party on matters of deregulation and ultimately the dangerous reliance on risky financial practices for economic growth which caused the crisis (see Witko 2016). In its aftermath, it seems that policymakers were more concerned with bolstering bank profits in the short term than with stimulating job growth, and many leading Democrats, most notably Treasury Secretary Timothy Geithner, were hesitant to reregulate the financial industry vigorously.

The stimulus packages that did get signed into law took the form of monetary stimulus (via increased government bond-buying) rather than the kind of fiscal stimulus which would arguably do more to create jobs (Perry and Vernengo 2014). Even the fiscal stimulus laws enacted contained more tax cuts than spending on infrastructure such as roads and bridges, which would spur employment for unionized workers in the construction industry. This was in marked contrast to responses to economic downturns prior to the 1980s, which routinely contained a large amount of construction spending to spur employment in these unionized fields (Dark 1999). The decision not to invest in infrastructure when the state of America's decrepit infrastructure is well known and the government could borrow money for free is bizarre, unless we look at the power of competing interests overall and within the Democratic Party. Put simply, unions do not appear to have as much influence within the party as they have in the past, and this has important broad policy consequences.

Arguably, from a strategic standpoint it was smart for the Democrats to court other interests, as structural economic change and hostile political and policy conditions weakened unions. After all, though union decline has continued since the early 1980s, the Democrats have sometimes had unified control of government in recent years. It is difficult to see how they might have accomplished this by relying mostly on the resources of labour unions and appealing mostly to union workers. And even when the Democrats are less influenced by unions, working class voters probably remain better off when Democrats are in control of government (Bartels 2008). However, waning union influence within the Democratic Party also means waning working class influence in the American political system.

NOTES

1. A table is not presented as there were no 'yes values' (coded judgments).
2. A table is not presented as there were no 'yes values' (coded judgments).
3. According to one comprehensive definition, 'Technically known as independent expenditure-only committees, super PACs may raise unlimited sums of money from corporations, unions, associations and individuals, then spend unlimited sums to overtly advocate for or against political candidates. Unlike traditional PACs, super PACs are prohibited from donating money directly to political candidates, and their spending must not be coordinated with that of the candidates they benefit.' See <https://www.opensecrets.org/pacs/superpacs.php>.
4. The data regarding union household voting presented in this section are all taken from the National Election Studies cumulative data file (NES 2014).
5. This is based on a conversation with Donald L. Fowler, who was DNC chair and co-chair during the late 1990s.

15

The Relationship between Left-of-Centre Parties and Trade Unions in Contemporary Democracies

Elin Haugsgjerd Allern, Tim Bale, and Simon Otjes

INTRODUCTION

The historical examples *par excellence* of close party–interest group relationships, both in Europe and elsewhere, were the old left-of-centre parties and trade unions. The overall motivation for writing this book has been to interrogate systematically the widespread assumption that these relationships, in organizational terms, are characterized today by distance. Since the 1960s, it has been argued that the traditional links between left-of-centre parties and trade unions have decayed as party–union collaboration has become less mutually beneficial, not least due to changes in the economy and the labour market. But as existing studies of those links have for the most part been ad hoc, indirect, and individual, scholars have been unable to draw clear conclusions across cases. Moreover, as we argued in Chapter 1, there is no determinism implied here even if one believes that structural and institutional factors matter.

This book is an attempt to come closer to the truth by means of a rigorous cross-national study of contemporary relationships. It also represents an attempt to examine whether old left-of-centre parties have forged links with employee associations other than the traditional blue-collar unions. Are they connected with other employee organizations in addition to, or even instead of, their traditional ally or allies. Are contemporary trade unions closely linked with only one left-of-centre party? Or do they prefer weaker connections with multiple parties, or prefer to keep their distance from political parties in general?

Covering a dozen countries that have been democracies since at least the mid to late 1940s, in Europe, North America, and Oceania, we are able to discover whether the relationships we are interested in look different or similar right across the world. Our country selection (described in more detail in Chapter 2) captures different types of economic, political, and institutional settings, country sizes, continents/regions, and provides us with historical examples of both strong and weak (or at least weaker) links. On the party side, we study old left-of-centre parties—social democratic/labour/socialist/communist and other parties associated with the historical labour movement (including surviving splinter parties), distinguishing between extra-legislative central party organizations (CPOs) and legislative party groups (LPGs). On the union side, we study all today's peak associations, and where these are relatively unimportant we have also included the major individual unions or super-unions as equivalents. In this way, we are able to examine if the parties have widened their organizational networks to include new employee groups, and whether different kinds of employee organizations differ in their approach to left-of-centre parties. That said, we mainly use pairs of parties and trade union confederations/unions as our unit of analysis. As shown in Chapter 2, our analytical focus means that we cover eighty-one (CPO) plus eighty-one (LPG) party-union dyads.

For the sake of tractability, we focus on the national/leadership level of politics. Analytically, we concentrate on party–trade union relationships in the limited organizational sense, assuming, as we noted in Chapter 1, that the notion of 'party–union relationship' refers to the extent to which—and how—parties and trade unions are connected as organizations, and how they deal with each other. Party–union links are those means by which a party and an interest group may communicate—such as formal affiliation and representation of unions in party executives, joint committees, actual personnel leadership over-laps, or more or less regular elite contact. By mapping organizational links we are able to measure *the general organizational closeness of relationships*, i.e. the strength/weakness of organizational links between, on the one hand, the party in question and the (confederations of) trade unions on the other.

The empirical mapping—unpacked in Chapter 2—is partly based on writ-ten sources, including party and union statutes, and partly based on a survey and structured interviews conducted among key informants in the parties and trade unions examined. The new and rich data allow us to draw broad conclusions about relationships that have impacted—and perhaps continue to impact—on politics the world over. We have created four new, innovative datasets based on the survey of links at the organizational level: one each for unions, CPOs, and LPGs, and one with the party-union dyads as units of analysis. The final dataset is based on the first three and is the one we mainly use for the analyses in this chapter. To solve the problem of some diverging party/union answers and some unreturned questionnaires, we have coded expert judgments based on the survey in combination with other sources in the dyadic file (see Chapter 2).[1]

We assume the dimension of closeness/distance *primarily* reflects the extent to which relationships are institutionalized—the degree to which party–union contact is incorporated into a structured and formalized system or set of arenas in which interaction takes place. This has to do both with the kind of and the number of connections—the extent, if you will, of durable and/or organized links for contact. In Chapter 2, we conducted a scaling analysis across the link items mapped in order to check whether they are hierarchically ordered as we assumed, and whether they vary along a unidimensional or multidimensional scale of closeness. The scaling results were strong at the transnational level. This means that pairs of parties and trade unions that have unusually strong links also tend to enjoy the links that occur in many, sometimes weaker party–union relationships too. Accordingly, we created an additive overall score of 'organizational closeness' by counting the number of 'yes values' for all the all links used in the scaling analysis for all those dyads without any 'unclear values'. On the basis of the scaling analysis, a low score points to the existence of only weak (albeit commonly occurring) ties, whereas the highest scores point to the existence of both weaker (common) and strong (less common) links.

We acknowledge, however, that intensive actual contact might also be established through completely informal connections at the individual level. Therefore, we have tried to assess personnel overlaps and transfers between unions (staff and officials) and the legislative party group. Finally, we are interested in the *overall range of left of centre party–trade union relationships*, mainly seen from the party side: are left-of-centre parties only or primarily linked to their traditional union allies, or have they established links with a wide range of employee organizations? We will also briefly touch upon the relationship of trade unions with other parties.

In the remainder of this chapter, we start by briefly summarizing the main conclusions of the empirical assessments presented in the preceding country chapters (Chapters 3–14). In the countries where union confederation/unions have been close to a centre-right party historically, this relationship has been outlined too. But here—in the comparative summary—we focus on the left-of-centre, seeing the links of other parties to unions as something that might constrain party–union relationships on the left. Thereafter, we move to comparing contemporary relationships via our dyadic dataset. After presenting the general descriptive statistics, we zoom in on the traditional relationships between the major left-of-centre parties and their traditional trade union ally or allies, before we compare the strength of these long-established organizational connections in different countries. Then we widen the perspective again and explore what characterizes party–union relationships in general in the different countries. Throughout, we address the question of possible differences between relationships involving the different 'faces' of parties (CPO/LPG), and look at the scores based on *both* CPO and LPG values in order to get a single measure. Finally, we compare these with available data on personnel overlaps and transfers, and also with the parties' and unions' own rating of the degree of organizational closeness/distance. In this way, we get an indication of whether taking account of informal organizational aspects modifies or confirms the picture.

COUNTRY ANALYSES: FROM CONTINUOUS INTEGRATION TO VIRTUAL SEPARATION

Taken together, the historical descriptions provided by the country chapters—of statutory links, inter-organizational links, and links at the individual level—support the idea that the strength of connections varied right from the outset, even if relationships were generally rather close: the most intimate—institutionalized—relationships developed in the UK, Australia, and the Nordic countries (i.e. Sweden and Finland). Close, though somewhat less integrated relations, characterized Israel and Austria as well. Relatively strong but somewhat weaker party–union links originally existed in the Netherlands, and between the German Social Democrats and the major trade union confederation. In Switzerland, the socialist party and the associated union confederation were both formally independent from the beginning, yet still aligned at the organizational level. Italy and France were from the start characterized by less institutionalized relationships but significant informal ties, albeit that unions there were most closely aligned to communist rather than socialist or social democratic parties. In the United States, relationships between labour unions and the traditional centre-left (Democratic) party have generally been less institutionalized than in many European countries, but based on significant informal links.

After describing how historical relationships have been challenged by social and economic developments, the country chapters provide a detailed empirical assessment of the contemporary relationship between established left-of-centre parties and all the major confederations of trade unions. Generally, party–union links have declined since the Second World War, but increased autonomy does not in most cases mean full separation, and some cases are characterized by relative stability rather than change, not least if we focus on the relationship between the main established left-of-centre party and its traditional trade union ally or allies.

Countries in which the decline of traditional party–union links has been relatively limited are the United Kingdom, Australia, Finland, and Sweden. Paul Webb and Tim Bale (Chapter 13) conclude that the relationship between the Labour Party and not least the major individual trade unions is still 'an integrated, organic one insofar as the formal affiliation of some unions continues to exist and continues to carry with it rights of representation and influence in the party's institutions and procedures, its structures, and its processes'. Phil Larkin and Charles Lees (Chapter 3) argue that the Australian Labour Party 'is the creation of the union movement and institutional links between the affiliated trade unions and the ALP remain strong'.

According to Tapio Raunio and Niko Laine (Chapter 5), the links between trade unions and the major left-of-centre party in Finland are 'solid and fairly well institutionalized', including 'routinized arrangements that draw on decades of experience of working together for mutual benefit'. Jenny Jansson's analysis of the Swedish case (Chapter 11) reminds us that, although collective affiliation of unions no longer exists, the SAP and unions still have joint committees and meetings on a regular basis, and that the Confederation of Trade Unions (LO) still enjoys representation in the party's board and executive committee: hence 'the relationship appears to be vital despite changes in social, economic, and institutional settings'.

Likewise, Roland Erne and Sebastian Schief (Chapter 12) conclude in their analysis of parties and trade unions in Switzerland that there continue to be significant links between the social democratic party and the union confederation SGB, and moreover 'a growing relationship between the formerly distant Travail.Suisse and the SP'. The relationship between the Austrian Social Democratic Party (SPÖ) and the social democratic faction of the peak association ÖGB has not been assigned a total score, and its traditional union ally PRO-GE is given only a medium score, but, as Richard Luther concludes in Chapter 4, the party–union relationships still 'include overlapping structures, inter-organizational links that are reciprocal and durable, as well as many others that are occasional' and 'a dense pattern of overlapping directorates'.[2]

According to our country chapters there are also places where the relationship between the left-of-centre parties and trade unions have grown relatively distant: namely the Israeli, Dutch, and Italian cases. In Israel the traditionally strong links between the Mapai/Labour Party and the Histadrut have dramatically weakened, although links between unions and politicians continue to play a role, as Ronen Mandelkern and Gideon Rahat show in Chapter 8. And Simon Otjes and Anne Rasmussen (Chapter 10) conclude that, in the Netherlands today, political parties and trade union confederations operate independently of each other and the fairly strong links that 'existed between Dutch political parties and trade unions during pillarization have disappeared'. The significant, if not very formal, links that existed between the Italian communist party and the confederation CGIL eventually faded and, after the transformation of the PCI into PD, the relationship became mainly ad hoc. Recently, Liborio Mattina and Mimmo Carrieri (Chapter 9) argue, 'the relationship between the CGIL and the PD has badly deteriorated, following the generational change which has occurred within the Democratic Party and the electoral success of Matteo Renzi'.

The German case seems to lie somewhere in between the poles of relative stability and significant decline. The *Gewerkschaftsrat,* a permanent advisory body of the social democratic SPD and trade unions, still exists; but the days of a privileged partnership between the SPD and the unions are over. Instead a new pluralized set of relationships came into existence, replacing some of the ties to Social Democracy with connections to other parties, most notably to Die Linke, Tim Spier concludes (Chapter 7). Similarly, but from a lower level of institutionalization at the outset, Christopher Witko suggests that the declining importance of union funds and votes have likely resulted 'in fewer links than in previous decades' between the Democratic Party and major trade unions in the United States (Chapter 14). Finally, we learn from Nick Parsons (Chapter 6) that party–union relations in France 'show both continuity and change'. The relationship between the Socialist Party and trade union confederations continues to be 'loose and ad hoc'. The closest relations are still maintained by the PS-CFDT dyad. Parsons suggests that 'these have not required any loosening as they have always been informal and not based on any durable organizational underpinning'. As a result, party–union relations in France are multi-directional, with no exclusivity in any relationship, on either the union or the party side.

Each and every one of the chapters by our country experts paints a fascinating and detailed picture of the relationship between that country's left-of-centre parties and its trade union confederations/super-unions. Yet the richness of their description need not prevent them from helping to tell a bigger story. We have seen that our concept and measurements have worked well across contexts, although they cannot capture everything: in Israel, for instance, we have learned that the party-based internal elections of the Histadrut confederation create some indirect connections with parties that our analytical focus misses. In Austria, the far from unitary structure of unions complicates the assessment of links; and, above all, in Sweden and the UK we see some organized links which are not included in our conceptualization and index, such as a joint youth organization and unions until very recently enjoying a privileged position in leadership elections. Generally speaking, however, major changes and variation do seem to be captured by the measurements developed in Chapter 2, and the country chapters have also been able to rely upon our index of organizational connections and perception data from the survey. In the remainder of this chapter we will directly compare the various party-union dyads examined in this book based on the different standardized measures developed, and try to assess what all or at least some of them can be said to have in common, and to what extent variation exists across and within countries.

GENERAL FREQUENCY OF LINK TYPES AND DISTRIBUTION OF TOTAL LINK SCORES TODAY

We begin, however, by simply showing the frequencies of the different links mapped at the organizational level. Table 15.1 suggests that such links certainly exist today: nearly all of the items we mapped via our party-union survey occur; some, indeed, could be seen as common.

The frequency varies significantly across link types. Statutory links, creating overlapping organizational structures, are rare. Collective affiliation of unions is reported in less than 10 per cent of the cases. About 7 per cent are connected through the union's right to send delegates to the national party conference, and barely any offer the union *ex officio* representation in the party executive or council. No pairs of parties and unions provide the party organization with

Table 15.1. Left-of-centre party–trade union relationships: shares of party-union dyads relying on different link types (%)

Variable (link items)	Party CPO-unions	Party LPG-unions
Collective union affiliation to party (local/national)	8.6	–
Union delegates at party conference	7.4	–
Party delegates at union conference	3.7	–
Party *ex officio seats* in union executive	0	–
Union *ex officio seats* in party executive	1.2	–
Party *ex officio seats* in union council	0	–
Union *ex officio seats* in party council	1.2	–
Tacit agreement about mutual representation	18.5	6.2
Permanent joint committee(s)	14.8	9.9
Temporary joint committee(s)	12.3	6.2
Formal agreement about regular meetings	3.7	2.5
Tacit agreement about regular meetings	35.8	24.7
Joint party-union conferences	16	7.4
Joint party-union campaigns	14.8	13.6
Party invited to union's conference	48.1	44.4
Union invited to party's conference	53.1	–
Union invited to party's ordinary meetings, seminars etc.	54.3	48.1
Party invited to union's ordinary meetings, seminars etc.	50.6	46.9
Union invited to party's special consultative arrangements	69.1	74.1
Party invited to union's special consultative arrangements	51.9	49.4
N	81	81

[1] This table concerns the relationships between communist, social-democratic, and other old left-of-centre parties and all confederations of trade unions/selected unions in every country (pairs of individual parties and confederations/unions). The empty cells (-) represent links we assume are mostly not applicable in the case of LPGs and that we have not surveyed.

guaranteed representation in the national executive or board of representative of unions, and only about 4 per cent allow the party to send delegates to the union conference.

Durable and reciprocal inter-organizational links are more common, albeit mainly outside the legislative arena. In nearly 20 per cent of the cases a tacit agreement exists about mutual representation in national decision-making organs—and it should be noted that this could include more than one party/ union body. A permanent joint (liaison) committee also exists in 15 per cent of the party CPO-union pairs examined. Some 36 per cent report having a formal or tacit cooperation agreement concerning regular meetings. As regards relationships between unions and legislative party groups, there are fewer durable links but about 25 per cent report tacit cooperation agreements about regular meetings.

As we move down the list to the occasional one-sided links, connections become more widespread both within and outside the legislative arena. Party/ union invitations to annual conferences, ordinary meetings, and seminars and special consultative arrangements are common, though not ubiquitous, both within and without the legislative arena. The most common—and even prevalent—link is the union being invited to parties' special consultative arrangements: this exists in 69 per cent of the pairs involving the CPO and 74 per cent of the pairs involving the LPG. Overall, the frequencies suggest that there are more durable links in the relationships involving the central organizations than in the dyads involving the legislative party groups.

We are, in line with the scaling analysis, able to assign an overall scale (index score) of closeness to the relationships examined. As shown in Chapter 2, 84/82 per cent of cases were included in the scaling analysis. Links exist in the excluded cases as well, but it is not possible to assign an overall score due to one or more 'unclear values'. As noted, we calculated separate total scores for the party-union pairs involving CPOs and LPGs (with 20 and 12 as maximum scores respectively) since we assume the strongest links (those creating overlapping structures) are not applicable in the case of LPGs.

If we focus on the joint link-items across the scale (0–12), ignoring statutory links like collective affiliation and formal representation rights, we find that the correlation between the scores for dyads involving CPOs and LPGs is very strong—0.92 for the left-of-centre/traditional ally dyads, and 0.74 for the others (0.82 in general). As explained in Chapter 2, we have therefore also calculated one combined party/union score to get a single score for the relationship between the union confederation/unions and the party/parties at large.[3] In what follows, we present the main results based on all three scores.

From Table 15.2 we see that the mean total link scores are low—4.5 in the case of the party CPO–union relationships, and just above 3 the case of party LPG–union relationships, suggesting that the 'average' left-of-centre party– trade union relationship today is characterized by a number of event-based links (regular invitations to congresses, seminars, and special consultative

Table 15.2. Descriptive statistics: total organizational link scores (0–12/20)

	N	Min.	Max.	Mean	Std. dev.
Party-union dyads					
Party CPO-Unions (0–20)	68	0	16	4.5	4.0
Party LPG-Unions (0–12)	66	0	11	3.3	2.8
Party (CPO/LPG)-Unions (0–20)	66	0	16	4.8	4.0

[1] The table concerns the relationships between communist, social-democratic, and other old left-of-centre parties and all confederations of trade unions/selected unions in every country (pairs of individual parties and confederations/unions)

arrangements, etc.) rather than by formally integrated or in other ways highly institutionalized relationships. However, we see that the range of the distribution is wide: the top score among those surveyed is 16 and 11 respectively (i.e. close to the theoretical maximum score both inside and outside the legislative arena), whereas other relationships are marked by complete separation and are thus virtually non-existent at the organizational level. The standard deviation is 4 and 2.8. For the combined score (ranging from 0–20), the mean value is 4.8, the standard deviation 4. Hence, there is substantial variation in link values to be examined.

Another way of looking at variation is by plotting histograms of scores. Figure 15.1, 15.2, and 15.3 show that the shapes are far from normal distributions: they are all more-or-less skewed to the right. There are very few relationships with very high link scores outside the legislative arena: only two dyads involving parties' central organizations have a truly high score (above 12, see Figure 15.1). Thus, integrated relationships still exist but are rare here: the highest scaling value of 16 points is obtained by the relationship between the British Labour Party and the GMB (a 'super-union' covering all sorts of sectors). The lowest/low scores are the most common. Among the party CPO-union pairs, 19 per cent have no links at the organizational level at all (13 out of 68).

However, it should be noted that a significant number of relationships (nearly one-third; 19 out of 68) obtain a total link score a between 6 and 10, and thus approaches the mid-level that includes durable inter-organizational links. A closer look at a few examples illustrates the existence of a one-dimensional scale: the British Labour Party–GMB links include collective union affiliation and mutual representation rights at party/union annual conferences plus all kinds of inter-organizational links. At the lower end we find, for example, the relationship between the French Socialist Party's central organization and one of France's federations, FO. This dyad obtains a scale value of 2, and a detailed look shows that it is based on two 'occasional' links, namely the union being invited to the party's conference and to party special meetings.

As far as the legislative party groups and trade unions are concerned, a similar, generally skewed pattern applies (Figure 15.2). One party-union pair

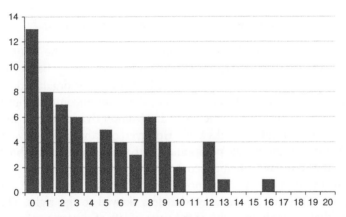

Figure 15.1. Frequency of total organizational link scores of central party organization–trade union relationships (0–20).[1]

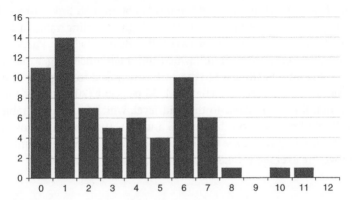

Figure 15.2. Frequency of total organizational link scores of legislative party group–trade union relationships (0–12).[1]

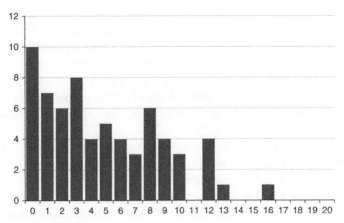

Figure 15.3. Frequency of total organizational link scores of party–trade union relationships (0–20).[1]

[1] All three figures concern the relationships between communist, social-democratic, and other old left-of-centre parties and all confederations of trade unions/selected unions in every country (pairs of individual parties and confederations/unions).

comes close to the highest possible score: once again, it is the British Labour Party and the GMB with 11. Next follows the relationship between Labour and Unite (another super-union) with 10. Strong inter-organizational links between left-of-centre parties and unions, then, are uncommon but they do occur. About 17 per cent of the party LPG-union dyads (11 out of 66) are reported to be without any links at all. However, one third of the dyads obtain a score between 4 and 6 scale points and approach the mid-level. About 14 per cent (9 out of 66) have a higher score.

The distribution for the combined score (i.e. for the parties' CPO and LPG put together, Figure 15.3) is somewhat less skewed to the right. The figure confirms that the large majority of the pairs of left-of-centre parties and trade union confederations/major unions enjoy organizational links. About 15 per cent of the dyads (10 of 66) have no links at all. The lowest/low scores are most common. Less than 10 per cent of the dyads obtain high link scores—12 and above. Integrated relationships are rare: the highest scaling value of 16 points is obtained by the relationship between the British Labour Party and two traditional allies (GMB and Unite), which, although much bigger than most of the other trade unions affiliated to the party, are linked to the party in more or less the same way as they are. That said, 30 per cent (20 out of 66) of dyads obtain a total link score close to the mid-level, which includes durable inter-organizational links (a score between 6 and 10). If we bundle those in with those that score highly, we see that about 40 per cent of the party-union dyads score above the average (of 4.8).

THE TRADITIONALLY CLOSE VS OTHER RELATIONSHIPS

After this general overview, we now turn to the main analytical focus of this book—*the relationship between the major left-of-centre party and its traditional union ally/allies* (Figure 15.4a and 15.4b). By 'traditional union ally' we mean a confederation/union known for having a historically fairly close/close relationship with one or more established left-of-centre parties or else a centre-right party.[4] We have values for this/these dyad(s) in all countries (see Chapter 2).

The average score is 7.5, i.e. below the mid-point of the scale for the central party organization–union relationships. As for the legislative party-trade union dyads, the average scale value of the relationships between the major left-of-centre party and its traditional union ally/allies across countries is 5.2— just below the mid-point again (Figure 15.3b). The traditionally closer party–union relationships still seem to be characterized by medium-strong links when it comes to the party in public office and somewhat weaker mean scores

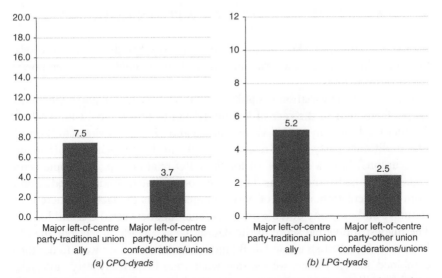

Figure 15.4. Total link scores of central party organization–trade union relationships and legislative party–trade union relationships: the main centre-left party and its traditional union ally/allies and other union confederations/unions (0–20/0–12), mean values, N = 42/38.[1]

[1] The scores represent the value of a single dyad or mean values (if there is more than one relationship). The theoretical maximum link score is 20 for the CPO-dyads and 12 for LPG-dyads since some link items are unlikely to apply to the legislative party group and were thus not included in this part of the survey. However, when comparing dyads involving CPOs with those involving LPGs, one should still keep in mind that the latter's maximum involves fewer links than the former's top scores.

as far as relationships between unions and central party organizations go, even if, when comparing dyads involving CPOs with those involving LPGs, one should bear in mind that the latter's maximum involves fewer links than the former's top scores.

So, have the major left-of-centre parties and *other* trade union confederations established links to each other as well? In most countries, there are peak associations and unions with roots outside what we might traditionally think of as 'the labour movement'. The second column in each figure (15.4a and 15.4b) shows the average scores of all these relationships. The average total link score is 3.7 and 2.5 for the CPO-dyads and the LPG-dyads respectively, and thus lower than for the traditional relationships.

Hence, the traditionally most intimate relationships, namely those involving today's major left-of-centre parties and their historical union allies, are generally closer in organizational terms than the relationships between the major left-of-centre parties and union confederations not belonging to the historical labour movement. However, on average, the differences are not huge.

VARIATION ACROSS AND WITHIN COUNTRIES

Figures 15.5 and 15.6 show how and to what extent traditionally close relationships differ across countries in terms of the strength of contemporary
organizational links.

We see that the variation is significant: the scale value outside public office
ranges from zero in the case of Labour-Histadrut (Israel) to 13 for SAP-LO
(Sweden), followed by SPD-SAK in Finland and SP-SGB (Switzerland) on 12.
The traditional party–union relationships in the United Kingdom (Labour-
TUC/unions) have a score of 10 for the CPO relationship, but would score
higher if we had removed the TUC, the non-affiliated union confederation,
from the calculation: a score of only 4 points reflects the fact that there is no
statutory and only one durable organizational link between TUC and Labour.
The highest individual score in the dataset is, as already noted, obtained by
Labour and the British union GMB (and, indeed, Unite if we were to use their
combined score). Hence, we see that what were historically very close relationships still seem to be characterized by fairly strong links today. At the mid-
level, with a score ranging from 8 to 9.4, we find the traditional left-of-centre
party–trade union relationships in Austria, Netherlands, and Germany.

In the case of the relationships involving the legislative party group, the
scale value for the traditional relationships ranges from 0 in Israel (Labour-
Histadrut), where there are barely any links, to 10.5 in the UK (Labour-TUC/
unions).[5] Overall, the differences in mean scores seem smaller than they do for
the relationships between unions and party CPOs. For instance, neither
Sweden nor Finland has a (much) higher score than the party-union dyad in
the Netherlands, Austria, and Germany. However, as regards Germany's
medium scores, one should recall that the scalability values of the German
union/LPG-dyads are unimpressive (Chapter 2). This means that in these
cases the link items relate somewhat differently than they do in the rest of
the cases. Dyads are connected by statutory and/or durable links but not
necessarily all those below the given level of institutionalization (see details
in Chapter 7).

Turning to the relationships between the major left-of-centre parties and
trade union confederations *without* historical roots in the labour movement,
we see that links exist but that the relationships are less organizationally
close across the board, both when it comes to the dyads involving central
party organizations and to those involving legislative parties (Figures 15.7
and 15.8).[6]

However, there are two major exceptions—relationships in Finland and
Austria. The links between the Social Democratic Party (SDP) and both the
professional and managerial and professional confederations, STTK and
AKAVA, adds up to an organizational scale value of 12—the same as the
traditional relationship between SDP and SAK. We do not have an overall

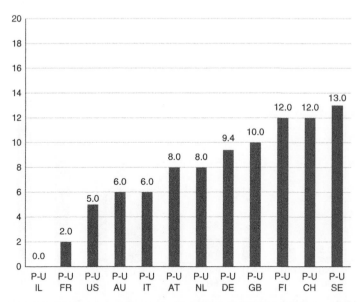

Figure 15.5. Total link scores of central party organization–trade union relationships: the major left-of-centre party and the traditional union ally/allies, by country (0–20), N = 20.[1]

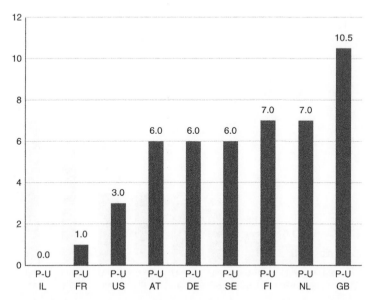

Figure 15.6. Total link scores of legislative party group–trade union relationships: the major left-of-centre party and the traditional union ally/allies, by country (0–12), mean values, N = 16.[1]

[1] The scores represent the value of a single dyad or mean values (if there is more than one relationship). P-U = party-union(s). Mean score across all countries: 7.5/5.2.

Elin Haugsgjerd Allern, Tim Bale, and Simon Otjes

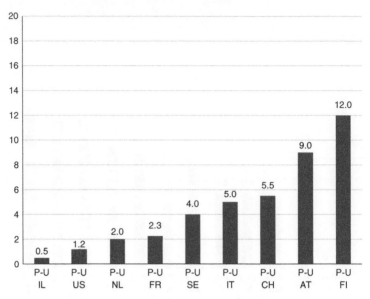

Figure 15.7. Total link scores of central party organization–trade union relationships: the major left-of-centre party and other union confederations/unions, by country (0–20), N = 22.[1]

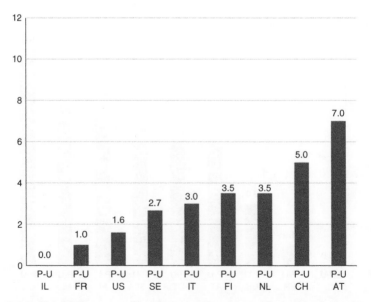

Figure 15.8. Total link scores of legislative party group-trade union relationships: the major left-of-centre party and other union confederations/unions, by country (0–12), mean values, N = 22.[1]

[1] The scores represent the value of a single dyad or mean values (if there is more than one relationship). P-U = party-union(s). Mean score across all countries: 3.7/2.55.

score for the relationship between the Austrian Social Democrats (SPÖ) and the major peak association ÖGB; but we see that the difference between the scores of the pairs which include the SPÖ and its traditional union ally, the blue-collar union PRO-GE, and the other—the large union GPA-djp—is minor. This finding is confirmed in Chapter 4, where additional interview data suggested that the party's relationships with the two unions were not that different.

Note also that party–union relationships in Germany are not included because the only full-blown trade union confederation and all the major unions are traditional allies of the left-of-centre party, the SPD. Likewise, there are no union confederations/major unions in the UK apart from those which have enjoyed a close relationship with Labour. In Australia, major unions without roots in the labour movement are included in the study, but these dyads do not have a total score and are thus excluded from the cross-country analysis. Finally, in Israel we note that the Labour party has no organized links to its traditional ally, Histadrut, but one to the Koach LaOvdim.[7] In other words, then, the conclusions of the country chapters are borne out in our cross-country comparison focusing on the organizational link score.

To simplify, we will now look at the combined scores, across parties' central organization and legislative party group, for the party-union dyads by country (Figure 15.9). When it comes to the relationship between the major left-of-centre party and its traditional union ally, the highest scores are to be found in Sweden, Germany, Switzerland, Finland, and the UK. As noted previously, the highest individual score is obtained by two of the UK relationships, due to the existence of statutory links. It should be noted that relationships between the Australian Labor Party and formally affiliated unions are not included here due to missing values. The Australian score would probably have been significantly higher if it had proved possible to include these dyads. In Israel, we see—again—that any organizational relationships have come to an end. As far as links between the major left-of-centre party and *other* union confederation/unions go, we see—again—generally lower scores, with the exception of Finland.

Additional analysis, we should note, demonstrates that, in countries with surviving communist parties (Finland, France, Germany, Sweden, and Israel) the (former) communist parties' relationships with the traditionally leftist unions tend to obtain lower link scores than the dyads involving the major left-of-centre party—but not always. In Finland, the relationship between the parliamentary group of the other left party—VAS—and the SAK union federation actually achieves around the same score as the SDP-SAK dyad.

To display the variation across all the possible left-of-centre party-trade union dyads in every country studied here, box plots are helpful. Figure 15.10

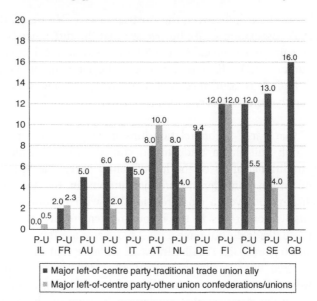

Figure 15.9. Total link scores of party–trade union relationships: the major left-of-centre party and its traditional union ally/allies compared to the major left-of-centre party and other unions, by country (0–20), N = 40.[1]

[1] The scores represent the value of a single dyad or mean values (if there is more than one relationship). P-U = party-union(s). Mean score across countries for traditional left-of-centre party-trade union dyad: 7.7, others: 4.1.

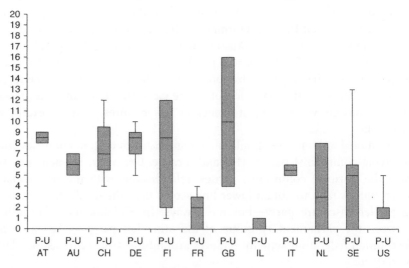

Figure 15.10. Distribution of total link scores of CPO–trade union relationships by country (0–20).

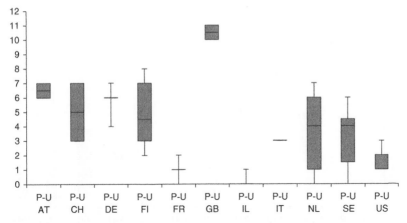

Figure 15.11. Distribution of total link scores of LPG–trade union relationships by country (0–12).

shows that cross-nationally the median value for the dyads involving the central party organizations varies from 0 (Israel) to 10 (United Kingdom). That said, we also notice that the degree of within-country variation is significant. The left-of-centre party-union pairs in Austria, Germany, Israel, Italy, and the United States display no or limited variation, but in Finland, the Netherlands, Switzerland, Sweden, and the United Kingdom the variation is significant—and to some extent also in France. The range in the United Kingdom is due to the 'deviant' Labour–TUC relationship: the median score is clearly higher. Israel is also a case apart—an example of a transition to almost complete detachment at the organizational level across all dyads. A similar pattern exists in the legislative sphere. As Figure 15.11 shows, the median value ranges from 0 in Israel to 10.5 in the UK. The TUC dyad is not included here, so we see limited variation among the party-union dyads in the United Kingdom, but again, significant variation in Finland, Netherlands, Switzerland, and Sweden.

We conclude by looking at the variation based on the combined party-union score (Figure 15.12). We notice that across countries the median value for the dyads still varies from 0 (party-union dyads in Israel) to 10 (party-union dyads in the UK). The figure confirms that the degree of within-country variation is considerable and follows the patterns mentioned above. However, the variation within the United States and Germany also appears somewhat more pronounced than for the separate organizational scores. Israel is certainly an example of barely any variation between party-union dyads at all, following a transition to nearly complete organizational detachment across the board.

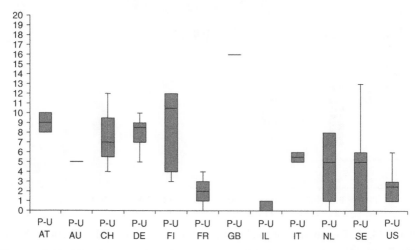

Figure 15.12. Distribution of total organizational link scores of party–trade union relationships by country (0–20).

INDIVIDUAL-LEVEL LINKS: PERSONNEL OVERLAPS AND TRANSFERS

Although our main focus is organizational, we also include less formal, but still politically relevant, links. While we cannot measure the intensity of informal contact, we can measure personnel overlaps/transfers that may well open up multiple opportunities for contact between decision makers. A high rate of transfers or overlaps of personnel between individual unions and confederations, on the one hand, and left-of-centre parties, on the other, would be another indication that the two sides of the labour movement are closer than many routinely assume. Moreover, we should try to look at the relationship *between* links at the organizational level and those materializing at the individual level: are statutory and inter-organizational links supplemented and reinforced by informal personnel links, or do such ties seem to be something which compensates for weak links at the organizational level?

First, what did our country experts discover when it came to the individual level? It was clearly much easier for some to come up with reliable data than others: for example, those researching the question in the Netherlands could use a Parliamentary Documentation Centre whereas others had to rely on a multiplicity of more or less reliable sources including personal websites where what is displayed is up to the legislator him or herself. The results are summarized in Table 15.3 for cases where shares of MPs in 2013/14 that hold or have held positions as officials or staff in the confederations of unions at the national level were presented in a graph in the country chapters.

Table 15.3. Share of MPs in 2013/14 that hold or have held positions as officials or staff in the confederations of unions at the national level[1]

Party-confederation dyad	Major old left-of-centre party-traditional union ally	Major old left-of-centre party-other trade unions	Other left-of-centre party-traditional left-of-centre union ally	Other left-of-centre party-other trade unions	Average across dyads
Israel	0	n.d.	0	n.d.	–
France	0.3	0	0	0	0.1
Italy	1.2	0.5	n.d.	n.d.	–
Netherlands	2.6	2.6	10.5	5.2	3.0
Germany	7.9	1.6	3.2	0	3.2
Sweden	8	0	0	10.5	4.6
Finland	19	4.8	50	0	18.5
Switzerland	19.6	6.5	n.d.	n.d.	–

[1] Only permanent representatives and deputy representatives who attend the entire term are included. For term years, see country chapters. The Dutch and Swiss shares concern MPs in the lower house. The Italian shares concern MPs in both houses. The German shares include both national and state-level positions. N of old-left-of-centre party MPs is 15 in Israel, 295 in France, 415 in Italy, 38 in Netherlands, 191 in Germany, 112 in Sweden, 42 in Finland, and 46 in Switzerland. N of other left-of-centre party MPs is 6 in Israel, 9 in France, 19 in Netherlands, 64 in Germany, 19 in Sweden, and 14 in Finland. 'n.d.' means no data.

It should be noted that not all these figures are directly comparable (see the notes beneath the table), but if we distinguish between weak (less than 10 per cent), medium (10–20 per cent), and strong (more than 20 per cent) links, we see that the major left-of-centre party (social democrats) and its traditional union ally have strong personnel ties in Finland and Switzerland, but that the strongest link is between the former communist party and the same trade unions in Finland (SAK): half of all Left Alliance (VAS) MPs had previously worked for SAK at the national level (but, of course, the total size of the latter's party group is also much smaller than the social democrats' number of MPs). The average across all dyads is as much as 18.5. It is also, according to Raunio and Laine (Chapter 5), very common for SDP officials to have worked previously for the traditional ally SAK, and vice versa. Two of the three most recent SDP party chairs are experienced trade union leaders.

Switzerland's Socialist Party seems to be maintaining its tradition of recruiting MPs with a background in the trade unions as well: fifteen of the forty-six members of the SP parliamentary party in the lower chamber (nearly 20 per cent) are, or have been, union officials at national *or* regional level. In the Senate, the proportion amounts to three out of eleven (see Chapter 12). Erne and Schief also emphasize noteworthy personnel overlaps at the very top-leadership level.

In Sweden, less than one in ten Social Democrat MPs in the 2010–14 parliament had worked for unions at the national level—but note that nearly 30 per cent had worked for them at the regional and local level (see Jansson, Chapter 11), so there is a question as to how big the difference between

Sweden and Switzerland actually is in this regard. Jansson also suggests that the quality of the data probably leads to underestimation, not the opposite. The average across dyads is about 5 per cent. That said, although the tradition of the LO chairman also being an SAP MP came to an end in the 1980s, Stefan Löfven was president of the metal workers union when he was elected SAP leader in 2012, becoming the first LO-affiliated union leader to become party leader in the party's long history.

In all other countries included in Table 15.3, there are few personnel overlaps and transfers (only weak links in this sense), although it should be noted that more MPs have a trade union background in Germany than in the Netherlands, Italy, France, or Israel. Figures from the Netherlands, taken from the 2013 parliament, show that only a handful of Labour Party and Socialist Party MPs have worked for trade unions on average. The numbers in Italy are similarly low, even if some of those with a union background hold relatively important positions in parliament. In France, too, only a handful of the nearly 300 Socialists in parliament in 2012 claimed to have worked for a union, although the Socialist government's recruitment of several union officials, albeit into mainly advisory roles, suggests that party–union relations may perhaps be closer than is commonly supposed, at least in this respect.

However, perhaps the strongest personnel links are to be found among parties and unions *not* included in the table? According to Larkin and Lees (Chapter 3), out of the eighty ALP members of the Australian Commonwealth Parliament, forty-three have previously worked for a union and/or ACTU in some capacity. Almost half of the ALP's MPs in the current parliament and almost all of its Senators—twenty-one out of a total of twenty-five—have previously worked for a union. Union officials are found both in the party leadership and in government. The authors conclude that a post of some sort in the unions' secretariat 'is probably the single most popular route to a seat in the Commonwealth parliament' (see Chapter 3 for a discussion of the organizational mechanism underpinning this recruitment pattern).

In Austria, we also find substantial personnel overlaps and transfers even if we do not have accurate figures for all dyad types. In the spring of 2014, some 27 per cent of SPÖ MPs held or had recently held positions as union officials or staff in sum. Five MPs were linked to the GPA-djp and four to the PRO-GE. Moreover, Chapter 4 shows that there are also personnel overlaps/transfers at the highest executive level of SPÖ and in government.

In contrast, Bale and Webb (Chapter 13) show that, until the election of Jeremy Corbyn (who had worked decades earlier as a union organizer) in 2015, the British Labour Party had not been led by anyone with a trade union background since Jim Callaghan (who had worked for a union as a young man before the Second World War) forty years previously. That said, in 2014 around a fifth of the 'shadow cabinet'—the parliamentary group awarded opposition portfolios by the Labour leader—appeared to have worked for trade unions before becoming MPs. More anecdotal evidence suggests a more two-way flow of personnel at the headquarters level, personified by the party's general secretary, who, after a career that began in student union politics, moved on to the Labour Party and then back into the union movement with the GMB, before being appointed to head up party HQ in 2011 (see Bale and Webb, Chapter 13). In the US, if there were ever many Democratic members of the House or the Senate with a union background they are—predictably enough given the very strong contemporary bias towards professional (and rich) candidates—very thin on the ground nowadays (see Witko, Chapter 14).

All in all, then, what we can probably say with some degree of confidence is that Australia, Austria, and Finland on the one hand, and Israel, France, and perhaps the US on the other, represent the opposite ends of the spectrum when it comes to personnel links. By and large, the dyads with the highest organizational link scores also tend to have strong links at the individual level, with the notable exception of the parties and major unions in the United Kingdom. Moreover, we see that the traditional party–union relationships in Australia and Austria strengthen their connection through personnel overlaps and transfer: while they have medium-level organizational scores they have perhaps the strongest personnel links. However, we also know that the organizational data are far from complete in these cases. Hence, albeit with a note of caution, we may perhaps conclude that, even if personnel overlaps and transfers may historically have compensated for limited formal links, this is not the case today. Indeed, if anything it seems as if links at the organizational level are positively correlated with links at the individual level among the established left-of-centre parties and trade unions.

When we look at the few available time series on the union background of MPs, we also see an overall decline (Table 15.4). We see that the links between the major old left-of-centre party (SDP) and its traditional union ally (SAK) in

Table 15.4. Changes in personnel overlaps and transfers at the national level over time: major left-of-centre party–traditional union ally and other left-of-centre party–traditional union ally (%)

	SDP-SAK (Finland)	VAS-SAK (Finland)	PvdA-NVV/FNV[1] (Netherlands)	SAP-LO (Sweden)	VP-LO (Sweden)	Labour-Histadrut (Israel)	Meretz-Histadrut (Israel)
1960s	–	–	18	–	–	–	–
1970s	–	–	8	11	0	44	25
1990s	–	–	14	–	–	46	25
2000s	53	42	11	–	–	–	–
2010s	19	50	9	8	0	0	0

[1] The secular, socialist Dutch Trade Union Confederation (*Nederlands Verbond van Vakverenigingen*, NVV) aligned with the PvdA, merged with the Catholic *Nederlands Katholiek Vakverbond* NKV to form the FNV in 1982.

Finland have declined from above 50 to 20 per cent since the turn of the millennium (whereas as the left party's share has increased somewhat). The share of Swedish social democratic MPs with backgrounds in the SAP's traditional ally (LO and its affiliates) at the national level has not changed much since the 1970s, although, in contrast to Finland, there seem to have been no such overlaps between the former communist party and the main union confederation.

In the Netherlands, the share of PvdA MPs holding or having held positions in the confederation NVV has declined from 18 to 9 per cent since the 1960s. And, once again, the Israeli case provides a paradigmatic example of precipitous decline. In the mid-1990s, as in the early 1970s, nearly half of all Labour members (and a quarter of all Meretz members) of the Knesset had worked for the trade unions. By the second decade of the twenty-first century, not one of the (admittedly much smaller) parliamentary delegation of either party had done so.

RATING OF OVERALL ORGANIZATIONAL CLOSENESS/DISTANCE BY ACTORS

So far the findings have been developed from scales and scores based on technical information about organizational arrangements, routines, and personnel. Does the picture change at all if we ask parties and unions (the key informants) about their own, necessarily more subjective perceptions?

To find out, we asked, 'Overall, how would you rate your party's degree of organizational closeness to/distance from the following confederations/unions in the last five years?' The response categories ranged from 'distant/separated' to 'integrated', and we asked respondents to report the *'the prevailing view within your party'* in order to minimize the subjective element. The results are presented in Figure 15.13. As both the CPO and the LPG was asked about the party as whole, there is only one column per party (see figure note).

Across all left-of-centre party-union dyads, about 20 per cent of them are reported to be involved in an 'integrated' relationship and 30 per cent in a 'fairly close' one. Hence, the reported party perceptions tend to imply a higher general level of closeness than our organizational scores. Fewer unions, however, report integrated and fairly close relationships, suggesting that the most common relationship is 'ad hoc', i.e. based on occasional links. Interestingly, on both sides, there seem to be few relationships that are perceived as distant or marked by complete detachment. Overall, the key informants' own assessments confirm that many left-of-centre parties and trade union confederations are involved in active relationships today, and that a significant number of these party-union dyads enjoy fairly strong or very strong links.

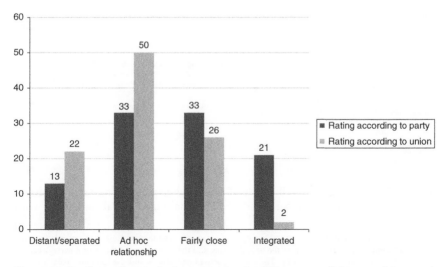

Figure 15.13. Share of parties/unions reporting the different overall degrees of closeness/distance of party–trade union relationships the last five years (*c*.2008–13), N = 65.[1]

[1] The party ratings reflect the mean value of the central party organization's and the legislative party's ratings. If the party ratings differed, the mean value has been rounded up (e.g. if the central party organization rated the relationship as distant/separated and the legislative party as ad hoc, the party's rating is ad hoc). In two cases, the answers differed with more than one category: Austria's SPÖ-GÖD (fairly close (CPO) vs distant/separated (LPG)), and Netherlands' PvdA-MHP (distant/separated (CPO) vs fairly close (LPG)). Then we chose the alternative in the middle. If only either the central party organization or the legislative party group answered the question, the rating reflects that answer. This is the case for eighteen of the party ratings.

To measure the exact correlation between the actors' rating and the organizational scale value we computed a measure based on the average of the LPG and CPO value and then the mean value of this party and the union score, and correlated this with the combined organizational score for the LPG and CPO. The result was a Pearson coefficient of 0.646 (significant at the 0.01 level). The correlation is similar if we look at the dyads involving CPO and the average of the party–union rating separately (0.645) and slightly lower if we only examine the correlation of the LPG–union relationships (0.621) (significant at the 0.01 level) (table not shown). In other words, the correlations are significant but far from absolute. Given that we explicitly asked the respondents to take into account individual-level contacts as well as organizational links, this is no big surprise. The most important finding is that actors consider themselves to be involved in more or less institutionalized relationships.

If we zoom in on the relationship between the major left-of-centre party and its traditional union ally/allies (Figure 15.14), the findings also echo the general tendencies revealed by our organizational mapping: in other words, we see that the answers indicate a similar although not identical order of countries (Figure 15.9). The relationship between the Swedish SAP and LO

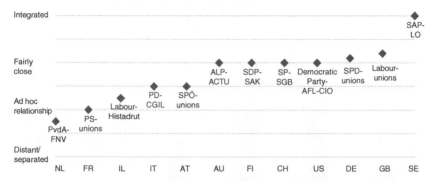

Figure 15.14. Rating of overall degree of closeness/distance (average score) between the major old left-of-centre party and its traditional union ally/allies, last five years (*c*.2008–13).[1]

[1] The ratings represent the value of a single dyad or mean values (if there is more than one relationship). The mean value is calculated based on the union's rating and the mean value of the central party organization's and the legislative party's rating. The central party organization's and the legislative party's ratings differed in two cases: Austria's SPÖ-PRO-GE (fairly close (CPO) vs ad hoc (LPG)), and Netherlands' PvdA-FNV (ad hoc (CPO) vs distant/separated (LPG)). If only either the central party organization or the legislative party group answered the question, the rating reflects that answer. This is the case for Germany, Israel, and the United Kingdom. The American, Australian, and French ratings reflect the union's rating only (the party's rating is missing). For one of the two Austrian dyads, the union's rating is missing.

comes top, followed by the UK Labour Party's traditional relationships, and then those enjoyed by the Finnish and Swiss. We should of course not read too much into this, but given the description provided by Jansson's country analysis of the Swedish case(s) (Chapter 11), it does not come as a surprise that the two sides still consider themselves to be closely aligned, and perhaps involved in a less contentious alliance than the British Labour Party and unions. The other changes in the rank order might reflect the fact that substantial informal interaction exists, or that the baseline for comparison used is perhaps more national than international.

It may also be worth noting that the German party and unions do not agree: the party informant suggests that the relationship is integrated, whereas the unions believe 'ad hoc' or 'fairly close' would be more accurate. Hence, as is the case when it comes to our more 'objective' organizational scores from Germany, it is difficult to decide exactly what characterizes the German dyads in comparative perspective. The most striking difference from the organizational scores, however, is the US score: the union confederation AFL-CIO reports having a 'fairly close relationship' with the Democratic Party despite weak organizational links and relatively few personnel overlaps and transfers. However, with no data from the party side, we cannot read much into this other than to note the possibility (no more than that) that significant informal interaction occurs at the individual level.

We might also note that in the Netherlands, PvdA and FNV report something in-between a distant and ad hoc relationship, despite having nearly as many organizational links as the German SPD-DGB dyad. In Italy, the CGIL considers its relationship with PD to be 'fairly close', whereas the party rate it as an 'ad hoc relationship', in line with the organizational score. Finally, we see that the relationships between the Austrian SPÖ, PRO-GE, and ÖGB are considered to be in-between fairly close to ad hoc, but both the party and union side consider the SPÖ and ÖGB, the traditional left-of-centre party-union confederation alliance, to enjoy a fairly close relationship. As we learned from Chapter 4, the complex partisan nature of the Austrian ÖGB and unions complicates the assessment, but given the organizational links and personnel overlaps that exist, 'fairly close' seems a more accurate description of these relationships than 'ad hoc'. Interestingly, though, not one of the traditional pairs of party and union confederation/unions consistently describes their relationship as distant/separated.

WEAKER LINKS, WIDER NETWORKS?

Taken together, the country case studies and the comparative analysis suggest that a few traditional party–union relationships have declined significantly, but also that several are still close—and that organizational links also exist between old left-of-centre parties and trade union confederations (or major unions) without roots in what was traditionally thought of as 'the labour movement'. Empirical assessment of the contemporary strength/weakness of links—from the well organized to the informal—reveals considerable variation across and within countries. Those with the most 'institutionalized' relationships also tend to have stronger informal links when it comes to personnel overlaps and transfers. In general, the organizational links between parties' central offices—their HQs—and trade unions are stronger than the ones between the legislative party groups and trade unions, although we also saw that there is a strong correlation between them.

When asked about whether the relationships had changed or not in the last ten years, the key party/union informants who did respond do not consistently report 'increased distance'. To some extent, answers vary between the two sides of specific dyads, emphasizing that we need to interpret the results with a degree of caution (table not shown). Still, it is worth noting that only in about a third of the pairs involving the major left-of-centre party's CPO and its traditional ally/allies, did *both sides* report 'a more distant relationship' (or one did while the other didn't respond).[8] Only in *one* case where the CPO answered 'more distant' did the LPG informant disagree. Thus, the party-union survey suggests that, with one or two notable exceptions, we are *not* about to witness a general disintegration of previously intimate relationships between parties and trade unions.

Seen from the party side, we may conclude that, in the second decade of the twenty-first century, a few established left-of-centre parties have a distant organizational relationship with trade unions, whereas others maintain medium-level links or even strong ones. Many of these parties also enjoy organized contacts with organizations other than their traditional ally/allies. A good number and variety of unions are linked to a given left-of-centre party through at least 'occasional' links, and unions are sometimes linked to more than one left-of-centre party. However, the connections tend to be stronger among the traditional partners of the old labour movement, than in other/ newer relationships. The networks have become wider on the left-of-centre but there are still some 'special relationships' around.

A look at the trade union confederations' reports on links with parties other than the left-of-centre parties and the centre-right with a history of ties to particular unions (Netherlands, Switzerland, and Israel),[9] confirms the impression that old and new acquaintances have yet to be put on an equal footing (Table 15.5). The strongest type of link that exists in this second set of

Table 15.5. Existence of links between trade union confederation/union and (any) other parties during the last five years (*c.*2008–13), according to trade union (%)[1]

Variable (link items)	Union-other parties' CPO			Union-other parties' LPG		
	Yes	No	Unclear	Yes	No	Unclear
Tacit agreement about mutual representation	0	64.2	35.8	0	50.9	49.1
Permanent joint committee(s)	0	64.2	35.8	0	50.9	49.1
Temporary joint committee(s)	0	62.3	37.7	0	50.9	49.1
Formal agreement about regular meetings	0	64.2	35.8	1.9	49.1	49.1
Tacit agreement about regular meetings	5.7	58.5	35.8	5.7	45.3	49.1
Joint conferences	3.8	60.4	35.8	0	49.1	50.9
Joint campaigns	5.7	58.5	35.8	1.9	47.2	50.9
Party invited to union's conference	32.1	30.2	37.7	20.8	30.2	49.1
Union invited to party's conference	32.1	32.1	35.8	N/A	N/A	N/A
Union invited to party's ordinary meetings, seminars, etc.	24.5	30.2	45.3	11.3	32.1	56.6
Party invited to union's ordinary meetings, seminars, etc.	20.8	34.0	45.3	11.3	30.2	58.5
Union invited to party's special consultative arrangements	28.3	34.0	37.7	20.8	26.4	52.8
Party invited to union's special consultative arrangements	20.8	41.5	37.7	11.3	35.8	52.8
N	53			53		

[1] The number of unions with missing data on at least one link item is pretty high (about 50 per cent), so we have not calculated total scores and simply show the percentage that reported having different types of links with other parties' central organization or legislative party group (one or more parties).

relationships is a tacit agreement about regular meetings, and only in about 6 per cent (i.e. three) of the cases. We see that occasional (event-oriented) links are more common, but not more than 20–30 per cent of the unions report being invited or inviting other parties to party/union arrangements like congresses and seminars (compared to 40–70 per cent for the established left-of-centre parties, see Chapter 2). Hence, some but not all unions have an organizational network reaching outside the left and centre-left, but existing links to other parties seem generally weaker. In short, there seems to be in most of the countries studied here, an 'inner core' of more strongly linked party-union dyads.

CONCLUSION

Party–union relationships consist of links that connect decision-makers on both sides. Using a novel comparative dyadic dataset covering twelve countries across three continents, we have assessed the strength of such links among left-of-centre parties and confederations of trade unions and/or major individual unions. We have shown that, even if previous research suggests that traditional party-union allies in these countries have moved apart, they are in many cases still involved with each other. The story is not the same everywhere, but that very variation is enough to question the existence (or at least the strength) of a general trend towards distance and drift.

Links still very much exist. Indeed, some are widespread. True, overlapping organizational structures are rare these days. But what we term 'durable links', rather than simply event-based 'occasional links', are still in evidence, although these are more common between unions and parties' central organization (i.e. their headquarters) than between unions and parties' parliamentary/legislative groups. In short, left-of-centre parties and unions that were once close are rarely completely estranged and a few remain almost as bound up with each other organizationally as they ever were. Even where parties have established links to unions other than their traditional ally (as the catch-all party and related theses would predict), they do not seem to have put them on an equal footing. Hence, by and large, our first hypothesis (H1) receives considerable support: the links between old left-of-centre parties and trade unions are generally not very strong, but significant variation exists in the strength of links, and in the range of each side's relationships with others, both within and across countries.

We have also examined the connection between *different kinds/types of links* and found that party–union relationships vary along a one-dimensional scale of organizational closeness/distance. Permanent/durable links indicating a particularly high degree of institutionalization are not that widespread these days, but the parties and unions that do still have them also have the kinds of occasional, weaker organizational links which are nowadays more common. In other words, the latter complement rather than replace the former.

Moreover, the available data on personnel overlaps and transfers suggest that links at the organizational level are positively correlated with links at the individual level among the old left-of-centre parties and trade unions. However, our main aim has been to examine to what extent left-of-centre parties and trade unions are interlinked by organized mechanisms. Of course, regular contact might occur, and some personnel overlaps may exist within party-union dyads which score low on the extent to which organized arrangements connect them. Future research should therefore look further at this individual level, and explore more thoroughly whether informal links may compensate for weak organizational links or are instead part of a single scale of closeness in the organizational sense. Unions' and parties' own subjective perceptions of closeness/distance suggested coherence, but also showed that some felt closer to each other than the arguably more objective measures suggested they would. Perhaps emotional commitments are sometimes stronger than organizational ties.

When comparing party-union dyads, we see above all that the relationships between the major left-of-centre parties and their traditional union allies, across parties' central organizations and legislative party groups, is organizationally closer than the relationships between these parties and other unions. Certainly, the relationship between a country's major left-of-centre party and union confederations without historical roots in the labour movement are more distant. We have also shown that these traditional relationships remain closer in the Nordic countries and in Australia, the UK, Switzerland, Germany, and probably also Austria, than in the other countries in continental Europe and the US. In Israel, relationships barely exist anymore.

The country differences more-or-less echo well-known historical differences: the most intimate party–union relationships are still to be found in Northern Europe, in the United Kingdom and Scandinavia, followed by Switzerland, Germany, and probably Austria, as well as in the Commonwealth country, Australia. In predominantly Catholic nations like France (and Italy), where relationships have historically been less institutionalized, the links are (still) much weaker. Austria, the Netherlands, and Switzerland are countries traditionally split along religious lines, but seem to have taken somewhat different paths. Links are largely maintained in Switzerland and so far also in Austria, but have declined significantly in the Netherlands. In the US, the relationship between the Democrats and trade unions seems to have declined even further than was once the case. In Israel, the traditional relationships are clearly not what they were: indeed, the links have radically decayed.

This is not to say that what we have observed here is simply a legacy of the past. In Chapter 16 we move on to summarize systematically what the country studies suggest might explain these changes in the relationships between the major left-of-centre parties and, primarily, their traditional union allies. Just as importantly, we run a cross-sectional analysis based on the additive scores presented in this chapter in order to test the exchange model hypotheses presented in Chapter 1.

NOTES

1. As noted in Chapter 2, all these datasets, and questionnaires and code books, will be made publicly available via Elin H. Allern's university website <http://www.sv.uio.no/isv/english/people/aca/elinal/>.
2. See Chapter 4 for details on how the country expert has handled the multi-partisan nature of the peak association/unions at large.
3. We computed this combined score by assigning a value of 1 if a union link exists either with the LPG or the CPO and by assigning a 0 if there is no link with either of them. For other cases, namely where there is a 0 ('no link') and at least one entry of 'unclear/don't know' as coded judgement, a missing value is entered. As shown in Chapter 2, these items scale very well (H = 0.80).
4. The coding has been done by the country experts. We focus on the main left-of centre party in all countries even if unions were, historically, perhaps most closely aligned with communist parties in France and Italy for sake of contemporary relevance.
5. The high score for the UK probably reflects the fact that the TUC is excluded from the analysis in the case of the LPG due to 'unclear values'.
6. By 'other union confederations/unions' we mean a confederation/union that is not known for having a fairly close/close relationship with the one or more old left-of-centre party or a centre-right party historically (the first union unit(s) we identified in each country). The coding has been done by the country experts.
7. Invitations to organizations regarding special consultative arrangements initiated by the party.
8. The two dyads where both sides reported the relationship to have become more distant in the last ten years were PvdA-FNV (Netherlands) and Labour-GMB UK).
9. We asked about links with Christian Democrats separately in countries with a history of such relationships.

16

Variations in Party–Union Relationships

Explanations and Implications

Elin Haugsgjerd Allern, Tim Bale, and Simon Otjes

In Chapter 15, we painstakingly mapped the relationships between left-of-centre parties and different confederations of trade unions and/or major unions across our selected countries. This exercise revealed, as we hypothesized in Chapter 1, a good deal of variation in the contemporary strength of organizational links. Our task now is to try to explain that variation using the cross-sectional data emerging from our survey combined with other data sources, and finally to try to throw some light on the possible political significance of the variation revealed.

As a first step towards systematically testing hypotheses generated from our analytical framework in Chapter 1, the analysis focuses exclusively on the organizations that, historically, have enjoyed the closest and most important relationships with each other: the major left-of-centre parties and their traditional allies in the union movement. As shown in Chapter 15, the variation across these relationships today is considerable. Given their legacies of common origins and strong links, a focused study of these can be seen as a tough test for the rational exchange model which we presented in Chapter 1.

We begin, however, with an attempt to summarize the main findings that come out of the case studies (Chapters 3–14) in order first to suggest some of the reasons that these long-lasting party–union relationships have changed—sometimes beyond all recognition, sometimes much less so—over time. We do this both by summarizing the conclusions of the country analyses and by looking for patterns across cases and countries over time in light of our analytical framework. To what extent is change—or, indeed, lack of change—associated with the changing usefulness of links—as seen from both sides of the labour movement? Is the pace of change primarily related to factors at the actor level or country level, or both?

We then move on to our main contribution, namely the cross-sectional analysis of variation between party-union dyads in terms of strength of organizational links today: why do some (still) prefer to have a fairly close relationship whereas others are separated organizationally—and why do others lie somewhere in between? Due to the limited number of cases, we will simply look for bivariate correlations that provide (preliminary) support for, or else lead us to dismiss, hypotheses that we laid out in detail towards the end of Chapter 1. Can variations in how individual parties and union confederations relate to each other be explained mainly by the various resources on offer (relative to the costs involved), as implied by the cost–benefit exchange model? To what extent are they (also) correlated with country and contextual factors, such as the density and fragmentation or the union movement? And what about the impact of (enduring) institutional features like the strength/weakness of corporatist structures? Finally, do the factors at the different levels seem to interplay?

WHY DECLINE AND STABILITY?

While we assume what happens at actor level is crucial for how party–union relationships develop, we start here by looking at the structural variables since these are the ones that have been highlighted in scholarly debate for decades and are those where most time series data are available. System-level trends in economies and societies certainly feature in the accounts offered by the authors of our country chapters, but the authors also confirm the need to look at the specific resource exchanges between unions and the left-of-centre parties on which we now focus.

All our contributors point to the shrinkage of the blue-collar working class in economies that have moved towards a service-based rather than a manufacturing economy. This change has left some (though not all) left-of-centre parties and their traditional allies struggling to adjust. The proportion of workers that unions are able to recruit also featured, but in different ways: some chapters suggest that steep declines in density may have eroded organizational links between major left-of-centre parties and the unions, but we also see that in other countries similar declines seem to have made little difference. Moreover, density figures can obscure as much as they reveal, not least about the composition of the unionized population. We learn in Chapter 9, for instance, that as many of half of Italy's trade union members are, in fact, retirees. We also learn in Chapter 7 that German unions continue to have a significant presence among blue-collar workers in the private sector—people who unions in Britain, which are increasingly becoming public sector bastions, find difficult to reach (Chapter 13). Swedish trade unions, on the other hand, seem to have done a reasonable job of bridging the divide between private and public sector workers (Chapter 11).

Possibly more important, many contributors hint, are the actual resources unions can offer parties, not least in terms of votes. The increasing disinclination of unionized workers to vote for left-of-centre parties, especially in those countries where parties and unions were originally part of fast-eroding subcultures or pillars and/or where populist radical right parties now represent a major electoral threat, have made traditionally blue-collar union confederations less attractive allies for electoral purposes. According to a number of our country studies, money also seems to matter, possibly helping to stabilize and reinforce relationships where unions are still willing and able to provide it.

Country experts also argue that changes in what parties can offer to unions might play a part. Union enthusiasm for continued links with left-of-centre parties, many chapters suggest, depends at least in part on whether those parties are still strong enough (presuming they ever were) to stand a reasonable chance of occupying national office. That said, the value of access to the left-of-centre party in office seems to have declined over time: when the centre-left embraces at least a degree of liberalization, parties' failure to deliver congenial policies (and to veto uncongenial policies) can cause considerable strain. Sometimes, authors report, those strains have led to ruptures that have proved difficult to repair, and may even lead to unions looking to other parties—some old, some new, nearly always more left-wing—to promote their agenda and to remind their traditional ally that they shouldn't be taken for granted.

History, our case studies suggest, still matters, though more in some places than others: for some parties and unions the past is a foreign country; for others, the legacy of a subcultural bond or foundation story continues to keep them together, even if their relationship nowadays is not nearly as harmonious or tight as it once may have been. Finally, as far as more or less enduring institutional constraints go, access to a party in office still seems to be valued by unions, even in the fairly strong corporatist systems where there continue to be significant alternative 'non-political' routes to influence. In short, the country experts paint a complex picture of the factors at play.

When we move beyond summarizing the individual country analyses, and compare across all cases at once, a similar pattern materializes. As noted in Chapter 2, developments in the class and occupational structures of the countries on which we focus have generally weakened the basis for a more or less close organizational relationship between major left-of-centre parties and their traditional union allies. There is no country where the working class at the beginning of the twenty-first century is anywhere near as large as it was in the middle of the twentieth, in many cases halving over that half-century. Rarely in social science do we see a trend without outliers, but this is one of them. Given that, traditionally, the blue-collar working class formed the core membership of unions and the core vote for the left, this was bound to hurt them both, and, from the parties' point of view, reduce what was probably the number one instrumental incentive for involvement with their traditional trade union allies. Moreover, the impact of this massive social change was undoubtedly amplified by the large decline in class voting that some (though this time not all) of the countries studied here experienced.

That said, there is clearly no determinism involved here. Obviously, the strength of party–union links has not declined in lockstep with the decline of the traditional industrial working class in most cases. Moreover, those places most affected by change in class composition or voting are not necessarily those where the two sides of the labour movement have been driven furthest apart. The decline of class voting has been particularly marked in, say, Finland, the UK, Germany, Austria, Australia, and Sweden—countries where parties and unions have by no means walked away from each other.

The decline in trade union density, namely the proportion of employees who are union members, is much less uniform across the spread of countries we focus on. Does the variation in the pace of change seem related to how much the trade union density has dropped? In Israel, where the two sides of the country's labour movement (such as it is) no longer have much to do with each other save in the sense of providing power bases for individual politicians, union density has dropped from 74 to 34 per cent from 1969 to 2006 (see Table 2.1a), and from an all-time high of 85 per cent in 1981 to just 23 per cent in 2012 (Visser 2015). By way of contrast, however, both the UK and Australia have also seen a big drop in density—down to 26 per cent in 2013 (from a high of 52 per cent in 1981) in the former and to 17 per cent in 2013 (from a high of 50 per cent in 1975) in the latter. Yet in both countries, the links between their respective Labour parties, although not without their stresses and strains, continue to be some of the tightest around. Links in Austria remain strong, too, despite the fact that nowadays the unions organize only just over a quarter of workers where once the proportion was over two thirds. The same could be said for Switzerland, where the relationship is similarly strong and where, although density has never been that high, it is, at 16 per cent in 2013, only just over half what it was in the early 1960s.

On the other hand, it is only fair to admit that we have no examples of countries where density remains relatively high (the most obvious cases being Sweden and Finland) where relations between parties and unions have markedly deteriorated in recent years. By the same token, it is also worth pointing out that those countries where union density has traditionally been low, namely France and the US, are not those in which parties and unions enjoy a particularly close relationship. In short, trade union density is not destiny. Where density remains rather high, party–union relationships seem to remain relatively tight, but even a big drop in density does not mean that parties and unions which were previously close will necessarily move apart. As hinted earlier, the composition of union members might also play a part in how likely it is that they have continued to be attractive to parties. Some traditionally blue-collar unions have recruited rapidly growing employee groups more successfully than have others—including those employed at the lower levels in the service sector, be it public or private.

The effective number of confederations has also changed, but not uniformly towards a higher number (Table 2.1a). We have no comparative data for Israel on trade union fragmentation, but see that in the other countries with the steepest decline in party–union links, Italy and the Netherlands, union fragmentation has, respectively, increased and decreased, and in the former case links have never been very strong. In the cases where links have declined but remain fairly strong—the United Kingdom, Australia, Sweden, Finland, and Switzerland—trade unions have both fragmented and consolidated. Hence, we do not see a clear pattern between the *direction* of changes in trade union fragmentation and how the relationship between the major-left-of centre party and the traditional union ally has developed.

The degree of competition from other left-of-centre parties is also a potentially important contextual factor. In Chapter 2, we saw that the fragmentation on this side of the party system had been particularly high in Israel (Table 2.1a), where links have declined the most. However, the same also goes for Finland, were the links between the social democrats and the traditional confederation ally have remained stronger. Indeed, the availability in more fragmented party systems of more left-wing alternatives does not seem to have persuaded unions in, say, Sweden or Switzerland to dump the social democrats either. We see that there is effectively only one left-wing party in Australia, the United Kingdom, and Switzerland—cases where the links have been strong historically. Yet the same goes for the United States—where links have never been strongly institutionalized and seem to have significantly declined.

We should also briefly address a change in one of the major institutional variables argued to affect party–union relationships—the degree of corporatism. Scholarly literature suggests there is a connection: empirically, strong party–union links have been associated with a high level of corporatism. Yet it could be argued that corporatism makes left-of-centre parties as such less attractive for unions, due to their regular access to government independent of party composition. If the latter is the case, party–union links would, in fact, have become more attractive over time because they help compensate for the decline of corporatism (see Lindvall and Sebring 2005). Table 2.1b, and chapters on, say, Austria, Germany, Finland, Sweden, and the Netherlands, make clear that this form of managed capitalism is not what it once was in its heyday and that this may well be associated with a weakening of the relationship between parties and unions.

However, the pattern is not clear. It is true that in Austria (where corporatism still seems relatively strong) and in Finland and Switzerland, links between the social democrats and their union allies are still relatively dense, whereas in the Netherlands, where its decline has been more obvious, those links are no longer that strong. But Sweden, too, has become less corporatist, and yet party–union links there remain some of the strongest in Europe and probably the world. Party–union links also remain strong in the UK, in spite of the fact that Labour (and the country as a whole) abandoned its half-hearted flirtation with corporatism as long ago as the late 1970s. On the other hand, Italy's experiment with social pacts in recent years—now abandoned in spite of the fact that there is evidence to show they confer electoral advantages to the governments which negotiate them (Hamann et al. 2015)—seemingly did little or nothing to bring the centre-left and the trade unions closer together. Hence, it is not easy to decide whether the general decline of corporatism has stimulated or rather tempered the decline in party–union links. Only the subsequent cross-sectional analysis can reveal whether the resulting variation in corporatism is correlated with contemporary strength of links.

All this suggests that even if structural changes constrain relationships, we need—if we want to find out why party–union links have not declined at the same rate everywhere and indeed remain vital in several countries—to look more closely at what unions and parties can actually offer each other in terms of resources. The most obvious place to begin is the precious resource that trade unions traditionally offered left-of-centre parties, namely votes. In this respect, things are definitely not what they used to be. We do not have systematic data on the tendency for union members to vote for left-of-centre parties since the 1960s, but we can glean some valuable information from some of the country chapters.

It remains the case in many countries (examples would include Austria, Germany, Sweden, Finland, the UK, and Australia) that union members are more likely to vote for the centre-left than many of their non-unionized work colleagues. Given the extent to which parties in some of those countries still seem to be relatively close to unions, it seems more than possible that the extent to which union voting for the left-of-centre has or has not declined might very well be associated with the extent to which party–union links have (or have not) weakened. If the union confederation's membership is still relatively high (due to recruitment of other employee groups than traditional blue-collar workers), and these union members are still significantly more disposed than voters in general to vote for the major centre-left party, this might explain why some traditional relationships have remained pretty close, as in many of the countries just mentioned. Previous case studies also suggest that union members' votes might still be regarded as valuable in some countries (see Chapter 1).

What, then, about union donations, especially during the period when state subventions to parties were introduced? Countries where union finance is no longer really an issue for parties include France, Italy, the Netherlands, and

Israel. The final two countries have seen what once was a relatively close relationship between the left-of-centre and the unions become more distant—in the case of Israel very much more distant. In the first two, they were never particularly close anyway. In the US, unions still make contributions to the campaigns of Democratic Party candidates, but their relative value has declined significantly as other sources of finance have increased and relations are not as close as they used to be.

In Germany, and in Australia and Finland, where party–union relationships are relatively tight, unions continue to give parties money (and sometimes 'donations in kind'). But this financial support is, according to the country experts, seen as very much a supplement to the funding provided by the state. In Sweden and Austria, notwithstanding state funding, both cold hard cash and other material resources still seem to reinforce the party–union relationship, although the lack of transparency in party funding in those countries makes it hard to know precisely what is going on. Lack of transparency applies—in spades—to Switzerland, except it is more obvious there that unions subsidize the social democrats, just as corporations and lobby groups support other parties (and maybe the social democrats too). Only in the UK, however, do we know for certain the extent to which the main left-of-centre party, Labour, relies on its affiliated trade unions and therefore, as Chapter 13 points out, how it has over the years become, if anything, more dependent on them than ever for its day-to-day running and, indeed, long-term survival.

In other words, while the age-old advice to 'follow the money' seems sensible in the sense that the countries where unions continue to contribute significantly to parties (whether transparently or not) are also those countries in which the relationships between them continue to be relatively close, we cannot definitively say that 'no pay means no say': state funding may facilitate but need not spell the death or the dwindling of ties between parties and unions. That said, our cross-sectional analysis will hopefully tell us more clearly whether today's size of union donations matters for the contemporary strength of links between the two sides.

So far, however, we have only discussed changes in what left-of-centre parties might get, or might no longer get, out of trade unions. What about what unions might get out of parties? This could include, we argued in Chapter 1, some or all of the following: a supply of potential members (perhaps via a formal recommendation of union membership); a friendly government (or at least sufficient parliamentary seats to influence government); and policies which are seen to favour (or at least do no harm to) either to union members or, because they are not always the same thing (see Davidsson and Emmenegger 2013), unions' organizational interests.

In all these respects, things seem to have been going downhill for some time but not necessarily any more so in countries where the relationship between party and unions is weak than in countries where it remains relatively strong.

Recommending party members to join a union is unusual nowadays—indeed, cross-national research would suggest that unions seeking to increase their membership may as well forget about a putative flow of members direct from parties and instead focus their efforts on getting governments to support the sort of union-friendly institutional regime that seems to make the biggest difference to workers either joining or not joining (Turner and D'Art 2012; see also Kelly 2015). Whatever the case, given that the two left-of-centre parties in our study which continue to explicitly recommend their members join unions, namely the Israeli and the British Labour parties, are poles apart when it comes to the strength of their links with those unions, the practice is clearly not confined to those countries where party–union links remain tight.

And when it comes to the occupation of office, and in turn, policy, things would appear to be far from clear-cut either. With the single exception of Switzerland (where the social democrats are, by virtue of that country's unique 'magic-formula' cabinet system, always in government) left-of-centre parties have, especially in recent decades, neither been in office as much as trade unions would have liked nor, when they have been in office, have they necessarily acted in ways that unions would have liked. More importantly, at least for our purposes, this includes—on both counts—countries where union links have not weakened as well as those in which they have.

Clearly, there are stand-out examples of left-of-centre parties which have found it more difficult of late to get into government than was once the case. The Israeli left, whose links with the unions have all but disappeared (at least outside the Histadrut's own internal elections), is the obvious case in point, but there are others. The US Democrats have long since lost the hold on Congress (if not the presidency) which they enjoyed for much of the post-war period, although they, like the centre-left in France and Italy (neither of which have ever been particularly successful office-seekers) never had that much of a union-link to lose.

However, one could also highlight, by way of contrast, Sweden, where the SAP has clearly lost what used to be its virtual lock on office but has not been abandoned by the LO. Left-of-centre parties in Finland and the Netherlands are no longer quite as likely as they once were to help run the country either, yet the party–union link has remained stronger in the former than in the latter. One could, of course, point to Austria, where the social democrats have rarely been out of office, as an example where the opportunities thus afforded to the unions have helped preserve relatively close ties. However, strong links continue to characterize the relationship between the Labour Party and British trade unions in spite of the fact that the party has endured long periods out of office—and, indeed, looks set to stay in opposition for at least another decade.

The UK, like Australia and Sweden, also shows that links between unions and parties can remain relatively strong in spite of the fact that, when the latter have made it into office, they have, much to the chagrin of their union allies, demonstrated a fair degree of autonomy and ideological flexibility—particularly when it comes to initiating economically liberal reforms or refusing to reverse them. Germany's SPD and the Dutch PvdA also provoked the wrath of their union movements by kick-starting or refusing to halt major programmes of welfare and labour market reforms. This may have affected the strength of their links with the unions negatively, which have, after all, grown weaker than those enjoyed by some of their counterparts in other countries. However, it would appear that in more recent times they are rather more inclined to listen to objections, perhaps due to concerns about being outflanked by parties on the radical left—parties whose support (Die Linke in Germany and the SP in the Netherlands are good examples) has led some trade union members (if not necessarily their leaders) to consider a closer relationship with them. Certainly, those alternatives, which, in the countries just mentioned, already enjoy some links with the unions, would welcome any chance to capitalize on unions' frustration with their more centrist competitors' policy shifts.

As the case of Italy shows (see Chapter 9), such shifts can be especially inimical to good relations between centre-left parties and unions when links are already relatively weak. Recently, there has been a very marked rupture between the unions and the Italian Democrats since the party was taken by the scruff of the neck by the modernizing faction led by Matteo Renzi, who from the moment he became prime minister in February 2014 made it obvious that he intended to liberalize the country's sclerotic, insider-dominated labour market in order to tackle its chronic lack of growth and jobs, especially for younger (non-unionized) people—and made it equally obvious that demonstrations orchestrated by unions would not blow him off course. Over the border in France, the Socialist Party, whose relationship with the country's tiny and fragmented labour movement is even weaker than the one the Democrats had with Italy's unions, likewise seems to have burned its bridges with the unions (and even some of its own parliamentarians) after President Hollande's decision to force his labour market reforms through parliament by decree. At least, though, the relationship between party and unions in France had enough vestigial meaning to prompt demonstrations, crippling strikes, and allegations of betrayal. Further afield, in the US one gets the sense from Chapter 14 that American unions—ever the realists—no longer expect too much in policy terms of a Democratic president, even where he (or she) has the rare good fortune to govern alongside a Democratic majority in Congress. All in all, it is not easy to identify a clear pattern when it comes to the stability/decline of party–union links and the long-term development of what the party involved can offer unions—at least in terms of access to office and policy.

All these observations, especially the last, are inevitably impressionistic, albeit gleaned from a close reading and comparison of our country studies. They suggest a pretty mixed picture. In sum, we seem to find support for our general assumption that, while differences in the national context make different rates of change more or less likely, nothing is inevitable. Pairs of parties and union confederations/unions that have been significantly challenged by the decline of the blue-collar working class and the degree of class voting, for example, continue to be involved in relatively close organizational relationships. It seems fair to say, however, that long-term changes in the resources the two sides can offer each other—in terms of votes and financial/material support and union members and policy influence—seemingly provide key pieces of the puzzle: where those traditional relationships have declined the most—in Israel, Italy, and the Netherlands—the two sides have clearly less to offer each other than they used to. Yet we also see that in countries in which relatively strong links continue—Sweden, Finland, Australia, and the UK– they continue in spite of the fact that both sides bring less to the table than was previously the case. Because of this, and because we lack time series and complete over-time data for many of the resource variables, we can only go so far as to say that, although we believe our argument that weakening of party–union links is primarily explained by a reduction in the instrumental incentives on both sides is convincing, there are enough exceptions and uncertainty to prevent us from concluding definitively that this is, indeed, the case. Furthermore, it is clearly difficult to establish a causal direction here: a decline of organizational links may have triggered a decline in resources provided, rather than the other way around. For example, we cannot know whether less union-friendly policies or the end of union donations to the party came before or after any significant weakening of party–union organizational links.

We are, however, in a position to say something more systematic and more definitive about contemporary variation in party–union links, and the extent to which it is related to how useful an organized relationship is seen to be by each side, as well as to enduring institutional variables like the size of state subventions, regulation of party finance, and varying degrees of corporatism. Clearly change over time matters. So, too, do starting points: it is rare for parties and unions which enjoyed the closest relationships at the beginning of the post-war period to be among those whose links are now the weakest. But that does not mean that their relationships now are unaffected by what each can offer the other today.

A CROSS-SECTIONAL ANALYSIS OF PARTY–UNION LINKS

In our data there are twenty-seven trade union-party dyads relating to the major left-of-centre parties and their traditional trade union allies across the parties' central organizations and legislative groups. As shown in Table A16.1

in this Chapter's Appendix, however, we are unable to assign a total organizational score to nine dyads and thus have to exclude these from the analysis: this includes one, or several, of the major left-of-centre parties' traditional relationships from Austria, the UK, and Australia. However, as these are also among the five countries where we had to include some major unions as only one confederation exists, we do not consider this a major caveat. We are still able to analyse traditional relationships in all twelve countries studied in this book.[1]

We will use the combined scores of legislative party groups and central party organizations when exploring the hypotheses developed in Chapter 1. To recapitulate, we assigned a value of 1 if a union link exists either with the LPG or the CPO and assigned a 0 if there is no link with either of them. For other cases, namely where there is no 0 and at least one entry where the country experts were unable to make a judgment, a missing value is entered. As documented in Chapter 2, these items scale very well (H=0.80), and this also applies to the twenty-seven major traditional relationships examined here (H=0.61). Table 16.1 shows that the units included in what follows differ to a significant extent on the dependent variable. The mean value of the additive organizational index is 7.7, which is nearly three points more than the average for all sixty-six left-of-centre party-trade union dyads mapped in Chapter 15 (Table 15.2). The standard deviation of 4.4 indicates considerable variation, however. The minimum value is 0 and the maximum value is 16 (out of a theoretical maximum of 20).

We briefly describe how we operationalize the independent variables as we proceed, but details can be found in the Appendix (Table A16.2). In general, we try to go back about five years—using averages—for the conditions that might fluctuate and that party/union actors would most likely have taken into account. The same time frame was used in the relevant survey questions too (for instance, on donations). The descriptive statistics for the independent variables are presented in Table 16.1, whereas the theoretical range (max.–min. values) of the variables is presented in Table A16.2. There are some variables with missing values, and we will comment on the implication of these in due course.

As far as the distributions go, we see that the cases examined differ significantly in many respects. It is worth noting that despite our focus on traditional, long-standing relationships, there is variation when it comes to organizational origins. However, we also note that the variation in the general left–right position of the parties involved is limited, due to our focus on the major left-of-centre parties. Limited variation characterizes the index of union financial/material support as well, with a mean value of 0.7 (out of maximum 7) and a standard deviation of 1.5. The latter could be caused by the number of missing values on this survey-based variable, but this is impossible to know. As far as the system variables go, we should note that the data—with twelve

Table 16.1. Descriptive statistics: dependent and independent variables

	N	Min.	Max.	Mean	Std. dev.
Dependent variable					
Combined score (CPO/LPG)	18	0	16	7.7	4.4
Independent variables					
Recommended membership	19	0	1	0.3	0.5
Welfare CMP 2008–13	26	7.12	36.6	16.0	6.5
Years in government between 2008 and 2013	27	0	5	2.4	1.7
Average share of seats between 2008 and 2013	27	0.1	0.5	0.4	0.1
Average share of unionized employees 2008–11	13	0.1	1	0.5	0.3
Union voting ESS 2008–12	20	16.2	42.7	37.0	7.3
Index of union financial/material support	18	0	6	0.8	1.8
EVS attitudes towards trade unions	12	25.1	54.2	39.6	11.4
Union history	26	0	2	0.7	0.9
Previous statutory links	25	0	1	0.4	0.5
Union density	26	7.7	69.1	24.0	14.8
Union fragmentation	26	1	8.1	2.6	2.1
Left-party fragmentation	27	1	3.4	1.6	0.7
Routine involvement	27	0	1	0.4	0.4
Index of party subsidies	27	0	1	0.4	0.3
Index of party finance restrictions	27	0	0.8	0.2	0.3
Federalism	27	0	1	0.4	0.4
Parliamentary government	27	0	1	0.8	0.3
Effective number of parties	27	2.2	7.7	4.5	1.2
Trade union = confederation	27	0	1	0.5	0.5

mainly European countries covered—are skewed towards parliamentary government and, to some extent, non-federal systems. We will get back to the possible implications of all these features when discussing the results.

All things considered, we can use our cases to shed light on the hypotheses on contemporary variation that we generated in Chapter 1, based on the cost–benefit model of resource exchange, although causal relationships cannot be established. As noted, we will study the possible effect of each resource variable individually and check whether party-union resources are equally important as we hypothesized. Then we will see if some types of resources seem more important than others, as we assumed they might be, due to their asset specificity (see Chapter 1). Owing to the limited number of cases, we only present bivariate correlations and no multivariate analysis (see Table 16.2). We will also present plots (graphs) of some of the bivariate correlations. Due to the missing values on the independent variables, the number of party-union dyads we can study as we explore individual hypotheses is never more than eighteen, meaning we need to be most careful when interpreting the results.

First, we will examine a number of party characteristics—i.e. what parties can offer unions (Hypotheses 2a–2d, Chapter 1). Is it the case that, when parties recommend their members become a member of a trade union, the

Table 16.2. Correlations between independent variables and strength of party–union links (additive score)

Variables	Correlation	N	Hypothesis number	
Recommended membership	−0.16	13	H2a	Not supported
Welfare CMP 2008–13	0.19	17	H2b	Not supported
Years in government between 2008 and 2013	−0.11	18	H2c	Not supported
Average share of seats between 2008 and 2013	−0.31	18	H2d	Not supported
Average share of unionized employees 2008–11	0.62*	10	H2e	Supported
Union voting ESS 2008–12	0.46**	14	H2f	Not supported
Index of union financial/material support	0.26	14	H2g	Not supported
EVS attitudes towards trade unions	−0.17	15	H5	Not supported
Union history	0.17	18	H6	Not supported
Previous statutory links	0.52**	17	H6	Supported
Union density	0.56**	17	H7a	Supported
Union fragmentation	−0.70***	17	H7b	Supported
Left-party fragmentation	−0.16	18	H8	Not supported
Routine involvement	0.44*	18	H9	Supported
Index of party subsidies	−0.86***	18	H10	Supported
Index of party finance restrictions	−0.72***	18	H11	Supported
Federalism	0.27	18	Control var.	Not significant
Parliamentary government	0.14	18	Control var.	Not significant
Effective number of parties	0.02	18	Control var.	Not significant
Trade Union = Confederation	−0.35	18	Control var.	Not significant

* $p < 0.1$, ** $p < 0.05$, *** $p < 0.01$.

relationships between the two actors are tighter (Hypothesis 2a)? In fact, only two parties in our study explicitly recommend trade union membership: the British and the Israeli Labour parties: the former has the strongest relationship with trade unions out of all our cases; the latter now has none whatsoever. In short, it makes no difference to the state of party–union links whether parties recommend membership or not.

Hypothesis 2b concerns the left–right position of the political parties, as a proxy for union-friendly policy. The underlying idea is that more centrist social-democratic parties become less appealing partners for trade union confederations because these parties are less likely to pursue the kinds of policies trade union confederations favour. Using data from the Comparative Manifesto Project (Volkens et al. 2015), which includes nearly all countries, to establish the parties' positions; we find no evidence for this. The relationship is not significant and very weak: in other words, the data do not support the hypothesis—party–union links do not seem to be influenced by how left-wing a left-of-centre party is.

What difference does whether the party is in office make—the subject of Hypothesis 2c? Intuitively, government parties are attractive partners for trade union confederations, while opposition parties are much less attractive because they cannot deliver policy benefits. We look at the number of years a party has been in government between 2008 and 2013, drawing data from a number of datasets on party composition of government (Goemans et al. 2009; Seki and Williams 2014; Döring and Manow 2016) and using, for the US, the length of time a Democratic president has been in office. We find that there is a negligible, non-significant, negative correlation between the time these left-of-centre parties have spent in government recently and the strength of their links with trade union confederations. This does not support the hypothesis: whether parties are in government or not does not seem to make any difference to the strength of party–union links.

Like participation in government, the size of the political party is a sign of a party's strength and may impact on its ability to deliver policies that trade union confederations desire (Hypothesis 2d). Yet, when we look at the average share of the seats in the lower house obtained by political parties in elections between 2008 and 2013 (Döring & Manow 2016; IPU 2016), we find that the *stronger* political parties are in this sense, the *weaker* their links with unions. However, the result is largely down to party systems such as France and the US, where, on average, parties of the centre-left get almost 50 per cent of the seats in the years on which we focus but have comparatively weak ties to trade union confederations, notwithstanding the fact that Congress and the notoriously weak *Assemblée Nationale* are at opposite ends of the spectrum when it comes to the strength of the legislature vis-à-vis the executive (see Wehner 2006; and Martin and Vanberg 2011). Rather, it is in multiparty systems with powerful parliaments, like Sweden's, where centre-left parties are still relatively strong (winning on average around 30 per cent of the seats) and at the same time still enjoy much stronger ties to trade unions. This notwithstanding, we can still say that our data seems to disconfirm the hypothesis that the ties between the parties we look at and trade unions will be closer the better those parties are represented in parliament.

All in all, then, we find no evidence that the resources political parties can offer lead to stronger relationships with trade unions in general. It is not the case that more left-wing, larger, or governing parties, or those that recommend trade union membership, have stronger relationships with trade unions.

Next we turn to the trade unions and to their resources (Hypotheses 2e–2g). The underlying idea is that the more they can offer political parties the stronger their ties with them will be. First, we can look at the size of the trade unions (Hypothesis 2e), expressed as the average share of employees these trade union confederations organize as a share of the country's employees that is a member of a trade union, with data drawn from Visser (2015). In this case we find a moderate significant correlation between the individual strength of the trade union confederations and the relationship with centre-left parties: the bigger the trade union confederation, the closer the relationship with the party/parties we study.

What about the extent to which trade unions can potentially boost the number of votes going to centre-left parties (Hypothesis 2f)? To explore this we can look at the average share of trade union members voting for centre-left parties in different surveys in the European Social Survey between 2008 and 2012, as this dataset includes the most cases, albeit not the ones in the United States. What we find is a moderately strong and significant relationship. Figure 16.1 presents a scatterplot of the cases: one can see that where union support for centre-left parties is low (e.g. Israel), the relationships are weaker than where union support is higher (e.g. UK and Sweden).

If, however, we look at data from the Comparative Survey of Electoral Systems (2006–11) or the World Values Survey (2005–9), which do include the United States, the patterns are not significant or even go in the opposite direction to what we would expect—mainly because the US case, with

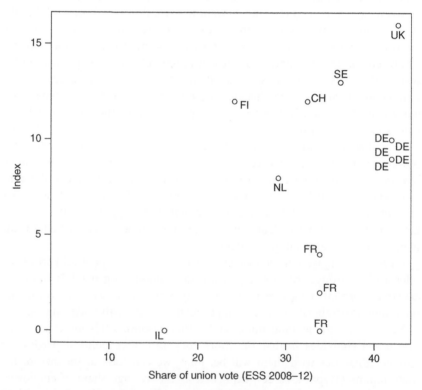

Figure 16.1. Strength of party–union links (additive score) and share of unions members voting for the left-of-centre party (US excluded).

Note: The United States is not included in the European Social Survey.

relatively weak ties between the Democratic Party and trade unions but strong support for the Democratic Party among trade union members, drives this pattern. Whatever the case, the party-union dyads in the US clearly under-mine the validity of the hypothesis that trade union support is positively correlated with the strength of left-of-centre party–union links.

Next, the question is does the trade union confederations' offer of material resources to political parties matter for the strength of organizational links (Hypothesis 2g)? In the survey, both trade union confederations and political parties were asked about whether the trade unions had supported the party or the campaigns of individual candidates financially, or supported campaigns by providing manpower, material support, or facilities. The distribution is, as already noted, skewed but the answers to these seven questions can be taken together in a single scale, the H-value for the seven items being 0.51. When we consider this index of financial and material support together with the strength of party–union ties, however, we find no correlation. As can be seen in Figure 16.2, the weak links between the Democrats and their tradition-al trade union allies undermine the story once again: the Democratic Party receives most resources from trade unions but has a weak relationship with them.

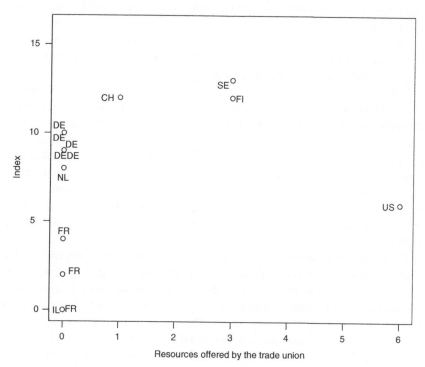

Figure 16.2. Strength of party–union links (additive score) and resources offered by unions to the left-of-centre party (additive score).

According to Christopher Witko's analysis (Chapter 14), the value of unions' support is reduced due the size of business donations to parties in the US. Generally, union support for political campaigns does not seem to tie the two more closely together.

When it comes, then, to unions' electoral resources, whether expressed through sheer size or else its members' electoral support for parties, we do find some support for the exchange model. Where it comes to material support for parties, however, we find no consistent significant patterns. In particular the case of the US, where trade unions offer the Democrats considerable electoral and material support, contradicts our expectations about exchange and relationship strength. Thus, we do not find evidence in favour of Hypothesis 3 on mutual exchange: the resources offered by parties and unions do not seem to be equally important for the strength of links between left-of-centre parties and trade unions.

As far as the nature of resources go it does seem as if the argument on asset specificity is echoed by our results. As some resources are harder to redeploy when invested we hypothesized (H4) that *the correlations are stronger between the strength of party–union links and the unions' financial party contributions, the share of union members voting for the party in recent years, and recommendation of union membership in party statutes than the correlations between the strength of party–union links and other resource variables.* True, recommendation of union membership is rare and without effect, but the number of votes and level of financial and material support from unions to parties seem to play a part, at least outside the United States.

It may be that parties find linking themselves closely with trade unions costly (Hypothesis 5). To measure that cost, we can use an indicator of popular attitudes towards trade unions from the European Values Survey, which covers all countries except for the US, Australia, and Israel. When we look for a link, however, we find that there is only a weak, insignificant correlation—and one that runs opposite to our expectations. It is *not* the case that, where trade unions have a better reputation with the public, parties are more inclined to engage with them: in the UK, for instance, fewer than a third of people trust them and yet they enjoy a strong (if sometimes strained) relationship with the Labour Party.

Hypothesis 6 proposes that the strength of relations may depend on the shared history of the political party and trade union. First, we asked in the survey and country experts whether there used to be statutory links between the parties and the trade unions or not. We then explored whether such links impact on the strength of current ties. There is a weak, only just significant correlation between these two variables. In other words, if links existed, then the current ties between parties and trade unions are slightly stronger. We might have expected, too, that that those unions whose origins were based on partisan considerations or which developed under the auspices of a party enjoy stronger links with parties today. However, there appears to be no significant relationship. History matters, then, but not always and not in every respect.

The final set of hypotheses concerns the political and economic context in which trade unions and parties enjoy links. First, there is the general strength of the union movement, the idea being that if union movements are stronger, either because they have a large total membership or because they enjoy a low level of fragmentation, then relations with parties are likely to be stronger than when in general the trade union movement is weaker. If we look at trade union density as the average share of employees who are members of a trade union for the period 2008–13 (OECD 2016), then there is a moderately strong significant relationship between the density of trade unions and the strength of their relationships with parties. Hence, Hypothesis 7a receives support: there tend to be stronger links between traditional allies when union membership is generally higher. Figure 16.3 visualizes this pattern: in countries that have low union density (e.g. France), the relationships are weaker than in countries with high union density (e.g. Sweden and Finland).

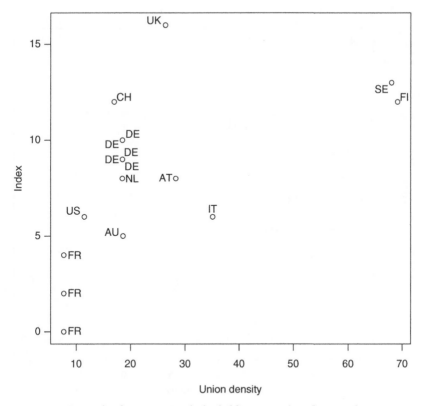

Figure 16.3. Strength of party–union links (additive score) and union density.

If we also look at trade union fragmentation (cf. Hypothesis 7b), measured as 'the effective number of confederations' much like the 'effective number of political parties' (Visser 2015), we find a similar but stronger pattern: countries that have more fragmented trade unions tend to see weaker relationships between left-of-centre parties and their trade union allies—typified (as can be seen in Figure 16.4) by France, where the effective number of trade union confederations is eight and where the Socialist Party has weak relations with its traditional ally. These analyses of fragmentation and density, then, support the idea that the more united the trade union movement, the stronger the links between parties and trade unions—a finding which is very much in line with recent research that uses policy alignment between the two to question, as we do, the conventional wisdom that there has been 'wide delinkage between the electoral left and labor as a consequence of internationalized markets and deindustrialization' (Simoni 2013, 314).

On the other side one may look at fragmentation of left-of-centre parties, expressed as the effective number of left-of-centre parties in elections in the

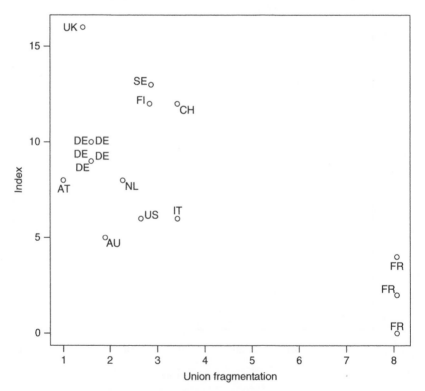

Figure 16.4. Strength of party–union links (additive score) and level of trade union fragmentation.

period 2010–13 with data on party positions and party size drawn from Döring and Manow (2016). The presence of multiple left-wing competitors makes it less likely that one party is able to offer stable access to government (Hypothesis 8). Here, however, we find no significant relationship: the existence of rivals for unions' affections does not preclude parties maintaining strong relationships with them.

Corporatism may also shape party–trade union relationships, although here theory and empirics point in different directions: when trade union confederations focus their attention on corporatist negotiations with the government and employers, there is arguably less need for direct interaction between them and political parties; yet previous studies point to strong links between parties and trade unions in corporatist countries. We hypothesized that there would be a systematic correlation between the degree of corporatism/pluralism and the strength of party–union links (Hypothesis 9). There are, of course, a large number of measures of corporatism. We are specifically interested in the extent to which trade unions are involved in the policymaking process. Visser (2015) offers a direct measurement of this: the routine involvement of trade unions and employers' organizations in government decisions on social and economic policy—something that applies most perhaps to the Dutch FNV and the Swiss SGB (see Figure 16.5). They have medium (FNV) and relatively strong ties (SGB) to social-democratic parties. However, party–union relationships in pluralist systems range from the strongest (UK) to to the weakest (Israel and France). Therefore, we find a weak and barely significant pattern.

It could also be that party finance context affects party–trade union links: parties that receive generous state support may be less enthusiastic about the benefits of close relationships with trade unions (Hypothesis 10), and the regulation of private donations makes financial contributions by trade unions to parties more sensitive or less likely (Hypothesis 11). To explore these hypotheses we construct two variables based on Casas-Zamora (2005: 19–20), updated by means of International IDEA (2016) and other sources. The first measures the extent to which there are electoral and permanent state subsidies that political parties can rely on, and the second measures the strength of restrictions on private donations: whether donations from individuals and/or trade unions are unregulated, regulated, or forbidden. The first two items do not form a single scale ($H = -0.54$), which is to be expected as the two kinds of subsidies can be complementary: if permanent subsidies exist, there is less need for electoral subsidies and vice versa. Still, we take the two items together and create an index, since there are countries with both subsidies and they are likely to have a more generous system of party finance than countries with only one kind. The items measuring restrictions on donations from individuals and trade unions scale extremely well ($H = 1.00$), and based on these two we create a composite measure for the strength of party finance regulations (see Appendix, Table A16.2).

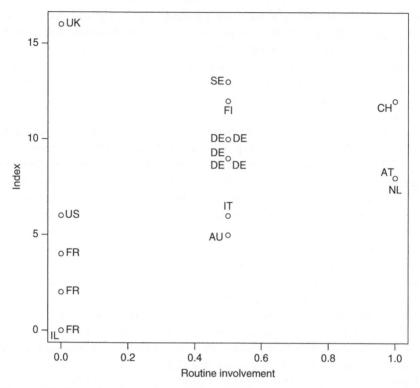

Figure 16.5. Strength of party–union links (additive score) and level of corporatism (degree of routine involvement).

The two relationships are visualized in Figure 16.6 and Figure 16.7. The data clearly show that in countries with both forms of party subsidies (such as France and Israel), the links between political parties and trade unions are weaker than in countries without subsidies (such as the United Kingdom and Switzerland). It also shows that in countries with stronger regulations about donations, such as France and the US, the relationships are less close than in most other countries where there are fewer regulations about donations. The mechanism underlying both these correlations is probably the same, since the countries that have restrictions on donations also tend to have extensive subsidies: in countries where the government has extensive control over party finance, the relationship between political parties and trade unions is weaker than in countries with relatively unregulated party finance. Hence, H10 and H11 receive support.

The basic structure of the political system may also shape the relations between political parties and trade unions. So we conclude by looking at these control variables. First, federalism may weaken party–trade union ties at the

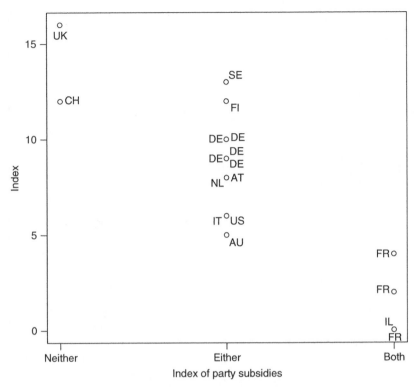

Figure 16.6. Strength of party–union links (additive score) and extent of state subsidies to parties' national organizations.

national level, because the national level matters less for policymaking and therefore strong ties at the national level are less worthwhile. Yet a correlation with a three-step federalism scale from Armingeon et al. (2014), which differentiates between non-federal, weakly federal, and strongly federal states, yields no significant results, although the level of variance is higher for unitary states compared to the strong federal states. Second, the separation of powers may weaken party–trade union links since, if multiple centres of power exist, it may be dangerous for trade unions to tie themselves too closely to one party. Utilizing a three-step scale from parliamentary via semi-parliamentary to presidential democracies from Cheibub et al. (2010), we find a weak and non-significant correlation. This does not of course mean we should dismiss out of hand the idea that party–union ties are slightly stronger in parliamentary compared to other systems: we would need to include more presidential and semi-presidential systems before we could make that assertion with more confidence.

What difference does the total effective number of political parties in a system make? Certainly, in a system with many different parties, allying with

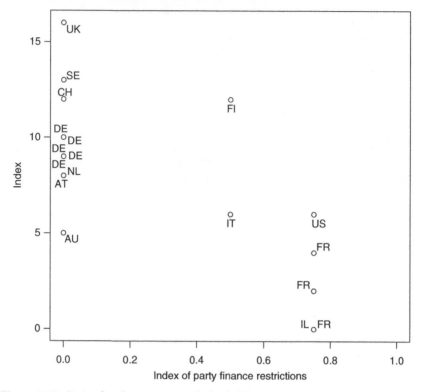

Figure 16.7. Strength of party–union links (additive score) and strength of party finance regulations.

just one of them would theoretically represent something of an opportunity cost for unions. To examine this we can look at the average effective number of political parties between 2008 and 2012 (Armingeon et al. 2014). We find that, contrary to what one might expect, there is a positive relationship between the number of parties and the strength of party–trade union links, even if it is not significant. We should therefore dismiss the idea that more parties mean weaker links. We should also, incidentally, note that there is no significant difference between the relationship political parties enjoy with confederations and the relationships they enjoy with individual trade unions.

Taken together, all this leaves us with a number of clear findings, as indicated in the right-hand column of Table 16.2, as well as some qualifications. Before summing up in our conclusion, however, we take time out to ask what might be termed 'the so-what question'. Irrespective of whether we can explain contemporary variation in organizational relationships between parties and trade unions, do they make a difference in real-world politics?

DOES THE VARIATION IN RELATIONSHIPS IMPACT ON POLICY?

We have seen that data on parties' general policy positions suggest that party–union links do not seem to be influenced by how left-wing a left-of-centre party is. However, as we go on to note, this does not preclude more concrete policy positions and actual policy outputs having an impact on the relationships. Those positions and outputs can confirm, strengthen, or weaken the incentives unions have to maintain organized links with a specific party. Moreover, the relationship can also obviously go in the opposite direction, since the strength of links might affect the party-union resources, including party policy over time: via a well-organized relationship with specific parties, trade unions seek more reliable access to legislation and may improve their own opportunities for policy rewards. However, we are not able to systematically investigate such developments. The assumption that changes and variation in organizational closeness/distance has political consequences is a major motivation behind this study, but an aspect that we have only been able to touch on briefly in our country studies. Taken together, however, country analyses may nevertheless help divine some patterns which may be worth pursuing further in future research. Whether the nature and strength of links between parties and trade unions has much influence on policy is an important question, and the final one we address in this book.

For instance, it seems fairly clear from our country studies, not least from recent experience in France and in Italy (where in the mid-1990s a centre-left government and trade unions managed to pull off a deal on pensions that had eluded its right-wing counterparts), that a weak and/or deteriorating relationship does have negative consequences for unions' policy influence in the sense of making it more difficult to prevent governments (including governments run by the centre-left) announcing policies, say, to liberalize the labour market that (according to the unions anyway) clash with the best interests of their members. This does not necessarily mean that said policies end up being implemented in full—in both countries unions, having failed to exert much influence in the early stages of the policy process, take to the streets and the airwaves to protest, sometimes very effectively.

The union movement in Israel has also proved it can have an effect on left-of-centre policy despite the disappearance of once close links between the two: characteristically, however, it was a personal intervention by the Chair of the Histadrut that persuaded it to join a coalition and negotiate a national response to the economic crisis that hit the country (and many others) after 2008. On the other hand, unions in the US, where connections with the Democrats are similarly weak, have had very little influence on policy in recent years, even when the Democrats have been able to set the agenda—one reason (although not of course the only reason) why the country's fiscal stimulus has centred mainly on tax reductions rather than on the kind of construction and infrastructure programmes that in previous decades would have been the natural response to an economic downturn.

That said, the existence of party–union relationships which are closer, sometimes much closer, than those in France, Italy, and Israel is no guarantee whatsoever that unions will be able to stop centre-left governments doing things they do not like—especially in an era where the emergence of new cleavages and constituencies may mean that alignment between their policy preferences is less likely than it once was (see Häusermann 2010). The paradigmatic example is surely German unions' failure, at the turn of the century, to prevent the SPD government adopting the Agenda 2020 and Harz IV liberal reforms to the labour market and welfare.

But there are others, notably Australian unions' having to accept the fact that the Labour Party, with which it continues to enjoy a relatively close organizational relationship, opted to dilute the previous right-wing govern-ment's WorkChoices legislation but not to abandon it altogether. By the same token, albeit two decades ago, British trade unions, which have even stronger organizational links with that country's centre-left party, were forced to accept the fact that the Labour government elected by landslides in 1997 and 2001 was not going to reverse the 'anti-trade union' legislation of its Conservative predecessors. On the other hand, when Labour began to worry about union support—particularly financial support—drying up in 2005, it negotiated the so-called 'Warwick Agreement' that, by acceding to a number of policies on the union movement's wish-list, rather undermined its earlier promise to suspicious floating voters to treat trade unions with 'fairness not favours'.

Meanwhile in Nordic countries like Sweden and Finland, where the rela-tionship between party and unions is still relatively solid and where it helped, at least in Sweden, to achieve significant pension reforms in 1990 (Ebbinghaus 2011, 324), recent years have seen more of an emphasis on defending past achievements and the status quo from right-wing attacks rather than proactive progressive policymaking—not least because, in both countries, the social democrats have lost their traditional grip on government.

In Switzerland, however—where the country's power-sharing government arrangement all but guarantees the centre-left a permanent presence in cabinet—the relatively strong links between party and unions have ensured not only that right-wing initiatives to deregulate the labour market and lower the pension age have been seen off, but also that progressive causes such as equal pay have made it onto the agenda.

Notwithstanding the above, we should avoid assuming that unions and parties, having fallen out with each other on policy, cannot come together again. After the bust-up between them under Gerhard Schröder, the SPD and the union movement managed to repair the damage sufficiently to see the SPD bring the unions' demands on a minimum wage and the retirement age into government with them when, after a period out of office, they joined a grand coalition with the CDU-CSU under Angela Merkel. And in the Netherlands, where the relationship between party and unions is more distant than it is in Germany, the two sides were able to put a disagreement over the raising of the retirement age behind them when, a couple of years later, they managed, after a conscious effort to build bridges, to secure compromise over labour market measures introduced by the coalition in which the Dutch Labour Party was a partner.

In short, then, relationships do seem to impact on policy inputs and outputs. Unions with weaker links to parties appear to find it difficult to stop those parties trying to push through policies they regard as inimical, although that does not necessarily mean that they will be unable to prevent those efforts coming to fruition. Moreover, even the strongest of organizational links are no guarantee that parties will not let unions down, and, even when they do not, their cooperation these days is more likely to revolve around blocking unwelcome initiatives from the centre-right than initiating game-changing progressive policies to rival those introduced in the golden age of the post-war boom. It nevertheless remains true that, on balance, it seems more useful—for these unions—to have left-of-centre parties occupying office (or at least occupying the role of veto-player) than it is to have the centre-right doing so instead. And thus, over time, *faute de mieux* may not be an inspiring policy reason to maintain organized links, but could be a good one nonetheless.

SUMMARY AND CONCLUSION

We wound up our qualitative comparison of the development of the relationships between major left-of-centre parties and their traditional union allies by stating that we found support for our general assumption that, even if differences in the national context make different rates of change more or less likely, we need to avoid any kind of determinism. We also suggested that long-term changes in the specific resources which the two sides can offer each other may provide pieces of the puzzle, but that lack of time series analysis makes it difficult to draw hard-and-fast conclusions. Contemporary variation in party–union links, we argued, is still significant and we therefore moved on to explore this in a quantitative cross-sectional analysis.

What significant patterns did that reveal? First, when it comes to the resources that *political parties* can offer *trade unions*, we can find no convincing support for the hypotheses we set out based on the exchange model. It is *not* the case that the traditional trade union allies of the left-of-centre have stronger ties with more left-wing and/or larger major left-of-centre parties. Admittedly, however, the manifestos of parties studied here do not vary that much along the left–right axis, and so the effect of policy proximity would perhaps be greater if one were to study a wider range of parties. A more concrete measure of 'union-friendly policy' might also give a different result, at least if it manages to capture policy delivery over time. That said, a party's recommendation of union membership and recent participation in government do not seem to affect the relationship with unions either.

In contrast, the resources that *trade unions* can offer *parties* do vary systematically with the strength of party–union links. Although no causality can be established, of course, the size of trade unions seems be correlated with party–union relationships: larger trade unions are involved in closer organizational relationships with parties. The hypothesis concerning union votes was not supported, but we saw that the more trade union members vote for major left-of-centre parties in Europe, the stronger the links between the two sides of the old labour movement.

Taken together, the results lend some weight to the resource exchange perspective as far as the traditional party–union cases go. These party–union relationships today are by no means just 'a legacy of the past'. Established partners that still have fairly strong links with each other seem to have greater incentives than others to maintain those links. Since these are cases of long-standing institutionalized relationships, with links that might be hard to unravel, we would argue that the results potentially indicate more general support for the cost–benefit exchange model too. Moreover, those resources that are specific to the relationships we study, and that are harder to redeploy, seem more important than other resources—in line with transaction cost theory underpinning the exchange model.

But our analysis also reveals that the relationship between left-of-centre parties and trade unions is essentially lopsided: any exchange of resources does not need to be mutual to matter, and as a consequence the cost–benefit model we formulated in Chapter 1 cannot be supported in full. For example, strong links exist even if parties cannot provide unions with stable access to government. The resources unions can offer parties appear to be considerably more important than those which parties can offer unions. Finally, our findings still provide some support for the argument that history matters, since a long-standing record of statutory links between parties and unions seems to make for stronger links between them today.

We have also seen that factors at the country level might play a part, even if the general institutional setting seems of limited importance. The less fragmented and the denser the trade union movement in a country, the stronger the traditional relationships between parties and trade unions. Financial donations that parties indicated receiving or trade unions indicated giving, however, do not affect the relationship. Yet the government subsidy regime seems closely related to party–trade union relationships: the more subsidies parties receive, and the more the regulatory regime constrains union donations, the weaker are party–trade union ties. In brief: *Left-of-centre party–trade union links are stronger where trade unions are larger, denser, and more unified, and where parties are less able to rely on the state to finance their organizational activities and electoral campaigns.*

All this could lead us to ask whether parties' roles as gatekeepers of the political system are more valuable *in themselves* than we have assumed. Does the exchange model rely on an unrealistic assumption of basic symmetry in the power relationship between parties and unions? One possible implication of this study is that, whereas unions inevitably covet access to an ideologically aligned party in the system, parties are more choosey. This seems at least to be the case as far as the relationships between the major left-of-centre parties and their tradition union ally go. Only by studying a wider range of parties and unions, and including systematic data on variation in parties' policy decisions and outputs over time compared to union preferences, can we explore this hypothesis further.

No doubt our analysis has its limitations if the aim is to draw more general conclusions. The number and variety of cases is relatively limited owing to our sharp analytical focus on traditional relationships and the number of countries involved. The next step will be to include all the party-union dyads mapped in the cross-sectional analysis. For now, we are unable to tell what significant correlations will hold when controlled for each other. Maybe some of the effects would lose significance if we were able to run a multivariate analysis. Indeed, future research, including more cases, might model and test the relationship in a multi-level fashion to check whether the country-level factors that matter influence (positively or negatively) the value of the resources parties and unions have to offer each other.

More information about the parties' competitors would probably also be relevant: do unions have good reasons to think they can 'seek out a higher bidder' elsewhere? Competition for working class votes is not necessarily strongest from the left, be it from old or new parties. In some countries, working class voters are plumping for populist radical right alternatives, with Austria, France, and Sweden being only the most obvious instances. Clearly, this does not necessarily mean that unions will do the same. As in other democracies similarly impacted by such parties, most trade unions— even those trade unions which are keen to reach out to other parties beyond their traditional allies—continue to treat them as beyond the pale. The Dutch are perhaps the best example of this, but Swedish and Finnish trade unions, too, display a marked reluctance to engage with the radical right parties for which many of their members are now voting. But the question is whether this shift will affect their ongoing willingness to commit to a major left-of-centre party through substantial organized links.

The negative correlation between union fragmentation and party–union links might also be related to a similar mechanism on the union side. How strongly the membership unions' recruitment base overlaps with other union confederations in the system might perhaps impinge on their calculations. If the competition for union members is very strong, this might weaken the reasons for allying organizationally with a particular left-of-centre party in order to avoid alienating potential members with different party preferences. Future analyses should include all union confederations/major unions and try to tease out the extent to which they compete or do not compete for the same members.

Clearly, however, we need further research on all this and on party–union links more generally, especially in the light of recent work that not only qualifies the common wisdom that who governs no longer makes much of a difference, but also confirms that centre-left administrations continue to protect trade union privileges—even if organizational links between parties and unions do not, on the face of it, appear to explain much (see Klitgaard et al. 2015 and Klitgaard and Nørgaard 2014; see also Simoni 2013). Further research is all the more important since it is now widely believed, at least in more coordinated market economies, that a strong union presence is positively associated with states' social expenditure (and indeed vice versa), and yet the reasons why this might be the case are by no means so clear: whether or not powerful unions are dealing with a left-of-centre government, for instance, does not seem to matter much (see Hooghe and Oser 2015), so what does? We have learned that the relationship between left-of-centre parties and unions without historical roots in the labour movement tend to be more distant but still organized, at least in the countries studied here. Future research should, if possible, take more countries into account and systematically study the complex relationship between party–union links and policy positions and outputs.

But while there is always more to be done, this book has nonetheless helped us take a significant step forward in understanding both how party–union relationships have developed over time and why they differ today. We have also seen indications of this variation having political consequences. As one useful study of divergent party and union preferences on welfare policies (Jensen 2012) is keen to remind us, we need to be careful not to assume that the two sides of the labour movement are necessarily 'two sides of the same coin'. If this was ever true, it is true no longer. Yet our study of their organizational links and their impact on each other suggests that it would be wrong, even implicitly, simply to write off that relationship as either already over or heading rapidly for the rocks. While left-of-centre parties and trade unions may not be as close as they once were, there are few countries in which we could say they may as well be strangers. Indeed, in some places, while old allies may no longer be in each other's pockets, they still see themselves as privileged partners, even if, in some cases, one side values what they have—or thinks they have—rather more than the other.

APPENDIX

Table A16.1. Missing cases from cross-sectional analysis

#	Country	Political party	Trade union
1	Austria	SPÖ	ÖGB
2	United Kingdom	Labour	TUC
3	United Kingdom	Labour	Unite
4	United Kingdom	Labour	Unison
5	United Kingdom	Labour	NUT
6	United Kingdom	Labour	USDAW
7	Australia	ALP	ACTU
8	Australia	ALP	AWU
9	Australia	ALP	SDA

Table A16.2. List of independent variables (operationalization and sources)

Recommended membership
Whether the party recommends union membership in its statutes. Coded 0 if no, 1 if yes. Question asked in the LPTU survey.

Welfare CMP 2008–2013
The average left–right party position between 2008 and 2013 measured using the Manifesto project's welfare variable. This consists of a positive view of equality ('concept of social justice and the need for fair treatment of all people') and 'favourable mentions of need to introduce, maintain or expand any public social service or social security scheme' (Volkens et al. 2015). The scale ranges theoretically from 0 to 100.

Years in government between 2008 and 2013
The average number of years a party has been in office between 2008 and 2013 (i.e. days in office divided by 365). For the United States, the length of Democratic presidents' time in office is used (Goemans et al. 2009; Seki and Williams 2014; Döring and Manow 2016).

Average share of seats between 2008 and 2013
The average share of seats in the lower house won by the party in elections between 2008 and 2013 (Döring and Manow 2016; IPU 2016).

Average share of unionized employees 2008–11
The union's average share of the country's total number of union members between 2008 and 2011 (Visser 2015).

Union voting ESS 2008–12
The average share of trade union members that voted for the party between 2008 and 2012 (European Social Survey 2014a; 2014b; 2014c).

Index of union financial/material support
Index based on seven questions asked in the LPTU survey. The questions concern whether the trade unions have supported the party or the campaigns of individual candidates financially, or supported campaigns by providing manpower, material support or facilities. The index goes from 0 (no support) to 7 (all types of support).

(continued)

Table A16.2. Continued

EVS attitudes towards trade unions
The share of respondents reporting they have 'a great deal' or 'quite a lot' of confidence in trade unions in the fourth EVS wave (2008–10) (European Values Study 2011).

Union history
Whether the confederation/trade union has been party political rather than non-aligned from its foundation. Coded 0 if not true, 1 if partially true, and 2 if fully true. Question asked in the LPTU survey.

Previous statutory links
Existence of previous statutory links between the party and union. Coded 0 if no, 1 if yes. From LPTU.

Union density
The average share of employees who were members of a trade union between 2008 and 2013 (OECD 2013a).

Union fragmentation
The average effective number of unions between 2008 and 2011, defined as the inverse of the Herfindahl index. The Herfindahl (H) index is given by $H_{cf} = \Sigma_i^n (p_i^2)$, where p_i is the proportion of total membership organized by the Ith union and n is the total number of unions. By discounting the weight of smaller confederations, the index conveys an idea of the actual degree of concentration at the central or peak level in a given country. The effective number of confederations is equal to the probability that any two union members are in the same confederation and thus a measure of the degree of fragmentation or unity at the central (political) level (Visser 1990: 172; 2015; Iversen 1999: 53).

Left party fragmentation
The effective number of left parties on the votes level between 2010 and 2013 according to Laakso and Taagepera's (1979) formula. Included are only vote shares of major, established left parties (communist, socialist, social democratic, and labour, and other various left-wing parties, e.g. left-libertarian parties) based on Swank's (2013) classification, with the exception of the US. In this case, we have not used the dataset's value of 0 as we in our study have included the Democrats as the US' equivalent to the left-of-centre parties in Europe. Israel is not included in Swank (2013). The left parties included in this case are the ones that got more than 1 per cent of the votes and with a score of less than 5 on Parlgov's left–right scale. This is a scale based on mean values in the left–right dimension with data from Castles and Mair (1984), Huber and Inglehart (1995), Benoit and Laver (2006), and Hooghe et al. (2010). Vote share source: Döring and Manow (2016).

Routine involvement
The routine involvement of trade unions and employers' organizations in government decisions on social and economic policy between 2008 and 2013 (Visser 2015). Coded 0 if no concertation, involvement is rare or absent, 0.5 if partial concertation, irregular and infrequent involvement, and 1 if full concertation, regular, and frequent involvement.

Index of party subsidies
Index of existence of permanent and/or electoral state subsidies. The index goes from 0 (no subsidies) to 1 (both subsidies). The coding is based on Casas-Zamora (2005: 19–20), and updated by means of International IDEA (2016). We checked the IDEA data against the Political Party Database <http://www.politicalpartydb.org/>, and supplemented this with Pacini and Piccio (2012) in the case of Italy.

Index of party finance restrictions
The index measuring the strength of party finance regulations is based on two items: existence of restrictions on donations to parties from individuals and existence of restrictions on donations to parties from trade unions (coded as 'no restrictions' (0), 'restrictions' (0.5), or 'forbidden' (1)).

Thus, it is an index of two items which have three points, making a total of six points possible. Values are assigned based on the average of the two items. The coding is based on Casas-Zamora (2005: 19–20), and updated by means of International IDEA (2016) and other sources.

Federalism
Three-step federalism scale that differentiates between non-federal (0), weakly federal (0.5), and strongly federal (1) states (Armingeon et al. 2014). Israel is not included in Armingeon et al. (2014), but has been coded as non-federal based on the comparative literature.

Parliamentary government
Three-step scale from parliamentary (1) via mixed (semi-presidential) (0.5) to presidential democracies (0) (Cheibub et al. 2010).

Effective number of parties
The average effective number of parties on the votes level between 2008 and 2012 according to Laakso and Taagepera's (1979) formula (Armingeon et al. 2014).

Trade union = confederation
Coded 0 if individual union, 1 if confederation. From LPTU.

NOTE

1. That said, we note that the Australian Labor party is almost certainly strongly linked to affiliated unions which we were not able to include.

Bibliography

Achterberg, Peter. 2006. 'Class Voting in the New Political Culture: Economic, Cultural and Environmental Voting in 20 Western Countries.' *International Sociology*, 21(2): 237–61.

Ackermann, Ewald. 2011. 'Nach wie vor starke gewerkschaftliche Deputation.' SGB press release, 26 October 2011: <http://www.sgb.ch/themen/gewerkschaftspolitik/artikel/details/nach-wie-vor-starke-gewerkschaftliche-deputation/>.

Afonso, Alexandre. 2010. 'Policy Concertation, Europeanization and New Political Cleavages: The Case of Switzerland.' *European Journal of Industrial Relations*, 16(1): 57–72.

Aitken, Don. 1982. *Stability and Change in Australian Politics*, 2nd edition. Canberra: Australian National University Press.

Alemann, Ulrich von, and Tim Spier. 2008. 'Doppelter Einsatz, halber Sieg? Die SPD und die Bundestagswahl 2005.' In Oskar Niedermayer (ed.), *Die Parteien nach der Bundestagswahl 2005*. Wiesbaden: VS Verlag für Sozialwissenschaften, 37–65.

Alemann, Ulrich von, and Tim Spier. 2011. 'Erholung in der Opposition? Die SPD nach der Bundestagswahl 2009.' In Oskar Niedermayer (ed.), *Die Parteien nach der Bundestagswahl 2009*. Wiesbaden: VS Verlag für Sozialwissenschaften, 57–77.

Allern, Elin H. 2010. *Political Parties and Interest Groups in Norway*. Colchester: ECPR Press.

Allern, Elin H., Nicholas Aylott, and Flemming J. Christiansen. 2007. 'Social Democrats and Trade Unions in Scandinavia: The Decline and Persistence of Institutional Relationships.' *European Journal of Political Research*, 46(5), 607–35.

Allern, Elin H., Nicholas Aylott, and Flemming J. Christiansen. 2010. 'Scenes from a Marriage: Social Democrats and Trade Unions in Scandinavia.' CVPA Working Paper, University of Copenhagen.

Allern, Elin H., and Tim Bale. 2012a. 'Political Parties and Interest Groups: Disentangling Complex Relationships.' Special Issue of *Party Politics*, 18(1): 7–25.

Allern, Elin H., and Tim Bale. 2012b. 'Conclusion: Qualifying the Common Wisdom.' Special Issue of *Party Politics*, 18(1): 99–106.

Almond, Gabriel A., and G. Bingham Powell. 1966. *Comparative Politics: A Developmental Approach*. Boston, MA: Little, Brown.

Altermatt, Urs. 2010. 'Christlichdemokratische Volkspartei (CVP).' *Historisches Lexikon der Schweiz*: <http://www.hls-dhs-dss.ch/textes/d/D17377.php>.

Andersson, Elisabeth. 2008. 'Fritzon: Samarbete kan bli nödvändigt. Ledaren för Skånes socialdemokrater: Valet ingen promenadseger.' *Sydsvenskan*, 13 November.

Andeweg, Rudy A. and Galen Irwin. 2008. *Governance and Politics in the Netherlands*. Houndsmills: Palgrave.

Andolfatto, Dominique, and Dominique Labbé. 2000. *Sociologie des syndicats*. Paris: Editions La Découverte.

Andolfatto, Dominique, and Jean-Yves Sabot. 2004. 'Les héritiers du mouvement ouvrier: CGT et CGT-FO.' In Dominique Andolfatto (ed.), *Les syndicats en France*. Paris: La Documentation française.

Angestellte Schweiz. 2013. *Jahresbericht 2013*. Zürich: Angestellte Schweiz <http://angestellte.ch/assets/Publikationen/Jahresbericht/Jahresbericht-2012-de.pdf>.

Anthonsen, Mette, and Johannes Lindvall. 2009. 'Party Competition and the Resilience of Corporatism.' *Government and Opposition*, 44(2): 167–87.

Anthonsen, Mette, Johannes Lindvall, and Ulrich Schmidt-Hansen. 2011. 'Social Democrats, Union and Corporatism: Denmark and Sweden Compared.' *Party Politics*, 17(1): 118–34.

Archer, Robin. 2010. *Why is there No Labor Party in the United States?* Princeton, NJ: Princeton University Press.

Armingeon, Klaus. 1997. 'Swiss Corporatism in Comparative Perspective.' *West European Politics*, 20(4): 164–79.

Armingeon Klaus, Christian Isler, Laura Knöpfel, David Weisstanner, and Sarah Engler. 2014. *Comparative Political Data Set 1960–2013*. Bern: Institute of Political Science, University of Berne.

Arter, David. 2009a. 'From a Contingent Party System to Party System Convergence? Mapping Party System Change in Postwar Finland.' *Scandinavian Political Studies*, 32(2): 221–39.

Arter, David. 2009b. 'Money and Votes: The Cost of Election for First-Time Finnish MPs.' *Politiikka*, 51(1): 17–33.

Atkinson, Anthony B. 1999. 'The Distribution of Income in the UK and OECD Countries in the Twentieth Century.' *Oxford Review of Economic Policy*, 15(4): 56–75.

Australian Bureau of Statistics. 2011. *6310.0—Employee Earnings, Benefits and Trade Union Membership, Australia, August*. Canberra: Australian Bureau of Statistics.

Aylott, Nicholas. 2003. 'After the Divorce: Social Democrats and Trade Unions in Sweden.' *Party Politics*, 9(3), 369–90.

Bailey, David J., Jean-Michel De Waele, Fabien Escalona, and Mathieu Vieira. 2014. *European Social Democracy during the Global Economic Crisis: Renovation or Resignation?* Manchester: Manchester University Press.

Bale, Tim. 2015. *Five Year Mission: The Labour Party under Ed Miliband*. Oxford: Oxford University Press.

Bale, Tim, and Paul Webb. 2014. 'The Selection of Party Leaders in the UK.' In Jean-Benoit Pilet and William Cross (eds), *The Selection of Political Party Leaders in Contemporary Parliamentary Democracies: A Comparative Study*. London: Routledge, 12–29.

Balmas, Meital, Gideon Rahat, Tamir Sheafer, and Shaul Shenhav. 2014. 'Two Routes to Personalized Politics: Centralized and Decentralized Personalization.' *Party Politics*, 20(1): 37–51.

Bank, Jan. 1985. 'De broederlijk relaties tussen de KAB/NKV en de KVP, 1945–1981.' In Jan Roes (ed.), *Katholieke arbeidersbeweging: studies over KAB en NKV in de economische en politieke ontwikkeling van Nederland na 1945*. Baarn: Ambo, 293–342.

Bank of Israel Report 2013. 2014. 'Number of Israeli Employees in the Principal Industries, 1969–2013.' Bank of Israel, 4 May: <http://www.boi.org.il/en/NewsAndPublications/RegularPublications/Pages/Boi.ashx?Command=DownloadFile&DocUrl=%2fen%2fNewsAndPublications%2fRegularPublications%2fDocuments%2fDochApp2013%2fe%2fe_4_e.xlsx>.

Barrling Hermansson, Katarina. 2004. *Partikulturer.* Uppsala: Acta Universitatis Upsaliensis.

Bartal, Gavriel. 1991. *Histadrut: Structure and Activity.* Tel Aviv: Histadrut Executive Committee.

Bartels, Larry. 2008. *Unequal Democracy: The Politics of the New Gilded Age.* Princeton, NJ: Princeton University Press.

Bartolini, Stefano. 2000. *The Political Mobilization of the European Left, 1860–1980.* Cambridge: Cambridge University Press.

Bartolini, Stefano. 2007. *The Political Mobilization of the European Left, 1860–1980: The Class Cleavage,* 2nd edition. Cambridge: Cambridge University Press.

Bates, Robert H., Avner Greif, Margaret Levi, Jean-Laurent Rosenthal, and Barry R. Weingast. 1998. *Analytic Narratives.* Princeton, NJ: Princeton University Press.

Baumgartner, Frank R., and Beth Leech. 1998. *Basic Interests: The Importance of Groups in Politics and in Political Science.* Princeton NJ: Princeton University Press.

Bellucci, Paolo, and Oliver Heath. 2012. 'The Structure of Party-Organization Linkages and the Electoral Strength of Cleavages in Italy, 1963–2008.' *British Journal of Political Science,* 42(1): 107–35.

Benoit, Kenneth, and Michael Laver. 2006. *Party Policy in Modern Democracies.* London and New York: Routledge.

Bergholm, Tapio. 2005. *Sopimusyhteiskunnan synty I. Työehtosopimusten läpimurrosta yleislakkoon. SAK 1944–1956.* Keuruu: Otava.

Bergholm, Tapio. 2007. *Sopimusyhteiskunnan synty II. Hajaannuksesta tulopolitiikkaan. SAK 1956–1969.* Keuruu: Otava.

Bergholm, Tapio. 2012. 'The Country Report of Finnish Trade Unions 2012: Strong Trade Union Movement in Gradual Decline.' Berlin: Friedrich Ebert Stiftung.

Bergholm, Tapio, and Andreas Bieler. 2013. 'Globalization and the Erosion of the Nordic Model: A Swedish–Finnish Comparison.' *European Journal of Industrial Relations,* 19(1): 55–70.

Bergstrand, Finn. 2003. *Daco 1931–1937: en svensk tjänstemannarörelse växer fram.* Stockholm: TAM-Arkiv.

Berry, Jeffrey M. 1997. *The Interest Group Society.* New York: Addison Wesley Longman.

Berry, Jeffrey M. 1999. *The New Liberalism: The Rising Power of Citizen Groups.* Washington, DC: Brookings Institution Press.

Bevort, Antoine. 2004. 'Du catholicisme social au réformisme: CFTC et CFDT.' In Dominique Andolfatto (ed.), *Les syndicats en France.* Paris: La Documentation française.

Beyers, Jan, Rainer Eising, and William Mahoney. 2008. 'Researching Interest Group Politics in Europe and Elsewhere: Much We Study, Little We Know.' *West European Politics,* 31(6): 1103–28.

Bille, Lars, and Flemming Juul Christiansen. 2001. 'Partier og interesseorganisationer I Danmark.' In Jan Sundberg (ed.), *Partier och interesseorganisationer i Norden.* Copenhagen: Nordisk Ministerråd.

Binderkrantz, Anne. 2005. 'Interest Group Strategies: Navigating Between Privileged Access and Strategies of Pressure.' *Political Studies,* 53(4): 694–715.

Blyth, Mark, and Richard S. Katz. 2005. 'From Catch-all Politics to Cartelization: The Political Economy of the Cartel Party.' *West European Politics,* 28(1): 33–60.

Bodah, Matthew M., Steve Ludlam, and David Coates. 2003. 'The Development of an Anglo-American Model of Trade Union and Political Party Relations.' *Labour Studies Journal*, 28(2): 45–66.

Borg, Sami (ed.). 2012. *Muutosvaalit 2011*. Helsinki: Oikeusministeriön julkaisu 16/2012.

Bourmaud, François-Xavier. 2013. 'Le PS recrute Edouard Martin.' *Le Figaro*, 18 December. <http://www.lefigaro.fr/conjoncture/2013/12/18/20002-20131218AR TFIG00511-le-ps-recrute-edouard-martin.php>.

Bracks, S., J. Faulkner, and R. Carr. 2010. *2010 National Review: Report to the ALP National Executive*. Canberra: ALP.

Brichta, Avraham. 2001. *Political Reform in Israel: The Quest for a Stable and Effective Government*. Brighton: Sussex Academic.

Bürgi, Markus. 2014. 'Demokratische Bewegung.' *Historisches Lexikon der Schweiz*: <http://www.hls-dhs-dss.ch/textes/d/D17382.php>.

Byggnads. 2012. *Verksamhetsberättelse*. Stockholm: Byggnads.

Böckerman, Petri, and Roope Uusitalo. 2006. 'Erosion of the Ghent System and Union Membership Decline: Lessons from Finland.' *British Journal of Industrial Relations*, 44(2): 283–303.

Cantone, Carla, and Massimo Franchi. 2014. *Di lotta e di memoria. Perché il sindacato ha ancora un ruolo. La CGIL vista dal di dentro*. Lecce: Manni Editori.

Carnes, Nicholas. 2013. *White Collar Government: The Hidden Role of Class in Economic Policy Making*. Chicago: The University of Chicago Press.

Carrieri, Mimmo. 2014. 'Le rappresentanze sociali nell'era neo-populista. Organizzare la democrazia per organizzare la rappresentanza.' *Quaderni di Rassegna sindacale*, XV(2): 141–57.

Casas-Zamora, Kevin. 2005. *Paying for Democracy: Political Finance and State Funding for Parties*. Colchester: ECPR Press.

Casparsson, Ragnar. 1947. *LO under fem årtionden 1898–1923, del I*. Stockholm: Tiden.

Castles, Francis G. and Peter Mair. 1984. 'Left–Right Political Scales: Some Expert Judgments.' *European Journal of Political Research*, 12(1): 73–88.

Cattaneo, Carlo. 1968. *Istituto di studi e ricerche La presenza sociale del Pci e della Dc*. Bologna: Il Mulino.

Celis, Karen, Anke Schouteden, and Bram Wauters. 2015. 'Cleavage, Ideology and Identity: Explaining the Linkage between Representatives and Interest Groups.' *Parliamentary Affairs*: 1–18, doi: 10.1093/pa/gsv040.

Cella, Gian P., and Tiziano Treu. 2001. 'National Trade Union Movements.' In Roger Blanpain and Chris Engels (eds), *Comparative Labour Law and Industrial Relations in Industrialized Market Economies*, 7th edition. Deventer: Kluwer.

Cella, Gian P., and Tiziano Treu. 2009. *Relazioni industriali e contrattazione collettiva*. Bologna: Il Mulino.

Cerri Marco, and Vladimiro Soli (eds). 2008. *I Mestieri del sindacalista. Tra rappresentazione soggettiva e ridefinizione professionale*. Quaderni Ires CGIL Veneto, maggio 2008.

Cesos Cisl-Ires Cgil. 1982. *Sindacalisti in Parlamento*. Roma: Eli-Esi.

CGIL. 1983. *Circolare no. 3691*, 8 June. Rome: CGIL.

Cheibub, José A., Jennifer Gandhi, and James R. Vreeland. 2010. 'Democracy and Dictatorship Revisited.' *Public Choice*, 143(1): 67–101.

Christiansen, Flemming Juul. 2012. 'Organizational De-integration of Political Parties and Interest Groups in Denmark.' *Party Politics*, 18(1): 27–43.

Cohen, Yinon, Yitchak Haberfeld, Tali Kristal, and Guy Mundlak. 2007. 'The State of Organized Labor in Israel.' *Journal of Labor Research*, 28(2): 255–73.

Cohen, Yinon, Yitchak Haberfeld, Guy Mundlak, and Ishak Saporta. 2003. 'Unpacking Union Density: Membership and Coverage in the Transformation of the Israeli IR System.' *Industrial Relations: A Journal of Economy and Society*, 42(4): 692–711.

Cook, T. nd. *Unions and the ALP: Between Dependence and Independence*. University of Sydney PhD.

Coombs, Clyde H. 1964. *A Theory of Data*. Hoboken: Wiley.

Courtois, Stéphane, and Dominique Andolfatto. 2008. 'France: The Collapse of the House of Communism.' In Uwe Backes and Patrick Moreau (eds), *Communist and Post-communist Parties in Europe*. Göttingen: Vandenhoeck and Ruprecht.

Crouch, Colin. 1993. *Industrial Relations and European State Traditions*. Oxford: Clarendon Press.

Crouch, Colin. 1999. *Social Change in Western Europe*. Oxford: Oxford University Press.

Crouch, Colin. 2004. *Postdemocracy*. Cambridge: Polity.

Daley, Anthony. 1993. 'Remembrance of Things Past: The Union–Party Linkage in France.' *International Journal of Political Economy*, Winter 1992–3: 53–71.

Daley, Anthony, and Michel Vale. 1992/93. 'Remembrance of Things Past: The Union–Party Linkage in France.' *International Journal of Political Economy*, 22(4): 53–71.

Dark, Taylor E. 1999. *The Unions and the Democrats: An Enduring Alliance*. Ithaca, NY: Cornell University Press.

Davidsson, Johan B., and Patrick Emmenegger. 2013. 'Defending the Organisation, not the Members: Unions and the Reform of Job Security Legislation in Western Europe.' *European Journal of Political Research*, 52(3): 339–63.

Davidsson, Lars. 2006. *I linje med partiet? Maktspel och lojalitet i den svenska riksdagen*. Stockholm: SNS förlag.

De Waele, Jean-Michel, Fabien Escalona, and Mathieu Vieira (eds) 2013. *The Palgrave Handbook of Social Democracy in the European Union*. Basingstoke: Palgrave.

Degen, Bernhard. 2012. 'Schweizerischer Arbeiterbund.' *Historisches Lexikon der Schweiz*: <http://www.hls-dhs-dss.ch/textes/d/D17398.php>.

Degen, Bernhard. 2013. 'Sozialdemokratische Partei der Schweiz.' *Historisches Lexikon der Schweiz*: <http://www.hls-dhs-dss.ch/textes/d/D17393.php>.

Demos and Pi. 2013. *Elezioni politiche 2013: com'è cambiata la composizione sociale del voto*. February 2013. Accessed April 2016: <http://www.demos.it/a00831.php>.

Demos and Pi. 2014. *Gli italiani e lo stato*. Survey, 15–19 December.

DN. 2008a. 'S och mp siktar på att regera ihop.' *Dagens Nyheter*, 8 October.

DN. 2008b. 'Mona Sahlin backar om v.' *Dagens Nyheter*, 10 October.

Döring, Holger, and Philip Manow. 2016. *Parliaments and Governments Database (ParlGov): Information on Parties, Elections and Cabinets in Modern Democracies*. Development version: <http://www.parlgov.org/>.

Dorling, P., and N. McKenzie. 2010. 'Unionists Boast of Backroom Power.' *Sydney Morning Herald*, 11 December.

Dunphy, Richard. 2007. 'In Search of an Identity: Finland's Left Alliance and the Experience of Coalition Government.' *Contemporary Politics*, 13(1): 37–55.

Duverger, Maurice. 1954/1972. *Political Parties: Their Organization and Activity in the Modern State*. London: Methuen.

Duverger, Maurice. 1968. *Sociologie Politique*. Paris: Presses Universitaires France.

Duverger, Maurice. 1972. *Party Politics and Pressure Groups: A Comparative Introduction*. New York: Crowell.

Ebbinghaus, Bernhard. 1995. 'The Siamese Twins: Citizenship Rights, Cleavage Formation, and Party-Union Relations in Western Europe.' *International Review of Social History*, 40(S3): 51–89.

Ebbinghaus, Bernhard. 2011. 'The Role of Trade Unions in European Pension Reforms: From "Old" to "New" Politics?' *European Journal of Industrial Relations*, 17(4): 315–31.

Ebbinghaus, Bernhard, and Claudia Göbel. 2014. 'Mitgliederrückgang und Organisationsstrategien deutscher Gewerkschaften.' In Wolfgang Schroeder (ed.), *Handbuch Gewerkschaften in Deutschland*, 2nd edition. Wiesbaden: Springer VS, 207–39.

Elektrikerna. 2010. *Verksamhetsberättelse*. Stockholm: Svenska Elektrikerförbundet.

Ellwood, David T., and Glenn Fine. 1987. 'The Impact of Right-to-Work Laws on Union Organizing.' *Journal of Political Economy*, 95(2): 250–73.

Elvander, Nils. 1980. *Skandinavisk arbetarrörelse*. Stockholm: Liber Förlag.

Englund, Rolf. 1984. *Rosornas krig: vad vilja socialdemokraterna?* Stockholm: Timbro.

Epstein, Leon D. 1967. *Political Parties in Western Democracies*. New York: Frederick A. Praeger.

Erne, Roland. 2003. 'Obligatorisches Referendum, Plebiszit und Volksbegehren—drei Typen direkter Demokratie im europäischen Vergleich.' In Theo Schiller and Volker Mittendorf (eds), *Direkte Demokratie*. Wiesbaden: Westdeutscher Verlag, 76–87. <http://link.springer.com/chapter/10.1007/978-3-322-80430-3_4>.

Erne, Roland. 2008. *European Unions: Labour's Quest for a Transnational Democracy*. Ithaca, NY: Cornell University Press.

Erne, Roland. 2014. 'Interest Groups.' In Daniele Caramani (ed.), *Comparative Politics*, 3rd edition. Oxford: Oxford University Press, 237–51.

Erne, Roland, and Natalie Imboden. 2015. 'Equal Pay by Gender and by Nationality: A Comparative Analysis of Switzerland's Unequal Equal Pay Policy Regimes across Time.' *Cambridge Journal of Economics*, 39(2): 655–74.

European Social Survey. 2014a. 'Round 4 Data. Data file edition 4.3.' Norwegian Social Science Data Services, Norway—Data Archive and distributor of ESS data for ESS ERIC.

European Social Survey. 2014b. 'Round 5 Data. Data file edition 3.2.' Norwegian Social Science Data Services, Norway—Data Archive and distributor of ESS data for ESS ERIC.

European Social Survey. 2014c. 'Round 6 Data. Data file edition 2.1.' Norwegian Social Science Data Services, Norway—Data Archive and distributor of ESS data for ESS ERIC.

European Values Study. 2011. *European Values Study Longitudinal Data File 1981–2008*. Cologne: GESIS Data Archive. ZA4804 Data file Version 2.0.0: <http://dx.doi.org/10.4232/1.11005>.

Fastighets. 2012. *Verksamhetsberättelse och årsredovisning*. Stockholm: Fastighetsanställdas förbund.

Feltrin, Paolo. 2010. 'Le scelte elettorali dell'ultimo quinquennio: voto di classe e voto degli iscritti al sindacato.' *Quaderni di Rassegna Sindacale. Lavori*, 11(4): 83–110.

Fenno, Richard F. 1978. *Home Style: House Members in their Districts*. New York: Pearson.

Fisher, Justin. 2015. 'Party Finance: The Death of the National Campaign?' *Parliamentary Affairs*, 68(S1): 133–53.

Fluder, Robert, and Beat Hotz-Hart. 1998. 'Switzerland: Still as Smooth as Clockwork?' In Antony Ferner and Richard Hyman (eds), *Changing Industrial Relations in Europe*. Oxford: Blackwell, 262–82.

Forester, Tom. 1976. *The Labour Party and the Working Class*. New York: Holmes & Meier.

Foster, Jody, and Christopher P. Muste. 1992. 'The United States.' In David Butler and Austin Ranney (eds), *Electioneering: A Comparative Study of Continuity and Change*. Oxford: Clarendon Press.

france-politique. n.d. 'Résultats électoraux du PCF.' Accessed September 2016: <http://www.france-politique.fr/elections-pcf.htm>.

Francia, Peter L. 2006. *The Future of Organized Labour in American Politics*. New York: Columbia University Press.

Francia, Peter L. 2010. 'Assessing the Labor-Democratic Party Alliance: A One-sided Relationship?' *Polity*, 42(3): 293–303.

Francia, Peter L. 2012. 'Do Unions Still Matter in U.S. Elections? Assessing Labor's Political Power and Significance.' *The Forum*, 10(1): Article 3.

Friedrich, Daniel, Kathleen Kollewe, Knut Lambertin, and Alexander Naujoks. 2009. 'Gemeinsam stark? Über die kontinuierliche Neubestimmung scheinbar altbewährter Verhältnisse: Gewerkschaften und Parteien.' *Forschungsjournal Neue Soziale Bewegungen*, 22(4): 79–87.

Gais, Thomas. 1996. *Improper Influence*. Ann Arbor: University of Michigan Press.

Galnoor, Itzhak. 1982. *Steering the Polity*. London: Sage.

Gardner, Amy. 2012. 'Union Leaders Support Obama Despite Tension with the Democratic Party.' *The Washington Post*, 5 September.

Gluchowski, Peter, and Ulrich von Wilamowitz-Moellendorff. 1998. 'The Erosion of Social Cleavages in Western Germany, 1971–97.' In Christopher J. Anderson and Carsten Zelle (eds), *Stability and Change in German Elections: How Electorates Merge, Converge, or Collide*. Westport: Praeger, 13–31.

Godfroid, D. J. 1995. 'FNV'er Suurhof: Er is geen alternatief voor de PvdA.' *Nederlands Dagblad*, 8 August.

Goemans, Henk E., Kristian Skrede Gleditsch, and Giacomo Chiozza. 2009. 'Introducing Archigos: A Dataset of Political Leaders.' *Journal of Peace Research*, 46(2): 269–83. Version 4.1: <http://www.rochester.edu/college/faculty/hgoemans/data.htm>.

Grant, Don S., and Michael Wallace. 1994. 'The Political Economy of Manufacturing Growth and Decline across the American States, 1970–1985.' *Social Forces*, 73(1): 33–66.

GRECO. 2013. *Compliance Report on Switzerland*. Strasbourg: Council of Europe: <http://www.coe.int/t/dghl/monitoring/greco/evaluations/round3/GrecoRC3(2013)17_Switzerland_EN.pdf>.

Greef, Samuel. 2014. 'Gewerkschaften im Spiegel von Zahlen, Daten und Fakten.' In Wolfgang Schroeder (ed.), *Handbuch Gewerkschaften in Deutschland*, 2nd edition. Wiesbaden: Springer VS, 659–755.

Greenstone, J. David. 1969. *Labour in American Politics*. New York: Knopf.

Greven, Michael Th. 1987. *Parteimitglieder. Ein empirischer Essay*. Opladen: Leske + Budrich.

Grinberg, Lev L. 1991. *Split Corporatism in Israel*. Albany: State University of New York Press.

Grunden, Timo. 2012. 'Die SPD. Zyklen der Organisationsgeschichte und Strukturmerkmale innerparteilicher Entscheidungsprozesse.' In Karl-Rudolf Korte and Jan Treibel (eds), *Wie entscheiden Parteien? Prozesse innerparteilicher Willensbildung in Deutschland*. Baden-Baden: Nomos, 93–119.

Grönlund, Kimmo, and Jussi Westinen. 2012. 'Puoluevalinta.' In Sami Borg (ed.), *Muutosvaalit 2011*. Helsinki: Oikeusministeriön julkaisu, 156–88.

Gumbrell-McCormick, Rebecca, and Richard Hyman. 2013. *Trade Unions in Western Europe: Hard Times, Hard Choices*. Oxford: Oxford University Press.

Haberfeld, Yitzhak, Yinon Cohen, Guy Mundlak, and Yitzhak Saporta. 2010. 'Union Density in Israel 2000–2006: Years of Stagnation.' *Avoda, Hevra ve Mishpat*, 10: 533–49.

Hacker, Jacob S., and Paul Pierson. 2010. *Winner-Take-All Politics: How Washington Made the Rich Richer—And Turned Its Back on the Middle Class*. New York: Simon and Schuster.

Hall, Peter A., and Rosemary C. R. Taylor. 1996. 'Political Science and the Three New Institutionalisms.' *Political Studies*, 44(5): 936–57.

Hamann, Kerstin, Alison Johnston, Alexia Katsanidou, John Jelly, and Phillip H. Pollock. 2015. 'Sharing the Rewards, Dividing the Costs? The Electoral Consequences of Social Pacts and Legislative Reform in Western Europe.' *West European Politics*, 38(1): 206–27.

Handrels. 2010. *Verksamhetsberättelse*. Stockholm: Handelsanställdas förbund.

Hansson, Sigfrid. 1936–9. *Svenska folkrörelser*. Stockholm: Lindfors.

Harpaz, Itzhak. 2007. 'The State of Trade Unionism in Israel.' In Craig Phelan (ed.), *Trade Union Revitalisation: Trends and Prospects in 34 Countries*. Oxford: Peter Lang, 445–9.

Harrison, Martin. 1960. *Trade Unions and the Labour Party*. London: Allen & Unwin.

Harrop, Andrew. 2015. *The Mountain to Climb: Labour's 2020 Challenge*. London: Fabian Society.

Hassels, Anke. 2006. 'Zwischen Politik und Arbeitsmarkt: Zum Wandel gewerkschaftlicher Eliten in Deutschland.' In Herfried Münkler, Grit Straßenberger, and Matthias Bohlender (eds), *Deutschlands Eliten im Wandel*. Frankfurt: Campus, 199–220.

Hassels, Anke. 2007. 'Gewerkschaften.' In Thomas von Winter and Ulrich Willems (eds), *Interessenverbände in Deutschland*. Wiesbaden: VS Verlag für Sozialwissenschaften, 173–96.

Häusermann, Silja. 2010. *The Politics of Welfare State Reform in Continental Europe: Modernization in Hard Times*. Cambridge: Cambridge University Press.

Hayward, Jack E. S. 1980. 'Trade Union Movements and their Politico-Erconomic Environments: A Preliminary Framework.' In Jack E. S. Hayward (ed.), *Trade Unions and Politics in Western Europe*. London: Frank Cass.

Hazenbosch, Piet. 2009. *Voor het Volk om Christus' Wil: Een geschiedenis van het CNV*. Hilversum: Verloren.

Heaney, Michael T. 2010. 'Linking Political Parties and Interest Groups.' In L. Sandy Maisel and Jeffrey M. Berry (eds), *The Oxford Handbook of American Political Parties and Interest Groups*. New York: Oxford University Press.

Hermann, Michael. 2013. *Das politische Profil des Geldes. Wahl- und Abstimmungswerbung in der Schweiz*. Study commissioned by the Swiss Federal Department of Justice and Police. Zürich: University of Zurich: <http://www.ejpd.admin.ch/dam/data/bj/aktuell/news/2012/2012-02-21/ber-wahlfinanzierung-d.pdf>.

Hernes, Gudmund. 1991. 'The Dilemmas of Social Democracies: The Case of Norway and Sweden.' *Acta Sociologica*, 34(4): 239–60.

Herrnson, Paul S. 2009. 'The Roles of Party Organizations, Party-Connected Committees, and Party Allies in Elections.' *Journal of Politics*, 71(4): 1207–24.

Hönigsberger, Herbert. 2008. *Der parlamentarische Arm: Gewerkschafter im Bundestag zwischen politischer Logik und Interessenvertretung*. Düsseldorf: Hans-Böckler-Stiftung.

Hönigsberger, Herbert, and Sven Osterberg. 2014. 'Gewerkschafter im Bundestag: Zwischen politischer Logik und Interessenvertretung.' In Thomas von Winter and Julia von Blumenthal (eds), *Interessengruppen und Parlamente*. Wiesbaden: Springer VS, 93–123.

Hooghe, Liesbet, Ryan Bakker, Anna Brigevich, Catherine De Vries, Erica Edwards, Gary Marks, Jan Rovny, Marco Steenbergen, and Milada Vachudova. 2010. 'Reliability and Validity of the 2002 and 2006 Chapel Hill Expert Surveys on Party Positioning.' *European Journal of Political Research*, 49(5): 687–703.

Hooghe, Marc, and Jennifer Oser. 2015. 'Trade Union Density and Social Expenditure: A longitudinal Analysis of Policy Feedback Effects in OECD Countries, 1980–2010.' *Journal of European Public Policy*, <http://dx.doi.org/10.1080/13501763.2015.1102952>.

Hotel and Gastro Union. 2012. *Statuten*. Luzern: Hotel und Gastro Union.

Howell, Chris. 1992. *Regulating Labor: The State and Industrial Relations Reform in Postwar France*. Princeton, NJ: Princeton University Press.

Howell, Chris. 2001. 'The End of the Relationship between Social Democratic Parties and Trade Unions?' *Studies in Political Economy*, 65: 7–37.

Howell, Chris, Anthony Daley, and Michel Vale. 1992. 'Introduction: The Transformation of Political Change.' *International Journal of Political Economy*, 22(4): 3–16.

Hrebenar, Ronald. 2001. 'Japan: Strong State, Spectator Democracy, and Modified Corporatism.' In Clive S. Thomas (ed.), *Political Parties and Interest Groups: Shaping Democratic Governance*. Boulder, CO: Lynne Rienner.

HRF. 2012. *Verksamhetsberättelse*. Stockholm: HRF.

Huber, John D., and Ronald Inglehart. 1995. 'Expert Interpretations of Party Space and Party Locations in 42 Societies.' *Party Politics*, 1(1): 73–111.

Hueting, Ernest, Frits de Jong, and Rob Neij. 1983. *Naar groter eenheid. De geschiedenis van het Nederlands Verbond van Vakverenigingen. 1906–1981*. Amsterdam: Van Gennep.

Hutson, James. 1991. *The Sister Republics: Switzerland and the United States from 1776 to the Present*. Washington, DC: Library of Congress.

Hyman, Richard, and Rebecca Gumbrell-McCormick. 2010. 'Trade Unions, Politics and Parties: Is a New Configuration Possible?' *Transfer: European Review of Labour and Research*, 16(3): 315–31.

ILO Labour Statistics. 2014. 'Total Employment, by Occupation (Thousands).' *LABORSTA* (database).

International IDEA. 2016. *Political Finance Database.* <http://www.idea.int/political-finance/>.

Interview NSS. 2007. 'Wat stemmen FNV stemmers? En wie vertrouwen ze het meest?' Report 29 March. <http://www.novatv.nl/uploaded/FILES/Karin/SP%20en%20FNV.doc>.

IPU. 2016. *Parline Database.* Inter-Parliamentary Union <http://www.ipu.org/parline-e/parlinesearch.asp>.

Iversen, Torben. 1999. *Contested Economic Institutions: The Politics of Macroeconomics and Wage Bargaining in Advanced Democracies.* Cambridge: Cambridge University Press.

Jacoby, Wade, and Martin Behrens. 2014. 'Breaking Up is Hard to Do: German Trade Unions within the Social Democratic Party.' *Comparative European Politics*: 1–25 <http://dx.doi.org/10.1057/cep.2014.29>.

Jaensch, D. 1983. *The Australian Party System.* Sydney: Allen and Unwin.

Jaensch, D. 1989. *The Hawke–Keating Hijack: The ALP in Transition.* Sydney: Allen and Unwin.

Jansson, Jenny. 2012. *Manufacturing Consensus: The Making of the Swedish Reformist Working Class.* Uppsala: Acta Universitatis Upsaliensis.

Jansson, Jenny. 2013. 'From Movement to Organization: Constructing Identity in Swedish Trade Unions.' *Labor History*, 54(3), 301–20.

Jensen, Carsten. 2012. 'Two Sides of the Same Coin? Left-wing Governments and Labour Unions as Determinants of Public Spending.' *Socio-Economic Review*, 10(2): 217–40.

Jobson, Richard, and Mark Wickham Jones. 2011. 'Reinventing the Block Vote? Trade Unions and the 2010 Labour Party Leadership Election.' *British Politics*, 63(3): 317–44.

Johansson, Anders L., and Magnusson, Lars. 2012. *LO: 1900-talet och ett nytt millennium.* Stockholm: Atlas.

Johansson, Göran, and Pettersson, Lars-Olof. 2009. 'Sahlins samarbete stort hot mot partiet.' *Dagens Nyheter*, 14 February.

Johansson, Joakim. 2000. *SAF och den svenska modellen: En studie av uppbrottet från förvaltningskorporatismen 1982–91.* Uppsala: Acta Universitatis Upsaliensis.

Jordan, Grant, and William A. Maloney. 2001. 'Britain: Change and Continuity within the New Realities of British Politics.' In Clive S. Thomas (ed.), *Political Parties and Interest Groups: Shaping Democratic Governance.* Boulder, CO: Lynne Rienner.

Karlhofer, Ferdinand. 2006. 'Arbeitnehmerorganisationen.' In Herbert Dachs, Peter Gerlich, Herbert Gottweis, Helmut Kramer, Volkmar Lauber, Wolfgang C. Müller, and Emmerich Tálos (eds), *Politik in Österreich: Ein Handbuch.* Vienna: Manz Verlag, 462–79.

Karreth, Johannes, Jonathan T. Polk, and Christopher S. Allen. 2012. 'Catchall or Catch and Release? The Electoral Consequences of Social Democratic Parties' March to the Middle in Western Europe.' *Comparative Political Studies*, 46(7): 791–822.

Karvonen, Lauri. 2010. *The Personalization of Politics: A Study of Parliamentary Democracies*. Wivenhoe Park: ECPR Press.

Karvonen, Lauri. 2014. *Parties, Governments and Voters in Finland: Politics under Fundamental Societal Transformation*. Colchester: ECPR Press.

Kassalow, Everett M. 1963. *National Labor Movements in the Postwar World*. Evanston, IL: Northwestern University Press.

Katz, Richard S. 2001. 'Are Cleavages Frozen in the English-speaking Democracies?' In Lauri Karvonen and Stein Kuhnle (eds), *Party Systems and Voter Alignments Revisited*. London: Routledge.

Katz, Richard S., and Peter Mair. 1995. 'Changing Models of Party Organization and Party Democracy: The Emergence of the Cartel Party.' *Party Politics*, 1(1): 5–28.

Katz, Richard S., and Peter Mair. 2009. 'The Cartel Party Thesis: A Restatement.' *Perspectives on Politics*, 7(4): 753–66.

Katzenstein, Peter. 1985. *Small States in World Markets: Industrial Policy in Europe*. Ithaca, NY: Cornell University Press.

Katzenstein, Peter. 1987. *Corporatism and Change: Austria, Switzerland, and the Politics of Industry*. Ithaca, NY: Cornell University Press.

Kazin, Michael. 2006. *A Godly Hero: The Life of William Jennings Bryan*. New York: Anchor Books.

Kelly, John. 2015. 'Trade Union Membership and Power in Comparative Perspective.' *The Economic and Labour Relations Review*, 26(4): 526–44.

Kenig, Ofer, and Anna Knafelman. 2013. 'The Decline of the Large Aggregative Parties: Israel in Comparative Perspective.' In Gideon Rahat, Shlomit Barnea, Chen Friedberg, and Ofer Kenig (eds), *Fixing The System of Government in Israel*. Jerusalem: The Israel Democracy Institute, 145–83.

Kenig, Ofer, Gideon Rahat, and Reuven Y. Hazan. 2005. 'The Political Consequences of the Introduction and the Repeal of the Direct Elections for the Prime Minister.' In Asher Arian and Michal Shamir (eds), *The Elections in Israel 2003*. New York: Transaction Books, 33–61.

Kirchheimer, Otto. 1966. 'The Transformation of the Western European Party Systems.' In Joseph LaPalombara and Myron Weiner (eds), *Political Parties and Political Development*. Princeton, NJ: Princeton University Press, 177–200.

Kitschelt, Herbert P. 1989. *The Logics of Party Formation: Ecological Politics in Belgium and West Germany*. Ithaca, NY: Cornell University Press.

Kitschelt, Herbert P. 1994. *The Transformation of European Social Democracy*. Cambridge: Cambridge University Press.

Kjellberg, Anders. 2001. *Fackliga organisationer och medlemmar i dagens Sverige*. Lund: Arkiv.

Klemm, Mary. 1944. 'The Rise of Independent Unionism and the Decline of Labour Oligopoly.' *The American Economic Review*, 34(1): 76–86.

Klitgaard, Michael B., and Asbjørn S. Nørgaard. 2014. 'Structural Stress or Deliberate Decision? Government Partisanship and the Disempowerment of Unions in Denmark.' *European Journal of Political Research*, 53(2): 404–21.

Klitgaard, Michael B., Gijs Schumacher, and Menno Soentken. 2015. 'The Partisan Politics of Institutional Welfare State Reform.' *Journal of European Public Policy*, 22(7): 948–66.

Koß, Michael. 2010. *The Politics of Party Funding: State Funding to Political Parties and Party Competition in Western Europe*. Oxford: Oxford University Press.

Koelbe, Thomas A. 1987. 'Trade Unionists, Party Activists, and Politicians: The Struggle for Power over Party Rules in the British Labour Party and the West German Social Democratic Party.' *Comparative Politics*, 19(3): 253–66.

Koelbe, Thomas A. 1992. 'Recasting Social Democracy in Europe: A Nested Games Explanation of Strategic Adjustment in Political Parties.' *Politics and Society*, 20(1): 51–70.

Koger, Gerogry, Seth E. Masket, and Hans Noel. 2009. 'Partisan Webs: Information Exchange and Partisan Networks.' *British Journal of Political Science*, 39(3): 633–53.

Koger, Gregory, Seth E. Masket, and Hans Noel. 2010. 'Cooperative Factions in American Politics.' *American Politics Research*, 38(1): 33–53.

Kok, Wim. 1984. 'Joop den Uyl en de vakbeweging: Enkele notities.' In Leo Casteleijn (ed.), *Tekens in de Tijd: 65 jaar Joop den Uyl*. Amsterdam: Arbeiderspers.

Kommunal. 2011. *Årsredovisning*. Stockholm: Hotell- och restaurangfacket.

König, Mario. 2009. 'Angestelltenorganisationen.' *Historisches Lexikon der Schweiz* <http://www.hls-dhs-dss.ch/textes/d/D16480.php>.

Koole, Wibo. 1986. 'Platform of doorgeefluik? Vijftien jaar Werkgroep Bedrijfsdemocratisering in de PvdA.' *Socialisme & Democratie*, 43(6): 190–4.

Kriesi, Hanspeter, and Philip van Praag Jr. 1987. 'Old and New Politics: The Dutch Peace Movement and the Traditional Political Organizations.' *European Journal of Political Research*, 15(3): 319–46.

Kriesi, Hanspeter, and Alexander Trechsel. 2008. *The Politics of Switzerland: Continuity and Change in a Consensus Democracy*. Cambridge: Cambridge University Press.

Kristal, Tali, and Yinon Cohen. 2007. 'Decentralization of Collective Agreements and Rising Wage Inequality in Israel.' *Industrial Relations*, 46(3): 613–35.

Kritzinger, Sylvia, Eva Zeglovits, Michael S. Lewis-Beck, and Richard Nadeau. 2013. *The Austrian Voter: Trends and Change in Vote Choice in Austria 1986–2008*. Göttingen: Vandenhoeck & Ruprecht.

Kunkel, Christoph, and Jonas Pontusson. 1998. 'Corporatism versus Social Democracy: Divergent Fortunes of the Austrian and Swedish Labour Movements.' *West European Politics*, 21(2): 1–31.

KV. 2013a. *Statuten*. Zürich: KV Schweiz, June.

KV. 2013b. *Corporate Goverance*. Zürich: KV Schweiz.

KV. 2014. *Der Zentralvorstand*. Zürich: KV Schweiz <http://www.kfmv.ch/de/1304/Zentralvorstand.htm>.

Kvavik, Robert B. 1976. *Interest Groups in Norwegian Politics*. Oslo: Universitetsforlaget.

Kyntäjä, Timo. 1993. *Tulopolitiikka Suomessa: Tulopoliittinen diskurssi ja instituutiot 1960–luvulta 1990-luvun kynnykselle*. Helsinki: Gaudeamus.

La Polis. 2013. 'Osservatorio elettorale. Survey on 4585 Cases Based on Data by Demos & Pi 2013 (January–February). Elections for the House of Deputies.' University of Urbino.

La Repubblica. 2014. 'Camusso: "Renzi è a Palazzo Chigi per volere dei poteri forti, lo ha ammesso Marchionne."' *La Repubblica*, 29 October.

Laakso, Markku, and Rein Taagepera. 1979. '"Effective" Number of Parties: A Measure with Application to West Europe.' *Comparative Political Studies*, 12(1): 3–27.

Labbé, Dominique, and Maurice Croisat. 1992. *La fin des syndicats?* Paris: L'Harmattan.

Landré, Marc. 2013. 'Le gouvernement promeut Chérèque et soigne la CFDT.' *Le Figaro*, 17 January. Accessed March 2014: <http://www.lefigaro.fr/conjoncture/2013/01/17/20002-20130117ARTFIG00695-le-gouvernement-promeut-chereque-et-soigne-la-cfdt.php>.

Landsorganisationen. 2011. *Röster om facket och jobbet. Rapport 4: Fackets uppgifter, fackets inflytande och facklig-politisk samverkan.* Stockholm: Landsorganisationen.

Landsorganisationen. 2013. *Facklig-politisk samverkan.* Stockholm: Landsorganisationen.

Landsorganisationen. 2014a. 'Presentation av LO' <http://www.lo.se/start/om_oss/en_presentation_av_lo.>.

Landsorganisationen. 2014b. *Verksamhetsberättelse 2013.* Stockholm: Landsorganisationen.

Latham, M. 2005. *The Latham Diaries.* Crow's Nest, NSW: Allen and Unwin.

Lauber, Volkmar. 1992. 'Changing Priorities in Economic Policy.' *West European Politics*, 15(1): 147–72.

Laurent, Agnès. 2012. 'CFDT: dur, dur d'être le chouchou du gouvernement.' *L'Expansion*, 18 September. Accessed February 2014: <http://lexpansion.lexpress.fr/actualite-economique/cfdt-dur-dur-d-etre-le-chouchou-du-gouvernement_1382604.html>.

Lavelle, A. 2005. 'Social Democrats and Neo-Liberalism: A Case Study of the Australian Labor Party.' *Political Studies*, 53(4): 753–71.

Lavelle, A. 2010. 'The Ties that Unwind: Social Democratic Parties and Unions in Australia and Britain.' *Labour History*, 98(May): 55–75.

Leigh, A. 2000. 'Factions and Fractions: A Case Study of Power Politics in the Australian Labor Party.' *Australian Journal of Political Science*, 35(3): 427–48.

Leigh, A. 2002. 'Trade Liberalisation and the Australian Liberal Party.' *Australian Journal of Politics and History*, 48(2): 487–508.

Leigh, A. 2006. 'How do Unionists Vote? Estimating the Causal Impact of Union Voting Behaviour from 1966 to 2004.' *Australian Journal of Political Science*, 41(4): 537–52.

Leimgruber, Matthieu. 2008. *Solidarity without the State? Business and the Shaping of the Swiss Welfare State, 1890–2000.* Cambridge: Cambridge University Press.

Lewin, Leif. 2002. *Ideologi och strategi: svensk politik under 130 år.* Stockholm: Norstedts juridik.

Lijphart, Arend. 1968a. *Verzuiling, pacificatie en kentering in de Nederlandse Politiek.* Amsterdam: De Bussy.

Lijphart, Arend. 1968b. 'Typologies of Democratic Systems.' *Comparative Political Studies*, 1(1): 3–44.

Lijphart, Arend. 1969. 'Consociational Democracy.' *World Politics*, 21(2): 207–25.

Lijphart, Arend. 1999. *Patterns of Democracy: Government Forms and Performance in Thirty-Six Countries.* New Haven, CT and London: Yale University Press.

Lindvall, Johannes, and Joakim Sebring. 2005. 'Policy Reform and the Decline of Corporatism in Sweden.' *West European Politics* 28(5): 1057–74.

Lipset, Seymour M., and Stein Rokkan. 1967. 'Cleavage Structures, Party Systems, and Voter Alignments.' In Seymour M. Lipset and Stein Rokkan (eds), *Party Systems and Voter Alignments: Cross-National Perspectives*. New York: The Free Press, 1–64.

Livs. 2013. *Motioner och utlåtanden till kongressen*. Stockholm: Livsmedelsarbetareförbundet.

Lizzi, Renata. 2014. 'Party–Group Disentanglement in the Italian Case: An Introduction.' *Contemporary Italian Politics*, 6(3): 238–48.

Loberg, Fredrik. 2012. *Håkan Juholt—utmanaren: vad var det som hände?* Stockholm: ETC.

Loveday, P., A. W. Martin, and R. S. Parker (eds). 1977. *The Emergence of the Australian Party System*. Sydney: Hale and Iremonger.

Luther, Kurt Richard. 1999a. 'A Framework for the Comparative Analysis of Political Parties and Party Systems in Consociational Democracy.' In Kurt Richard Luther and Kris Deschouwer (eds), *Party Elites in Divided Societies: Political Parties in Consociational Democracy*. London and New York: Routledge, 3–19.

Luther, Kurt Richard. 1999b. 'Must What Goes Up Always Come Down? Of Pillars and Arches in Austria's Political Architecture.' In Kurt Richard Luther and Kris Deschouwer (eds), *Party Elites in Divided Societies: Political Parties in Consociational Democracy*. London and New York: Routledge, 43–73.

Luther, Kurt Richard. 2012. 'Of Goals and Own Goals: A Case Study of Right-wing Populist Party Strategy For and During Incumbency.' *Party Politics*, 17(4): 453–80.

Mach, André. 2006. *La Suisse entre internationalisation et changements politiques internes: législation sur les cartels et relations industrielles dans les années 1990*. Zürich: Rüegger Verlag.

Magnusson, Lars. 2000. *Den tredje industriella revolutionen*. Stockholm: Prisma/ Arbetslivsinstitutet.

Magnusson, Lars. 2006. *Håller den svenska modellen? Arbete och välfärd i en globaliserad värld*. Stockholm: Norstedts akademiska förlag.

Mair, Peter. 2013. *Ruling the Void: The Hollowing-Out of Western Democracy*. London: Verso.

Mandelkern, Ronen. 2015. 'What Made Economists so Politically Influential? Governance-related Ideas and Institutional Entrepreneurship in the Economic Liberalisation of Israel and Beyond.' *New Political Economy*, 20(6): 924–41.

Mandelkern, Ronen, and Michael Shalev. 2010. 'Power and the Ascendance of New Economic Policy Ideas: Lessons from the 1980s Crisis in Israel.' *World Politics*, 62(3): 459–95.

Mania, Roberto. 2013. 'Sindacato, se ci sei batti un colpo.' *Il Mulino*, 3: 403–10.

Mania, Roberto, and Gaetano Sateriale. 2002. *Relazioni pericolose: sindacati e politica dopo la concertazione*. Bologna: Il Mulino.

Mariaucourt, Laurence. 2013. 'Le PS recase les Ex-CFDT.' *L'Humanité*, 24 January. Accessed March 2014: <http://www.humanite.fr/social-eco/le-ps-recase-les-ex-cfdt-513591>.

Martin, Cathie Jo, and Duane Swank. 2012a. 'Contemporary data.' <http://www.marquette.edu/polisci/documents/MartinSwankcontemporarydata.xlsx>.

Martin, Cathie Jo, and Duane Swank. 2012b. 'Data Codebook, STATA Code, and Supplemental Material for Quantitative Analysis of Contemporary Era.' <http://www.marquette.edu/polisci/documents/MartinSwankcontemporarydatacode.pdf>.

Martin, Lanny W., and Georg Vanberg. 2011. *Parliaments and Coalitions: The Role of Legislative Institutions in Multiparty Governance.* Oxford: Oxford University Press.

Martos Nilsson, Mårten. 2012. 'TCO-basen: LO:s koppling till S försvårar samarbete.' Stockholm: Arbetet.

Masket, Seth E., Michael Heaney, and Dara Strolovitch. 2014. 'Mobilizing Marginalized Groups among Party Elites.' *The Forum*, 12(2): 257–80.

Mavrogordatos, George Th. 2009. 'Models of Party–Interest Group Relations and the Uniqueness of the Greek Case.' Paper presented at the ECPR Joint Sessions of Workshops, Lisbon, 14–19 April 2009.

Mazzoleni, Oscar, André Mach, and Andrea Pilotti. 2010. 'Entre professionnalisation et proximité. L'évolution du profil des candidats et des élus socialistes depuis les années 1950.' In Sarah Nicolet and Pascal Sciarini (eds), *Le destin électoral de la gauche: Le vote socialiste et vert en Suisse.* Genève: Georg, 331–60.

McAllister, I. 1991. 'Party Adaptation and Factionalism within the Australian Party System.' *American Journal of Political Science*, 35(1): 206–27.

McIlroy, John. 1998. 'The Endurance Alliance? Trade Unions and the Making of New Labour, 1994–1997.' *British Journal of Industrial Relations*, 36(4): 537–64.

McLean, Ian. 1987. *Public Choice: An Introduction.* Oxford: Basil Blackwell.

Medlingsinstitutet. 2016. *Avtalsrörelsen och lönebildningen 2015.* Stockholm: Medlingsinstitutet (Swedish National Mediation Office).

Mergen, Bernard. 1972. 'Blacksmiths and Welders: Identity and Phenomenal Change.' *Industrial and Labour Relations Review*, 25(3): 354–62.

Merkel, Wolfgang. 1993. *Ende der Sozialdemokratie? Machtressourcen und Regierungspolitik im westeuropäischen Vergleich.* Frankfurt: Campus.

Metall. 2014. *Beslutsbok kongress.* Stockholm: IF Metall.

Mickelsson, Rauli. 2007. *Suomen puolueet: historia, muutos ja nykypäivä.* Tampere: Vastapaino.

Minkin, Lewis. 1991. *The Contentious Alliance: Trade Unions and the Labour Party.* Edinburgh: Edinburgh University Press.

Mokken, Robert J. 1971. *A Theory and Procedure of Scale Analysis: With Applications in Political Research.* Berlin: De Gruyter.

Moore, William J. 1998. 'The Determinants and Effects of Right-to-Work Laws: A Review of the Recent Literature.' *Journal of Labor Research*, 19(3): 445–69.

Morlino, Leonardo. 1998. *Democracy between Consolidation and Crisis: Parties, Groups, and Citizens in Southern Europe.* Oxford: Oxford University Press.

Mulder, Bertus. 2012. *Het hart van de sociaal-democratie: Over het belang van Arbeid en Zeggenschap.* Den Haag: Wiardi Beckman Stichting.

Müller, Wolfgang C. 2002. 'Parties and the Institutional Framework.' In Kurt Richard Luther and Ferdinand Müller-Rommel (eds), *Political Parties in the New Europe: Political and Analytical Challenges.* Oxford: Oxford University Press.

Müller, Wolfgang C. 2006. 'Die Österreichische Volkspartei.' In Herbert Dachs, Peter Gerlich, Herbert Gottweis, Helmut Kramer, Volkmar Lauber, Wolfgang C. Müller, and Emmerich Tálos (eds), *Politik in Österreich. Ein Handbuch.* Vienna: Manz Verlag, 341–63.

Mundlak, Guy. 2007. *Fading Corporatism: Israel's Labor Law and Industrial Relations in Transition*. Ithaca, NY: ILR Press/Cornell University Press.

Mundlak, Guy, Ishak Saporta, Yitchak Haberfeld, and Yinon Cohen. 2013. 'Union Density in Israel 1995–2010: The Hybridization of Industrial Relations.' *Industrial Relations: A Journal of Economy and Society*, 52(1): 78–101.

Nachtwey, Oliver. 2009. *Marktsozialdemokratie: Die Transformation von SPD und Labour Party*. Wiesbaden: VS Verlag für Sozialwissenschaften.

Nachtwey, Oliver, and Tim Spier. 2007. 'Political Opportunity Structures and the Success of the German Left Party in 2005.' *Debatte: Journal of Contemporary Central and Eastern Europe*, 15(2): 123–54.

Nathanson, Roby. 2002. 'Union Responses to a Changing Environment: The New Histadrut—The General Federation of Labour in Israel.' In A. V. Jose (ed.), *Organized Labour in the 21st Century*. Geneva: International Institute for Labour Studies, 167–98.

Nationalrat. 2015a. *Register der Interessenbindungen*. Accessed April 2015: <http://www.parlament.ch/d/organe-mitglieder/nationalrat/Documents/ra-nr-interessen.pdf>.

Nationalrat. 2015b. *Liste der Zugangsberechtigen. Nationalrat 5.12.2011–29.11.2015*. Accessed 9 April 2015: <http://www.parlament.ch/d/organe-mitglieder/nationalrat/Documents/zutrittsberechtigte-nr.pdf>.

Neumann, Sigmund. 1956. 'Toward a Comparative Study of Political Parties.' In Sigmund Neumann (ed.), *Modern Political Parties: Approaches to Comparative Politics*. Chicago: University of Chicago Press.

Neusser, Christian. 2013. *Pluralisierte Partnerschaften: Über den Wandel der Parteien-Gewerkschafts-Beziehungen*. Berlin: Edition Sigma.

NES. 2014. 'The American National Election Studies Time Series Cumulative Data File (Dataset).' Stanford University and the University of Michigan (producers and distributors), 2010 <http://www.electionstudies.org/studypages/download/datacenter_all_NoData.php>.

Nieuwbeerta, Paul. 1996. 'The Democratic Class Struggle in Postwar Societies: Class Voting in Twenty Countries, 1945–1990.' *Acta Sociologica*, 39(4): 345–83.

Nilsson, Tommy. 1985. *Från kamratföreningar till facklig rörelse: de svenska tjänstemännens organisationsutveckling 1900–1980*. Lund: Arkiv.

Nollert, Michael. 1995. 'Neocorporatism and Political Protest in Western Democracies: A Cross-National Analysis.' In J. Craig Jenkins and Bert Klandermans (eds), *The Politics of Social Protest: Comparative Perspectives on States and Social Movements*. Minneapolis: University of Minnesota Press, 139–64.

Norberg, Anders, Björn Asker, and Andreas Tjerneld. 1985–92. *Tvåkammarriksdagen 1867–1970: ledamöter och valkretsar*. Stockholm: Almqvist & Wiksell.

Öberg, PerOla. 1994. *Särintresse och allmänintresse: Korporatismens ansikte*. Uppsala: Acta Universitatis Upsaliensis.

Öberg, PerOla, Torsten Svensson, Peter Munk Christiansen, Asbjørn Sonne Nørgaard, Hilmar Rommetvedt, and Gunnar Thesen. 2011. 'Disrupted Exchange and Declining Corporatism: Government Authority and Interest Group Capability in Scandinavia.' *Government and Opposition*, 46(3), 365–91.

OECD. 2011. 'Employment in General Government and Public Corporations.' In *Government at a Glance 2011*. Paris: OECD Publishing: <http://dx.doi.org/10.1787/gov_glance-2011-27-en>.

OECD. 2013a. 'Trade Unions: Trade Union Density.' *OECD Employment and Labour Market Statistics* (database): <http://dx.doi.org/10.1787/data-00371-en>.

OECD. 2013b. 'Employment in General Government and Public Corporations.' In *Government at a Glance 2013*. Paris: OECD Publishing: <http://dx.doi.org/10.1787/gov_glance-2013-32-en>.

OECD. 2014. 'Labour Force Statistics: Employment by Activities and Status.' *OECD Employment and Labour Market Statistics* (database): <http://dx.doi.org/10.1787/a6bdf274-en>.

OECD. 2015. 'Employment in the Public Sector.' In *Government at a Glance 2015*. Paris: OECD Publishing: <http://dx.doi.org/10.1787/gov_glance-2015-22-en>.

OECD. 2016. 'Trade Unions: Trade Union Density.' *OECD Employment and Labour Market Statistics (database)*: <http://dx.doi.org/10.1787/data-00371-en>.

Oesch, Daniel. 2006. *Redrawing the Class Map: Stratification and Institutions in Britain, Germany, Sweden and Switzerland*. London: Palgrave Macmillan.

Oesch, Daniel. 2007. 'Weniger Koordination, mehr Markt? Kollektive Arbeitsbeziehungen und Neokorporatismus in der Schweiz seit 1990.' *Schweizerische Zeitschrift für Politikwissenschaft*, 13(3): 337–68.

Olofsson, Gunnar. 1979. *Mellan klass och stat: om arbetarrörelse, reformism och socialdemokrati*. Lund: Arkiv.

Oscarsson, Henrik. 2016. *Flytande väljare*. Stockholm: Statistics Sweden.

Oscarsson, Henrik, and Sören Holmberg. 2011. *Eight Parties Election 2010: General Elections, Election Study*. Stockholm: Statistics Sweden.

Otjes, Simon. 2016. 'Wat is er over van de rode familie? De bijzondere relatie tussen de PvdA en NVV/FNV.' In F. Becker and G. Voerman (eds), *De Partij van de Arbeid 1946–2014*. Amsterdam: Boom.

Otjes, Simon, and Anne Rasmussen. 2015. 'The Collaboration between Interest Groups and Political Parties in Multi-party Democracies: Party System Dynamics and the Effect of Power and Ideology.' *Party Politics*, 29 January, doi: <http://dx.doi.org/10.1177/1354068814568046>.

Pacini, Chiara Maria, and Daniela Romee Piccio. 2012. 'Party Regulation in Italy and its Effects.' *The Legal Regulation of Political Parties: Working Paper 26*. March 2012. Leiden: Leiden University.

Padgett, Stephen, and William E. Paterson. 1991. *A History of Social Democracy in Postwar Europe*. London: Longman.

Parkin, A. 1983. 'Party Organisation and Machine Politics: The ALP in Perspective.' In Andrew Parkin and John Warhurst (eds), *Machine Politics in the Australian Labor Party*. Sydney: George Allen and Unwin.

Parsons, Nick. 2005. *French Industrial Relations in the New World Economy*. London: Routledge.

Parsons, Nick. 2013. 'France.' In Carola M. Frege and John Kelly (eds), *Comparative Employment Relations in the Global Economy*. London: Routledge.

Parsons, Nick. 2015. 'Left Parties and Trade Unions in France.' *French Politics*, 13(1): 64–83.

Pauli, Petra. 2012. *Rörelsens ledare: karriärvägar och ledarideal i den svenska arbetarrörelsen under 1900-talet*. Göteborg: Institutionen för historiska studier, Göteborgs universitet.

Pemberton, Hugh, and Mark Wickham-Jones. 2013. 'Brothers all? The Operation of the Electoral College in the 2010 Labour Leadership Contest.' *Parliamentary Affairs*, 66(4): 708–31.

Pernot, Jean-Marie. 2010. *Syndicats: Lendemains de crise?* Paris: Gallimard.

Perry, Nathan, and Matias Vernengo. 2014. 'What Ended the Great Depression? Re-evaluating the Role of Fiscal Policy.' *Cambridge Journal of Economics*, 38(2): 349–67.

Persson, Göran, and Kask, Peeter-Jaan. 1997. *Den som är satt i skuld är icke: min berättelse om hur Sverige återfick sunda statsfinanser.* Stockholm: Atlas.

Peters, B. Guy. 1999. *Institutional Theory in Political Science: The 'New Institutionalism.'* London: Continuum.

Piazza, J. 2001. 'Delinking Labor: Labor Unions and Social Democratic Parties Under Globalization.' *Party Politics*, 7(4): 413–35.

Pierson, C., and F. G. Castles. 2002. 'Australian Antecedents of the Third Way.' *Political Studies*, 50(4): 683–702.

Pierson, Paul. 2000. 'The Limits of Design: Explaining Institutional Origins and Change.' *Governance: An International Journal of Policy and Administration*, 13(4): 475–99.

Piketty, Thomas. 2014. *Capital in the Twenty-First Century.* Cambridge, MA: Harvard University Press.

Poguntke, Thomas. 1998. 'Party Organizations.' In Jan W. van Deth (ed.), *Comparative Politics: The Problem of Equivalence*. London: Routledge.

Poguntke, Thomas. 2000. *Parteiorganisation im Wandel: Gesellschaftliche Verankerung und organisatorische Anpassung im europäischen Vergleich.* Wiesbaden: Westdeutscher Verlag.

Poguntke, Thomas. 2002. 'Parties without Firm Social Roots? Party Organisational Linkage.' In Kurt Richard Luther and Ferdinand Müller-Rommel (eds), *Political Parties in the New Europe: Political and Analytical Challenges.* Oxford: Oxford University Press.

Poguntke, Thomas. 2006. 'Political Parties and Other Organizations.' In Richard S. Katz and William Crotty (eds), *Handbook of Party Politics.* London: SAGE.

Poguntke, Thomas. 2015. 'Living in Separate Worlds? Left-wing Parties and Trade Unions in European Democracies.' In Thomas Poguntke, Sigrid Rossteutscher, Rüdiger Schmitt-Beck, and Sonja Zmerli (eds), *Citizenship and Democracy in an Era of Crisis: Essays in honour of Jan W. van Deth.* London and New York: Routledge.

Poppe, Stan. 1980. 'Een goede verhouding tussen PvdA en vakbeweging is gewenst.' *Socialisme En Democratie*, 37(11): 523–30.

Przeworski, Adam, and Sprague, John. 1986. *Paper Stones: A History of Electoral Socialism.* Chicago: University of Chicago Press.

Quinn, Thomas. 2002. 'Block Voting in the Labour Party.' *Party Politics*, 8(2): 207–26.

Quinn, Thomas. 2004. *Modernising the Labour Party: Organisational Change since 1983.* Basingstoke: Palgrave.

Quinn, Thomas. 2010. 'New Labour and the Trade Unions in Britain.' *Journal of Elections, Public Opinion and Parties*, 20(3): 357–80.

Radcliff, Benjamin, and Martin Saiz. 1998. 'Labour Organization and Public Policy in the American States.' *The Journal of Politics*, 60(1): 113–25.

Rahat, Gideon, and Tamir Sheafer. 2007. 'The Personalization(s) of Politics: Israel 1949–2003.' *Political Communication*, 24(1): 65–80.

Rasmussen, Anne. 2012. 'Interest Group–Party Interaction in EU Politics.' *Party Politics*, 18(1): 81–98.

Rasmussen, Anne, and Gert-Jan Lindeboom. 2013. 'Interest Group–Party Linkage in the Twenty-First Century: Evidence from Denmark, the Netherlands and the United Kingdom.' *European Journal of Political Research*, 52(2): 264–89.

Raunio, Tapio. 2010. 'The EU and the Welfare State are Compatible: Finnish Social Democrats and European Integration.' *Government and Opposition*, 45(2): 187–207.

Rawson, Donald W. 1969. 'The Life Span of Labour Parties.' *Political Studies*, 17(3): 313–33.

RD. 1990/91. *Konstitutionsutskottet betänkande 1990/91:KU40*. Stockholm: Sveriges Riksdag.

Regan, Patrick M., Richard W. Frank, and David H. Clark. 2009. 'New Datasets on Political Institutions and Elections, 1972—2005.' *Conflict Management and Peace Science*, 26(3): 286–304.

Regini, Marino. 1997. 'Still Engaging in Corporatism? Recent Italian Experience in Comparative Perspective.' *European Journal of Industrial Relations*, 3(3): 259–78.

Reinhardt, Max. 2009. 'Parteiflügelkämpfe seit der Bundestagswahl 2002: Der Kampf um die Macht in der SPD.' In Heiko Geiling (ed.), *Die Krise der SPD: Autoritäre oder partizipative Demokratie*. Münster: Lit Verlag, 53–112.

Rennwald, Linn. 2014. 'Class (Non) Voting in Switzerland 1971–2011: Ruptures and Continuities in a Changing Political Landscape.' *Swiss Political Science Review*, 20(4): 550–72.

Reynaud, Jean-Daniel. 1975. 'Trade Unions and Political Parties in France: Some Recent Trends.' *Industrial and Labour Relations Review*, 28(2): 208–25.

Riksdagen. 2011. *Fakta om folkvalda: riksdagen 2010–2014*. Stockholm: Riksdagens förvaltningskontor.

Riksdagen. 2015. 'Partistöd.' 27 April: <http://www.riksdagen.se/sv/Sa-funkar-riksdagen/Sa-arbetar-partierna/Partistod/>.

Rokkan, Stein. 1966. 'Norway: Numerical Democracy and Corporative Pluralism.' In Robert A. Dahl (ed.), *Political Oppositions in Western Democracies*. New Haven, CT: Yale University Press.

Rommetvedt, Hilmar, Gunnar Thesen, Peter M. Christiansen, and Asbjørn S. Nørregard. 2012. 'Coping with Corporatism in Decline and the Revival of Parliament: Interest Group Lobbyism in Denmark and Norway: 1980–2005.' *Comparative Political Studies*, 46(4): 457–85.

Rothstein, Bo. 1992. 'Labor-market Institutions and Working-class Strength.' In S. Steinmo, K. Thelen, and F. Longstreth (eds.), *Structuring Politics: Historical Institutionalism in Comparative Analysis*. Cambridge: Cambridge University Press.

Rozell, Mark J., Clyde Wilcox, and David Madland. 2006. 'Interest Groups and American Politics.' In Mark J. Rozell, Clyde Wilcox, and David Madland (eds), *Interest Groups in American Campaigns: The New Face of Electioneering*, 2nd edition. Washington, DC: CQ Press.

Rudén, Janne, and Lars-Anders Häggström. 2008. 'Socialdemokratin måste bilda front med vänstern.' *Dagens Nyheter*, 9 October.

Ruostetsaari, Ilkka. 2014. *Vallan sisäpiirissä*. Tampere: Vastapaino.

Russell, Meg. 2005. *Building New Labour: The Politics of Party Organisation*. Basingstoke: Palgrave.

Saco. 2013a. 'Fredrik Reinfeldt talade till kongressen.' 8 September 2014: <http://www.saco.se/saco-kongress-2013/nyheter/fredrik-reinfeldt-talade-till-kongressen/>.

Saco. 2013b. *Årsredovisning*. Stockholm: Saco.

SCB. 1970. *Riksdagsmannavalen 1965–1968. Del 2*. Stockholm: Statistiska Centralbyrån.

SCB. 2008. *General Elections in 2006: Part 4*. Stockholm: Statistics Sweden.

Schattschneider, Elmer E. 1942. *Party Government*. New York: Rinehart.

Schattschneider, Elmer E. 1960. *The Semi-Sovereign People: A Realist's View of Democracy in America*. New York: Holt, Rinehart and Winston.

Schlesinger, Joseph A. 1984. 'On the Theory of Party Organization.' *The Journal of Politics*, 46(2): 369–400.

Schnabel, Claus, and Joachim Wagner. 2007. 'The Persistent Decline in Unionization in Western and Eastern Germany, 1980–2004: What Can We Learn from a Decomposition Analysis?' *Industrielle Beziehungen*, 14(2): 118–32.

Schoen, Harald. 2014. 'Soziologische Ansätze in der empirischen Wahlforschung.' In Jürgen W. Falter and Harald Schoen (eds), *Handbuch Wahlforschung*, 2nd edition. Wiesbaden: Springer VS, 169–239.

Schönhoven, Klaus. 2014. 'Geschichte der deutschen Gewerkschaften: Phasen und Probleme.' In Wolfgang Schroeder (ed.), *Handbuch Gewerkschaften in Deutschland*, 2nd edition. Wiesbaden: Springer VS, 59–83.

Schroeder, Wolfgang. 2005. 'Sozialdemokratie und Gewerkschaften.' *Berliner Debatte Initial*, 16(5): 12–21.

Schroeder, Wolfgang. 2008. 'SPD und Gewerkschaften: Vom Wandel einer privilegierten Partnerschaft.' *WSI-Mitteilungen*, 61(5): 231–7.

Schwartz, Mildred A. 2005. 'Linkage Processes in Party Networks.' In Andrea Römmele, David M. Farrell, and Piero Ignazi (eds), *Political Parties and Political Systems: The Concept of Linkage Revisited*. Westport, CT: Praeger.

Seki, Katsunori, and Laron K. Williams. 2014. 'Updating the *Party Government* Data Set.' *Electoral Studies*, 34: 270–9. <http://web.missouri.edu/~williamslaro/data.html>.

Seko. 2013. *Motioner och utlåtanden kongressen*. Stockholm: Seko.

SEKOväst. 2009. *SEKOnden. Medlemsblad för SEKO väst, nr 3*. Stockholm: Seko.

Selle, Per. 1997. 'Parties and Voluntary Organizations: Strong or Weak Ties?' In Kaare Strøm and Lars G. Svåsand (eds), *Challenges to Political Parties: The Case of Norway*. Ann Arbor: University of Michigan Press.

Settle, A. 2016. 'McCluskey Intervention Set to Intensify Labour's Internal Strife on Trident.' *Herald Scotland*, 12 January.

SGB. 2010. *Statuten des Schweizerischen Gewerkschaftsbundes*, 7 November. SGB: Bern. Accessed March 2014: <http://www.sgb.ch/uploads/media/Statuten_D_2010.pdf>.

SGB. 2014. *Zur Mitgliederentwicklung der Gewerkschaften 2013*. SGB Dossier 105. September: <http://www.sgb.ch/themen/gewerkschaftspolitik/schweiz/artikel/details/dossier-105-zur-mitgliederentwicklung-der-gewerkschaften-2013/>.

Shalev, Michael. 1992. *Labour and the Political Economy in Israel*. Oxford: Oxford University Press.

Shalev, Michael. 1999. 'Have Globalization and Liberalization "Normalized" Israel's Political Economy?' *Israel Affairs*, 5(2–3): 121–55.

Siaroff, Alan. 1999. 'Corporatism in 24 Industrial Democracies: Meaning and Measurement.' *European Journal of Political Research*, 36(2): 175–205.

Silvia, Stephen J. 2013. *Holding the Shop Together: German Industrial Relations in the Postwar Era*. Ithaca, NY: Cornell University Press.

Simoni, Marco. 2013. 'The Left and Organized Labor in Low-inflation Times'. *World Politics*, 65(2): 314–49.

Socialdemokraterna. 1970. *Verksamheten 1969*. Borås.

Socialdemokraterna. 1986. *Verksamheten 1986*. Stockholm: Socialdemokraterna.

Socialdemokraterna. 2009a. *Verksamhetsberättelse 2008*. Stockholm: Socialdemokraterna.

Socialdemokraterna. 2009b. *Verksamhetsberättelse 2009*. Stockholm: Socialdemokraterna.

Socialdemokraterna. 2010. *Valanalys 2010: Rapport från den socialdemokratiska kriskommissionen*. 5 February 2015: <http://www.socialdemokraterna.se/valanalys2010>.

Socialdemokraterna. 2013a. *Stadgar: Antagna av den ordinarie partikongressen 2013*. 30 May 2014: <www.socialdemokraterna.se>.

Socialdemokraterna. 2013b. *Årsredovisning 2009–2011*. Stockholm: Socialdemokraterna.

Socialdemokraterna. 2013c. *Årsredovisning 2012*. Stockholm: Socialdemokraterna.

Socialdemokraterna. 2014. *Verksamhetsberättelse 2013*. Stockholm: Socialdemokraterna.

Spier, Tim, and Ulrich von Alemann. 2015. 'In ruhigerem Fahrwasser, aber ohne Land in Sicht? Die SPD nach der Bundestagswahl 2013.' In Oskar Niedermayer (ed.), *Die Parteien nach der Bundestagswahl 2013*. Wiesbaden: Springer VS, 49–69.

Spier, Tim, and Markus Klein. 2015. 'Party Membership in Germany. Rather Formal, Therefore Uncool?' In Anika Gauja and Emilie van Haute (eds), *Party Members and Activists*. London: Routledge, 84–99.

Ständerat. 2015a. *Register der Interessenbindungen*. Accessed April 2015: <http://www.parlament.ch/d/organe-mitglieder/staenderat/documents/ra-sr-interessen.pdf>.

Ständerat. 2015b. *Liste der Zugangsberechtigen. Ständerat 5.12.2011–29.11.2015*. Accessed April 2015: <http://www.parlament.ch/d/organe-mitglieder/staenderat/Documents/zutrittsberechtigte-sr.pdf>.

Strand, Sven-Erik. 2013. *Saco i historiens backspegel: en studie om fackliga arbetstagarorganisationers funktioner i ett demokratiskt politiskt system*. Stockholm: TAM-Arkiv.

Streeck, Wolfgang, and Anke Hassel. 2003. 'Trade Unions as Political Actors.' In John T. Addison and Claus Schnabel (eds), *International Handbook of Trade Unions*. Cheltenham: Edward Elgar.

Strøm, Kaare. 1990. 'A Behavioral Theory of Competitive Political Parties.' *American Journal of Political Science*, 34(2): 565–98.

Strøm, Kaare, and Wolfgang C. Müller. 1999. 'Political Parties and Hard Choices.' In Wolfgang C. Müller and Kaare Strøm (eds), *Policy, Office or Votes? How Political Parties in Western Europe Make Hard Decisions*. Cambridge: Cambridge University Press.

STTK. 2013. *Toimihenkilöbarometri 2013*. Helsinki: STTK.

Suhonen, Daniel. 2014. *Partiledaren som klev in i kylan: berättelsen om Juholts fall och den nya politiken*. Stockholm: Leopard.

Sundberg, Jan (ed.). 2001. *Partier och interesseorganisationer i Norden*. Copenhagen: Nordisk Ministerråd.

Sundberg, Jan. 2003. *Parties as Organized Actors: The Transformation of the Scandinavian Three-Front Parties*. Helsinki: The Finnish Society of Sciences and Letters.

Sundberg, Jan. 2008. 'Puolueiden organisaatiot ja suhteet etujärjestöihin.' In Heikki Paloheimo and Tapio Raunio (eds), *Suomen puolueet ja puoluejärjestelmä*. Helsinki: WSOY, 61–83.

Svensson, Torsten. 1994. *Socialdemokratins dominans*. Uppsala: Acta Universitatis Upsaliensis.

Svensson, Torsten, and PerOla Öberg. 2002. 'Labour Market Organisations' Participation in Swedish Public Policy-Making.' *Scandinavian Political Studies*, 25(4): 295–315.

SVT. 2014. *Kampen om identiteten*. Dokumentär.

Swank, Duane. 2013. *Comparative Political Parties Dataset: Electoral, Legislative, and Government strength of Political Parties by Ideological Group in 21 Capitalist Democracies, 1950–2011*. Electronic Database, Department of Political Science, Marquette University <http://www.marquette.edu/polisci/faculty_swank.shtml>.

Sydsvenskan. 2014. 'LO låter S välja kompisar själv.' *Sydsvenskan*, 28 April.

Tálos, Emmerich. 2008. *Sozialpartnerschaft: Ein zentraler politischer Gestaltungsfaktor in der Zweiten Republik*. Innsbruck, Vienna, and Bozen: Studienverlag.

Tanner, Jakob. 2015. *Geschichte der Schweiz im 20: Jahrhundert*. München: Beck.

Taylor, Andrew J. 1987. *Trade Unions and the Labour Party*. London: Croom Helm.

Taylor, Andrew J. 1993. 'Trade Unions and the Politics of Social Democratic Renewal.' In Richard Gillespie and William E. Patterson (eds), *Rethinking Social Democracy in Western Europe*. London: Frank Cass.

TCO. 2013. *TCOs verksamhetsberättelse 2012*. Stockholm.

Thomas, Clive S. (ed.). 2001a. *Political Parties and Interest Groups: Shaping Democratic Governance*. Boulder, CO: Lynne Rienner.

Thomas, Clive S. 2001b. 'Preface.' In Clive S. Thomas (ed.), *Political Parties and Interest Groups: Shaping Democratic Governance*. Boulder, CO: Lynne Rienner.

Thomas, Clive S. 2001c. 'Studying the Political Party–Interest Group Relationship.' In Clive S. Thomas (ed.), *Political Parties and Interest Groups: Shaping Democratic Governance*. Boulder, CO: Lynne Rienner.

Thomas, Clive S. 2001d. 'The United States: The Paradox of Loose Party–Group Ties in the Context of American Political Development.' In Clive S. Thomas (ed.), *Political Parties and Interest Groups: Shaping Democratic Governance*. Boulder, CO: Lynne Rienner.

Thomas, Clive S. 2001e. 'Towards a Systematic Understanding of Party–Group Relations in Liberal Democracies.' In Clive S. Thomas (ed.), *Political Parties and Interest Groups: Shaping Democratic Governance*. Boulder, CO: Lynne Rienner.

Thörn, Ylva. 2013. 'Interview with the Spokes Person for Union–Party Cooperation at SAP', 12 April.

Tiihonen, Aino. 2015. *Etujärjestöjen, puolueiden ja yhteiskuntaluokkien suhde Suomessa 2000-luvulla*. Master's thesis, University of Tampere, Finland.

Tope, Daniel, and David Jacobs. 2009. 'The Politics of Union Decline: The Contingent Determinants of Union Recognition Elections and Victories.' *American Sociological Review*, 74(5): 842–64.

Trampusch, Christine. 2011. *Der erschöpfte Sozialstaat: Transformation eines Politikfeldes*. Frankfurt: Campus.

Transport. 2013. *Verksamhetsberättelse*. Stockholm: Svenska Transportarbetareförbundet.

Travail.Suisse. 2009. *Statuten*. Travail.Suisse, Bern, 24 April: <http://www.travailsuisse. ch/system/uploadedfiles/3344/original/Statuten_090514.pdf?1430442073>.

Travail.Suisse. 2013a. *Über uns—Aufgabe und Struktur*. <http://www.travailsuisse.ch/ portraet/aufgabe_und_struktur>.

Travail.Suisse. 2013b. *Mitgliedsverbände*. <http://www.travailsuisse.ch/portraet/ mitgliedsverbaende>.

Tribune 1997. 'Het Poldermodel' 33:9, 19 September.

Tribune 2002. 'Hoe zit het met de vakbonden en de SP?' 38:7, 4 July.

Trivellato, Ugo. 2015. 'Jobs act, un vaso di Pandora con tante ambiguità.' *lavoce.info*, 20 February: <http://www.lavoce.info>.

Turner, Thomas, and Daryl D'Art. 2012. 'Public Perceptions of Trade Unions in Countries of the European Union: A Causal Analysis.' *Labor Studies Journal*, 37(1): 33–55.

Upchurch, Martin, Graham Taylor, and Andrew Mathers. 2009. *The Crisis of Social Democratic Trade Unionism in Western Europe: The Search for Alternatives*. London: Ashgate.

Valen, Henry, and Daniel Katz. 1964. *Political Parties in Norway: A Community Study*. Oslo: Universitetsforlaget.

Van Biezen, Ingrid, Peter Mair, and Thomas Poguntke. 2012. 'Going, Going, . . . Gone? The Decline of Party Membership in Contemporary Europe.' *Party Politics*, 51(1): 24–56.

Van Biezen, Ingrid, and Thomas Poguntke. 2014. 'The Decline of Membership-based Politics.' *Party Politics*, 20(2): 205–16.

Van der Velden, Sjaak. 2005. *Werknemers georganiseerd: Een geschiedenis van de vakbeweging bij het honderdjarig jubileum van de Federatie Nederlandse Vakbeweging (FNV)*. Amsterdam: Aksant.

Van Praag, Philip. 1987. 'Een mislukte campagne: FNV en de verkiezingen van 1986.' *Namens*, 2(7).

Van Schuur, Wijbrandt H. 2003. 'Mokken Scale Analysis: Between the Guttman Scale and Parametric Item Response Theory.' *Political Analysis*, 11(2): 139–63.

Vänsterpartiet. 2004. *Partiprogram*. Stockholm: Vänsterpartiet.

Vänsterpartiet. 2012. *Facklig-politisk plattform*. Stockholm: Vänsterpartiet.

Vänsterpartiet. 2013. *Särskild partigemensam intäktsanalys år 2013*. Stockholm: Vänsterpartiet.

Vänsterpartiet-kommunisterna. 1988. *Avskaffa kollektivanslutningen*. VPK/2263/F/8/ 14, ARAB. Stockholm: Vänsterpartiet.

Venho, Tomi. 2008. *Piilotettua julkisuutta: Suomalaisen puolue- ja vaalirahoituksen avoimuusintressi normeissa ja käytännössä*. Väitöskirja. Turku: Turun yliopisto, valtio-opin laitos.

Verge, Tània. 2012. 'Party Strategies towards Civil Society in New Democracies: The Spanish Case.' *Party Politics*, 18(1): 45–60.

Visser, Jelle. 1990. 'In Search of Inclusive Unionism.' *Bulletin of Comparative Labour Relations*, 18: 5–278.

Visser, Jelle. 2006. 'Union Membership Statistics in 24 Countries.' *Monthly Labor Review*, 129(1): 38–49.

Visser, Jelle. 2015. *ICTWSS Data Base (Version 5.0)*. Amsterdam: Amsterdam Institute for Advanced Labour Studies AIAS. October 2015: <www.uva-aias.net/208>.

Volkens, Andrea, Pola Lehman, Theres Matthieß, Nicolas Merz, Sven Regel, and Annika Werner. 2015. *The Manifesto Data Collection. Manifesto Project. (MRG/CMP/MARPOR). Version 2015a*. Berlin: Wissenschaftszentrum Berlin für Sozialforschung (WZB).

Von Beyme, Klaus. 1985. *Political Parties in Western Democracies*. Aldershot: Gower.

Wallerstein, Michael, and Bruce Western. 2000. 'Unions in Decline? What Has Changed and Why.' *Annual Review of Political Science*, 3(1): 355–77.

Wandruszka, Adam. 1954. 'Österreichs politische Struktur: Die Entwicklung der Parteien und politischen Bewegungen.' In Heinrich Benedikt (ed.), *Geschichte der Republik Österreich*. Vienna: Verlag für Geschichte und Politik, 289–485.

Ware, Alan. 1996. *Political Parties and Party Systems*. Oxford: Oxford University Press.

Warner, Carolyn M. 2000. *Confessions of an Interest Group: The Catholic Church and Political Parties in Europe*. Princeton, NJ: Princeton University Press.

Webb, Paul D. 1992. *Trade Unions and the British Electorate*. Aldershot: Dartmouth.

Webb, Paul D. 1994. 'Party Organizational Change in Britain: The Iron Law of Centralization?' In Richard S. Katz and Peter Mair (eds), *How Parties Organize*. London: Sage.

Webb, Paul D. 1995. 'Reforming the Labour Party–Trade Union Link: An Assessment.' In David Broughton, David M. Farrell, David Denver, and Colin Rallings (eds), *British Elections and Parties Yearbook 1994*. London: Frank Cass, 1–14.

Wehler, Hans-Ulrich. 1995. *Deutsche Gesellschaftsgeschichte, 1849–1914*. München: C. H. Beck.

Wehler, Hans-Ulrich. 2003. *Deutsche Gesellschaftsgeschichte, 1914–1949*. München: C. H. Beck.

Wehler, Hans-Ulrich. 2008. *Deutsche Gesellschaftsgeschichte, 1949–1990*. München: C. H. Beck.

Wehner, Joachim. 2006. 'Assessing the Power of the Purse: An Index of Legislative Budget Institutions.' *Political Studies*, 54(4): 767–85.

Weinblum, Shay. 2010. 'A Work in Progress: Union Revitalization in the Israeli "New Genreal Federation of Labour".' MA thesis, University of Kassel and Berlin School of Economics and Law, Germany.

Wenger, Simon. 2010. 'Zwischen Markt und Plan: Energiebewirtschaftung im Zweiten Weltkrieg.' In Bernard Degen, Hans Schäppi, and Adrian Zimmermann (eds), *Robert Grimm: Marxist, Kämpfer, Politiker*. Zürich: Chronos, 137–54.

Westerlund, Uno. 2011. *En glansfull framtid: ur TCO:s historia 1944–2010*. Stockholm: Premiss.

Wilson, Graham. 1990. *Interest Groups*. Oxford: Blackwell.

Wintour, Patrick. 2015. 'Jeremy Corbyn to give Greater Decision-making Power to Labour Grassroots.' *The Guardian*, 20 November.

Witko, Christopher. 2009. 'The Ecology of Party–Organized Interest Relationships.' *Polity*, 41(2): 211–34.

Witko, Christopher. 2013. 'When does Money buy Votes? Campaign Contributions and Policy-making.' In Matt Grossmann (ed.), *New Directions in Interest Group Politics*. New York: Routledge.

Witko, Christopher. 2016. 'The Politics of Financialization in the United States, 1949–2005.' *British Journal of Political Science*, 46(2) 349–70.

Witko, Christopher, and Sally Friedman. 2008. 'Business Backgrounds and Congressional Behavior.' *Congress and the Presidency*, 35(1): 71–86.

Wright, J. 2012. 'Gillard Rebukes Hawke on Unions.' *Sydney Morning Herald*, 4 January.

Wright, John R. 2000. 'Interest Groups, Congressional Reform and Party Government in the United States.' *Legislative Studies Quarterly*, 25(2): 217–35.

Wyler, Rebekka. 2012. *Schweizer Gewerkschaften und Europa: 1960–2005*. Münster: Westfälisches Dampfboot.

Yishai, Yael. 1991. *Land of Paradoxes: Interest Politics in Israel*. Albany: State University of New York Press.

Yishai, Yael. 1999. 'Interest Politics in a Comparative Perspective: The (Ir)regularity of the Israeli Case.' *Israel Affairs*, 5(2): 73–86.

Yishai, Yael. 2001. 'Bringing Society Back In: Post-cartel Parties in Israel.' *Party Politics*, 7(6): 667–87.

Zalmanovitch, Yair. 1998. 'Transitions in Israel's Policymaking Network.' *The Annals of the American Academy*, 555(1): 193–208.

Zilliacus, Kim O. K. 2001. '"New Politics" in Finland: The Greens and the Left Wing in the 1990s.' *West European Politics*, 24(1): 27–54.

Ziloni, Efraim. 2010. 'Is Union Multiplicity Good for the Workers?' *Hadshot Mashabei Enosh* 72. <http://www.hrisrael.co.il/home/doc.aspx?mCatID=68102>.

Index

activists 189, 199
ACTU *see* Australian confederation of trade unions
AEU *see* Australian Education Union
AfA see *Arbeitgemeinschaft für Arbeitnehmerfragen*
AFL *see* American Federation of Labour
AFT *see* American Federation of Teachers
Agenda 2010 133–4, 142, 144, 146–7
agreements
  for cooperation 287
  between dyads 191*t*–2*t*, 212*t*–13*t*
  for labour market 98
  SPD Manheim agreeement 134
  Warwick Agreement 260, 334
AKAVA *see* Unions for Professional and Managerial Staff in Finland
alliances 155, 168
  as enduring 14
  Left Alliances 96, 97, 102
  as new 243
  as partisan 129
ALP *see* Australian Labor Party
Am Echad (national party) 156, 156*t*, 157*t*
American Federation of Labour (AFL) 265
American Federation of Teachers (AFT) 267
ANMF *see* Australian Nursing and Midwifery Federation
Anthonsen, Mette 19
Anti-Revolutionary Party (*Anti-Revolutionaire Partij*, ARP) 188
Arbeitgemeinschaft für Arbeitnehmerfragen (AfA) 137
Armingeon, Klaus 331
ARP *see* Anti-Revolutionary Party
Aubert, Josiane 237
Australia 48*t*
  corporatism in 64
  strikes in 69n1
Australian confederation of trade unions (ACTU) 45
  ALP and 65
  campaigns from 61
  relationships party between 64, 64*f*
Australian Education Union (AEU) 57
Australian Labor Party (ALP) 56
  ACTU and 65
  ANMF and 61

  Hawke-Keating and 67, 68
  MPs from 54
Australian Nursing and Midwifery Federation (ANMF) 57, 64*f*
  ALP and 61
  as unaffiliated union 65
Australian Workers Union (AWU) 56
Austria 48*t*
  cartel democracy in 70–92
  labour movement in 90
  media in 86
  pillarization in 87
  social democrats in 317
  strikes in 73
Austrian Trade Union Federation (*Österreichischer Gewerkschaftsbund*, ÖGB) 70
  questionnaires from 80
AWU *see* Australian Workers Union

Baumgartner, Frank R. 53n8
Berlusconi, Silvio 182
biographies 122, 256
Blair, Tony 260
Blairite Third Way 68
Bonn Republic 145
Bontems, Jacky 123
British Labour Party 14
Brown, Gordon 248
Bundestag 130, 138

Cahill, Mary Beth 272
campaigns
  from ACTU 61
  apparatus for 206
  against Coalition's Work Choices 68
  contributions to 230, 237, 276
  for elections 106
  financing for 267
  Poverty Does Not Work as 193
  referendums for 245n2
cartel democracy 70–92
cartel party thesis 7
Casas-Zamora, Kevin 329
Catholic/Catholics
  cantons as 227
  countries as 1
  labour movement as 244

Catholic/Catholics (*cont.*)
  parties as 2
  unions as 11
  workers organization of 171
CBI *see* Confederation of British Industry
CDA *see* Christian Democratic Appeal
central party organizations (CPOs) 35, 41*t*,
    43*t*, 48–52*t*, 60*t*, 62*t*, 76*t*
  arrangements with 118
  as dependent variables 321
  independence from 209
  link scores for 104*f*, 104n1, 124*f*, 143*f*, 163*f*,
    178*f*, 198*f*, 219*f*, 239*f*, 257*f*, 273*f*, 289*f*
  party-confederation dyads as 60*t*, 62*t*, 78*t*,
    81*t*–2*t*, 85*f*, 99*t*, 101*t*, 116*t*–17*t*, 119*t*–20*t*,
    135*t*–6*t*, 139*t*–40*t*, 154*t*, 159*t*–60*t*,
    174*t*, 191*t*–2*t*, 195*t*–6*t*, 198*f*, 212*t*–13*t*,
    215*t*–16*t*, 253*t*, 255*t*, 257*f*, 270*t*
  party-union as 286
  relationships between confederations
    and 36
  relationships for LPGs and 40
  unions and 45
Central Union of Agricultural Producers and
    Forest Owners (MTK) 102
Central Union of Swedish Speaking
    Agricultural Producers in Finland
    (SLC) 103
centre-right parties 24
  Finland and 98
  governments and 179
CFDT *see* Democratic French Confederation
    of Labour
CFTC *see* French Confederation of Christian
    Workers
CGB see *Christlicher Gewerkschaftsbund*
CGIL see *Confederazione italiana generale del
    lavoro*
CGL *see* General Confederation of Labour
CGT see *Confédération générale du travail*
Chamber of Labour (*Arbeiterkammer*,
    AK) 71
Change-to-Win (CTW) 268
Cheibub, José 331
Chérèque, François 123
Christian Democratic Appeal (*Christen-
    Democratisch Appèl*, CDA) 187, 193
Christian Democrats (DC) 170
Christian Historical Union (*Christelijk-
    Historische Unie* CHU) 188
Christian National Trade Union
    Confederation (CNV)
  GreenLeft and 200
  PvdA and 194
Christlicher Gewerkschaftsbund (CGB) 131
CHU *see* Christian Historical Union

Cinque stelle (Five Stars) 182
CIO *see* Congress of Industrial Organizations
CISL *see* Italian Confederation of Union
    Workers
Clinton, Bill 276, 277
Clinton, Hillary 271
closeness
  concept of 27–9
  definition of 26
  degree of 44, 63–4, 65*f*, 84–8, 86*f*, 103–5,
    105*f*, 123–5, 125*f*, 144*f*, 147, 162*t*, 164*f*,
    165, 177–9, 178*f*, 218–19, 220*f*, 240*f*
  differences in 15, 203
  as historical 35
  of organizations 12
  as perceived 274
  perceptions of 37
  of relationships 39, 202, 303*f*
  scale of 23, 46
CNV *see* Christian National Trade Union
    Confederation
Coalition's Work Choices 68
Cohen, Yinon 151
Cold War 113, 171
Combet, Greg 63
communism
  Maoist split from 188
  after Second World War 171
  unions and 171–2
Communist Party (PCI) 170
  after second World War 171
  statutes of 173
  transformation for 180
Comparative Manifesto Project 322
Comparative Survey of Electoral Systems 324
Confederation for Middle and Higher
    Personnel (*Vakcentrale voor Middlebar
    en Hoger Personnel*, MHP) 187
  as white collar 194
Confédération générale du travail (CGT)
  Charter of Amiens by 112, 127
  PCF and 112, 128
Confederation of British Industry (CBI) 247
Confederation of Finnish Employers
    (STK) 94
Confederation of Finnish Industries (EK) 98
  National Coalition and 105
Confederation of Finnish Trade Unions
    (SAK)
  Left Alliance within 97
  SDP and 93, 104, 110
confederations 53n4
  ACTU as 45
  CFTC as 113
  CGIL as 170–1, 173, 174*t*, 175, 178*f*, 179
  CISL as 172, 174*t*

cooperation with 214
CPOs and 76*t*
Dutch parties and 186–205
FNV as 188
as independence 176
Israel labour parties and
    149–69
in Italy 36
positions held in 198*f*
SAK as 93
shift in 118
STK as 94
STTK as 94, 97
see also dyads, party-confederation as
Confederazione italiana generale del lavoro
    (Italian General Confederation of
    Labour-CGIL) 170–1, 173, 174*f*,
    175, 178*f*
  isolation of 179
conferences 61, 211
  congresses and 214
  for Histadrut 156*t*
  invitations to 62*t*, 81*t*–2*t*, 100, 118,
    139*t*–40*t*, 159*t*–60*t*
  outcome control over 56
Congress of Industrial Organizations
    (CIO) 265
context
  background and 95–111, 131–4
  as political and institutional 150
cooperation 335
  agreements for 287
  with confederations 214
  loyalty and 271
  support for 223*f*
Corbyn, Jeremy 25n3, 249, 250
  nomination of 252
  support for 263
corporatism 32*t*
  in Australia 64
  coalition government and 201–3
  decline of 19
  level of 330*f*
  as neo 73, 77, 90–1
  in Netherlands 189, 197
  as norm 109
  politics and 204, 228
  in structures 202
  in Switzerland 228
  UK and 246
corruption 73
cost-benefit exchange model 112, 126,
    167, 223
  expectations of 22
  support for 336
  of transactions 5, 12–14, 17, 321

countries
  case selection of 30, 31*t*–2*t*
  as Catholic 1
  decline of links 283
  in EU 96
  with fragmented unions 328*f*
  with high union density 327*f*
  level factors for 310, 336–7
  level hypotheses for 18–21
  results for 46
  with subsidies 329–30, 331*f*
CPOs *see* central party organizations
Crean, Simon 63
CTW *see* Change-to-Win

DAG *see Deutsche Angestellten-Gewerkschaft*
data 46, 111n1, 319
  as biographical 38
  collection of 37–8
  from Comparative Manifesto Project 322
  on party policy positions 333
  on relationships 26–7
  sets of 53n6
  sources of 110n4
DBB *see Deutscher Beamten-Bund*
DC *see* Christian Democrats
democracy
  cartel 70–92
  contemporary 26–53
  liberal 168
  links in 34
  mature 4, 23
  social 91
Democratic French Confederation of Labour
    (CFDT) 113
Democratic Leadership Council 277
Democratic National Convention 269
Democratic National Council (DNC) 268
  Democratic National Convention after 269
Democratic Party (PD) 170
  CGIL and 174*t*, 175, 178*f*
  CISL and 174*t*, 178*f*
  as opposition 179
Deutsche Angestellten-Gewerkschaft
    (DAG) 131
Deutscher Beamten-Bund (DBB) 131
Deutscher Gewerkschaftsbund (DGB) 130
  member unions of 137
  unitary unionism (*Einheitsgewerkschaft*)
    for 131
development 5
  factors for 24
  OECD and 71
DGB *see Deutscher Gewerkschaftsbund*
directorates 70–92, 200
DNC *see* Democratic National Council

Durazo, Maria Elena 272
Dutch Federation Trade Union Movement
    (*Federatie Nederlandse Vakbeweging,*
    FNV) 187, 188, 193
  activists from 189, 199
  PvdA and 190, 199
Duverger, Maurice 2, 8, 10*t*
dyads 11, 22, 48–52*t*, 58*t*, 76*t*
  agreements between 191*t*–2*t*, 212*t*–13*t*
  categorization as 29
  CGT-PCF as 128
  comparisons across 122
  as core 24
  data for 39
  as institutionalized 15
  party-confederation as 60*t*, 62*t*, 78*t*,
    81*t*–2*t*, 85*f*, 99*t*, 101*t*, 116*t*–17*t*, 119*t*–20*t*,
    135*t*–6*t*, 139*t*–40*t*, 159*t*–60*t*, 174*t*,
    191*t*–2*t*, 195*t*–6*t*, 198*f*, 212*t*–13*t*,
    215*t*–16*t*, 253*t*, 255*t*, 257*f*, 270*t*
  party-union as 36–7, 288*t*
  reporting on 164n1
  scaling analysis 44
  between unions and CPOs 45
  variation between 167

Ebbinghaus, Bernhard 2, 25n4
Economic and Monetary Union (EMU) 97
economy 3, 68, 145, 150
  as agrarian 126
  crisis of 227
  downturns in 278
  as industrial 131, 184
  policy and 88
  politics and 19
  Second World War and 227
  transformation of 110
  in turmoil 55
Eduskunta
  elections in Finland 95, 96, 97, 102, 108*t*
  representation in 105, 110
  survey on 97
Eini, Ofer 156
electrician's union (IBEW) 272
employees 33n2c, 33n2b
  FIOM for 177
  GPA-djp 74
  SDA for 56
  sectors of 87
  TCO for 210
employment
  Employment Relations Act about 248
  as full 206, 246
  issues of 2
  new patterns of 12, 30
  threat to 220

Employment Relations Act (1999) 248
EMU *see* Economic and Monetary Union
Engström, Hillevi 218
Epifani, Guglielmo 177
Ernst, Klaus 138
Erziehung und Wissenschaft (GEW) 132
European Social Survey 324
European Union (EU)
  power of 3
  as single market 228
  trade dependence on 96
EVP *see* Protestant People's Party
ex officio
  positions as 155
  representation as 40, 286
  seats as 27, 43*t*, 79
  as service capacity 69n4

Fahimi, Yasmin 138
Faymann, Werner 74
FCG *see* *Fraktion Christlicher
    Gewerkschafterinnen und Gewerkschafter*
FDP *see* Liberal Party
federalism 265, 321*t*
  scale of 330–1
Federatie Nederlandse Vakbeweging see Dutch
    Federation Trade Union Movement
Féderation des syndicats unifiée (FSU) 114
  in public sector 118
Federation of Employees and Metal Workers
    (FIOM) 177
FEN *see* National Education Federation
FIM *see* National Federation of Metalworkers
finance
  for campaigns 267
  contributions of 34
  parties and 32*t*, 111n7, 257, 329, 332*f*
  politics and 20, 166, 181, 248, 330, 332*t*
  as resources 229, 248
  see also funding
Finland 48*t*
  AKAVA in 94
  centre-right coalition in 98
  Eduskunta elections in 95, 96, 97, 102, 108*t*
  EK and National Coalition in 105
  Hakaniemi in 100
  Intellectual Employment Union in 97
  Lapua movement in 93
  party-union links in 93–111
  as rural society 96
  SDP and SAK in 93, 104, 110
  as welfare state 109
Finnish Confederation of Professionals
    (STTK) 94, 97
Finnish People's Democratic Union
    (FPDU) 95

Finnish Trades Organization (SAJ) 94
Finns Party 109
FIOM *see* Federation of Employees and Metal
    Workers
First World War 171
Five Stars (*Cinque stelle*) 182
FNV *see* Dutch Federation Trade Union
    Movement
Force Ouvriére (FO) 113
The Fourth Republic 127
FPDU *see* Finnish People's Democratic Union
FPÖ *see* Freedom Party of Austria
fragmentation 30, 31*t*
    of labour movement 206
    of party systems 92, 107, 189
    of unions 92, 107, 114, 328, 338, 340
*Fraktion Christlicher Gewerkschafterinnen
    und Gewerkschafter im ÖGB* (FCG) 71
    ÖVP and 89
*Fraktion Sozialdemokratischer
    GewerkschafterInnen im ÖGB* (FSG) 71
    domination of unions 80, 83, 87
France 48*t*–9*t*
    as agrarian economy 126
    Auroux Laws in 114
    The Fourth Republic of 127
    National Assembly of 122
    parties and unions in 112–29
Freedom Party of Austria (FPÖ) 71, 72
French Communist Party (PCF)
    CGT and 112, 128
    decline of 125–6
French Confederation of Christian Workers
    (CFTC) 113
FSG see *Fraktion Sozialdemokratischer
    GewerkschafterInnen*
FSU see *Féderation des syndicats unifiée*
funding 89
    disclosures of 111n8
    by donors 229
    as public 106
    see also finance

Gabriel, Sigmar 138
gay marriage 67
Geithner, Timothy 278
General Confederation of Labour (CGIL) 171
    PD and 175, 178*f*
geography 100
German Social Democrats
    (*Sozialdemokratische Partei
    Deutschlands*, SPD) 130, 142
    advisory body (*Gewerkschaftsrat*) of 137
    Die Linke and 141f
    Manheim agreement with 134
    Neue Mitte (Third Way) by 146

Germany 49*t*
    Bonn Republic in 145
    Bundestag in 130, 138, 142
    as federal state 21
    labour law in 131
    trade union membership in 132–3
    unification of 133
    Ver.di in 132, 138, 142
GEW see *Erziehung und Wissenschaft*
GewSPÖ *see* Trade Unionists in the SPÖ
Gillard, Julia 66
globalization 3
GLP *see* Green Liberal Party
GÖD *see* Public Services Union
government
    centre-right parties and 179
    as coalition 223
    composition of 323
    connections to 190
    as conservative 247
    corporatism and 201–3
    as parliamentary 21
    positions in 145
    as power sharing 334
    as representative 1
    unions and 23
    years in 339*t*
GP *see* Greens
GPA-djp *see* Salaried Private Sector
        Employees, Printers, Journalists and
        Paper Workers
Graber, Konrad 241
GRECO *see* Group of States against
        Corruption of the Council of Europe
Green Liberal Party (GLP) 243
Greens (*Grüne Partei/Les Verts* GP) 230
Group of States against Corruption of the
        Council of Europe (GRECO) 229
Grüne Partei see Greens
Gumbrell-McCormick, Rebecca 25n4
Gusenbauer, Alfred 73–4, 77

Halonen, Tarja 106
Hassel, Anke 6
Hawke, Bob 64, 66
    Keating and 67, 68
HDC *see* House Democratic Caucus
Heaney, Michael 8–9
hierarchy 29, 44
Histadrut (*Histadrut Ha'Ovdim Ha'Hadasha*,
        New Labour Federation) 149–51
    conferences for 156*t*
    decline of 152
    House of Representatives for 157
    as Israel's main federation 165
    positions *as ex officio* 155

Histadrut Ha'ovdim Ha'Le'umit (National
  Labour Federation) (HL) 150, 151
  Likud and 161, 165
Hollande, François 123, 127, 318
Hotel and Gastro Union 231
House Democratic Caucus (HDC) 268
Howard, John 59, 61, 68
Howell, Chris 2–3
human capital 16
Hyman, Richard 25n4

IBEW *see* electrician's union
ideology 165, 266
  cohesion of 172
  debate about 55–6
  differences in 167, 222
  of legacy 239
  role of 55
  socialism as 246
IG BCE see *Industriegewerkschaft Bergbau,*
  Chemie Energie
IG Metall see *Industriegewerkschaft Metall*
Ihalainen, Lauri 107
Industriegewerkschaft Bergbau, Chemie
  Energie (IG BCE) 132, 148
Industriegewerkschaft Metall (IG Metall) 132
  as Germany's largest union 141
Intellectual Employment Union 97
International Brotherhood of Carpenters and
  Joiners (the Carpenters) 268
invitations
  to conferences 62t, 81t–2t, 100, 118,
    139t–40t, 159t–60t
  to KL activities 158
  as mutual 175
  to and from unions 139t–40t, 159t–60t,
    195t–6t, 270t
Israel 49t, 162f
  interest group system in 151
  Knesset in 155, 162
  left wing decline in 157
  Likud in 150, 158
  national party (Am Echad) in 156,
    156t, 157t
  parties and labour federations in 149–69
  partisanship in 163
  political parties in 152–3
  political system changes in 166
Israeli Labour Party 152–3, 162f
Italian Confederation of Union Workers
  (CISL)
  DC and 172
  PD and 174t
Italy 50t
  CGIL in 170–1, 173, 179
  Cinque stelle in 182

CISL in 172, 174t
confederations in 36
DC in 170
Jobs Act in 184
Parliament in 176
PCI in 170
PD in 170, 174t
Popolo delle libertà in 182
SPI in 181

Jaensch, D. 54
Johnson, Lyndon 274
Jositch, Daniel 238
Juholt, Håkan 220

Katz, Daniel 29
Katz, Haim 161
Katz, Richard 20
  cartel party thesis by 7
Keynesianism 3, 208
Kirchheimer, Otto 4, 133
Kitschelt, Herbert P. 9, 10t, 52n2, 353
KL see *Ko'ach La'Ovdim*
Knesset 155, 162
Ko'ach La'Ovdim (Power to the Workers,
  KL) 151
  fragmentation of 152
  Meretz and 161
  paramilitary group of 158
Koskimaa, Vesa 111n5
Kvavik, Robert B. 10t, 29

labour market
  agreements for 98
  liberalization of 145
  reforms for 203–4, 205, 318, 334
  regulation of 1, 127
labour movement, Catholics and 244
Labour Party (*Partij van de Arbeid,*
  PvdA) 186, 187, 189
  CNV and 194
  FNV and 190, 199
Labour Representation Committee, the
  (LRC) 246
Lafontaine, Oskar 146
Laigo, Laurence 123
Lama, Luciano 185n7
language 38
Latham, Mark 66
laws 278
Leech, Beth 53n8
Left Alliance 96, 97, 102
left-of-centre parties 40
  decline of 157
  in Finland and Netherlands 317
  in France 112–29

in Italy 170–85
links to 42, 43*t*
unions and 1–25
USA unions and 280–309
left-wing parties *see* left-of-centre parties
legislative party groups (LPGs) 35, 41*t*, 43*t*,
    76n1, 153n1
  as dependent variables 321
  link scores for 104*f*, 104n1, 124*f*, 143*f*, 163*f*,
    178*f*, 198*f*, 219*f*, 239*f*, 257*f*, 273*f*, 289*f*
  overlap of 84
  party-confederation dyads as 60*t*, 62*t*,
    78*t*, 81*t*–2*t*, 85*f*, 99*t*, 101*t*, 116*t*–17*t*,
    119*t*–20*t*, 135*t*–6*t*, 139*t*–40*t*, 159*t*–60*t*,
    174*t*, 191*t*–2*t*, 195*t*–6*t*, 198*f*, 212*t*–13*t*,
    215*t*–16*t*, 253*t*, 255*t*, 257*f*, 270*t*
  relationships for CPOs and 40
Leigh, A. 55
Letta, Enrico 180
Liberal Party (FDP) 238
Lijphart, Arend 30
Likud 162*f*
  and HL 161
Die Linke 285
  as new party 134
  as pro-labour 147
  SPD and 141f
  union relations with 137
links 13
  categories of 23, 27–30
  correlation between variables and 322*t*
  decline of 5–7, 204, 283
  in democracy 34
  as dichotomous variables 37
  extinction of 153
  hypothesis on 12
  importance of 224
  as individual 41*t*, 61, 63, 83–4,
    121–3, 217
  intensity of 53n7
  as inter-organizational 6–7, 77–88, 78*t*,
    81*t*–2*t*, 109, 115–21, 116*t*–17*t*, 135*t*–6*t*
  to left-of-centre parties 42, 43*t*
  mapping of 57–69, 60*t*, 62*t*, 98–105, 99*t*,
    115, 116*t*–17*t*, 172–7
  as one way and occasional 101*t*, 119*t*–20*t*,
    139*t*–40*t*, 158, 159*t*–60*t*, 174*t*, 175,
    195*t*–6*t*, 214, 215*t*–16*t*, 239*f*,
    255*t*, 270*t*
  perception of 143
  as reciprocal and durable 169n1, 173,
    191*t*–2*t*, 212*t*–13*t*, 253*t*, 287
  strength of 15, 16, 17, 20, 24, 42–6, 324*f*,
    325*f*, 327*f*, 330*f*, 332*f*, 333
  as superfluous 77
  as weakened 180

link scores
  for CPOs and LPGs 104*f*, 104n1, 124*f*, 143*f*,
    163*f*, 178*f*, 198*f*, 219*f*, 239*f*, 257*f*, 273*f*, 289*f*
  distribution of 286
Lipponen, Paavo 97
Lipset, Seymour M. 107
literature 8, 22
LO *see* Trade Union Confederation
Löfven, Stefan 218
Loomes, Gemma 92n1
LPGs *see* legislative party groups
LRC *see* Labour Representation Committee,
    the
Lynch, Stephen 272

Mair, Peter 20
  cartel party thesis by 7
Maire, Jacques-André 237
Malm, Stig 217
Mapai/Labour 150
  dominance of 167–8
Mapam (United Workers Party) 153
mapping 11
  of achievement 15
  of links 57–69, 60*t*, 62*t*, 98–105, 99*t*, 115,
    116*t*–17*t*, 172–7
  of organizations 303
  of relationships 26–53
Martin, Cathie Jo 30, 33n8a
Martin, Edouard 123
Masket, Seth E. 269
Mavrogordatos, George Th. 9, 10*t*
Meany, George 274
media
  as mass 47
  as social 40, 41*t*, 161
membership
  as collective 28, 190
  decline in 57, 166, 181
  fees for 145
  as recommended 339*t*
  recruitment and 63
  research on 317
  role of 59
  structure for 209
  of unions 3, 4, 16, 202
Menzies, Robert 59, 66
Meretz 152–3, 158
  KL and 161
  MKs from 162*f*
Merkel, Angela 148, 335
MHP *see* Confederation for Middle and
    Higher Personnel
Miliband, Ed 25n3
  proposals by 252
  reforms by 257, 260

Mitterrand, François 114, 127
Mokken scaling 44
Movement for Civil Rights, The (Ratz) 153
MTK *see* Central Union of Agricultural
　　Producers and Forest Owners
Müller-Altermatt, Stefan 240

National Coalition 111n7
　EK and 105
National Education Federation (FEN) 114
National Executive Committee
　　(NEC) 249–50
National Federation of Metalworkers
　　(FIM) 176
National Labour Federation see *Histadrut*
　　Ha'ovdim Ha'Le'umit
national party (Am Echad) 156, 156*t*, 157*t*
National Pensioners Union (SPI) 181
NEC *see* National Executive Committee
Netherlands 50*t*
　ARP in 188
　CDA in 187
　CHU in 188
　confederations and parties in 186–205
　corporatism in 189, 197
　FNV in 188
　GreenLeft in 200
　PvdA in 186, 187, 189, 190
　SER in *189*
　SP in 187
　subcultures in 186
Neue Mitte (Third Way) 146
Neugebauer, Fritz 79
New Labour Federation *see* Histadrut
　　(*Histadrut Ha'Ovdim Ha'Hadasha*, New
　　Labour Federation)

Obama, Barack 271
OECD *see* Organisation for Economic
　　Co-operation and Development
ÖGB *see* Austrian Trade Union Federation
Organisation for Economic Co-operation and
　　Development (OECD) 71
organizations 60*t*
　of Catholic workers 171
　closeness of 12
　as collateral 27, 52n1
　as independent 226–45
　links between 6–7, 109, 115–21,
　　116*t*–17*t*
　overlap between 28, 29, 41*t*, 58*t*, 76*t*
　scores for 103, 164, 197, 219, 320
　for youth 210, 285
Österreichischer Gewerkschaftsbund
　　see Austrian Trade Union
　　Federation

Österreichische Volkspartei (ÖVP) 71
　election votes for 72
　FCG and 89
　GÖD and 83, 86
　questionnaires from 80
　unions and 75
overlap
　in leadership 77, 84, 102, 103*f*
　between organizations 28, 29, 41*t*, 58*t*, 76*t*
　of personnel 42, 61, 63, 83–4, 121–3, 138,
　　141, 161, 175–7, 224, 271, 283
　of recruitment base 338
　of structures 75, 154*t*, 175, 210
ÖVP see *Österreichische Volkspartei*

PACs *see* political action committees
Padgett, Stephen 6
Palestine 149, 150
Parliamentary Labour Party (PLP) 249
Partei des Demokratischen Sozialismus
　　(PDS) 147
Partij van de Arbeid see Labour Party
partisanship 309n2
　alliances as 129
　as attachment 265
　as complex 305
　considerations of 326
　in Israel 163
　as non 232, 237
Paterson, William E. 6
PCF *see* French Communist Party
PCI *see* Communist Party
PD *see* Democratic Party
PDS see *Partei des Demokratischen Sozialismus*
Pearson coefficient 303
Pelizzari, A. 237n2
pension
　age of 203–4, 205, 244
　management of 150
　reforms for 254n2
People of Freedoms (*Popolo delle libertà*) 182
Peretz, Amir 156
Persson, Göran 208
Piazza, J. 25n2
pillarization 186–205
　in Austria 87
　parties and 90–1
　of subcultures 91
PLP *see* Parliamentary Labour Party
pluralism 20, 228
　American-style of 151
　society and 4
Poguntke, Thomas 10*t*
　on collateral organizations 27, 52n1
　on integration of interest groups 28
　on organizational links 6–7

political action committees (PACs) 34
  for labour 275
  as super 279n3
political science 1, 8, 244
Popolo delle libertà (People of Freedoms)
  182
Poverty Does Not Work 193
power
  balance of 173, 228
  concentration of 229
  as decentralized 168
  government sharing of 334
Power to the Workers see *Ko'ach La'Ovdim*
practices 100
PRO-GE *see* Union of Production Workers
Protestant People's Party (EVP) 243
Protestants
  EVP as 243
  parties as 201
  Swiss federation founders as 226
  as urban 241
PSU *see* Unified Socialist Party
Public Services Union (GÖD) 74, 80
  as interlocutor 86
  ÖVP and 83, 86
PvdA *see* Labour Party

Quinn, Thomas 14

Ratz (The Movement for Civil Rights) 153
Rawson, Donald W. 2
regulation 34
  of interest groups 20
  of labour market 1
religious groups 189; *see also* Catholics;
  Protestants
Renzi, Matteo 180, 184, 185, 285
representation
  in Eduskunta 105, 110
  as ex officio 40, 286
  in government 1
  of unions 40
Republican Party 265
resources 264, 311, 336
  access to 223–4
  changes in 319, 335
  decline of 266, 276
  exchange of 13, 145, 207, 221, 247
  as financial 229, 248
  in politics 323, 335
  redirection of 94
  role of 202
  under supply of 14
  of unions 326, 336
  value of 18, 19, 337
  as variable 319

Riksdag 209
Rinne, Antti 95
Robbiani, Meinrado 240
Rokkan, Stein 107
Rommetvedt, Hilmar 19
Rudd, Kevin 56

SAC 210
Saco *see* Swedish Confederation of
  Professional Associations
Sahlin, Mona 219–20
SAJ *see* Finnish Trades Organization
SAK *see* Confederation of Finnish Trade
  Unions
Salaried Private Sector Employees, Printers,
  Journalists and Paper Workers (GPA-
  djp) 74
  leadership of 79, 90
  SPÖ relationship with 79
Sanchez, Linda 272
SAP *see* Swedish Social Democrats
scaling analysis 44–6, 52t, 282, 287
Schröder, Gerhard 133–4, 142, 144, 146–7
Schüssel, Wolfgang 73, 74
SDA *see* Shop, Distributive and Allied
  Employees Association
SDC *see* Senate Democratic Caucus
SDP *see* Social Democratic Party
Second World War
  Communist Party after 171
  economy and 227
  party-union relationships after 112–15
SEIU *see* Service Employees International
  Union
Senate Democratic Caucus (SDC) 268
SER *see* Social-Economic Council
Service Employees International Union
  (SEIU) 268
Shop, Distributive and Allied Employees
  Association (SDA) 56
Shorten, Bill 63
SLC *see* Central Union of Swedish Speaking
  Agricultural Producers in Finland
Social Democratic Party (SDP) 108t
  chairs of 102
  as dominant party 97
  funding for 106
  importance of 109
  SAK and 93, 104, 110
  working groups of 100
Social-Economic Council (*Sociaal-
  Economische Raad*, SER) 189, 197
Socialist Party (*Socialistische Partij* SP) 187
  FNV and 193
Solidaires unitaires démocratiques (SUD) 114
Soviet Union 96

Sozialdemokratische Partei Deutschlands see
German Social Democrats
Sozialdemokratische Partei Österreichs
(SPÖ) 71
election votes for 72
as governing party 87
GPA-djp relationship with 79
SP *see* Socialist Party
SPD *see* German Social Democrats
SPI *see* National Pensioners Union
SPÖ see *Sozialdemokratische Partei Österreichs*
Stekelenburg, Johan 205n1
STK *see* Confederation of Finnish Employers
Strandhäll, Annika 218
Streeck, Wolfgang 6
strikes 318
in Australia 69n1
in Austria 73
miners and 247
STTK *see* Finnish Confederation of Professionals
subcultures 70, 71, 88
as eroding 312
in Netherlands 186
pillarization of 91
subsidies 259, 331, 331*f*
countries with 329–30, 331*f*
for parties 321*t*, 322*t*, 330, 337
types of 329
SUD see *Solidaires unitaires démocratiques*
survey 185n4, 214
coded judgment and 45, 101n2, 134, 136n1, 268, 279n2, 309n3
Comparative Survey of Electoral Systems as 324
DNC, HDC and SDC and 268
European Social Survey as 324
interviews for 87, 100, 110, 193
questionnaires for 37–8, 88, 245n6
on relationships 173, 183
responses to 39, 75, 77, 80, 82n1, 83, 85, 86, 119n1, 124, 144, 158, 164, 175, 179, 200*f*, 237
World Values Survey as 324
Swank, Duane 30, 33n7, 33n8a, 340*t*
Sweden 45, 50*t*
LO in 207, 211, 217
party-union links in 206–25
Riksdag in 209
as unitary state 207
voting as volatile in 224
'war of the roses' in 207–8
Sweden Democrats
(*Sverigedemokraterna*) 214, 222

Swedish Confederation for Professional Employees (*Tjänstemännens centralorganization*, TCO) 210
LO and 211
SAP voting for 222*f*
Swedish Confederation of Professional Associations (*Sveriges akademikers centralorganisation*, Saco) 210, 222*f*
Swedish People's Party 103
Swedish Social Democrats
(*Socialdemokrastika*, SAP) 206
executive committee for 210
Keynesianism for 208
Swedish syndicalist union (*Sveriges arbetares centralorganisation*, SAC) 210
Switzerland 45, 50*t*
Constitution of 227
corporatism in 228
EVP in 243
FDP in 238
GLP in *243*
government of 334
GP *in* 230
Hotel and Gastro Union in 231
House and Senate of 229
Travail.Suisse of 231
unions and parties in 226–45
University of Zürich in 238

taxes
cuts for 278
policy changes for 277
reductions for 334
as revenue 262
TCO *see* Swedish Confederation for Professional Employees
Tessin, Canton 240
Thatcher, Margaret 247
Thibault, Bernard 113
Third Way (*Neue Mitte*) 146
Thomas, Clive S. 10*t*
on decline 6
on parliamentary government 21
on party-interest group relationships 9
Thomson, Craig 56
Thorwaldsson, Karl-Petter 218
Tjänstemännens centralorganization see
Swedish Confederation for Professional Employees
Trades Union Congress (TUC) 247
Trade Union Confederation
(*Landsorganisationen*, LO) 207, 217
SAP voting for 222*f*
TCO and 211
Trade Unionists in the SPÖ (GewSPÖ) 75

Trade Unions Coordinating Committee
(TUCC) 254
Trade Unions for Labour Victory
(TULV) 254
transaction costs theory 16
Travail.Suisse 231, 240
TUC *see* Trades Union Congress
TUCC *see* Trade Unions Coordinating
Committee
TULV *see* Trade Unions for Labour
Victory

UAW *see* United Auto Workers
UIL *see* Union of Italian Workers
unemployment 95
benefits for 203
insurance for 209
rise in 181, 183, 208
Unified Socialist Party (PSU) 113–14
Union nationale des syndicats autonomes
(UNSA) 114, 118
Union of Italian Workers (UIL) 172
Union of Production Workers (PRO-GE)
74, 89
Unions for Professional and Managerial Staff
in Finland (AKAVA) 94
Union syndicale solidaire (USS) 114
United Auto Workers (UAW) 268
United Kingdom 51*t*
CBI in 247
corporatism and 246
Employment Relations Act (1999) in 248
LRC in 246
NEC in 249–50
PLP in 249
the TUC 247
TUCC in 254
TULV in 254
Warwick Agreement in 260, 334
United States 51*t*
AFL-CIO in 277
Democratic Leadership Council in 277
DNC, HDC and SDC in 268
infrastructure of 278
pluralism in 151
Republican Party in 265
SEIU in 268
UAW in 268
United Workers Party (Mapam) 153
University of Zürich 238
UNSA see *Union nationale des syndicats
autonomes*

Urpilainen, Jutta 95
USS 114

Valen, Henry 29
Vall, Emmanuel 122
Vallaud-Belkacem, Najat 123
variables 24, 39
contextual 26, 31*t*–2*t*
dependent 320
independent 9, 11, 38, 320, 321*t*, 322*t*, 339*t*
links as 37, 43*t*, 286*t*
at system-level 30
variation 22, 310–39
Vereinte Dienstleistungsgewerkschaft (Ver.
di) 132, 138, 142
Les Verts see Greens
Viannet, Louis 113
Visser, Jelle 323
Von Beyme, Klaus 2, 8, 10*t*
voting 3, 13, 31*t*
for centre-left-parties 324
class levels of 33n3, 189, 201, 207, 221–2,
279, 313, 319, 337
electoral systems for 229, 238
in exchange for policies 202
power of 5
union households and 276
universal suffrage and 220
value of 16
as volatile 224
working class and 279

wages 228
federal minimum for 148
inequality of 206
system of talks for 98
Wahlalternative Arbeit & Soziale Gerechtigkeit
(WASG) 134
Warner, Carolyn M. 14
War of the Roses 207–8
Warwick Agreement 260, 334
WASG see *Wahlalternative Arbeit & Soziale
Gerechtigkeit*
Whitlam, Gough 67
Wilson, Graham 25n9
WorkChoices 334
World Values Survey 324
World Zionist Organization 149

Yishai, Yael 8, 10*t*, 151

Zimmermann, Sabine 138